# Lecture Notes in Computer Science 4784

*Commenced Publication in 1973*
Founding and Former Series Editors:
Gerhard Goos, Juris Hartmanis, and Jan van Leeuwen

## Editorial Board

Willy Susilo   Joseph K. Liu
Yi Mu (Eds.)

# Provable Security

First International Conference, ProvSec 2007
Wollongong, Australia, November 1-2, 2007
Proceedings

 Springer

Volume Editors

Willy Susilo
University of Wollongong
School of Computer Science and Software Engineering
Wollongong NSW 2522, Australia
E-mail: wsusilo@uow.edu.au

Joseph K. Liu
Institute for Infocomm Research
21 Heng Mui Keng Terrace, Singapore 119613, Singapore
E-mail: ksliu@i2r.a-star.edu.sg

Yi Mu
University of Wollongong
School of Computer Science and Software Engineering
Wollongong NSW 2522, Australia
E-mail: ymu@uow.edu.au

Library of Congress Control Number: 2007937100

CR Subject Classification (1998): D.4.6, E.3, K.4.4

LNCS Sublibrary: SL 4 – Security and Cryptology

ISSN        0302-9743
ISBN-10     3-540-75669-8 Springer Berlin Heidelberg New York
ISBN-13     978-3-540-75669-9 Springer Berlin Heidelberg New York

Springer is a part of Springer Science+Business Media

springer.com

© Springer-Verlag Berlin Heidelberg 2007
Printed in Germany

Typesetting: Camera-ready by author, data conversion by Scientific Publishing Services, Chennai, India
Printed on acid-free paper        SPIN: 12172443        06/3180        5 4 3 2 1 0

# Preface

The First International Conference on Provable Security 2007 (ProvSec 2007) was held in Wollongong, Australia, November 1–2, 2007. The conference was sponsored by iCORE Information Security Laboratory and RNSA (Research Network for a Secure Australia). We are grateful to these organizations for their support of the conference.

The conference proceedings, representing both full papers and short papers, were published in time for the conference in this volume of Lecture Notes in Computer Science series by Springer. This year the program committee invited an international keynote speaker: Colin Boyd from Queensland University of Technology, Australia. Prof. Boyd's talk addressed the topic of "On One-Pass Key Establishment".

The Program Committee received 51 submissions. Ten submissions were selected for full paper presentation and seven were selected for short paper presentation. The reviewing process was run using the iChair software, written by Thomas Baignères and Matthieu Finiasz (EPFL, Switzerland). It took seven weeks; each paper was carefully evaluated by at least three members of the Program Committee. We appreciate the hard work of the members of the Program Committee and the external referees, who gave many hours of their valuable time.

We would like to thank all the people involved in organizing this conference. In particular we would like to thank the General Chair Yi Mu, the Organizing Committee Man Ho Au and Xinyi Huang and the Webmaster, Lan Zhou, for their time and efforts.

Finally, we would like to thank all authors for submitting interesting new research papers to ProvSec, providing us with an embarrassment of riches out of which we could only accept a total of 17 contributed papers, even though many more would have been worth publishing.

November 2007

Willy Susilo
Joseph K. Liu

# First International Conference on Provable Security 2007 (ProvSec 2007)

## General Chair

Yi Mu — University of Wollongong, Australia

## Program Chairs

Willy Susilo — University of Wollongong, Australia
Joseph K. Liu — Institute for Infocomm Research, Singapore

## Program Committee

Joonsang Baek — Institute for Infocomm Research, Singapore
Feng Bao — Institute for Infocomm Research, Singapore
Emmanuel Bresson — CELAR, France
Xavier Boyen — Voltage Inc., Palo Alto, USA
Liqun Chen — Hewlett-Packard Laboratories, UK
Kim-Kwang Raymond Choo — Australian Institute of Criminology, Australia
Sherman S.M. Chow — New York University, USA
Nelly Fazio — IBM Almaden Research Centre, USA
Dengguo Feng — Chinese Academy of Sciences, China
David Galindo — University of Nijmegen, Netherlands
Craig Gentry — Stanford University, USA
Swee-Huay Heng — Multimedia University, Malaysia
Marc Joye — Thomson R&D, France
Eike Kiltz — CWI, Netherlands
Kwangjo Kim — ICU, Korea
Fabien Laguillaumie — University of Caen, France
Benoit Libert — UCL, Belgium
Javier Lopez — University of Malaga, Spain
Atsuko Miyaji — Japan Advanced Institute of Science and Technology, Japan
Chanathip Namprempre — Thammasat University, Thailand
Miyako Ohkubo — Information-Technology Promotion Agency, Japan
Tatsuaki Okamoto — NTT Labs, Japan
Juanma Gonzalez Nieto — Queensland University of Technology, Australia
Duong Hieu Phan — France Telecom R&D and University of Paris 8, France

| Raphael C.W. Phan | EPFL, Switzerland |
| Josef Pieprzyk | Macquarie University, Australia |
| Pascal Paillier | Gemplus, Security Technology Department, France |
| David Pointcheval | CNRS and ENS, France |
| Jean-Jacques Quisquater | UCL CryptoGroup, Belgium |
| Rei Safavi-Naini | University of Calgary, Canada |
| Palash Sarkar | Indian Statistical Institute, India |
| Alice Silverberg | U.C. Irvine, USA |
| Martijn Stam | EPFL, Switzerland |
| Ron Steinfeld | Macquarie University, Australia |
| Tsuyoshi Takagi | Future University-Hakodate, Japan |
| Damien Vergnaud | b-it, Computer Security Group (Bonn), Germany |
| Huaxiong Wang | Nanyang Technological University, Singapore |
| Duncan S. Wong | City University of Hong Kong, Hong Kong |
| Fangguo Zhang | Sun Yat-sen University, China |

## Organizing Committee

| Man Ho Au | University of Wollongong, Australia |
| Xinyi Huang | University of Wollongong, Australia |
| Lan Zhou | University of Wollongong, Australia |

## External Referees

Masayuki Abe
Mohamad Yusoff Alias
Patrick Amon
Vivien Dubois
Georg J. Fuchsbauer
Emeline Hufschmitt
Sozo Inoue
Marcelo Kaihara
Tadayoshi Kohno
Shinichiro Matsuo
Yoichi Omori
Olivier Pereira

Masaaki Shirase
Masakazu Soshi
Francois-Xavier Standaert
Xiaojian Tian
Elvis Tombini
Bogdan Warinschi
Yuji Watanabe
Go Yamamoto
Guomin Yang
Wei-Chuen Yau

# Table of Contents

## Authentication and Symmetric Encryption (Short Papers)

## Signature (Short Papers)

## Asymmetric Encryption (Short Papers)

# Stronger Security of Authenticated Key Exchange

Brian LaMacchia[1], Kristin Lauter[2], and Anton Mityagin[3]

[1] Microsoft Corporation, 1 Microsoft Way, Redmond, WA
bal@microsoft.com
[2] Microsoft Research, 1 Microsoft Way, Redmond, WA
klauter@microsoft.com
[3] Microsoft Live Labs, 1 Microsoft Way, Redmond, WA
mityagin@microsoft.com

**Abstract.** Recent work by Krawczyk [12] and Menezes [16] has highlighted the importance of understanding well the guarantees and limitations of formal security models when using them to prove the security of protocols. In this paper we focus on security models for authenticated key exchange (AKE) protocols. We observe that there are several classes of attacks on AKE protocols that lie outside the scope of the Canetti-Krawczyk model. Some of these additional attacks have already been considered by Krawczyk [12]. In an attempt to bring these attacks within the scope of the security model we extend the Canetti-Krawczyk model for AKE security by providing significantly greater powers to the adversary. Our contribution is a more compact, integrated, and comprehensive formulation of the security model. We then introduce a new AKE protocol called NAXOS and prove that it is secure against these stronger adversaries.

## 1 Introduction

In this paper we extend the Canetti-Krawczyk [11,12] security model for authenticated key exchange (AKE) to capture attacks resulting from leakage of ephemeral and long-term secret keys. Our security model for authenticated key exchange is defined in the spirit of Bellare and Rogaway [3] and Canetti and Krawczyk [11] by an experiment in which the adversary is given many corruption powers for various key exchange sessions and must solve a challenge on a test session. We extend adversarial capabilities to the following extent: the only corruption powers we do not give an adversary in the experiment are those that would trivially break an AKE protocol. We also define a new AKE protocol which is secure in our new model.

More specifically, in an authenticated key exchange protocol, two parties exchange information and compute a secret key as a function of at least four pieces of secret information: their own long-term (static) and ephemeral secret keys and the other party's long-term and ephemeral secret keys. Of the four pieces of

W. Susilo, J.K. Liu, and Y. Mu. (Eds.): ProvSec 2007, LNCS 4784, pp. 1–16, 2007.

information, we allow an adversary to *reveal*[1] any subset of the four which does not contain both the long-term and ephemeral secrets of one of the parties. To explain this more precisely, we divide AKE test sessions (sessions which are subject to attack by an adversary) into two types. In sessions of the first type ("passive" sessions), the adversary does not cancel or modify communications between the two parties. In sessions of the second type ("active" sessions), the adversary may forge the communication of the second party. Another way to phrase the distinction, as done by Krawczyk in the analysis of the HMQV protocol [12], is whether the adversary actively intervenes in the key exchange session or is a passive eavesdropper.

In addition to distinguishing between passive and active sessions, we identify which pieces of secret information the adversary can reveal without being able to trivially break the AKE protocol (compute the session key for any AKE protocol). In both types of sessions, if an adversary can reveal the long-term and the ephemeral secret keys of one of the parties in the session, then the adversary can trivially compute a session key as it has all the secret information of one of the legitimate parties in the session.

For passive sessions, an adversary may reveal both ephemeral secret keys, both long-term secret keys, or one of each from the two different parties without trivially breaking the protocol. Thus security in our model implies weak Perfect Forward Secrecy, defined by Krawczyk to be security against revelation of long-term secret keys after the session is completed (without active adversarial intervention in the session establishment).

For active sessions, the adversary may forge communications from one of the parties. Thus, if the adversary can also reveal the long-term secret key of that same party, then the adversary can trivially compute the session key. The same argument was used by Krawczyk to show that no 2-round AKE protocol can achieve full perfect forward secrecy (PFS). Still, an adversary can reveal a long-term secret key or ephemeral secret key of the other party without trivially breaking the session. So for another example, our extension to the Canetti-Krawczyk model also implies security against Key Compromise Impersonation (KCI) attacks, where the adversary first reveals a long-term secret of a party and then impersonates others to this party.

Considering attacks involving both types of sessions, it is natural to define a single security model which captures all of them. In our model, in passive test sessions we allow the adversary to reveal any subset of the four pieces of secret information which does not contain both the long-term and ephemeral secrets of one of the parties. In active test sessions, we allow the adversary to reveal only the long-term secret or the ephemeral secret key of the party which is executing the test session. In our security experiment, a test session is still considered *clean* even if the adversary has revealed any of the allowable combinations of secret keys of the two parties.

---

[1] We say that an adversary "reveals" a piece of secret information when that adversary chooses to learn the value of that information by performing the corresponding key reveal query as defined in Section 3.2.

Security in this extended Canetti-Krawczyk model also implies security against a number of other attacks not covered by the Canetti-Krawczyk model (see Section 2.2). In a sense, our model is just an extension of an instance of the Canetti-Krawczyk model, since we define the session state of a party to be the ephemeral secret key. On the other hand, *some* instance of the Canetti-Krawczyk model must be chosen when considering the security of any protocol, since the definition of the session-state reveal query must be specified, and our model is stronger than a model which does not include the ephemeral secret key as part of the session state for the session state reveal query. In addition, the Canetti-Krawczyk model does not allow the adversary to attack sessions against which a session state reveal query has been made. They consider such sessions broken, while our definition covers the security of these partially corrupted sessions. Krawczyk does extend the model in [12], but still some attacks are not covered because those sessions are not considered clean. Our model extends the notion of a clean session further, giving the adversary more power to reveal long-term and ephemeral secret keys. Our motivation to include revelations of ephemeral secret keys in the model comes from "practical" (i.e. engineering) considerations and scenarios such as active adversarial attacks or compromise of the random number generator (RNG) used by one of the parties.

We stress that our extension of the security model allows the adversary to register arbitrary public keys for adversary-controlled parties without any checks such as proof-of-possession done by the certificate authority. In contrast, some of the protocols in the literature [13,14] were proved secure assuming that the key registration is done honestly. Namely, that initially a trusted party generates keys for all, even adversary-controlled parties.

Finally, we present a new AKE protocol, called NAXOS, which provably meets our definition of AKE security. We prove the security of NAXOS under the standard Gap Diffie-Hellman assumption. We also improve the concrete security of NAXOS under the related Pairing Diffie-Hellman assumption. A version of the NAXOS protocol with key confirmation is also possible.

In Figure 1 we compare the efficiency and security of NAXOS with four other recent authenticated key exchange protocols: HMQV, KEA+ [15], protocol $\mathcal{TS}3$ by Jeong, Katz and Lee [13] and Kudla-Paterson [14][2]. The second column in the table, "Efficiency," lists the relative efficiency of the protocol as measured by the number of exponentiations executed by one party. (Communication costs in all of these protocols, except for Jeong-Katz-Lee, is the same as in the original Diffie-Hellman protocol.) Column 3, "Key Registration," specifies whether adversary-controlled parties can register arbitrary public keys or if honest key-registration is assumed. The fourth column, labeled "Ephemeral," indicates whether an adversary is allowed to reveal ephemeral secret information of the parties. Column 5 lists

---

[2] Kudla and Paterson [14] define partnership via matching session identifiers (computed by the parties), although for their protocol this appears to be equivalent to matching conversations.

| Protocol | Effic. | Key Reg. | Ephemeral | Security | Assumptions |
|---|---|---|---|---|---|
| NAXOS | 4 | Arbitrary | yes | Extended CK | GDH (or PDH) + RO |
| HMQV | 2.5 | Arbitrary | yes | CK + wPFS + KCI | GDH + KEA1 + RO |
| KEA+ | 3 | Arbitrary | yes | CK + wPFS + KCI | GDH (or PDH) + RO |
| Jeong-Katz-Lee | 3 | Honest | no | BR + wPFS | DDH + secure MACs |
| Kudla-Paterson | 3 | Honest | no | BR + KCI | GDH + RO |

**Fig. 1.** Comparison of recent AKE protocols

the security model for each protocol[3]. Finally, the sixth column ("Assumptions") lists the security assumptions upon which each protocol depends[4]. We refer the reader to Chapter 7 of [6] for a good overview of Diffie-Hellman assumptions.

We begin with a brief review in Section 2 of the Canetti-Krawczyk security model and discuss some attacks not covered by their definition in Section 2.2. We introduce our extension of the Canetti-Krawczyk security model in Section 3. In Section 4 we describe the NAXOS protocol and prove its security in the extended model.

## 2  Previous Models

### 2.1  Overview of the Canetti-Krawczyk Model

The Canetti-Krawczyk security model is among a family of security models for authenticated key exchange that includes those of Bellare and Rogaway [3,5] and Bellare, Pointcheval and Rogaway [2]. We refer the reader to Choo et al. [9] for a concise summary of the differences among these various models. We give a high-level overview of the Canetti-Krawczyk model and introduce some notation which will be useful later in the paper. We remark that the model we describe differs from the original definition in that we use session identifiers defined via matching conversations. The same definition was used by Krawczyk when analyzing the security of the HMQV protocol [12] and it is now a commonly used variant of the Canetti-Krawczyk model.

The AKE security experiment involves multiple honest parties and an adversary $\mathcal{M}$ connected via an unauthenticated network. The adversary selects parties to execute key-exchange sessions and selects an order in which the sessions will be executed. Actions the adversary is allowed to perform include taking full

---

[3] CK denotes Canetti-Krawczyk security without perfect forward secrecy, assuming that partnership is defined via matching conversations. BR denotes the Bellare-Rogaway model [3], which appears to be equivalent to the Canetti-Krawczyk model with no ephemeral reveals allowed and key-registration done honestly [9]. KCI denotes security against key-compromise impersonation. wPFS denotes weak perfect forward secrecy. Extended CK denotes our extension of the Canetti-Krawczyk model.

[4] RO – random oracle model [4], DDH – Decisional Diffie-Hellman, GDH – Gap Diffie-Hellman [17], PDH – Pairing Diffie-Hellman [15] and KEA1 – knowledge of exponent assumption [1].

control of any party (a Corrupt query), revealing the session key of any session (a Reveal query), or revealing session-specific secret information of any session (a Session-State Reveal query).

We stress that an AKE session is executed by a single party: since all communication is controlled by an adversary, a party executing a session cannot know for sure with whom it is communicating. The party executing the session is called the *owner* of the session and the other party is called the *peer*. The *matching session* to an AKE session (by the owner with the peer) is the corresponding AKE session which is supposed to be executed by the peer with the owner. The matching session might not exist if the communications were modified by the adversary. The *session identifier* of an AKE session consists of the parties' identities concatenated with messages they exchanged in the session[5]. In [12], a completed session is definied to be "clean" if the session as well as its matching session (if it exists) is not corrupted (neither session key nor session state were revealed by $\mathcal{M}$) and if none of the participating parties were corrupted.

At some point in the experiment, the adversary is allowed to make one Test query: it can select any clean completed session (called the *test session*) and it is given a challenge which consists either of the session key for that session or a randomly selected string. The adversary's goal is to guess correctly which of the cases was selected.

Additionally, the Canetti-Krawczyk [11] definition has an optional perfect forward secrecy (PFS) requirement. In the variant of Canetti-Krawczyk security with PFS, the adversary is allowed to corrupt a participant of the test session (either owner or peer) after the test session is completed. As noted by Krawczyk [12], the PFS requirement is not relevant for 2-round AKE protocols since no 2-round protocol can achieve PFS. Krawczyk introduced the notion of *weak perfect forward secrecy* (wPFS) which can be achieved by 2-round protocols and which he demonstrated is achieved by HMQV [12]. Weak PFS guarantees perfect forward secrecy only for those AKE sessions where the adversary didn't modify communications between the parties. (Using the above terminology, the matching session exists for the test session and both test and matching sessions are clean.)

## 2.2 Attacks Not Covered by the Existing Definitions

We point out several attacks which are not captured by the previous definitions and explain which components of the Canetti-Krawczyk model prohibit these attacks from being considered. First, we observe that although the adversary is allowed to reveal the session state of the parties, he is not allowed to make Session-State Reveal queries against the session he wants to attack (the test session). That is, existing security models do not provide any security guarantees for a session if the ephemeral secret key of either party has been leaked. While Krawczyk ([12]) extends the Canetti-Krawczyk model by making a definition of clean session that allows him to consider resistance to Key Compromise

---

[5] We remark that for protocols, where participants do not have full view of the messages exchanged (for example, see [10]), it might not be possible to define such session identifiers.

Impersonation (KCI) attacks and achieve weak Perfect Forward Secrecy (wPFS), this extension still does not include attacks such as revelation of both ephemeral secret keys or both long-term secret keys. Krawczyk does consider resistance to revelation of both ephemeral secret keys separately, and proves HMQV secure against this attack under the stronger assumptions of GDH and KEA1.

Second, when the adversary corrupts an honest party, he takes full control over this party and reveals all its secret information. This definition of the Corrupt query does not allow attacks where the adversary reveals a long-term secret key of some party prior to the time when that party executes the test session. Here we summarize some attacks which are not allowed by the Canetti-Krawczyk model but are permitted under our new definition:

- Key-compromise impersonation (KCI) attack [7,12]: the adversary reveals a long-term secret key of a party and then impersonates others to this party.
- An adversary reveals the ephemeral secret key of a party and impersonates others to this party.
- Two honest parties execute matching sessions, and the adversary reveals the ephemeral secret keys of both of the parties and tries to learn the session key.
- Two honest parties execute matching sessions. The adversary reveals the ephemeral secret key of one party, the long-term secret key of the other party and tries to learn the session key
- Two honest parties execute matching sessions. The adversary reveals the long-term keys of both of the parties prior to the execution of the session and tries to learn the session key.

## 3   Definitions

### 3.1   Motivation for Our Security Definition

We modify the Canetti-Krawczyk model in the definition of adversarial power and in the notion of cleanness of the test session. Specifically, we replace the Session-State Reveal query with an "Ephemeral Key Reveal" query which reveals the ephemeral secret key of the party. Additionally, we give the adversary the power to reveal a long-term secret key, by making a Long-Term Key Reveal query, without corrupting the party. We remove the Corrupt query as it is no longer necessary: the adversary can achieve the same result as the Corrupt query by revealing all the secret information of the party through Long-Term Key Reveal, Ephemeral Key Reveal and Reveal queries and by computing everything on behalf of that party. We also modify the definition of a "clean session" by allowing the adversary to reveal the maximum possible amount of data. We disallow only those corruptions which allow the adversary to trivially break any AKE protocol.

We classify the test sessions as either "passive" or "active" depending on whether the adversary is able to cancel or modify the information sent between two honest participants. Formally, passive sessions are those where the matching session was completed at some point in the experiment, and active sessions are those where no matching session was completed at any time in the experiment.

For passive sessions we allow the adversary to reveal any subset of the four secret keys (each party's ephemeral and long-term secret keys) which does not contain both the ephemeral and long-term secret keys of a single party. Note that the knowledge of both the ephemeral and long-term keys of one of the parties allows the adversary to compute the session key for any AKE protocol.

For active sessions the communication sent by the peer might be corrupted and thus we cannot define the ephemeral key of the peer. In this case we only allow the adversary to reveal either the ephemeral or the long-term secret key of the owner, as revealing both keys would trivially compromise the protocol. Note that we cannot allow the adversary to reveal the long-term secret of the peer (even after the test session is completed), since Krawczyk [12] shows that in this case one can break any AKE protocol. (This is the same attack which shows the impossibility of the full perfect forward secrecy requirement.)

### 3.2   Security Experiment for Extended Canetti-Krawczyk

Assume that the identities of the parties are binary strings (they can be derived from the actual names of the parties). We will use letters $\mathcal{A}$, $\mathcal{B}$, $\mathcal{C}$, ..., both for referring to the parties and for their identities. The adversary is given the power to select each party's identity (the binary string) if it so chooses.

There are a number of honest parties which are connected to the certificate authority, $\mathcal{CA}$, and to the adversary, $\mathcal{M}$. That is, the communication between the parties is fully controlled by $\mathcal{M}$ (and $\mathcal{M}$ cannot interfere with communication between a single party and the $\mathcal{CA}$). $\mathcal{M}$ is also connected to the certificate authority and can register fictitious parties. The adversary plays a central role in the experiment and is responsible for activating all other parties.

We call a particular instantiation of an AKE protocol executed by one of the parties an *AKE session*. Since all communication is controlled by the adversary, a party can never know if the second party actually exists and if the communication it receives was computed by an honest party or by the adversary. Legitimate execution of an AKE protocol by two parties $\mathcal{A}$ and $\mathcal{B}$ consists of two AKE sessions, matching sessions executed by $\mathcal{A}$ and by $\mathcal{B}$ respectively. Note that an instantiation of the AKE protocol is different depending on whether the executor is the owner or the peer.

We do not assume the existence of explicit session identifiers. Instead, we define a session identifier to consist of the identities of the 2 participants and the information they exchanged. Specifically, a session identifier

$$sid = (role, \mathrm{ID}, \mathrm{ID}^*, \mathrm{comm}_1, \ldots, \mathrm{comm}_n),$$

where $\mathrm{ID} \in \{0,1\}^*$ is the identity of the party executing the session, $role \in \{O, P\}$ is its role (owner/peer) in the protocol, $\mathrm{ID}^*$ is the identity of the other party and $comm_i \in \{0,1\}^*$ is the $i$-th communication sent by the parties. As in the Canetti-Krawczyk model, we define the *matching session* to an AKE session to be the session executed by the other party with the same communications being transmitted, albeit in different order. For example, in a 2-round protocol, if $\mathcal{A}$ executes the session $(O, \mathcal{A}, \mathcal{B}, comm_\mathcal{A}, comm_\mathcal{B})$, then the matching session is executed by $\mathcal{B}$ and has session identifier $(P, \mathcal{B}, \mathcal{A}, comm_\mathcal{A}, comm_\mathcal{B})$.

A party computes a communication $comm_i$ as a function of its own ephemeral and long-term secret keys, its partner's public key and previous messages exchanged. Once a party receives all the communications, it computes a session key as a function of its own ephemeral and long-term secret keys, its partner's public key, and all communications, and completes the session.

The experiment proceeds as follows. Initially $\mathcal{M}$ selects the identities of all honest parties (which can be arbitrary distinct binary strings) and honest parties generate and register their public keys with the $\mathcal{CA}$. The adversary can register arbitrary public keys (even the same as those of some honest parties) on behalf of adversary-controlled parties. Then the adversary makes any sequence of the following queries:

- Send($\mathcal{A}, \mathcal{B}, comm$). Sends a message $comm$ to $\mathcal{A}$ on behalf of $\mathcal{B}$. Returns $\mathcal{A}$'s response to this message. This query allows $\mathcal{M}$ to order $\mathcal{A}$ to start an AKE session with $\mathcal{B}$ and to provide communications from $\mathcal{B}$ to $\mathcal{A}$.
- Long-Term Key Reveal($\mathcal{A}$). Reveals a long-term key of a party $\mathcal{A}$.
- Ephemeral Key Reveal($sid$). Reveals an ephemeral key of a session $sid$ (possibly incomplete).
- Reveal($sid$). Reveals a session key of a completed session $sid$.

Eventually (at any time in the experiment), $\mathcal{M}$ selects a completed session $sid$, makes a query Test($sid$) and is given a challenge value $C$. $\mathcal{M}$ continues the experiment after the Test query. The experiment terminates as soon as $\mathcal{M}$ makes the Guess($b'$) query. The experiment answers the adversary's queries as follows:

- Test($sid$) // can be made only once.
  Pick $b \xleftarrow{\$} \{0, 1\}$. If $b = 1$, let $C \leftarrow$ Reveal($sid$); otherwise pick $C \xleftarrow{\$} \{0, 1\}^\lambda$.
  Return $C$.
- Guess($b'$) // $\mathcal{M}$ terminates after making this query.
  If $b' = b$, return 1, otherwise return 0.

An adversary $\mathcal{M}$ *wins* the experiment if the selected test session is *clean* and if he guesses the challenge correctly (that is, if the Guess query returns 1).

We now define what it means for a test session to be *clean*. Let $sid$ be an AKE session completed by a party $\mathcal{A}$ with some other party $\mathcal{B}$, and denote by $sid^*$ the matching session to $sid$, supposedly executed by $\mathcal{B}$ ($sid^*$ may not exist in the experiment). Denote by $sk_\mathcal{A}$ and $sk_\mathcal{B}$ long-term secret keys of $\mathcal{A}$ and $\mathcal{B}$. Denote by $esk_\mathcal{A}$ and $esk_\mathcal{B}$ ephemeral secret keys generated by $\mathcal{A}$ and $\mathcal{B}$ in $sid$ and $sid^*$ (the latter is defined only if $sid^*$ exists). We say that an AKE session $sid$ is *not clean* if an adversary can trivially compute the session key. That is, a session $sid$ is not clean if any of the following conditions hold:

- $\mathcal{A}$ or $\mathcal{B}$ is an adversary-controlled party. This means in particular that $\mathcal{M}$ chooses or reveals both the long-term and ephemeral secret keys for the party and performs all communications and computations on behalf of the party.

- $\mathcal{M}$ reveals the session key of $sid$ or $sid^*$ (if the latter exists).
- Session $sid^*$ exists and $\mathcal{M}$ reveals either both $sk_A$ and $esk_A$, or both $sk_B$ and $esk_B$.
- Session $sid^*$ doesn't exist and $\mathcal{M}$ reveals either $sk_B$ or both $sk_A$ and $esk_A$.

A session $sid$ is clean if *none* of these conditions hold. We remark that the cleanness of the test session can be identified only after the experiment is completed: the third and fourth conditions above can only be determined in the end of the experiment. That is, the adversary wins the experiment if he correctly guesses the challenge for the test session and this session remains clean until the end of the experiment.

**Definition 1 (Extended Canetti-Krawczyk security).** *The* advantage *of the adversary $\mathcal{M}$ in the AKE experiment with AKE protocol $\Pi$ is defined as*

$$\mathbf{Adv}_{\Pi}^{AKE}(\mathcal{M}) \;=\; \Pr[\mathcal{M} \; wins] - \frac{1}{2}.$$

*We say that an AKE protocol is secure (in the extended Canetti-Krawczyk model) if matching sessions compute the same session keys and no efficient adversary $\mathcal{M}$ has more than a negligible advantage in winning the above experiment.*

## 4 NAXOS AKE Protocol

### 4.1 Assumptions

All the arithmetic in this section is assumed to be in a mathematical group $G$ of known prime order $q$. We denote by $g$ a generator of $G$ and write the group operation multiplicatively.

The discrete logarithm function $DLOG(\cdot)$ in $G$ takes input an element $a \in G$ and returns $x \in \mathbb{Z}_q$ such that $a = g^x$. The computational Diffie-Hellman (CDH) function $CDH(\cdot, \cdot)$ takes as input a tuple of elements $(a, b) \in G^2$ and returns $g^{DLOG(a) \cdot DLOG(b)}$. The Decisional Diffie-Hellman (DDH) function $\mathrm{DDH}(\cdot, \cdot, \cdot)$ takes as input a triple of elements $(a, b, c) \in G^3$ and returns 1 if $c = CDH(a, b)$ and 0 otherwise.

The *advantage* of an algorithm $\mathcal{M}$ in solving the Discrete Logarithm problem, $\mathbf{Adv}^{DLOG}(\mathcal{M})$, is the probability that, given $a \overset{\$}{\leftarrow} G$, $\mathcal{M}$ correctly returns $DLOG(a)$. Similarly, the advantage of an algorithm $\mathcal{M}$ in solving the Gap Diffie-Hellman (GDH) problem, $\mathbf{Adv}^{GDH}(\mathcal{M})$, is the probability that, given as input $(a, b) \overset{\$}{\leftarrow} G^2$ and oracle access to $\mathrm{DDH}(\cdot, \cdot, \cdot)$, $\mathcal{M}$ correctly outputs $CDH(a, b)$. We say that $G$ satisfies the GDH assumption if no feasible adversary can solve the GDH problem with non-negligible probability. The GDH assumption was introduced by Okamoto and Pointcheval [17] and is now a standard cryptographic assumption used to establish the security of many protocols.

Let $G'$ be another group of order $q$. A function $e : G \times G \to G'$ is a bilinear pairing if it is non-degenerate and if for any pair $g^a, g^b \in G$, $e(g^a, g^b) = e(g, g)^{ab}$. The Pairing Diffie-Hellman (PDH) problem recently introduced by Mityagin and

Lauter [15] is to solve the CDH problem when given access to the pairing oracle $e$. The advantage $\mathbf{Adv}^{\mathrm{PDH}}(\mathcal{M})$ of an algorithm $\mathcal{M}$ in solving the PDH problem is the probability that $\mathcal{M}$, given $(a, b) \overset{\$}{\leftarrow} G^2$ and a pairing oracle $e$, computes $CDH(a, b)$. We say that $G$ satisfies the PDH assumption if no feasible adversary solves the PDH problem with non-negligible probability. In groups which have a bilinear pairing, the PDH problem is equivalent to the original CDH problem, although one can also consider the PDH problem in groups where no efficient pairing operation is known. We find the Pairing Diffie-Hellman assumption to be as justified as the GDH assumption since the only known way to compute DDH in groups where CDH is hard is via a pairing function.

### 4.2 Protocol Description

The NAXOS AKE protocol uses a mathematical group $G$ and two hash functions, $H_1 : \{0,1\}^* \to \mathbb{Z}_q$ and $H_2 : \{0,1\}^* \to \{0,1\}^\lambda$ (for some constant $\lambda$). A long-term secret key of a party $\mathcal{A}$ is an exponent $sk_\mathcal{A} \in \mathbb{Z}_q$, and the corresponding long-term public key of $\mathcal{A}$ is the power $pk_\mathcal{A} = g^{sk_\mathcal{A}} \in G$. In the following description of an AKE session of NAXOS executed between the parties $\mathcal{A}$ and $\mathcal{B}$ we assume that each party knows the other's public key and that public keys are in the group $G$. Additionally, we use the syntax $H(x_1, x_2, ...)$ to represent the application of the hash function $H$ to the concatenation of its arguments $x_1||x_2||....$

The session execution proceeds as follows. The parties pick ephemeral secret keys $esk_\mathcal{A}$ and $esk_\mathcal{B}$ at random from $\{0,1\}^\lambda$. Then the parties exchange values $g^{H_1(esk_\mathcal{A}, sk_\mathcal{A})}$ and $g^{H_1(esk_\mathcal{B}, sk_\mathcal{B})}$, check if received values are in the group $G$ and only compute the session keys if the check succeeds. The session key $K \in \{0,1\}^\lambda$ is computed as

$$H_2(g^{H_1(esk_\mathcal{B}, sk_\mathcal{B})sk_\mathcal{A}}, g^{H_1(esk_\mathcal{A}, sk_\mathcal{A})sk_\mathcal{B}}, g^{H_1(esk_\mathcal{A}, sk_\mathcal{A})H_1(esk_\mathcal{B}, sk_\mathcal{B})}, \mathcal{A}, \mathcal{B}).$$

The last two components in the hash are the identities of $\mathcal{A}$ and $\mathcal{B}$, which we assume to be binary strings. Figure 2 depicts the protocol.

**Theorem 1.** *NAXOS satisfies Extended Canetti-Krawczyk security if $H_1$ and $H_2$ are modeled by independent random oracles.*

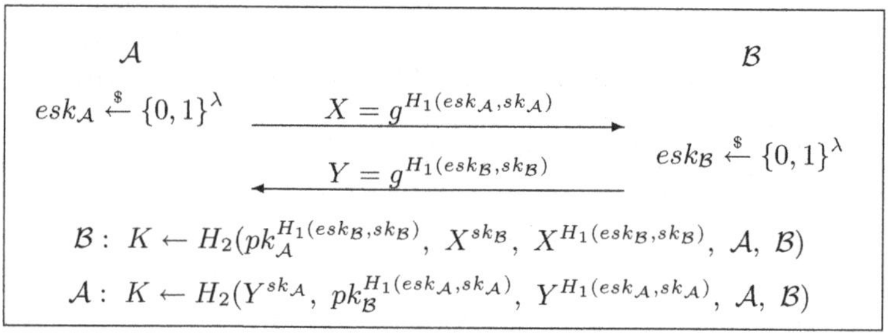

**Fig. 2.** NAXOS AKE Protocol

*For any AKE adversary $\mathcal{M}$ against NAXOS that runs in time at most $t$, involves at most $n$ honest parties and activates at most $k$ sessions, we show that there exists a GDH solver $\mathcal{S}$, a PDH solver $\mathcal{R}$ and a DLOG solver $\mathcal{T}$ such that*

$$\mathbf{Adv}^{GDH}(\mathcal{S}) = \mathbf{Adv}^{PDH}(\mathcal{R})$$

$$\geq \frac{1}{2}\left(\min\left\{\frac{2}{k^2}, \frac{1}{nk}\right\} \cdot \mathbf{Adv}^{AKE}_{NAXOS}(\mathcal{M}) - 2n \cdot \mathbf{Adv}^{DLOG}(\mathcal{T}) - O\left(\frac{k^2}{2^\lambda}\right)\right),$$

*where $\mathcal{S}$ runs in time $O(tk)$, $\mathcal{R}$ runs in time $O(t\log t)$ and $\mathcal{T}$ runs in time $O(t)$.*

The proof of Theorem 1 is given in Appendix A.

# References

1. Bellare, M., Palacio, A.: The Knowledge-of-Exponent Assumptions and 3-Round Zero-Knowledge Protocols. In: Franklin, M. (ed.) CRYPTO 2004. LNCS, vol. 3152, pp. 273–289. Springer, Heidelberg (2004)
2. Bellare, M., Pointcheval, D., Rogaway, P.: Authenticated Key Exchange Secure Against Dictionary Attacks. In: Preneel, B. (ed.) EUROCRYPT 2000. LNCS, vol. 1807, pp. 139–155. Springer, Heidelberg (2000)
3. Bellare, M., Rogaway, P.: Entity Authentication and Key Distribution. In: Stinson, D.R. (ed.) CRYPTO 1993. LNCS, vol. 773, pp. 110–125. Springer, Heidelberg (1994)
4. Bellare, M., Rogaway, P.: Random Oracles are Practical: A Paradigm for Designing Efficient Protocols. ACM Conference on Computer and Communications Security, 62–73 (1993)
5. Bellare, M., Rogaway, P.: Provably Secure Session Key Distribution: the Three Party Case. In: STOC 1995. Proc. 27th Annual Symposium on the Theory of Computing, ACM Press, New York (1995)
6. Bellare, M., Rogaway, P.: Introduction to Modern Cryptography. Course notes for UCSD cryptography course, available at http://www-cse.ucsd.edu/users/mihir/cse207/classnotes.html
7. Blake-Wilson, S., Johnson, D., Menezes, A.: Key Agreement Protocols and their Security Analysis. In: Darnell, M. (ed.) Cryptography and Coding. LNCS, vol. 1355, pp. 30–45. Springer, Heidelberg (1997)
8. Choo, K.-K.R., Boyd, C., Hitchcock, Y.: Errors in Computational Complexity Proofs for Protocols. In: Roy, B. (ed.) ASIACRYPT 2005. LNCS, vol. 3788, pp. 624–643. Springer, Heidelberg (2005)
9. Choo, K.-K.R., Boyd, C., Hitchcock, Y.: Examining Indistinguishability-Based Proof Models for Key Establishment Protocols. In: Roy, B. (ed.) ASIACRYPT 2005. LNCS, vol. 3788, pp. 585–604. Springer, Heidelberg (2005)
10. Choo, K.-K.R.: A Proof of Revised Yahalom Protocol in the Bellare and Rogaway (1993) Model. The Computer Journal, Oxford University; also available at Cryptology ePrint Archive: Report 2007/188 ( to appear, 2007)
11. Canetti, R., Krawczyk, H.: Analysis of Key-Exchange Protocols and Their Use for Building Secure Channels. In: Pfitzmann, B. (ed.) EUROCRYPT 2001. LNCS, vol. 2045, pp. 453–474. Springer, Heidelberg (2001)

12. Krawczyk, H.: HMQV: A High-Performance Secure Diffie-Hellman Protocol. In: Shoup, V. (ed.) CRYPTO 2005. LNCS, vol. 3621, pp. 546–566. Springer, Heidelberg (2005)

13. Jeong, I.R., Katz, J., Lee, D.H.: One-Round Protocols for Two-Party Authenticated Key Exchange. In: Jakobsson, M., Yung, M., Zhou, J. (eds.) ACNS 2004. LNCS, vol. 3089, Springer, Heidelberg (2004)

14. Kudla, C., Paterson, K.G.: Modular Security Proofs for Key Agreement Protocols. In: Roy, B. (ed.) ASIACRYPT 2005. LNCS, vol. 3788, pp. 549–565. Springer, Heidelberg (2005)

15. Lauter, K., Mityagin, A.: Security Analysis of KEA Authenticated Key Exchange. In: Yung, M., Dodis, Y., Kiayias, A., Malkin, T.G. (eds.) PKC 2006. LNCS, vol. 3958, pp. 378–394. Springer, Heidelberg (2006)

16. Menezes, A.: Another look at HMQV. Journal of Mathematical Cryptology (to appear)

17. Okamoto, T., Pointcheval, D.: The Gap Problems: A New Class of Problems for the Security of Cryptographic Schemes. In: Kim, K.-c. (ed.) PKC 2001. LNCS, vol. 1992, pp. 104–118. Springer, Heidelberg (2001)

# A    Security Proof for NAXOS

Let $\mathcal{A}$ be any AKE adversary against NAXOS. We start by observing that since the session key of the test session is computed as $K = H_2(\sigma)$ for some 5-tuple $\sigma$, the adversary $\mathcal{M}$ has only two ways to distinguish $K$ from a random string:

1. Forging attack. At some point $\mathcal{M}$ queries $H_2$ on the same 5-tuple $\sigma$.
2. Key-replication attack. $\mathcal{M}$ succeeds in forcing the establishment of another session that has the same session key as the test session.

A similar argument was used in the security proofs of the HMQV [12] and KEA+ [15] AKE protocols. If random oracles produce no collisions, the key-replication attack is impossible as equality of session keys implies equality of the corresponding 5-tuples (which are hashed to produce session keys). In turn, distinct AKE sessions must have distinct 5-tuples. Therefore, if random oracles produce no collisions (collisions happen with probability $O(k^2/2^\lambda)$), $\mathcal{M}$ must perform a forging attack. Next we show that if $\mathcal{M}$ can mount a successful forging attack, then we can construct a Gap Diffie-Hellman solver $\mathcal{S}$ which uses $\mathcal{M}$ as a subroutine. Most of the remaining proof is devoted to the construction of $\mathcal{S}$.

$\mathcal{S}$ takes as input a GDH challenge $(X_0, Y_0)$. Then $\mathcal{S}$ executes the Extended Canetti-Krawczyk (ECK) experiment with $\mathcal{M}$ the adversary against the NAXOS protocol, and modifies the data returned by the honest parties in such a way that if $\mathcal{M}$ breaks security of NAXOS, then $\mathcal{S}$ can reveal the solution to the GDH problem from $\mathcal{M}$.

We distinguish between two cases of $\mathcal{M}$'s behavior: whether $\mathcal{M}$ selects a test session for which the matching session exists or if the test session has no matching session. We handle analysis of these cases differently and note that at least one of them happens with probability $\geq 1/2$.

## A.1   Matching Session Exists

Assume that $\mathcal{M}$ selects a test session for which the matching session exists. Then $\mathcal{S}$ modifies the experiment as follows. $\mathcal{S}$ selects at random matching sessions executed by some honest parties $\mathcal{A}$ and $\mathcal{B}$ (in fact, $\mathcal{S}$ selects two sessions at random and continues only if they are matching – $\mathcal{S}$ successfully guesses them with probability $2/k^2$). Denote by $comm_A$ and $comm_B$ the communications sent by the respective parties in these matching sessions. When either of these sessions is activated, $\mathcal{S}$ does not follow the protocol. Instead, $\mathcal{S}$ generates $esk_A$ and $esk_B$ normally but sets $comm_A \leftarrow X_0$ (in place of $g^{H_1(sk_A, esk_A)}$) and $comm_B \leftarrow Y_0$ (in place of $g^{H_1(sk_B, esk_B)}$).

With probability $1/k^2$ $\mathcal{M}$ picks one of the selected sessions as the test session and another as its matching session. We claim that if $\mathcal{M}$ wins in the forging attack, $\mathcal{S}$ can solve the CDH challenge. Indeed, the supposed session key for the selected session is $H_2(\sigma)$, where the 5-tuple $\sigma$ includes the value $CDH(X_0, Y_0)$. To win, $\mathcal{M}$ must have queried $\sigma$ to the random oracle $H_2$.

If the selected session is indeed the test session, $\mathcal{M}$ is allowed to reveal a subset of $\{\ sk_A,\ sk_B,\ esk_A\ \text{and}\ esk_B\ \}$, but it is not allowed to reveal both $(sk_A, esk_A)$ or both $(sk_B, esk_B)$. We observe that in this case, the only way that $\mathcal{M}$ can distinguish this simulated ECK experiment from a true ECK experiment is if $\mathcal{M}$ queries $(sk_A, esk_A)$ or $(sk_B, esk_B)$ to $H_1$ (this way, $\mathcal{M}$ will find out that $comm_A$ and $comm_B$ were not computed correctly). Proposition 1 shows that the probability that $\mathcal{M}$ makes such queries is at most

$$2n \cdot \mathbf{Adv}^{\mathrm{DLOG}}(\mathcal{T})$$

for some discrete logarithm solver $\mathcal{T}$.

Therefore (assuming that $\mathcal{M}$ always selects a test session which has a matching session)

$$\mathbf{Adv}^{\mathrm{GDH}}(\mathcal{S}) \ \geq\ \frac{2}{k^2} \cdot \mathbf{Adv}^{\mathrm{AKE}}_{\mathrm{NAXOS}}(\mathcal{M}) - 2n \cdot \mathbf{Adv}^{\mathrm{DLOG}}(\mathcal{T}) - O\left(\frac{k^2}{2^\lambda}\right).$$

Note that in this case $\mathcal{S}$ doesn't make any queries to the DDH oracle and runs in time $O(t)$.

## A.2   No Matching Session

Now assume that $\mathcal{M}$ selects a test session for which no matching session exists. In this case $\mathcal{S}$ modifies the experiment as follows. $\mathcal{S}$ selects a random party $\mathcal{B}$ and sets $pk_B \leftarrow X_0$. Note that $\mathcal{S}$ doesn't know the secret key corresponding to this public key and thus it cannot properly simulate ECK sessions executed by $\mathcal{B}$. $\mathcal{S}$ handles ECK sessions executed by $\mathcal{B}$ as follows (assume that $\mathcal{B}$ is the owner). $\mathcal{S}$ randomly selects $esk_B$, picks $h$ at random from $\mathbb{Z}_q$ and sets $comm_B = g^h$ instead of $g^{H_1(esk_B, DLOG(X_0))}$. $\mathcal{S}$ sets a session key $K$ (which is supposed to be $H_2(CDH(X_0, comm_C), pk_C^h, comm_C^h, \mathcal{B}, \mathcal{C})$) to be a random value. Note that $\mathcal{S}$ can handle session key and ephemeral secret key reveals by revealing $K$ and $esk_B$, but cannot handle long-term secret key reveals.

If $\mathcal{C}$ is an adversary-controlled party, $\mathcal{M}$ can compute the session key on its own, reveal $K$ and detect that it is fake. To address this issue, $\mathcal{S}$ watches $\mathcal{M}$'s random oracle queries and if $\mathcal{M}$ ever queries $(Z, pk_{\mathcal{C}}^h, comm_{\mathcal{C}}^h, \mathcal{B}, \mathcal{C})$ to $H_2$ (for some $Z \in G$), $\mathcal{S}$ checks if $DDH(X_0, comm_{\mathcal{C}}, Z) = 1$ and if yes, replies with the key $K$. Similarly, on the computation of $K$, $\mathcal{S}$ checks if $K$ should be equal to any previous response from the random oracle. Because of these checks $\mathcal{S}$ runs in quadratic time of the number of random oracle's queries.

$\mathcal{M}$ cannot detect that it is in the simulated ECK experiment unless it either queries $(esk_{\mathcal{B}}, DLOG(X_0))$ to $H_1$ or reveals a long-term secret key of $\mathcal{B}$. The first event reveals $DLOG(X_0)$ and allows $\mathcal{S}$ to solve the CDH problem – by Proposition 1 it happens with probability at most

$$n \cdot \mathbf{Adv}^{\mathrm{DLOG}}(\mathcal{T})$$

for some discrete logarithm solver $\mathcal{T}$. The second event is impossible as otherwise the test session will no longer be clean.

$\mathcal{S}$ also randomly selects an ECK session in which $\mathcal{B}$ is the peer. Denote the owner of this session by $\mathcal{A}$. When the selected session is activated, $\mathcal{S}$ follows the protocol only partially: $\mathcal{S}$ generates $esk_{\mathcal{A}}$ normally but sets $comm_{\mathcal{A}} \leftarrow Y_0$ (in place of $g^{H_1(sk_{\mathcal{A}}, esk_{\mathcal{A}})}$).

With probability at least $1/nk$ ($1/n$ to pick the correct party $\mathcal{B}$ and $1/k$ to pick the correct session), $\mathcal{M}$ picks the selected session as the test session, and if it wins, it solves the CDH problem. The supposed session key for the selected session is $H_2(\sigma)$, where the 5-tuple $\sigma$ includes the value $CDH(X_0, Y_0)$. To win, $\mathcal{M}$ must have queried $\sigma$ to the random oracle $H_2$.

If the selected session is indeed the test session, $\mathcal{M}$ is not allowed to reveal both $sk_{\mathcal{A}}$ and $esk_{\mathcal{A}}$ and is not allowed to corrupt $\mathcal{B}$. In this case, the only way that $\mathcal{M}$ can distinguish this simulated ECK experiment from a true ECK experiment is if M queries $(sk_{\mathcal{A}}, esk_{\mathcal{A}})$ to $H_1$. However, by Proposition 1 it happens with probability at most

$$n \cdot \mathbf{Adv}^{\mathrm{DLOG}}(\mathcal{T})$$

for some discrete logarithm solver $\mathcal{T}$.

Overall, if $\mathcal{M}$ always selects a test session which doesn't have a matching session then the success probability of $\mathcal{S}$ is at most

$$\mathbf{Adv}^{\mathrm{GDH}}(\mathcal{S}) \geq \frac{1}{nk} \cdot \mathbf{Adv}^{\mathrm{AKE}}_{\mathrm{NAXOS}}(\mathcal{M}) - 2n \cdot \mathbf{Adv}^{\mathrm{DLOG}}(\mathcal{T}) - O\left(\frac{k^2}{2^\lambda}\right),$$

where $\mathcal{T}$ is some discrete logarithm solver. $\mathcal{S}$ runs in time $O(kt)$.

### A.3   Efficiency Analysis

We observe that the running time of $\mathcal{S}$ is $O(kt)$. For each session key computation done by $\mathcal{B}$ (where $Y$ is the incoming communication in that session) the solver $\mathcal{S}$ has to go over all previous $H_2$ queries and for each $H_2$ query of the form $(\ldots, Z, \ldots)$ check if $\mathrm{DDH}(X_0, Y, Z) = 1$. Similarly, on each DDH query of the form $(\ldots, Z, \ldots)$, $\mathcal{S}$ has to go over all previous session key computations done by $\mathcal{B}$ and for each such computation $\mathcal{S}$ checks if $DDH(X_0, Y, Z)$ (where $Y$ the incoming communication in that session). Since $\mathcal{M}$ can activate at most $k$ sessions and make at most $t$ $H_2$ queries, the total running time is $O(tk)$.

The running time of the solver can be improved if the solver has access to the pairing oracle instead of to the DDH oracle. We construct the PDH solver $\mathcal{R}$ in the same way as $\mathcal{S}$ with the only difference being that $\mathcal{R}$ must also handle the checks discussed above. Note that $DDH(X_0, Y, Z) = 1$ if and only if $e(Z, g) = e(X_0, Y)$. Therefore $\mathcal{R}$ can store corresponding values $e(Z, g)$ in a balanced binary tree and on each session executed by $\mathcal{B}$ check for $X_0$, $Y$ by computing $e(X_0, Y)$ and searching for this value in the binary tree (which can be done in $\log t$ steps). Therefore, $\mathcal{R}$ has the same advantage as $\mathcal{S}$ and runs in time $O(t \log t)$.

## A.4  Reduction to the Discrete Logarithm Problem

Finally, we are left to prove the proposition which reduces breaking secret keys of honest parties to solving the Discrete Logarithm problem.

Consider any adversary $\mathcal{M}$ against the NAXOS protocol. $\mathcal{M}$ can obtain long-term secret keys of some honest parties via Long-Term Key Reveal queries and can attempt to break long-term keys of uncorrupted parties. We claim that he cannot do so unless he solves the discrete logarithm problem. Let "$\mathcal{M}$ breaks a secret key" denote an event that $\mathcal{M}$ makes a random oracle query $H_1(*, sk_A)$ for some honest party $\mathcal{A}$ against which $\mathcal{M}$ didn't make the Long-Term Key Reveal query.

**Proposition 1.** *For any adversary $\mathcal{M}$ against the NAXOS protocol who runs in time $t$ and involves at most $n$ honest parties, there exists a discrete logarithm solver $\mathcal{T}$ such that*

$$Prob[\text{``}\mathcal{M} \text{ breaks a secret key''}] < nAdv^{DLOG}(\mathcal{T}),$$

*where $\mathcal{T}$ runs in time $O(t)$.*

**Proof.** Since the security experiment involves at most $n$ honest parties, we can assume that $\mathcal{M}$ queries $(*, sk_A)$ to $H_1$ for a certain party $\mathcal{A}$ with probability at least

$$\frac{1}{n} Prob[\text{``}\mathcal{M} \text{ breaks a secret key''}].$$

The discrete logarithm solver $\mathcal{T}$ is given a challenge $X$; T runs the AKE experiment with $\mathcal{M}$ and sets the public key of a party $\mathcal{A}$ to be $X$.

$\mathcal{T}$ can perfectly simulate all actions of the parties except for computing $H_1(esk_A, sk_A)$ during key-exchange sessions involving $\mathcal{A}$ (here $sk_A$ is supposed to be $DLOG(X)$). In these cases $\mathcal{T}$ randomly selects distinct random oracle values for distinct values of $esk_A$.

The only way that $\mathcal{M}$ can distinguish this simulation from the true experiment is by querying $(esk_A, DLOG(X))$ to the random oracle. However in this case (as we see below) $\mathcal{T}$ automatically wins the DLOG experiment.

Whenever $\mathcal{M}$ makes a query of the form $(y, z)$ to the random oracle $H_1$, $\mathcal{T}$ verifies whether $X = g^z$ and if true, submits $z$ as an answer to the DLOG experiment. Note that in the simulated experiment $\mathcal{M}$ makes a random oracle query $(*, sk_{\mathcal{A}} = DLOG(X))$ with probability at least

$$\frac{1}{n}\mathrm{Prob}[\text{``}\mathcal{M} \text{ breaks a secret key''}].$$

Therefore, $\mathcal{T}$ succeeds in solving discrete logarithm of $X$ at least with this probability.

# An Hybrid Approach for Efficient Multicast Stream Authentication over Unsecured Channels

Christophe Tartary[1,2], Huaxiong Wang[1,3], and Josef Pieprzyk[3]

[1] Division of Mathematical Sciences
School of Physical and Mathematical Sciences
Nanyang Technological University
Singapore
[2] Institute for Theoretical Computer Science
Tsinghua University
Beijing, 100084
P.R. China
[3] Centre for Advanced Computing - Algorithms and Cryptography
Department of Computing
Macquarie University
NSW 2109 Australia
{ctartary,josef}@ics.mq.edu.au,
HXWang@ntu.edu.sg

**Abstract.** We study the multicast stream authentication problem when an opponent can drop, reorder and inject data packets into the communication channel. In this context, bandwidth limitation and fast authentication are the core concerns. Therefore any authentication scheme is to reduce as much as possible the packet overhead and the time spent at the receiver to check the authenticity of collected elements. Recently, Tartary and Wang developed a provably secure protocol with small packet overhead and a reduced number of signature verifications to be performed at the receiver.

In this paper, we propose an hybrid scheme based on Tartary and Wang's approach and Merkle hash trees. Our construction will exhibit a smaller overhead and a much faster processing at the receiver making it even more suitable for multicast than the earlier approach. As Tartary and Wang's protocol, our construction is provably secure and allows the total recovery of the data stream despite erasures and injections occurred during transmission.

**Keywords:** Stream Authentication, Polynomial Reconstruction, Unsecured Channel, Merkle Hash Tree, Erasure Code.

## 1 Introduction

With the expansion of communication networks, broadcasting has become a major technology to distribute digital content from a single user to a large audience via a public communication channel such as the Internet for instance. Online games, military defense systems, satellite television and financial quotes are a few examples of multicast distribution of information. Nevertheless, in large-scale broadcasts, a lost piece of a data stream[1] could generate a flood of retransmission requests from the receivers that

---

[1] In broadcasting, the sequence of information sent into the network is called *stream*.

W. Susilo, J.K. Liu, and Y. Mu. (Eds.): ProvSec 2007, LNCS 4784, pp. 17–34, 2007.

congregate at the sender's side. Furthermore the network can be under the influence of malicious users performing illegal and damaging operations on the stream. As a consequence, the security of a multicast authentication protocol relies on the network properties and the opponents' computational power. Several unconditionally secure schemes have been developed [5, 9, 36] but either these are one-time protocols or they require too large storage capacities. In this work, we consider that adversaries have polynomially bounded computational abilities.

An application like a pay-TV channel broadcasting programs 24 hours a day and seven a week suggests that the stream can be considered as infinite. Nevertheless the receivers must be able to authenticate data within a short period of time upon reception. Since many protocols will distribute private or sensitive content, non-repudiation of the sender is required for most of them as using data from an uncertain origin can have disastrous consequences during military operations for instance. Unfortunately signing each data packet[2] is impractical as digital signatures are generally very expensive to generate and/or verify. Furthermore bandwidth limitations prevent one-time and $k$-time signatures [11, 35] from being used due to their large size. Boneh et al. constructed short signatures in [6] but their verification time is prohibitive to be a practical solution for authenticated broadcast [3, 37]. Thus a general approach is to generate a single signature and to amortize its computational cost and overhead over several data packets using a chain of hash functions for instance.

Several constructions relying on hash functions have been developed to deal with packet loss [12, 21, 31, 32]. A signature is generated from time to time and is always assumed to be received correctly. This provides authentication and non-repudiation of the sender and allows new receivers to join the communication group at any block[3] boundary. Using Markov chains [10, 30, 42] to model the network packet loss, the authors of the previous constructions determined bounds on the packet authentication probability. Unfortunately, the main issue in those schemes is the fact that they rely on the reliable reception of signature packets. Since networks like the Internet only provide a best effort delivery of data, the reliability requirement limits the area of applications of those constructions.

In order to overcome this issue, a general solution is to split the signature into $k$ parts where only $\ell$ of them $(\ell < k)$ are enough to guarantee the recovery of the whole signature. Many schemes have been developed using this idea [1, 26, 27, 28, 29] but none of them tolerates a single packet injection. Using a Merkle hash tree [20], Wong and Lam developed a construction dealing with both erasures and injections [41]. Nevertheless, it is vulnerable to denial of service attacks (DoS) against the computational resources of the receiver as each packet carries the block signature. Thus, in the worst case, the number of signature verifications to be performed per block of $n$ packets is $\Theta(n)$. In [15], Karlof et al. overcame this problem by using Merkle hash trees as one-way accumulators [2, 4, 24, 25]. Their approach requires $O(1)$ signature verifications per block in any case and each augmented packet[4] has to carry $\lceil \log_2 n \rceil$ hashes which may be too

---

[2] Since the data stream is large, it is divided into fixed-size chunks called *packets*.

[3] In order to be processed, packets are gathered into fixed-size sets called *blocks*.

[4] We call *augmented packets* the elements sent into the network. They generally consist of the original data packets with some redundancy used to prove the authenticity of the element.

large for resource limited receivers. In [17], Lysyanskaya et al. used a polynomial representation as well as an algorithm by Guruwami and Sudan [14] to deal with packet drops and data injections. As in Karlof et al.'s construction, their technique requires $O(1)$ signature verifications but its packet overhead is $O(1)$ bits. Recently, Lysyankaya et al.'s approach has been extended by Tartary and Wang [39]. This scheme uses Maximum Distance Separable (MDS) codes [18] and is denoted as TWMDS in our paper. It requires $O(1)$ signature verifications per block, $O(1)$ bit packet overhead and enables all data packets to be recovered at the receiver despite erasures and injections thanks to the erasure correcting code. This feature is important when the application processing the data packets is not loss tolerant as it may be the case for military applications where obtaining all information about the enemy target is vital or for high quality video streaming where this technique prevents frozen images to happen.

In this work, we present an hybrid construction based on Merkle hash trees and TWMDS which will be provably secure in the random oracle model. This idea of using a Merkle hash tree for multicast authentication is note new but this technique enables fast authentication as only hash computations are performed. As in TWMDS, our new scheme will enable the whole data packets to be recovered at the receiver despite erasures and injections and will allow new members to join the communication group at any block boundary. As noted earlier, both the packet overhead and the speed of authentication at the receiver are the core concerns for multicast stream authentication. Since the relation between overhead and speed is central in this context and limits the scope of applications of many schemes, we will emphasize that our protocol exhibits a smaller overhead and a much faster authentication process than TWMDS making our scheme more suitable for broadcast applications. As TWMDS, the non-repudiation of the stream origin will be guaranteed using a digital signature.

The plan of this paper is as follows. In the next section, we introduce our network model and recall a few results from [14]. Our authentication scheme is described in Sect. 3 while its security and recovery property will be discussed in Sect. 4. In Sect. 5, we present the benefits of our approach in term of overhead as well as authentication speed at the receiver. Finally, we will sum up our contribution to the multicast authentication problem over unsecured channels in Sect. 6.

## 2   Preliminaries

We now present our network model as well as an erasure correcting code we use in our construction. We also recall a modified version of the algorithm Poly-Reconstruct by Guruswami and Sudan [14] which will be used to deal with data injections and packet drops as in [17, 39].

**Network Model.** We consider that the communication channel is under the influence of an opponent $\mathcal{O}$ who can drop and rearrange packets of his choice as well as can inject bogus data into the network. This corresponds to the unsecured communication channel model described by Menezes et al. in [19]. We investigate the multicast stream authentication problem. Thus we can assume that a reasonable number of original augmented packets reaches the receivers and not too many incorrect chunks of data are injected by $\mathcal{O}$. Indeed, if too many original packets are dropped then data transmission becomes the main problem to treat since a small number of received packets would be probably useless even if authenticated. On the other hand, if $\mathcal{O}$ injects a large number of forged packets then the main problem becomes increasing the resistance against DoS attacks. In order to build our signature amortization scheme, we need to split the data stream into blocks of $n$ packets: $P_1, \ldots, P_n$. We define two parameters: $\alpha\,(0 < \alpha \leq 1)$ (the *survival* rate) and $\beta\,(\beta \geq 1)$ (the *flood* rate). It is assumed that at least a fraction $\alpha$ and no more than a multiple $\beta$ of the number of augmented packets are received. This means that at least $\lceil \alpha n \rceil$ original augmented packets are received amongst a total which does not exceed $\lfloor \beta n \rfloor$ elements.

**Code Construction.** In our construction, we focus on linear codes to correct erasures. As in [39], we use *Maximum Distance Separable* (MDS) codes [18]. As our scheme works with any MDS code, we refer the reader to [39] for a discussion about which family of MDS codes to choose for best efficiency. Note that any linear code can be represented by a *generator matrix* $G$. *Encoding* a message $m$ (represented as a row vector) means computing the corresponding codeword $c$ as: $c := m\,G$ (see [18]).

**Polynomial Reconstruction Algorithm.** In [14], Guruswami and Sudan developed an algorithm Poly-Reconstruct to solve the polynomial reconstruction problem. They proved that if $T$ points were given as input then their algorithm output the list of all polynomials of degree at most $K$ passing through at least $N$ of the $T$ points provided: $T > \sqrt{KN}$. We will use the same version of Poly-Reconstruct as in [39] where it was named MPR. Denote $\mathbb{F}_{2^q}$ the field representing the coefficients of the polynomial. Every element of $\mathbb{F}_{2^q}$ can be represented as a polynomial of degree at most $q - 1$ over $\mathbb{F}_2$ (see [16]). Operations in $\mathbb{F}_{2^q}$ are performed modulo a polynomial $\mathcal{Q}(X)$ of degree $q$ ($\mathcal{Q}(X)$ is irreducible over $\mathbb{F}_2$).

**MPR**

Input:The maximal degree $K$ of the polynomial $Q(X)$, the minimal number $N$ of agreeable points, $T$ points $\{(x_i, y_i), 1 \leq i \leq T\}$ and the polynomial $\mathcal{Q}(X)$ of degree $q$.
1. If there are no more than $\sqrt{KN}$ distinct points then the algorithm stops.
2. Using $\mathcal{Q}(X)$, run Poly-Reconstruct on the $T$ points to get the list of all polynomials of degree at most $K$ over $\mathbb{F}_{2^q}$ passing through at least $N$ of the points.
3. Given the list $\{L_1(X), \ldots, L_\mu(X)\}$ obtained at Step 2. For each polynomial $L_i(X) := \mathcal{L}_{i,0} + \ldots + \mathcal{L}_{i,K} X^K$ where $\forall i \in \{0, \ldots, K\} \mathcal{L}_{i,j} \in \mathbb{F}_{2^q}$, form the elements: $\mathcal{L}_i := \mathcal{L}_{i,0} \| \cdots \| \mathcal{L}_{i,K}$.
Output: $\{\mathcal{L}_1, \ldots, \mathcal{L}_\mu\}$: list of candidates

Note that Poly-Reconstruct runs in time quadratic in $N$ and outputs a list of size at most quadratic in $N$ as well (see Theorem 6.12 and Lemma 6.13 from [13]). Algorithms for implementing Poly-Reconstruct can be found in [22].

## 3   Our Hybrid Authentication Protocol

In order to guarantee the security of our construction, we need a collision resistant hash function $h$ (see [33]) and an unforgeable signature scheme (Sign$_{\mathrm{SK}}$,Verify$_{\mathrm{PK}}$) (see [38]) the key pair of which (SK,PK) is created by a generator KeyGen as in [15, 17, 39].

**Scheme Overview.** Each block contains $n$ data packets $P_1, \ldots, P_n$ and is located within the whole stream using its identification value BID. Our algorithms apply two steps.

The first step works as follows. Due to our network model, we want to generate $n$ augmented packets $AP_1, \ldots, AP_n$ such that we can reconstruct the sequence of packets $P_1, \ldots, P_n$ from any $\lceil \alpha n \rceil$-subset of $\{AP_1, \ldots, AP_n\}$. Thus we need to encode $P_1, \ldots, P_n$ using a code which can correct up to $n - \lceil \alpha n \rceil$ erasures. Therefore we employ a $[n, \lceil \alpha n \rceil, n - \lceil \alpha n \rceil + 1]$ code. Notice that the use of such a code implies that the elements of the code alphabet are larger than the size of a data packet as the message to be encoded $(M_1 \cdots M_{\lceil \alpha n \rceil})$ should represent the concatenation $P_1 \| \cdots \| P_n$.

The second step of our algorithm consists of building Merkle hash trees. If we denote $(C_1 \cdots C_n)$ the codeword corresponding to the message $(M_1 \cdots M_{\lceil \alpha n \rceil})$ then we partition the digests $h(C_1), \ldots, h(C_n)$ into $f$ families of $\lceil \frac{n}{f} \rceil$ elements where $f$ is an efficiency parameter (see Sect. 5). Remark that if $f$ does not divide $n$ then the last family will be completed with dummy packets (consisting of zeros for simplicity). This family padding has no effect on the number of augmented packets sent into the network as those dummy elements will only be used to construct the last family tree. Since $f$ and $n$ will be public, each receiver knows how many dummy packets to add for the last family. For each family $F_j := \{h(C_{(j-1)\lceil \frac{n}{f} \rceil + 1}), \ldots, h(C_{j \lceil \frac{n}{f} \rceil})\}$ (for $j \in \{1, \ldots, f\}$) we build the Merkle hash tree the leaves of which are the elements of $F_j$ (see Fig. 1 for an example).

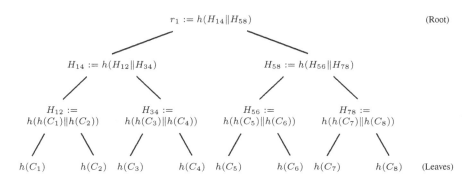

**Fig. 1.** the Merkle hash tree of $F_1$ when $\lceil \frac{n}{f} \rceil = 8$

To provide authentication and non-repudiation and allow new members to join the communication group at block boundaries, we sign the digest $h(r_1 \| \cdots \| r_f)$ where $r_1, \ldots, r_f$ are the $f$ tree roots. As in [39], we construct a polynomial $A(X)$ of degree at most $\rho n$ (for some rational constant $\rho$), the coefficients of which represent $r_1 \| \cdots \| r_f \| \sigma$ where $\sigma$ is the signature. We build the augmented packets as:

$$\forall i \in \{1, \ldots, n\} \; AP_i := BID \| i \| C_i \| A(i) \| \operatorname{path}(i)$$

where $\operatorname{path}(i)$ denotes the $\lceil \log_2 \lceil \frac{n}{f} \rceil \rceil$ hashes needed to reconstruct the path from $h(C_i)$ to the root of his family tree. For instance on Fig. 1, we have $\operatorname{path}(2) = h(C_1) \| H_{34} \| H_{58}$. As said earlier, BID denotes the position of the block $P_1, \ldots, P_n$ within the stream.

Upon reception of data, the receiver checks the signature by reconstructing $A(X)$ using MPR. Once the signature $\sigma$ is verified, the receiver knows the original tree roots $r_1, \ldots, r_f$. Thus he can identify the correct $C_i$'s amongst the list of elements he got by checking which paths are correct within the $f$ trees. According to the definition of $\alpha$ there must be at least $\lceil \alpha n \rceil$ symbols from $C_1, \ldots, C_n$ in his list. Finally, he corrects the erasures using the MDS code and recovers the data packets $P_1, \ldots, P_n$.

**Formal Scheme Construction.** As in [39], we assume that $\alpha$ and $\beta$ are rational numbers so that we can represent them over a finite number of bits using their numerator and denominator. In order to run Poly-Reconstruct as a part of MPR, we have to choose $\rho \in (0, \frac{\alpha^2}{\beta})$. Remark that it is suggested in [39] to choose $\rho = \frac{\alpha^2}{2\beta}$ to get a small list returned by Poly-Reconstruct. Notice that $\rho$ has to be rational since $\rho n$ is an integer. We also consider that the $[n, \lceil \alpha n \rceil, n - \lceil \alpha n \rceil + 1]$ code is uniquely determined (i.e. its generator matrix $G$ is known) when $n, \alpha, \beta$ and $\rho$ are known. Denote $\mathbb{F}_{2^{\tilde{q}}}$ the field of this MDS code. Due to space limitations, we omitted the construction of $q, \tilde{q}$ as well as the different pads used by our scheme which can be found in the full version of this paper. Table 1 summarizes the scheme parameters which are assumed to be publicly known.

**Table 1.** Public parameters for our authentication scheme

| | |
|---|---|
| $n$: Block length | $\tilde{\mathcal{Q}}(X)$: Polynomial representing the field for the MDS code |
| $f$: Number of families | $\mathcal{P}$: bit size of data packets |
| $\alpha, \beta$: Network rates | $G$: Generating matrix of the MDS code |
| $\rho$: Ratio | $\mathcal{Q}(X)$: Polynomial representing the field for polynomial interpolation |

The hash function $h$ as well as the signature verification algorithm Verify and the signature public key PK are also assumed to be publicly known. We did not include them in Table 1 since they can be considered as general parameters. For instance $h$ can be SHA-256 [23] while the digital signature is a 1024-bit RSA signature [34]. We denote $\mathcal{H}$ the digest bit length and $\mathcal{S}$ the bit length of a signature. Since $h$ and the digital signature are publicly known, so are $\mathcal{H}$ and $\mathcal{S}$.

**Authenticator**

Input: The secret key SK, the block number BID, Table 1 and $n$ data packets $P_1, \ldots, P_n$.

/* Packet Encoding */

1. Parse $P_1 \| \cdots \| P_n$ as $M_1 \| \cdots \| M_{\lceil \alpha n \rceil}$ after padding. Encode the message $(M_1 \cdots M_{\lceil \alpha n \rceil})$ into the codeword $(C_1 \cdots C_n)$ using the MDS code.

/* Tree Construction */

2. For $j$ from 1 to $f$ do

Compute the digests $h(C_{(j-1) \lceil \frac{n}{f} \rceil + 1}), \ldots, h(C_{j \lceil \frac{n}{f} \rceil})$ and build the Merkle hash tree having the previous digests as leaves (as said earlier some padding with zeros values may be needed when $j = f$). Denote $r_j$ its root.

/* Signature Generation */

3. Write $R$ as $R := r_1\|\cdots\|r_f$. Compute the family signature $\sigma$ as $\sigma := \mathrm{Sign}_{\mathrm{SK}}(h(\mathrm{BID}\|f\|n\|\alpha\|\beta\|\mathcal{P}\|R))$. Parse $R\|\sigma$ as $a_0\|\cdots\|a_{\rho n}$ where each $a_i \in \mathbb{F}_{2^q}$ after padding.

4. Construct the block polynomial $A(X) := a_0 + a_1 X + \cdots + a_{\rho n} X^{\rho n}$ and evaluate it at the first $n$ points[5] of $\mathbb{F}_{2^q}$.

/* Construction of Augmented Packets */

6. Build the augmented packet $\mathrm{AP}_i$ as $\mathrm{AP}_i := \mathrm{BID}\|i\|C_i\|A(i)\|\,\mathrm{path}(i)$ where $\mathrm{path}(i)$ is defined as in the scheme overview section.

Output: $\{\mathrm{AP}_1, \ldots, \mathrm{AP}_n\}$: set of augmented packets.

As in [39], assuming that $\alpha$ and $\beta$ are rational enabled us to write $\alpha\|\beta$ over a finite number of bits. It should be noticed that when $(n, f, \alpha, \beta, \mathcal{P}, \rho)$ are given, each step of Authenticator is uniquely determined as soon as $(\mathcal{Q}(X), G, \widetilde{\mathcal{Q}}(X))$ are provided. Furthermore since $\rho$ only depends on $\alpha$, $\beta$ and $n$, it is realistic to presume that when $(n, \alpha, \beta)$ are given, $\rho$ is also uniquely determined. For instance, consider the remark made in [39] where $\rho$ is suggested to be set as $\frac{\alpha^2}{2\beta}$. As a consequence, we can consider that when $(n, f, \alpha, \beta, \mathcal{P})$ are given, $(\rho, \mathcal{Q}(X), G, \widetilde{\mathcal{Q}}(X))$ are uniquely determined. This consideration is identical to what is assumed in [39].

**Decoder**
Input: The public key PK, the block number BID, Table 1 and the set of received packets RP.

/* Signature Verification and Root Recovery */

1. Write the packets as $\mathrm{BID}_i\|j_i\|C'_{j_i}\|A_{j_i}\|\,\mathrm{path}'_{j_i}$ and discard those having $\mathrm{BID}_i \neq \mathrm{BID}$ or $j_i \notin \{1, \ldots, n\}$. Denote $\mathcal{N}$ the number of remaining elements. If $(\mathcal{N} < \lceil \alpha n \rceil$ or $\mathcal{N} > \lfloor \beta n \rfloor)$ then the algorithm stops.

2. Rename the remaining elements as $\{\mathrm{AP}'_1, \ldots, \mathrm{AP}'_{\mathcal{N}}\}$ and write each element as: $\mathrm{AP}'_i = \mathrm{BID}\|j_i\|C'_{j_i}\|A_{j_i}\|\,\mathrm{path}'_{j_i}$ where $j_i \in \{1, \ldots, n\}$. Run MPR on the set $\{(j_i, A_{j_i}),$ $1 \le i \le \mathcal{N}\}$ to get a list $L := \{\mathcal{C}_1, \ldots, \mathcal{C}_\mu\}$ of candidates for signature verification. If MPR rejects that set then the algorithm stops.

3. Set $r'_k = \emptyset$ for $k \in \{1, \ldots, f\}$. While the signature has not been verified and the list $L$ has not been exhausted, pick a new candidate $\tilde{r}_1\|\cdots\|\tilde{r}_f\|\tilde{\sigma}$ after removing the pad. If $\mathrm{Verify}_{\mathrm{PK}}(h(\mathrm{BID}\|f\|n\|\alpha\|\beta\|\mathcal{P}\|\tilde{r}_1\|\cdots\|\tilde{r}_f), \tilde{\sigma}) = \mathrm{TRUE}$ then $\tilde{\sigma}$ is considered as the authentic block signature $\sigma$ and we set $r'_k = \tilde{r}_k$ for $k \in \{1, \ldots, f\}$ as authentic tree roots. If $L$ is exhausted before the signature is verified then our algorithm stops.

/* Packet Decoding */

4. Set $\mathcal{C}' := (\emptyset, \ldots, \emptyset)$. For each of the $\mathcal{N}$ remaining packets, $\mathrm{BID}\|j_i\|C'_{j_i}\|A_{j_i}\|\,\mathrm{path}'_{j_i}$,

---

[5] Any element of $\mathbb{F}_{2^q}$ can be represented as $\lambda_0 Y^0 + \lambda_1 Y_1 + \ldots + \lambda_{q-1} Y^{q-1}$ where each $\lambda_i$ belongs to $\mathbb{F}_2$. We define the first $n$ elements as $(0, \ldots, 0)$, $(1, 0, \ldots, 0)$, $(0, 1, 0, \ldots, 0)$, $(1, 1, 0, \ldots, 0)$ and so on until the binary decomposition of $n - 1$.

we first compute its family number $\ell_{j_i}$ as $\ell_{j_i} := \left\lceil \frac{j_i}{\lceil n/f \rceil} \right\rceil$. Second, if the path from $h(C'_{j_i})$ to the value $r'_{\ell_{j_i}}$ can be reconstructed using path$'_{j_i}$ then we set the $j_i^{\text{th}}$ coordinate of $\mathcal{C}'$ to $C_{j_i}$.

5. If $\mathcal{C}'$ has less than $\lceil \alpha n \rceil$ non-erased coordinates then the algorithm stops.
   Else
   5.1. Correct the erasures of $\mathcal{C}'$ using the MDS decoding process and denote $(M'_1, \ldots, M'_{\lceil \alpha n \rceil})$ the corresponding message.
   5.2. Remove the pad from $M'_1 \| \cdots \| M'_{\lceil \alpha n \rceil}$ and write the resulting string as $P'_1 \| \cdots \| P'_n$.

Output: $\{P'_1, \ldots, P'_n\}$: set of authenticated packets.

Note that when Decoder stops then the whole content of block BID is lost. Nevertheless the definitions of $\alpha$ and $\beta$ ensure that this will never happen (see Theorem 2).

## 4    Security and Recovery Analysis

**Security of the Scheme.** We recall the security definition as presented in [39].

**Definition 1 ([39]).** (KeyGen,Authenticator,Decoder) *is a* secure *and* $(\alpha, \beta)$-correct *multicast authentication scheme if no probabilistic polynomial-time opponent* $\mathcal{O}$ *can win with a non-negligible probability to the following game:*

   i. *A key pair* $(\mathrm{SK}, \mathrm{PK})$ *is generated by* KeyGen.
   ii. $\mathcal{O}$ *is given:* (a) *The public key* PK *and* (b) *Oracle access to* Authenticator *(but* $\mathcal{O}$ *can only issue at most one query with the same block identification tag* BID*).*
   iii. $\mathcal{O}$ *outputs* $(\mathrm{BID}, f, n, \alpha, \beta, \mathcal{P}, \rho, \mathcal{Q}(X), \widetilde{\mathcal{Q}}(X), G, \mathrm{RP})$.

$\mathcal{O}$ *wins if one of the following happens:*

   a. *(correctness violation)* $\mathcal{O}$ *succeeds to output* RP *such that even if it contains* $\lceil \alpha n \rceil$ *packets (amongst a total number of elements which does not exceed* $\lfloor \beta n \rfloor$*) for some block identification tag* BID*,* Decoder *fails to identify all the correct packets.*
   b. *(security violation)* $\mathcal{O}$ *succeeds to output* RP *such that* Decoder *outputs* $\{P'_1, \ldots, P'_n\}$ *that was never authenticated by* Authenticator *for parameters* $(\mathrm{BID}, f, n, \alpha, \beta, \mathcal{P}, \rho, \mathcal{Q}(X), \widetilde{\mathcal{Q}}(X), G)$.

We now show that our construction also satisfies the above security definition. The proof of the following theorem can be found in Appendix A.

**Theorem 1.** *Our scheme* (KeyGen,Authenticator,Decoder) *is secure and* $(\alpha, \beta)$-correct.

**Recovery Property.** We now show that our scheme enables any receiver to recover the $n$ data packets and the number of signature verifications to be performed per block is upper bounded by the same value as for TWMDS. We recall the following definition:

**Definition 2** ([39]). *Given a flow of $n$ symbols, we say that the survival and flood rates $(\alpha, \beta)$ are accurate if: (1) data are sent per block of $n$ elements through the network and (2) for any block of $n$ elements $\{E_1, \cdots, E_n\}$ emitted by the sender, if we denote $\{\tilde{E}_1, \ldots, \tilde{E}_\mu\}$ the set of received packets then $\mu \leq \lfloor \beta n \rfloor$ and at least $\lceil \alpha n \rceil$ elements of $\{E_1, \cdots, E_n\}$ belong to $\{\tilde{E}_1, \ldots, \tilde{E}_\mu\}$. Condition (2) must be true for each receiver belonging to the communication group.*

From this point onwards, we assume that $(\alpha, \beta)$ is accurate for our network flow $n$. As in [39], we have the following result whose proof can be found in Appendix B.

**Theorem 2.** *For any* BID*, each receiver recovers the $n$ original data packets $P_1, \ldots, P_n$. In addition the number of signature verifications to be performed is upper bounded by $U(n) := \min(\lfloor U_1(n) \rfloor, \lfloor U_2(n) \rfloor)$ where:*

$$
\begin{cases}
U_1(n) = \dfrac{1}{\rho n} \left( \dfrac{1}{\sqrt{\alpha^2 - \beta\rho}} - 1 \right) + \dfrac{\beta}{\alpha^2 - \beta\rho} + \dfrac{1}{\rho} \\[3mm]
U_2(n) = \dfrac{\beta}{2(\alpha^2 - \beta\rho)} + \dfrac{1}{\rho} + \dfrac{\sqrt{\beta^2 + \frac{4}{\rho^2 n^2}(1 - \rho\alpha)}}{2(\alpha^2 - \beta\rho)} - \dfrac{1}{\rho n}
\end{cases}
$$

*which is $O(1)$ as a function of the block length $n$.*

## 5  Efficiency Analysis

As said in Sect. 1, bandwidth limitations and authentication delay are two major concerns for authentication protocols. In this section we will see that for a suitable choice of $f$ our construction can achieve smaller overhead than TWMDS while exhibiting a much faster authentication at the receiver.

**Packet Overhead.** The packet overhead is the length of the extra tag of information used to provide authentication. Notice that an augmented packet without a tag is assumed to be written as: $\text{BID}\|i\|P_i$. Remember that the bit size of packets $P_i$ is $\mathcal{P}$.

Our augmented packets are written as $\text{BID}\|i\|C_i\|A(i)\|\,\text{path}(i)$. The element $C_i$ is represented by $\left\lceil \frac{n\mathcal{P}}{\lceil \alpha n \rceil} \right\rceil$ bits while $A(i)$ requires $\left\lceil \frac{f\mathcal{H} + \mathcal{S} + \lambda}{\rho n + 1} \right\rceil$ bits where $\lambda$ is the smallest element of $\mathbb{N}$ such that:

$$
\left\lceil \frac{f\mathcal{H} + \mathcal{S} + \lambda}{\rho n + 1} \right\rceil \geq \lceil \log_2 n \rceil
$$

is verified (see the full version of the paper for details). The element $\text{path}(i)$ consists of $\lceil \log_2 \lceil \frac{n}{f} \rceil \rceil$ digests computed by $h$. Therefore, our packet overhead $\omega$ is equal to:

$$
\omega := \left( \left\lceil \frac{n\mathcal{P}}{\lceil \alpha n \rceil} \right\rceil - \mathcal{P} + \left\lceil \frac{f\mathcal{H} + \mathcal{S} + \lambda}{\rho n + 1} \right\rceil + \left\lceil \log_2 \left\lceil \frac{n}{f} \right\rceil \right\rceil \right) \mathcal{H} \text{ bits}
$$

The augmented packets of TWMDS are written as $\text{BID}\|i\|C_i\|A(i)$ where $C_i$ is represented over $\left\lceil \frac{n\mathcal{P}}{\lceil \alpha n \rceil} \right\rceil$ bits while $A(i)$ requires $\left\lceil \frac{n\mathcal{H} + \mathcal{S}}{\rho n + 1} \right\rceil$ bits. Therefore, the overhead $\omega_{\text{TWMDS}}$ of TWMDS is equal to:

$$\omega_{\text{TWMDS}} := \left\lceil \frac{n\,\mathcal{P}}{\lceil \alpha\, n\rceil} \right\rceil - \mathcal{P} + \left\lceil \frac{n\,\mathcal{H} + \mathcal{S}}{\rho\, n + 1} \right\rceil \text{ bits}$$

To illustrate the benefits of our approach over TWMDS, we will compute the ratio $\frac{\omega}{\omega_{\text{TWMDS}}}$ for different choices of $\mathcal{P}, \alpha, \beta$. We choose the network rates as in [39] and the packet size to 512 and 4096 bits as in [32]. We pick $n = 1000$ as in those two works and set $\rho$ to $\frac{\alpha^2}{2\beta}$ as suggested in [39]. We used SHA-256 as a hash function and a 1024-bit RSA signature scheme. The first step is to compute $f$ minimizing our overhead $\omega$. These values are shown in Table 2 while the corresponding overhead $\omega$ is in Table 3.

**Table 2.** Number of families $f$ minimizing $\omega$ when $n = 1000$

|   |      | $\mathcal{P} = 512$ | | | | $\mathcal{P} = 4096$ | | | |
|---|------|------|------|-----|-----|------|------|-----|-----|
|   |      | $\alpha$ | | | | $\alpha$ | | | |
|   |      | 0.5 | 0.75 | 0.8 | 0.9 | 0.5 | 0.75 | 0.8 | 0.9 |
|        | 1.1  | 125 | 500 | 500 | 500 | 125 | 500 | 500 | 500 |
| $\beta$ | 1.25 | 125 | 250 | 500 | 500 | 125 | 250 | 500 | 500 |
|        | 1.5  | 125 | 250 | 250 | 500 | 125 | 250 | 250 | 500 |
|        | 2    | 125 | 250 | 250 | 250 | 125 | 250 | 250 | 250 |

**Table 3.** Overhead of our construction $\omega$ when $f$ is chosen as in Table 2 and $n = 1000$

|   |      | $\mathcal{P} = 512$ | | | | $\mathcal{P} = 4096$ | | | |
|---|------|------|------|------|------|------|------|------|------|
|   |      | $\alpha$ | | | | $\alpha$ | | | |
|   |      | 0.5 | 0.75 | 0.8 | 0.9 | 0.5 | 0.75 | 0.8 | 0.9 |
|        | 1.1  | 1569 | 930  | 827  | 663  | 5153 | 2125 | 1723 | 1062 |
| $\beta$ | 1.25 | 1607 | 971  | 887  | 710  | 5191 | 2166 | 1783 | 1109 |
|        | 1.5  | 1672 | 1028 | 944  | 790  | 5256 | 2223 | 1840 | 1189 |
|        | 2    | 1801 | 1143 | 1044 | 889  | 5385 | 2338 | 1940 | 1288 |

Our comparison to TWMDS is depicted in Table 4. It clearly shows that our construction exhibits a smaller overhead than TWMDS. Our benefits get larger over networks with small reliability (i.e. $\alpha$ is small) or highly polluted by $\mathcal{O}$ (i.e. $\beta$ is large). Our construction also seems to perform even better when the data packets are small.

**Table 4.** Ratio $\frac{\omega}{\omega_{\text{TWMDS}}}$ when $n = 1000$

|   |      | $\mathcal{P} = 512$ | | | | $\mathcal{P} = 4096$ | | | |
|---|------|--------|--------|--------|--------|--------|--------|--------|--------|
|   |      | $\alpha$ | | | | $\alpha$ | | | |
|   |      | 0.5 | 0.75 | 0.8 | 0.9 | 0.5 | 0.75 | 0.8 | 0.9 |
|        | 1.1  | 56.95% | 79.28% | 81.96% | 87.93% | 81.29% | 89.74% | 90.45% | 92.11% |
| $\beta$ | 1.25 | 52.57% | 74.18% | 78.57% | 83.73% | 78.17% | 86.50% | 88.05% | 88.93% |
|        | 1.5  | 46.97% | 66.97% | 71.08% | 78.53% | 73.57% | 81.43% | 82.73% | 84.63% |
|        | 2    | 39.50% | 57.55% | 60.52% | 67.30% | 66.12% | 73.50% | 74.02% | 74.88% |

**Authentication Efficiency.** We now compare the authentication delay at the receiver between our construction and TWMDS. It should be noticed that the authentication part of Decoder consists of Steps 1 to 4. Indeed Step 5 is dedicated to erasure correction which is a non-authentication related feature. In those four steps, two points matter: the number of signature verification queries and the quantity of information to be processed by $h$. In our comparison, we focus on the worst case, i.e. we assume that the number of signature verification is $U(n)$. Note this is the same value as in [39]. In this situation, the number of bits $\mathfrak{h}_1$ processed by $h$ is:

$$U(n)\left(|\mathrm{BID}| + f\,\mathcal{H} + |f| + \lceil\log_2 n\rceil + |\alpha| + |\beta| + \lceil\log_2 \mathcal{P}\rceil\right) + \lfloor\beta\,n\rfloor\left(\mathcal{P} + 2\,\lceil\log_2\lceil\tfrac{n}{f}\rceil\rceil\mathcal{H}\right)$$

As $f \leq n$, we can assume that $|f| = \lceil\log_2 n\rceil$ bits. Considering TWMDS, the number of bits $\mathfrak{h}_2$ processed by the hash function is:

$$U(n)\left(|\mathrm{BID}| + n\,\mathcal{P} + \lceil\log_2 n\rceil + |\alpha| + |\beta| + \lceil\log_2 \mathcal{P}\rceil\right) + \lfloor\beta\,n\rfloor\,\mathcal{P}$$

Table 5 represents the ratio $\mathcal{T} := \dfrac{U(n)\,t_{\mathcal{S}} + \mathfrak{h}_1\,t_{\mathcal{H}}}{U(n)\,t_{\mathcal{S}} + \mathfrak{h}_2\,t_{\mathcal{H}}}$ where $t_{\mathcal{S}}$ denotes the number of seconds required to perform one signature verification and $t_{\mathcal{H}}$ is the number of seconds to hash one bit. In [31], it is assumed that there are about 500 packets sent per second in the network in the case of video broadcast. As $n = 1000$, we buffer roughly 2 seconds of video per block. So if BID is represented over 30 bits, then it provides a stream which can last at least 68 years. It is also realistic to assume that $|\alpha|$ and $|\beta|$ are negligible in comparison to $|\mathrm{BID}|$, $\mathcal{H}$, $\lceil\log_2 n\rceil$ and $\lceil\log_2 \mathcal{P}\rceil$. Our results are based on Dai's benchmarks [8].

**Table 5.** Ratio $\mathcal{T}$ when $n = 1000$

| | | $\mathcal{P} = 512$ | | | | $\mathcal{P} = 4096$ | | | |
| | | $\alpha$ | | | | $\alpha$ | | | |
| | | 0.5 | 0.75 | 0.8 | 0.9 | 0.5 | 0.75 | 0.8 | 0.9 |
|---|---|---|---|---|---|---|---|---|---|
| $\beta$ | 1.1 | 37.98% | 54.08% | 56.98% | 60.85% | 10.49% | 19.14% | 21.18% | 23.89% |
| | 1.25 | 38.31% | 56.40% | 56.46% | 59.64% | 10.62% | 19.41% | 20.82% | 23.04% |
| | 1.5 | 38.14% | 55.22% | 58.35% | 60.26% | 10.55% | 18.84% | 20.34% | 23.48% |
| | 2 | 37.93% | 53.85% | 58.35% | 68.25% | 10.47% | 18.19% | 20.34% | 25.03% |

Table 5 shows that our construction is much faster than TWMDS. Note that we deliberately removed the query to Poly-Reconstruct happening at Step 2 of Decoder. Nevertheless TWMDS also performs such a request. So if the time needed to run Poly-Reconstruct is added to both numerator and denominator of $\mathcal{T}$ then the values of Table 5 will be flattened but our scheme will nonetheless remain faster.

In [40], Tartary and Wang suggested to use the provably collision resistant trapdoor hash function Very Smooth Hash (VSH) [7] instead of a digital signature to speed up the running time at the receiver. Based on Contini et al.'s work, VSH is 25 times slower than SHA-1 while it requires to use a 1516-bit modulus to achieve the same security level as a 1024-bit RSA signature modulus. Table 6 describes the overhead for our construction,

**Table 6.** Minimal overhead of our construction for $n = 1000$ when using VSH

| | | $\mathcal{P} = 512$ | | | | $\mathcal{P} = 4096$ | | | |
| | | $\alpha$ | | | | $\alpha$ | | | |
| | | 0.5 | 0.75 | 0.8 | 0.9 | 0.5 | 0.75 | 0.8 | 0.9 |
|---|---|---|---|---|---|---|---|---|---|
| | 1.1 | 1573 | 932 | 828 | 664 | 5157 | 2127 | 1724 | 1063 |
| $\beta$ | 1.25 | 1612 | 973 | 888 | 712 | 5196 | 2168 | 1784 | 1111 |
| | 1.5 | 1678 | 1031 | 946 | 791 | 5262 | 2226 | 1842 | 1190 |
| | 2 | 1808 | 1146 | 1047 | 891 | 5392 | 2341 | 1943 | 1290 |

**Table 7.** Ratio $\frac{\omega}{\omega_{\text{TWMDS}}}$ for $n = 1000$ when using VSH

| | | $\mathcal{P} = 512$ | | | | $\mathcal{P} = 4096$ | | | |
| | | $\alpha$ | | | | $\alpha$ | | | |
| | | 0.5 | 0.75 | 0.8 | 0.9 | 0.5 | 0.75 | 0.8 | 0.9 |
|---|---|---|---|---|---|---|---|---|---|
| | 1.1 | 57.10% | 79.45% | 82.06% | 88.06% | 81.35% | 89.82% | 90.50% | 92.19% |
| $\beta$ | 1.25 | 52.73% | 74.33% | 78.65% | 83.96% | 78.24% | 86.58% | 88.10% | 89.09% |
| | 1.5 | 47.13% | 67.17% | 71.23% | 78.63% | 73.66% | 81.54% | 82.82% | 84.70% |
| | 2 | 39.65% | 57.70% | 60.70% | 67.45% | 66.21% | 73.59% | 74.13% | 75.00% |

**Table 8.** Ratio $\mathcal{T}$ for $n = 1000$ when using VSH

| | | $\mathcal{P} = 512$ | | | | $\mathcal{P} = 4096$ | | | |
| | | $\alpha$ | | | | $\alpha$ | | | |
| | | 0.5 | 0.75 | 0.8 | 0.9 | 0.5 | 0.75 | 0.8 | 0.9 |
|---|---|---|---|---|---|---|---|---|---|
| | 1.1 | 26.81% | 43.71% | 46.82% | 50.97% | 8.95% | 17.72% | 19.79% | 22.54% |
| $\beta$ | 1.25 | 27.15% | 46.02% | 46.26% | 49.74% | 9.07% | 17.98% | 19.42% | 21.68% |
| | 1.5 | 26.97% | 44.79% | 48.06% | 50.33% | 9.01% | 17.41% | 18.92% | 22.12% |
| | 2 | 26.75% | 43.36% | 48.06% | 58.38% | 8.92% | 16.74% | 18.92% | 23.68% |

Table 7 depicts the ratio $\frac{\omega}{\omega_{\text{TWMDS}}}$ and Table 8 represents the speed ratio $\mathcal{T}$ when VSH is used instead of RSA.

One notices that using VSH slightly increases the overhead with respect to the digital signature approach but it reduces the authentication time at the receiver even further.

## 6   Conclusion

In this paper, we presented an hybrid construction based on Merkle hash trees and TWMDS. Our scheme is provably secure under the random oracle model and enables new participants to join the communication group at every block boundary. As TWMDS, our approach allows the whole data packets to be recovered at the receiver. The tradeoff between overhead and authentication speed limits the application of many constructions. The main benefits of this interaction between MDS codes and Merkle hash tree is that our packet overhead and authentication speed are much smaller than for TWMDS. If the number of families $f$ is suitably chosen then, when using 512-bit packets, our overhead is between $39\%$ and $88\%$ of TWMDS while the authentication speed is between $66\%$ and $92\%$. When using larger packets, the benefits of our construction increase even further as the overhead then represents between $38\%$ and $68\%$ of TWMDS while the authentication speed is between $11\%$ and $25\%$. The advantages of our scheme are important when the reliability of the network is small and the pollution due to the attacker is large.

We also saw that when we employed a trapdoor hash function such a VSH instead of a digital signature as suggested in [40], the benefits of our scheme increased even further.

## Acknowledgement

The authors are grateful to the anonymous reviewers for their comments to improve the quality of this paper. This work was supported by the Australian Research Council under ARC Discovery Projects DP0558773, DP0665035 and DP0663452. This work was supported in part by the National Natural Science Foundation of China Grant 60553001 and the National Basic Research Program of China Grant 2007CB807900, 2007CB807901. Christophe Tartary did some of this work while at Macquarie University where his research was supported by an iMURS scholarship. The research of Huaxiong Wang is partially supported by the Minitry of Education of Singapore under grant T206B2204.

## References

[1] Al-Ibrahim, M., Pieprzyk, J.: Authenticating multicast streams in lossy channels using threshold techniques. In: Lorenz, P. (ed.) ICN 2001. LNCS, vol. 2094, pp. 239–249. Springer, Heidelberg (2001)

[2] Barić, N., Pfitzmann, B.: Collision-free accumulators and fail-stop signature schemes without trees. In *Advances in Cryptology - Eurocrypt'97*. In: Fumy, W. (ed.) EUROCRYPT 1997. LNCS, vol. 1233, pp. 480–494. Springer, Heidelberg (1997)

[3] Barreto, P.S., Kim, H.Y., Lynn, B., Scott, M.: Efficient algorithms for pairing-based cryptosystems. In: Yung, M. (ed.) CRYPTO 2002. LNCS, vol. 2442, pp. 354–369. Springer, Heidelberg (2002)

[4] Benaloh, J., de Mare, M.: One-way accumulators: A decentralized alternative to digital signatures. In: Helleseth, T. (ed.) EUROCRYPT 1993. LNCS, vol. 765, pp. 274–285. Springer, Heidelberg (1994)

[5] Blundo, C., De Santis, A., Herzberg, A., Kutten, S., Vaccaro, U., Yung, M.: Perfectly-secure key distribution for dynamic conferences. In: Brickell, E.F. (ed.) CRYPTO 1992. LNCS, vol. 740, pp. 471–486. Springer, Heidelberg (1993)

[6] Boneh, D., Lynn, B., Shacham, H.: Short signatures from the Weil pairing. In: Boyd, C. (ed.) ASIACRYPT 2001. LNCS, vol. 2248, pp. 514–532. Springer, Heidelberg (2001)

[7] Contini, S., Lenstra, A.K., Steinfeld, R.: VSH: an efficient and provable collision resistant hash function. In: Vaudenay, S. (ed.) EUROCRYPT 2006. LNCS, vol. 4004, pp. 165–182. Springer, Heidelberg (2006)

[8] Dai, W.: Crypto++ 5.2.1 benchmarks (July 2004)

[9] Desmedt, Y., Frankel, Y., Yung, M.: Multi-receiver/multi-sender network security: Efficient authenticated multicast/feedback. In: IEEE INFOCOM 1992, vol. 3, pp. 2045–2054. IEEE Computer Society Press, Los Alamitos (1992)

[10] Fu, J.C., Lou, W.Y.W.: Distribution Theory of Runs and Patterns and its Applications. World Scientific Publishing, Singapore (2003)

[11] Gennaro, R., Rohatgi, P.: How to sign digital streams. In: Kaliski Jr., B.S. (ed.) CRYPTO 1997. LNCS, vol. 1294, pp. 180–197. Springer, Heidelberg (1997)

[12] Golle, P., Modadugu, N.: Authenticating streamed data in the presence of random packet loss. In: Symposium on Network and Distributed Systems Security, pp. 13–22. Internet Society (2001)

[13] Guruswami, V.: List Decoding of Error-Correcting Codes. Springer, Heidelberg (2004)

[14] Guruswami, V., Sudan, M.: Improved decoding of Reed-Solomon and algebraic-geometric codes. IEEE Transactions on Information Theory 45(6), 1757–1767 (1999)

[15] Karlof, C., Sastry, N., Li, Y., Perrig, A., Tygar, J.D.: Distillation codes and applications to DoS resistant multicast authentication. In: 11th Network and Distributed Systems Security Symposium (NDSS) (2004)

[16] Lidl, R., Niederreiter, H.: Introduction to Finite Fields and their Applications - Revised Edition. Cambridge University Press, Cambridge (2000)

[17] Lysyanskaya, A., Tamassia, R., Triandopoulos, N.: Multicast authentication in fully adversarial networks. In: IEEE Symposium on Security and Privacy, pp. 241–253. IEEE Computer Society Press, Los Alamitos (2003)

[18] MacWilliams, F.J., Sloane, N.J.A.: The Theory of Error-Correcting Codes. North-Holland, Amsterdam (1977)

[19] Menezes, A.J., van Oorschot, P.C., Vanstone, S.A.: Handbook of Applied Cryptography. CRC Press, Boca Raton, USA (1996)

[20] Merkle, R.: A certified digital signature. In: Brassard, G. (ed.) CRYPTO 1989. LNCS, vol. 435, pp. 218–238. Springer, Heidelberg (1990)

[21] Miner, S., Staddon, J.: Graph-based authentication of digital streams. In: IEEE Symposium on Security and Privacy, pp. 232–246. IEEE Computer Society Press, Los Alamitos (2001)

[22] Moon, T.K.: Error Correction Coding: Mathematical Methods and Algorithms. Wiley, Chichester (2005)

[23] National Institute of Standards and Technology. FIPS 180-2: Secure Hash Standard (SHS) (August 2002. Amended 25 (February 2004)), Available online at:
http://csrc.nist.gov/publications/fips/fips180-2/
fips180-2withchangenotice.pdf

[24] Nguyen, L.: Accumulators from bilinear pairings and applications. In: Menezes, A.J. (ed.) CT-RSA 2005. LNCS, vol. 3376, pp. 275–292. Springer, Heidelberg (2005)

[25] Nyberg, K.: Fast accumulated hashing. In: Gollmann, D. (ed.) Fast Software Encryption. LNCS, vol. 1039, pp. 83–87. Springer, Heidelberg (1996)

[26] Pannetrat, A., Molva, R.: Authenticating real time packet streams and multicasts. In: 7th International Symposium on Computers and Communications, IEEE Computer Society Press, Los Alamitos (2002)

[27] Park, J.M., Chong, E.K.P., Siegel, H.J.: Efficient multicast packet authentication using signature amortization. In: IEEE Symposium on Security and Privacy, pp. 227–240. IEEE Computer Society Press, Los Alamitos (2002)

[28] Park, J.M., Chong, E.K.P., Siegel, H.J.: Efficient multicast stream authentication using erasure codes. ACM Transactions on Information and System Security 6(2), 258–285 (2003)

[29] Park, Y., Cho, Y.: The eSAIDA stream authentication scheme. In: Laganà, A., Gavrilova, M., Kumar, V., Mun, Y., Tan, C.J.K., Gervasi, O. (eds.) ICCSA 2004. LNCS, vol. 3046, pp. 799–807. Springer, Heidelberg (2004)

[30] Paxson, V.: End-to-end Internet packet dynamics. IEEE/ACM Transactions on Networking 7(3), 277–292 (1999)

[31] Perrig, A., Canetti, R., Tygar, J.D., Song, D.: Efficient authentication and signing of multi-cast streams over lossy channels. In: IEEE Symposium on Security and Privacy, pp. 56–73. IEEE Computer Society Press, Los Alamitos (2000)

[32] Perrig, A., Tygar, J.D.: Secure Broadcast Communication in Wired and Wireless Networks. Kluwer Academic Publishers, Dordrecht (2003)

[33] Pieprzyk, J., Hardjono, T., Seberry, J.: Fundamentals of Computer Security. Springer, Heidelberg (2003)

[34] Rivest, R.L., Shamir, A., Adelman, L.: A method for obtaining digital signatures and public key cryptosystems. Communication of the ACM 21(2), 120–126 (1978)

[35] Rohatgi, P.: A compact and fast hybrid signature scheme for multicast packet authentication. In: 6th ACM Conference on Computer and Communications Security, pp. 93–100. ACM Press, New York (1999)

[36] Safavi-Naini, R., Wang, H.: New results on multi-receiver authentication code. In: Nyberg, K. (ed.) EUROCRYPT 1998. LNCS, vol. 1403, pp. 527–541. Springer, Heidelberg (1998)

[37] Scott, M., Costigan, N., Abdulwahab, W.: Implementing cryptographic pairings on smartcards. In: Goubin, L., Matsui, M. (eds.) CHES 2006. LNCS, vol. 4249, pp. 134–147. Springer, Heidelberg (2006)

[38] Stinson, D.R.: Cryptography: Theory and Practice, 3rd edn. Chapman & Hall/CRC (2006)

[39] Tartary, C., Wang, H.: Achieving multicast stream authentication using MDS codes. In: Pointcheval, D., Mu, Y., Chen, K. (eds.) CANS 2006. LNCS, vol. 4301, pp. 108–125. Springer, Heidelberg (2006)

[40] Tartary, C., Wang, H.: Efficient multicast stream authentication for the fully adversarial network. International Journal of Security and Network (Special Issue on Cryptography in Networks) 2(3/4), 175–191 (2007)

[41] Wong, C.K., Lam, S.S.: Digital signatures for flows and multicasts. IEEE/ACM Transactions on Networking 7(4), 502–513 (1999)

[42] Yajnik, M., Moon, S., Kurose, J., Towsley, D.: Measurement and modeling of the temporal dependence in packet loss. In: IEEE INFOCOM 1999, vol. 1, pp. 345–352. IEEE Computer Society Press, Los Alamitos (1999)

# A    Proof of Theorem 1

Assume that the scheme is either insecure or not $(\alpha, \beta)$-correct. By definition an opponent $\mathcal{O}$ can break the scheme security or correctness with a non-negligible probability $\pi(k)$ where $k$ is the security parameter setting up the digital signature and the hash function. Therefore we must have either cases:

(1) With probability at least $\pi(k)/2$, $\mathcal{O}$ breaks the scheme correctness
(2) With probability at least $\pi(k)/2$, $\mathcal{O}$ breaks the scheme security

It should be noticed that since $\pi(k)$ is a non-negligible function of $k$, so is $\pi(k)/2$.

Point (1). We claim that if $\mathcal{O}$ can break the scheme correctness in polynomial time then either he can forge the digital signature or he can find a collision for the hash function in polynomial time as well.

This will be proved by turning an attack breaking the $(\alpha, \beta)$-correctness of our construction into a successful attack against either primitive.

For this attack, $\mathcal{O}$ will have access to the signing algorithm $\mathrm{Sign}_{\mathrm{SK}}$ (but $\mathcal{O}$ will not have access to SK itself). He can use the public key PK as well as the collision resistant hash function $h$. $\mathcal{O}$ will be allowed to run Authenticator whose queries are written as $(\mathrm{BID}_i, f_i, n_i, \alpha_i, \beta_i, \mathcal{P}_i, \rho_i, \mathcal{Q}_i(X), \widetilde{\mathcal{Q}}_i(X), \mathrm{DP}_i)$ where $\mathrm{DP}_i$ is the set of $n_i$ data packets to be authenticated. In order to get the corresponding output, the signature is obtained by querying $\mathrm{Sign}_{\mathrm{SK}}$ as a black-box at Step 3 of Authenticator.

According to our hypothesis, $\mathcal{O}$ broke the correctness of the construction. This means that, following the previous process, $\mathcal{O}$ managed to obtain values BID, $f, n, \alpha, \beta, \mathcal{P}, \rho$, $\mathcal{Q}(X), \widetilde{\mathcal{Q}}(X)$ and a set of received packets RP such that:

– There exists a query value $i$ such as:

$$(\mathrm{BID}, f, n, \alpha, \beta, \mathcal{P}, \rho, \mathcal{Q}(X), \widetilde{\mathcal{Q}}(X)) = (\mathrm{BID}_i, f_i, n_i, \alpha_i, \beta_i, \mathcal{P}_i, \rho_i, \mathcal{Q}_i(X), \widetilde{\mathcal{Q}}_i(X))$$

Denote $\mathrm{DP} = \{P_1, \dots, P_n\} (= \mathrm{DP}_i)$ the $n$ data packets associated with this query and AP the response given to $\mathcal{O}$. In particular we denote $\sigma$ the signature corresponding to DP and generated as in Step 3 of Authenticator.

– $|\mathrm{RP} \cap \mathrm{AP}| \geq \lceil \alpha n \rceil$ and $|\mathrm{RP}| \leq \lfloor \beta n \rfloor$.

– $\{P'_1, \dots, P'_n\} = \mathrm{Decoder}(\mathrm{PK}, \mathrm{BID}, f, n, \alpha, \beta, \mathcal{P}, \rho, \mathcal{Q}(X), \widetilde{\mathcal{Q}}(X), \mathrm{RP})$ where $P'_\zeta \neq P_\zeta$ for some $\zeta \in \{1, \dots, n\}$.

Assume that the digital signature is unforgeable and the hash function is collision resistant.

Since $|\mathrm{RP} \cap \mathrm{AP}| \geq \lceil \alpha n \rceil$ and $|\mathrm{RP}| \leq \lfloor \beta n \rfloor$, Step 1 of Decoder ends successfully. The consistency of Poly-Reconstruct involves that the list returned by MPR at Step 2 contains the element $r_1 \| \cdots \| r_f \| \sigma$ corresponding to DP once the pad is removed. Note that the length of the pad is uniquely determined once $\mathcal{H}, \mathcal{S}, n$ and $\rho$ are known. The first two ones are general parameters while the others correspond to query $i$ on DP.

The presence of $r_1 \| \cdots \| r_f \| \sigma$ within the list returned by MPR involves that at least one pair message/signature will go through the verification process at Step 3 of Decoder. As the digital signature is unforgeable and the hash function is collision resistant, this pair will be the only one for which $\mathrm{Verify}_{\mathrm{PK}}$ ends successfully. Indeed denote $\widetilde{R} \| \widetilde{\sigma}$ an element from the list such that:

$$\mathrm{Verify}_{\mathrm{PK}}(h(\mathrm{BID}\|f\|n\|\alpha\|\beta\|\mathcal{P}\|\widetilde{R}), \widetilde{\sigma}) = \mathrm{TRUE}$$

By hypothesis, $\mathcal{O}$ is allowed to perform a polynomial number of queries to Authenticator and no more than one query per block identification value. Denote $\ell$ the number of queries done by $\mathcal{O}$, $\mathrm{BID}_1, \dots, \mathrm{BID}_\ell$ the $\ell$ block identification values and $R_1 \| \sigma_1, \dots$, $R_\ell \| \sigma_\ell$ the corresponding $\ell$ concatenations of tree roots/signatures. Note that we are currently working with iteration number $i$ since $\mathrm{BID} = \mathrm{BID}_i$.

Since the signature scheme is secure we get $\widetilde{\sigma} \in \{\sigma_1, \dots, \sigma_\ell\}$. This means: $\exists i_0 \in \{1, \dots, \ell\}/\widetilde{\sigma} = \sigma_{i_0}$. The security of the digital signature involves $i_0 = i$ as $\mathcal{O}$ cannot query Authenticator more than once per block identification value. Thus: $\widetilde{\sigma} = \sigma_i = \sigma$. For the same reason we get:

$$h(\mathrm{BID}\|f\|n\|\alpha\|\beta\|\mathcal{P}\|\underbrace{R_i}_{R}) = h(\mathrm{BID}\|f\|n\|\alpha\|\beta\|\mathcal{P}\|\widetilde{R})$$

Since $h$ is collision resistant we get: $\widetilde{R}\|\widetilde{\sigma} = R\|\sigma$ which corresponds to the data packets DP $(=$ DP$_i)$.

Therefore at the end of Step 3 we have recovered the $f$ tree roots, that is:

$$\forall i \in \{1, \ldots, f\} \quad r'_i = r_i$$

Since $h$ is collision resistant, it is obvious that, for any element of RP written as BID$\|j_i\|C'_{j_i}\|A_{j_i}\|$ path$'_{j_i}$, if path$'_{j_i}$ can be used to recover the path of $h(C'_{j_i})$ to the root of his tree $r'_{\ell_{j_i}} = r_{\ell_{j_i}}$ then $C'_{j_i} = C_{j_i}$. This corresponds to the use of the Merkle hash trees as collision resistant accumulators as in [15]. This involves that, at the end of Step 4 of Decoder, we have:

$$\forall \xi \in \{1, \ldots, n\} \quad C'_\xi \in \{\emptyset, C_\xi\} \quad \text{where } C' = (C'_1 \cdots C'_n)$$

Since $|\text{RP} \cap \text{AP}| \geq \lceil \alpha\, n \rceil$, we deduce that at least $\lceil \alpha\, n \rceil$ coordinates of $C'$ are non-empty at the end of Step 4. Since the code can correct up to $n - \lceil \alpha\, n \rceil$ erasures we get:

$$\forall \xi \in \{1, \ldots, \lceil \alpha\, n \rceil\} \quad M'_\xi = M_\xi$$

at the end of Step 5.1. Therefore we get:

$$\forall \xi \in \{1, \ldots, n\} \quad P'_\xi = P_\xi$$

We obtain a contradiction with our original hypothesis which stipulated $\exists j \in \{1, \ldots, n\}\, P'_j \neq P_j$. As a consequence, we deduce that either the hash function is not collision resistant or the digital signature is not secure.

Point (2). We claim that if $\mathcal{O}$ can break the scheme correctness in polynomial time then either he can forge the digital signature or he can find a collision for the hash function in polynomial time as well.

We consider the same kind of reduction as in Point (1). The opponent $\mathcal{O}$ breaks the security of the scheme if one of the following holds:

I. Authenticator was never queried on input BID, $f, n, \alpha, \beta, \mathcal{P}, \rho, \mathcal{Q}(X), \widetilde{\mathcal{Q}}(X)$ and the decoding algorithm Decoder does not reject RP, i.e. $\{P'_1, \ldots, P'_n\} \neq \emptyset$ where $\{P'_1, \ldots, P'_n\} = \text{Decoder}(\text{BID}, f, n, \alpha, \beta, \mathcal{P}, \rho, \mathcal{Q}(X), \widetilde{\mathcal{Q}}(X), \text{RP})$.
II. Authenticator was queried on input BID, $f, n, \alpha, \beta, \mathcal{P}, \rho, \mathcal{Q}(X), \widetilde{\mathcal{Q}}(X)$ for some data packets DP $= \{P_1, \ldots, P_n\}$. Nevertheless the output of Decoder verifies $P'_j \neq P_j$ for some $j \in \{1, \ldots, n\}$.

Case I. Since Decoder output some non-empty packets, Step 3 had to terminate successfully. In particular it has been found a pair $(h(\text{BID}\|f\|n\|\alpha\|\beta\|\mathcal{P}\|R), \sigma)$ (after removing the pad) such that:

$$\text{Verify}_{\text{PK}}(h(\text{BID}\|f\|n\|\alpha\|\beta\|\mathcal{P}\|R), \sigma) = \text{TRUE}$$

If $\mathcal{O}$ never queried Authenticator for block tag BID then the previous pair is a forgery of the digital signature.

If $\mathcal{O}$ queried Authenticator for block tag BID then denote (BID, $f_i, n_i, \alpha_i, \beta_i, \mathcal{P}_i, \rho_i,$ $\mathcal{Q}_i(X), \widetilde{\mathcal{Q}}_i(X)$) his query. By hypothesis we have:

$$(\text{BID}, f_i, n_i, \alpha_i, \beta_i, \mathcal{P}_i, \rho_i, \mathcal{Q}_i(X), \widetilde{\mathcal{Q}}_i(X)) \neq (\text{BID}, f, n, \alpha, \beta, \mathcal{P}, \rho, \mathcal{Q}(X), \widetilde{\mathcal{Q}}(X))$$

As said in Sect. 3, when $(n, f, \alpha, \beta, \mathcal{P})$ are given, $(\rho, \mathcal{Q}(X), G, \widetilde{\mathcal{Q}}(X))$ are uniquely determined. Thus the previous relation is equivalent to:

$$(\text{BID}, f_i, n_i, \alpha_i, \beta_i, \mathcal{P}_i) \neq (\text{BID}, f, n, \alpha, \beta, \mathcal{P})$$

Therefore either the previous pair message/signature is a forgery of the signature scheme or the pair $(\text{BID}\|f_i\|n_i\|\alpha_i\|\beta_i\|\mathcal{P}_i\|R_i, \text{BID}\|f\|n\|\alpha\|\beta\|\mathcal{P}\|R)$ is a collision for the hash function $f$.

*Case II.* We have the same situation as Point (1).

# B    Proof of Theorem 2

Let BID be fixed. Due to the accuracy of $(\alpha, \beta)$, we could demonstrate as in [39] that, at the end of Step 3 of Decoder, the receiver has recovered the signature $\sigma$ as well as the $f$ tree roots $r_1, \ldots, r_f$. Similarly to Wong and Lam's and Karlof et al.'s approaches [15, 41] which both relies on a Merkle hash tree construction, Step 4 enables us to identify all correct codeword coordinates amongst the set of received elements since $h$ is a collision resistant hash function. Due to the accuracy of $(\alpha, \beta)$, we have at least $\lceil \alpha n \rceil$ values which are consistent with $(C_1 \cdots C_n)$. Thus Step 5 successfully ends since the code can correct up to $n - \lceil \alpha n \rceil$ erasures. As a consequence, Decoder outputs the whole $n$ original packets, that is: $\forall i \in \{1, \ldots, n\}\ P'_i = P_i$.

As we use the same settings as in [39], we deduce that $U(n) \in O(1)$ is also a bound on the size of the list output by Poly-Reconstruct for our construction. The reader interested in the details is referred to [39].

# CCA2-Secure Threshold Broadcast Encryption with Shorter Ciphertexts

Vanesa Daza[1], Javier Herranz[2], Paz Morillo[3], and Carla Ràfols[3]

[1] Dept. D'Enginyeria Informàtica i Matemàtiques,
Universitat Rovira i Virgili
Av. Països Catalans 26, E-43007 Tarragona, Spain
`vanesa.daza@urv.cat`
[2] IIIA, Artificial Intelligence Research Institute
CSIC, Spanish National Research Council
Campus UAB s/n, E-08193 Bellaterra, Spain
`jherranz@iiia.csic.es`
[3] Dept. Matemàtica Aplicada IV,
Universitat Politècnica de Catalunya
C. Jordi Girona 1-3, E-08034 Barcelona, Spain
`{paz,crafols}@ma4.upc.edu`

**Abstract.** In a threshold broadcast encryption scheme, a sender chooses (ad-hoc) a set of $n$ receivers and a threshold $t$, and then encrypts a message by using the public keys of all the receivers, in such a way that the original plaintext can be recovered only if at least $t$ receivers cooperate. Previously proposed threshold broadcast encryption schemes have ciphertexts whose length is at least $n + \mathcal{O}(1)$. In this paper, we propose new schemes, for both PKI and identity-based scenarios, where the ciphertexts' length is $n - t + \mathcal{O}(1)$. The constructions use secret sharing techniques and the Canetti-Halevi-Katz transformation to achieve chosen-ciphertext security. The security of our schemes is formally proved under the Decisional Bilinear Diffie-Hellman (DBDH) Assumption.

## 1 Introduction

In a threshold public key encryption scheme a message is encrypted and sent to a group of receivers, in such a way that the cooperation of at least $t$ of them (where $t$ is the threshold) is necessary in order to recover the original message. Such schemes have many applications in situations where one wants to avoid that a single party has all the power/responsibility to protect or obtain some critical information. The usual strategy to implement this idea is the following: the set of receivers, which is decided on from the beginning, runs an interactive setup protocol which takes as input a threshold (chosen by themselves) and outputs a public key for the set and shares of the matching secret key.

The fact that the set of receivers and the threshold are set from the beginning can limit the applications of these schemes in real life. One can imagine that the sender of the message, who wants to protect some information, may want

W. Susilo, J.K. Liu, and Y. Mu. (Eds.): ProvSec 2007, LNCS 4784, pp. 35–50, 2007.

to decide who will be the designated receivers in an ad-hoc way, just before encrypting the message, and also decide the threshold of receivers which will be necessary to recover the information (e.g. depending on the secrecy level desired for the message). With this motivation in mind, a scheme for this situation would have the following properties:

1. There is no setup phase or predefined groups. Each potential receiver has his own pair of secret/public keys.

2. The sender chooses (ad-hoc) the set of receivers $\mathcal{P}$ and the threshold $t$ for the decryption. Then he encrypts the message by using the public keys of all the receivers in $\mathcal{P}$.

3. A ciphertext corresponding to the pair $(\mathcal{P}, t)$ can only be decrypted if at least $t$ members of $\mathcal{P}$ cooperate by using their secret keys. Otherwise, it is computationally infeasible to obtain any information about the plaintext.

Note that, when $t = 1$, the resulting scheme will be a *broadcast encryption scheme* [15], where a sender encrypts a message in such a way that any member of the set of receivers can decrypt it. For this reason, we have decided to use the name *threshold broadcast encryption scheme* (TBE scheme, for short) to refer to this kind of schemes. Other possible names could be dynamic threshold encryption (as used in [16]) or ad-hoc threshold encryption. To the best of our knowledge, very few works have dealt with this extension of the concept of broadcast encryption. In [16] the authors propose a scheme based on RSA; even if the authors claim that the length of the ciphertexts is constant, the ciphertext contains an integer modulo $N$, where $N$ is the product of all the RSA moduli of the receivers. Therefore, the actual length of the ciphertext is $\mathcal{O}(n)$, where $n$ is the number of receivers. A different scheme where the length of the ciphertexts is again $n + \mathcal{O}(1)$ is included in [17]. In [12], the authors propose a TBE scheme for identity-based scenarios; again, the length of the ciphertexts is $n + \mathcal{O}(1)$. In this same work [12], and previously in [10], a naive solution to the problem of threshold broadcast encryption was sketched: the sender distributes the message $m$ into $n$ pieces $m_i$, by using a threshold secret sharing scheme [19], and then encrypts each $m_i$ by using the public key of the $i$-th receiver. The length of the ciphertext is also $\mathcal{O}(n)$.

In this paper we propose two new threshold broadcast encryption schemes, one for PKI-based scenarios and one for identity-based scenarios, where the length of the ciphertexts is $n - t + \mathcal{O}(1)$, being $n$ the number of receivers and $t$ the threshold for the decryption. We do not include the description of the set of receivers when we measure the length of the ciphertext; such a description can be quite short (for example, if the receivers are all the members of a company) or can be $\mathcal{O}(n)$-long, if the best/only way to describe the set is by including all the public keys of the receivers.

The idea in the design of our schemes is to combine the following tools: (1) a chosen plaintext selective-ID secure identity-based encryption scheme; (2) some secret sharing techniques to create, for each encryption, an ad-hoc master public key whose matching master secret key will be distributed among the receivers of the message; (3) and the generic transformation due to Canetti, Halevi and Katz [11], to achieve chosen-ciphertext security. This last transformation has already been used by Boneh, Boyen and Halevi to construct a standard threshold encryption scheme [6] where interaction is not required among the decrypting servers (which differs from other previous schemes [21,10]). This property is very desirable in our scenario of threshold broadcast encryption, where the receivers are chosen ad-hoc and maybe they do not know each other.

Our scheme for PKI-based scenarios uses a scheme by Boneh and Boyen [5] as the selective-ID secure identity-based encryption scheme. In this way, security of the resulting threshold broadcast encryption scheme under chosen-ciphertext attacks can be proved in the standard model. For the identity-based scenario, it is necessary to combine the techniques in the scheme of Boneh-Franklin [8] and the techniques in [5]; as a result, the security of the obtained identity-based threshold broadcast encryption scheme is proved in the random oracle model.

The rest of the work is organized as follows. In Section 2 we recall some tools (secret sharing, bilinear pairings, one-time signatures) that will be necessary for the construction of our schemes. In Section 3 we give the general definitions of the protocols and the security definitions for threshold broadcast encryption schemes. We propose our PKI-based scheme in Section 4, and we formally prove its security by reduction to the hardness of the Decisional Bilinear Diffie-Hellman (DBDH) problem. The description of our identity-based scheme is sketched in Section 5. The conclusions of our work and some related open problems are given in Section 6.

## 2  Preliminaries

### 2.1  Threshold Secret Sharing Schemes

The idea of *secret sharing schemes* was independently introduced by Shamir [19] and Blakley [4]. A $(d, N)$-threshold secret sharing scheme is a method by means of which a special figure, usually called *dealer*, distributes a secret $s$ among a set $\mathcal{P} = \{R_1, \ldots, R_N\}$ of $N$ players. Each player $R_i$ privately receives from the dealer a piece of information $s_i$ (or *share*). Then, those subsets with at least $d$ players can recover the secret $s$ from their shares, while subsets containing less than $d$ players do not obtain any information at all about the secret.

*Shamir's secret sharing scheme* [19] solves this problem by means of polynomial interpolation. Let $GF(q)$ be a finite field with $q > N$ elements, and let $s \in GF(q)$ be the secret to be shared. The dealer picks a polynomial $f(x)$ of degree at most $d - 1$, where the constant term of $f(x)$ is $s$ and all other coefficients $a_j$ are selected from $GF(q)$, uniformly and independently, at random. That is, $f(x)$ has the form $f(x) = s + \sum_{j=1}^{d-1} a_j x^j$.

Every player $R_i$ is publicly and uniquely associated to a field element $\alpha_i$. The dealer privately sends to player $R_i$ his share $s_i = f(\alpha_i)$, for $i = 1, \ldots, N$.

Now, players in a set $A \subset \mathcal{P}$ such that $|A| \geq d$ can recover the secret $s = f(0)$, by using Lagrange interpolation. Actually, players in $A$ can compute the value of the polynomial $f(x)$ evaluated on any point $\alpha_j$, with the formula:

$$f(\alpha_j) = \sum_{R_i \in A} \lambda_{ij}^A f(\alpha_i) = \sum_{R_i \in A} \lambda_{ij}^A s_i,$$

where $\lambda_{ij}^A = \prod_{R_\ell \in A, \ell \neq i} \frac{\alpha_j - \alpha_\ell}{\alpha_i - \alpha_\ell}$.

On the other hand, it can be proved that players in a subset $B \subset \mathcal{P}$ such that $|B| < d$ do not obtain any information about the polynomial $f(x)$, apart from their shares $\{f(\alpha_k)\}_{R_k \in B}$, of course.

## 2.2   Bilinear Pairings and Assumptions

Given an additive group $\mathbb{G}_1 = \langle P \rangle$ and a multiplicative group $\mathbb{G}_2$, both with prime order $q$, we say that they admit a bilinear pairing if there exists a map $e : \mathbb{G}_1 \times \mathbb{G}_1 \to \mathbb{G}_2$ satisfying the following properties:

1. it is bilinear: $e(aP, bP) = e(P, P)^{ab} = e(bP, aP)$, for all $a, b \in \mathbb{Z}_q$;
2. it can be efficiently computed for any possible input pair;
3. it is non-degenerate, which means that $e(P, P) \neq 1$.

Bilinear pairings like the Tate or Weil pairings can be constructed over groups defined on elliptic curves. In the last years, bilinear pairings have been widely used in cryptography, for example in the design of identity-based cryptographic protocols. Identity-based cryptography was introduced by Shamir [20] as an alternative to traditional PKI-based cryptography, to avoid the efficiency problems related to the management of digital certificates which link a user with his public key. In identity-based cryptography, the public key of each user can be directly and publicly obtained from his identity, so an external link is not necessary. The negative point is that the secret keys of the users must be computed by a totally trusted (master) entity.

The security of these cryptographic schemes employing bilinear pairings is based on the assumption that some problems are hard to solve. These problems are adaptations to the bilinear pairing setting of more studied and standard computational problems, like the Decisional Diffie-Hellman (DDH) problem. The security of the schemes that we propose in this paper is based on the hardness of the following problem.

**Definition 1.** *(Decisional Bilinear Diffie-Hellman problem). We say that an algorithm $\mathcal{S}$ is a $\varepsilon'$-solver of the DBDH problem if it distinguishes with probability at least $1/2 + \varepsilon'$ between the two following probability distributions:*
*$\mathcal{D}_{BDH} = (P, aP, bP, cP, e(P, P)^{abc})$, where $a, b, c$ are chosen uniformly and independently in $\mathbb{Z}_q$,*
*$\mathcal{D}_{rand} = (P, aP, bP, cP, T)$, where $a, b, c$ are chosen uniformly and independently in $\mathbb{Z}_q$ and $T$ is chosen uniformly and independently in $\mathbb{G}_2$.*

In other words, a challenger chooses at random a bit $d \in \{0, 1\}$. If $d = 1$, a tuple taken at random from $\mathcal{D}_{BDH}$ is given to $\mathcal{S}$. If $d = 0$, a tuple taken at random from

$\mathcal{D}_{rand}$ is given to $\mathcal{S}$. The goal of $\mathcal{S}$ is to guess the bit $d$ with better probability than at random. The Decisional Bilinear Diffie Hellman Assumption states that there does not exist any $\varepsilon'$-solver of the DBDH problem for non-negligible values of $\varepsilon'$.

### 2.3   One-Time Signatures

A one-time signature scheme $\Sigma = (\Sigma.KG, \Sigma.\text{Sign}, \Sigma.\text{Verify})$ consists of the three typical protocols of a digital signature scheme. $\Sigma.KG(1^k) \rightarrow (SK, VK)$ is the key generation protocol, which outputs a secret signing key $SK$ and a public verification key $VK$. The signing protocol $\Sigma.\text{Sign}(SK, M) \rightarrow \sigma$ takes as input the signing key and a message $M$, and outputs a signature $\sigma$. Finally, the verification protocol $\Sigma.\text{Verify}(VK, M, \sigma) \rightarrow 1$ or 0 takes as input the verification key, a message and a signature, and outputs 1 if the signature is valid, or 0 otherwise.

Regarding security, we consider an adversary who first receives a verification key $VK$ obtained from $\Sigma.KG(1^k) \rightarrow (SK, VK)$. He can make at most one signature query for a message $M$ of his choice, obtaining as answer a valid signature $\Sigma.\text{Sign}(SK, M) \rightarrow \sigma$, and finally outputs a pair $(M', \sigma')$. We say that the adversary succeeds if $(M', \sigma') \neq (M, \sigma)$ and $\Sigma.\text{Verify}(VK, M', \sigma') \rightarrow 1$.

A one-time signature scheme $\Sigma$ is $\varepsilon_\Sigma$-secure if any polynomial-time adversary against $\Sigma$ has a success probability bounded by $\varepsilon_\Sigma$.

## 3   Threshold Broadcast Encryption

Roughly speaking, the operations of a threshold broadcast encryption scheme work as follows: the sender chooses a set of receivers and a threshold $t$, and then encrypts a message by using the public keys of these receivers. Given the resulting ciphertext, the original message can be recovered by any set of at least $t$ of the designated receivers: they use their secret keys to compute partial decryptions which are then combined to obtain the message.

More formally, a threshold broadcast encryption scheme TBE= (TBE.Setup, TBE.KG, TBE.Enc, TBE.PartDec, TBE.Dec) consists of five algorithms:

- The randomized setup algorithm TBE.Setup takes as input a security parameter $k$ and outputs some public parameters **params**, which will be common to all the users of the system. We write **params** $\leftarrow$ TBE.Setup$(1^k)$.
- The randomized key generation algorithm TBE.KG is run by each user $R_i$. It takes as input some public parameters **params** and returns a pair $(PK_i, SK_i)$ consisting of a public key and a matching secret key; we denote an execution of this protocol as $(PK_i, SK_i) \leftarrow$ TBE.KG(**params**).
- The randomized encryption algorithm TBE.Enc takes as input a set of public keys $\{PK_i\}_{R_i \in \mathcal{P}}$ corresponding to a set $\mathcal{P}$ of $n$ receivers, a threshold $t$ satisfying $1 \leq t \leq n$, and a message $m$. The output is a ciphertext $C$, which contains the description of $\mathcal{P}$ and $t$; we write $C \leftarrow$ TBE.Enc$(\mathcal{P}, \{PK_i\}_{R_i \in \mathcal{P}}, t, m)$.
- The (possibly randomized) partial decryption algorithm TBE.PartDec takes as input a ciphertext $C$ for the pair $(\mathcal{P}, t)$ and a secret key $SK_i$ of a receiver

$R_i \in \mathcal{P}$. The output is a partial decryption value $\kappa_i$ or a special symbol $\perp$. We denote with $\kappa_i \leftarrow$ TBE.PartDec$(C, SK_i)$ an execution of this protocol.
- The deterministic final decryption algorithm TBE.Dec takes as input a ciphertext $C$ for the pair $(\mathcal{P}, t)$ and $t$ partial decryptions $\{\kappa_i\}_{R_i \in A}$ corresponding to receivers in some subset $A \subset \mathcal{P}$. The output is a message $m$ or a special symbol $\perp$. We write $\tilde{m} \leftarrow$ TBE.Dec$(C, \{\kappa_i\}_{R_i \in A}, A)$.

An important parameter of such schemes is the length of the ciphertext $C$. When measuring this length, we will not consider the description of the set $\mathcal{P}$: in some cases, the description can consist of the list of all the public keys, which already has length $\mathcal{O}(n)$. In some other cases, the description can be much simpler, for example if the set of receivers is formed by the workers of a company. For the previous TBE schemes in the literature [16,17,12], the length of the ciphertexts is $n + \mathcal{O}(1)$. In this paper we will propose new schemes where the length of the ciphertexts is $n - t + \mathcal{O}(1)$.

## 3.1   Security of Threshold Broadcast Encryption Schemes

When formalizing security of standard public key encryption schemes, one usually considers a single challenged public key. This is because it has been shown [2] that security in this model is equivalent to security in a model which considers many public keys.

In threshold broadcast encryption schemes, however, we must consider many public keys when we formalize security, because each encryption and decryption in the system involves many public/secret keys. An attacker can corrupt different users, in two possible ways: registering new public keys for such users, or obtaining the secret key matching with the public key of some previously honest users. The final goal of the attacker is to obtain some information about a message which has been encrypted for a pair $(\mathcal{P}^*, t^*)$ such that the number of corrupted players in $\mathcal{P}^*$ is less than $t^*$.

For simplicity, we will not consider the first kind of user corruption, where the adversary registers new public keys. The reason is that, in the real world, certification authorities (should) require users to prove the knowledge of the secret key which matches with the public key they are registering. This can be done by means of a Proof of Knowledge [3]. In the game which models the security of threshold broadcast encryption schemes, the attacker is required to perform such a Proof of Knowledge of the secret keys which match with the new public keys he wants to register. Because of the 'proof of knowledge' property of the employed Proof of Knowledge system [3], this is equivalent to requiring the adversary to supply the matching secret key, each time he registers a public key. Therefore, registering new public keys does not give any useful information to the adversary.

Taking all this into consideration, indistinguishability for threshold broadcast encryption schemes is defined by considering the following game that an attacker $\mathcal{A}_{atk}$ plays against a challenger:

$\mathcal{U} = \emptyset$
params $\leftarrow$ TBE.Setup($1^k$)
Each time $\mathcal{A}_{atk}$ requires the creation of a new user $R_i$,
$(PK_i, SK_i) \leftarrow$ TBE.KG(params) is executed and $R_i$ is added to $\mathcal{U}$
$(St, \mathcal{P}^*, t^*, m_0, m_1) \leftarrow \mathcal{A}_{atk}^{Corr, \mathcal{O}_1(\cdot)}$(find, params, $\{PK_i\}_{R_i \in \mathcal{U}}$)
$\beta \leftarrow \{0, 1\}$ at random; $C^* \leftarrow$ TBE.Enc($\mathcal{P}^*, \{pk_i\}_{R_i \in \mathcal{P}^*}, t^*, m_\beta$)
$\beta' \leftarrow \mathcal{A}_{atk}^{Corr, \mathcal{O}_2(\cdot)}$(guess, $C^*, St$).

In both phases of the attack, $\mathcal{A}_{atk}$ has access to a corruption oracle $Corr$: $\mathcal{A}_{atk}$ submits to the oracle a user $R_i \in \mathcal{U}$, and must receive as answer his secret key $SK_i$. Let $\mathcal{U}' \subset \mathcal{U}$ be the subset of users that $\mathcal{A}_{atk}$ has corrupted during the attack. In order to consider meaningful and successful such an attack, we require $|\mathcal{P}^* \cap \mathcal{U}'| < t^*$. Otherwise, $\mathcal{A}_{atk}$ knows the secret key of at least $t^*$ players in $\mathcal{P}^*$ and can decrypt $C^*$ by himself, obtaining $m_\beta$.

Depending on the considered kind of attacks, $\mathcal{A}_{atk}$ can also have access to a decryption oracle for ciphertexts $C$ of his choice. As answer, $\mathcal{A}_{atk}$ receives all the information that would be broadcast in a complete decryption process for this tuple; this includes all the partial decryption values and the resulting plaintext. If $atk$ is a chosen plaintext attack (CPA), then there is no access at all, i.e. $\mathcal{O}_1 = \mathcal{O}_2 = \epsilon$. If $atk$ is a partial chosen ciphertext attack (CCA1), then $\mathcal{O}_1 = $ TBE.PartDec($\cdot$) $\cup$ TBE.Dec($\cdot$) and $\mathcal{O}_2 = \epsilon$. Finally, if $atk$ is a full chosen ciphertext attack (CCA2), then $\mathcal{O}_1 = \mathcal{O}_2 = $ TBE.PartDec($\cdot$) $\cup$ TBE.Dec($\cdot$). In this last case, $\mathcal{A}_{CCA2}$ is not allowed to query the oracle $\mathcal{O}_2$ with the challenge ciphertext $C^*$.

The advantage of such an adversary $\mathcal{A}_{atk}$ is defined as

$$\text{Adv}(\mathcal{A}_{atk}) = \Pr[\beta' = \beta] - \frac{1}{2}.$$

A threshold broadcast encryption scheme is said to be $\varepsilon$-indistinguishable under $atk$ attacks if $\text{Adv}(\mathcal{A}_{atk}) < \varepsilon$ for any attacker $\mathcal{A}_{atk}$ which runs in polynomial time. The CCA2 level of security is quite restrictive; for example, a CCA2 attack can be easily constructed against the naive solution to the problem of threshold broadcast encryption, where the message is divided into $n$ shares and each share is encrypted for one different receiver.

Note that the definitions in this section (with slight changes) are valid also for identity-based scenarios: params will include a master public key, whereas the corresponding master secret key is used to compute secret keys for the users (identities) in a Key Extraction protocol. The sets of receivers will be sets of identities $\mathcal{P} = \{ID_1, \ldots, ID_n\}$. In the security game, the adversary is allowed to make key extraction (i.e. corruption) queries in order to obtain the secret keys for identities of his choice; this is reflected by the oracle $Corr$ in the game above.

## 4    A PKI-Based Threshold Broadcast Encryption Scheme with $|C| \approx n - t$

The idea behind the design of our scheme is to combine some threshold secret sharing techniques with the Canetti et al. [11] generic transformation, applied to the first selective-ID secure identity-based encryption scheme proposed by Boneh and Boyen in [5]. Note that the same idea has been used to construct a standard threshold encryption scheme (with fixed threshold and set of receivers) in [6]. The resulting schemes (ours and the one in [6]) enjoy two very good properties: security can be proved in the standard model and no interaction is needed among the receivers at the time of decryption.

The public parameters of our TBE scheme will be the public parameters of the scheme in [5] along with part (all but one element) of the master public key. The remaining element of the master public key will be computed ad-hoc by the sender of the message, from the public keys of the $n$ receivers, in such a way that the corresponding ad-hoc master secret key is distributed into the secret keys of the receivers, by means of a $(n, N)$-threshold secret sharing scheme, where $N = 2n - t$.

Then, the sender generates a fresh pair of keys $(SK, VK)$ for a one-time signature scheme, and encrypts the desired message by using the resulting identity-based public parameters and the identity $ID = VK$. Intuitively, $n$ shares of the master secret key would be necessary to compute the secret key for the identity $ID = VK$ and therefore decrypt the ciphertext. The sender creates a subset of $n - t$ dummy users, out of the set of receivers, and adds to the ciphertext the secret decryption information that these users would provide. As a result, only $t$ other partial decryption values, coming from the designated set of receivers, will be necessary to correctly perform decryption. Following the techniques in [11], the ciphertext is signed with $SK$. The resulting signature and the verification key $VK$ are appended to the ciphertext.

There are some alternative to the use of one-time signatures in the generic constructions in [11], which provide the same security level with a better efficiency; for example, by using message authentication codes and commitments [7] or chamaleon hash functions [1]. These techniques could also be applied to our constructions, but we have chosen one-time signatures for simplicity of the scheme description and the proofs. Note that all these techniques are needed to achieve chosen-ciphertext (CCA2) security. For chosen-plaintext (CPA) security only, it is possible to design simple schemes, based on ElGamal for example, which do not employ bilinear pairings (see [14]).

In the two following sections, we detail the protocols of the proposed scheme for PKI scenarios and the security proof.

### 4.1   The Scheme

Let $\Sigma = (\Sigma.KG, \Sigma.\text{Sign}, \Sigma.\text{Verify})$ be a secure one-time signature scheme. The five algorithms of the new TBE scheme work as follows.

*Setup.* Given a security parameter $k$, it generates a prime number $q$ with $k$ bits, and groups $\mathbb{G}_1 = \langle P \rangle$, $\mathbb{G}_2$ with order $q$ which admit a bilinear pairing $e : \mathbb{G}_1 \times \mathbb{G}_1 \to \mathbb{G}_2$, as described in Section 2.2. A hash function $h : \{0,1\}^* \to \mathbb{Z}_q$ is chosen, along with two random elements $P_1$ and $Q$ from $\mathbb{G}_1$. The output of the protocol is $\text{params} = (q, \mathbb{G}_1, \mathbb{G}_2, P, e, h, P_1, Q)$. Any user $R_i$ of the scheme will be publicly associated to a different element $\alpha_i \in \mathbb{Z}_q$ (for the secret sharing scheme). This can be done by defining $\alpha_i = g(R_i)$ for some public and collision-resistant hash function $g : \{0,1\}^* \to \mathbb{Z}_q$.

*Key Generation.* Each player (potential receiver) $R_i$ chooses at random a value $\gamma_i \in \mathbb{Z}_q^*$. The public key is $PK_i = \gamma_i P$, whereas the secret key is $SK_i = \gamma_i P_1$.

*Encryption.* The goal is to encrypt a message $m \in \mathbb{G}_2$ addressed to some set $\mathcal{P} = \{R_1, \ldots, R_n\}$ of $n$ receivers, with threshold $t$ for the decryption. The $n$ public keys of the receivers implicitly define a $n-1$ degree polynomial. The idea is to compute the values of this polynomial in the points $\alpha_0 = 0$ (this will be the value $P_2$) and in some dummy points $\alpha_j$ (these will be values $\tilde{PK}_j$), by using the corresponding Lagrange coefficients, defined in Section 2.1. Note that these values $P_2, \{\tilde{PK}_j\}_{P_j \in \tilde{\mathcal{P}}}$ are univocally determined from the public keys of the receivers, so they can be re-used every time a message is encrypted for this set of players (independently of the decryption threshold). Specifically, the sender must act as follows.

1. Run $\Sigma.KG(1^k) \to (SK, VK)$.
2. Define $P_2 = \sum_{R_i \in \mathcal{P}} \lambda_{i0}^{\mathcal{P}} PK_i$.
3. Choose at random $s \in \mathbb{Z}_q^*$ and compute $C_1 = sP$.
4. Compute $C_2 = m \cdot e(P_1, P_2)^s$.
5. Compute $C_3 = s[h(VK)P_1 + Q]$.
6. Choose a set $\tilde{\mathcal{P}}$ of $n-t$ (dummy) players, such that $\tilde{\mathcal{P}} \cap \mathcal{P} = \emptyset$. For each $R_j \in \tilde{\mathcal{P}}$, consider the corresponding $\alpha_j \in \mathbb{Z}_q$ and then define $\tilde{PK}_j = \sum_{R_i \in \mathcal{P}} \lambda_{ij}^{\mathcal{P}} PK_i$.

   Note that this dummy value $\tilde{PK}_j$ is not necessarily equal to the real public key $PK_j$ of user $R_j$.
7. For each $R_j \in \tilde{\mathcal{P}}$, choose $r_j \in \mathbb{Z}_q$ at random and compute

$$\kappa_j = \frac{e(C_3, r_j P)}{e(\tilde{PK}_j, sP_1) \cdot e(C_1, r_j[h(VK)P_1 + Q])}.$$

8. Define $C' = (\mathcal{P}, t, \tilde{\mathcal{P}}, C_1, C_2, C_3, \{\kappa_j\}_{R_j \in \tilde{\mathcal{P}}})$.
9. Run $\Sigma.\text{Sign}(SK, C') \to \sigma$.
10. Define the final ciphertext as $C = (VK, C', \sigma)$.

Note that, excluding the description of the sets $\mathcal{P}$ and $\tilde{\mathcal{P}}$, which can have different lengths depending on the case, a ciphertext $C$ contains $n-t+3$ elements. The description of the set $\tilde{\mathcal{P}}$ can actually be very short; for example, the sender can look for an interval of $n-t$ integers $J = \{j_0, j_0 + 1, \ldots, j_0 + n - t - 1\}$ (modulo $q$) such that $\alpha_i \notin J$ for all $P_i \in \mathcal{P}$, and define the set $\tilde{\mathcal{P}}$ simply as the $n-t$ dummy users $P_j$ (real or not) whose associated values are $\alpha_j \in J$. Note that in this case, the value $j_0$ is enough to describe the set $\tilde{\mathcal{P}}$. Such an interval $J$ exists as long as $n(n-t) < q - 1$, which is very likely to happen since $q$ is a very large number.

The cost to pay for this improvement in the ciphertexts' length is a more inefficient encryption protocol. Compared with the proposal in [12] (which is the only previous TBE scheme which achieves CCA2 security), our encryption protocol requires $n - t + 3$ pairing computations, whereas the scheme in [12] does not require any pairing computation. The efficiency for the rest of the protocols of our scheme is very similar to the efficiency of [12].

*Partial Decryption, EG_TBE.PartDec.* Given a ciphertext $C = (VK, C', \sigma)$, any receiver $R_i \in \mathcal{P}$ first runs $\Sigma.\text{Verify}(VK, C', \sigma)$. If the result is 0 (invalid ciphertext), then the special symbol $\perp$ is output. Otherwise (valid ciphertext) let $C' = (\mathcal{P}, t, \tilde{\mathcal{P}}, C_1, C_2, C_3, \{\kappa_j\}_{R_j \in \tilde{\mathcal{P}}})$. Receiver $R_i$ chooses $r_i \in \mathbb{Z}_q$ at random; the partial decryption that is broadcast by $R_i$ is

$$\kappa_i = \frac{e(C_3, r_i P)}{e(C_1, SK_i + r_i[h(VK)P_1 + Q])}.$$

*Final Decryption, EG_TBE.Dec.* Given a valid ciphertext $C = (VK, C', \sigma)$, with $C' = (\mathcal{P}, t, \tilde{\mathcal{P}}, C_1, C_2, C_3, \{\kappa_j\}_{R_j \in \tilde{\mathcal{P}}})$, and a set of $t$ partial decryptions $\kappa_i$, corresponding to a subset $A \subset \mathcal{P}$ with $|A| = t$, a combiner algorithm considers the whole set of partial decryptions in $B = A \cup \tilde{\mathcal{P}}$ and then computes

$$\kappa = \prod_{R_i \in B} \kappa_i^{\lambda_{i0}^B} = \ldots = \frac{1}{e(P_1, P_2)^s}.$$

The plaintext $m$ is recovered by computing $m = C_2 \cdot \kappa$.

## 4.2   Provable Security

**Theorem 1.** *Suppose $\Sigma$ is $\varepsilon_\Sigma$-secure, which means that any polynomial-time forger against $\Sigma$ has a success probability bounded by $\varepsilon_\Sigma$.*

*If there exists a CCA2 attack $\mathcal{A}$ against the proposed TBE scheme, with advantage $\varepsilon$ and corrupting at most $q_c$ users, then the Decisional Bilinear Diffie-Hellman (DBDH) problem can be solved with advantage $\varepsilon' \geq \frac{\varepsilon(1-\varepsilon_\Sigma)}{6(q_c+1)}$.*

*Proof.* Let $\mathcal{D} = (P, aP, bP, cP, T)$ be an instance of the DBDH problem (which includes the description of $\mathbb{G}_1 = \langle P \rangle, \mathbb{G}_2, e$). The goal of a solver $\mathcal{S}$ is to decide if $\mathcal{D} \in \mathcal{D}_{BDH}$ (that is, if $T = e(P, P)^{abc}$), or if $\mathcal{D} \in \mathcal{D}_{rand}$ (that is, if $T$ is a random value in $\mathbb{G}_2$). In the first case, the output of a solver is the bit $d = 1$, whereas in the second case, the output is the bit $d = 0$. We are going to construct such a solver $\mathcal{S}$ for this problem. $\mathcal{S}$ first runs $\Sigma.KG(1^k) \to (SK^*, VK^*)$. $\mathcal{S}$ chooses two suitable hash functions $h, g : \{0, 1\}^* \to \mathbb{Z}_q$. The solver chooses at random $\eta \in \mathbb{Z}_q$ and defines $P_1 = aP$ and $Q = -h(VK^*)P_1 + \eta P$. At this point, $\mathcal{S}$ initializes the hypothetical attacker $\mathcal{A}$ against the TBE scheme, with input $\text{params} = (q, \mathbb{G}_1, \mathbb{G}_2, P, e, h, g, P_1, Q)$.

Each time $\mathcal{A}$ asks for the creation of a new user $R_i$, the solver $\mathcal{S}$ chooses at random $\gamma_i \in \mathbb{Z}_q^*$. Let $\mu \in (0, 1)$ be a real number to be determined later. With probability $\mu$, the value $c_i = 0$ is chosen, and then $\mathcal{S}$ defines $PK_i = \gamma_i P$ (in this case, $SK_i = \gamma_i P_1$ is known to $\mathcal{S}$). On the other hand, with probability $1 - \mu$, the value $c_i = 1$ is chosen, and $\mathcal{S}$ defines $PK_i = \gamma_i(bP)$ (in this case, $\mathcal{S}$ does not know the value of $SK_i$). The public key $PK_i$ is sent back to $\mathcal{A}$. These values are stored in a table.

$\mathcal{A}$ is allowed to corrupt some users. If $\mathcal{A}$ sends a corruption query for user $R_i$, the solver $\mathcal{S}$ looks for $c_i$ in the table. If $c_i = 0$, then the value $SK_i = \gamma_i P_1$ (along with $\gamma_i$, if required by $\mathcal{A}$) is sent to $\mathcal{A}$. Otherwise, if $c_i = 1$, the solver $\mathcal{S}$ aborts and outputs a random bit $d \in \{0, 1\}$. If the number of corruption queries from $\mathcal{A}$ is $q_c$, then the probability that $\mathcal{S}$ does not abort in this phase is $\mu^{q_c}$.

The CCA2 attacker $\mathcal{A}$ can make decryption queries for ciphertexts $C = (VK, C', \sigma)$ of his choice. The solver $\mathcal{S}$ acts as follows:

- If $VK = VK^*$, then $\mathcal{S}$ runs $\Sigma.\text{Verify}(VK, C', \sigma)$. If the output is 0, $\mathcal{S}$ replies with $\perp$. If the output is 1 (valid signature), then $\mathcal{S}$ aborts and outputs a random bit $d \in \{0, 1\}$.
- If $VK \neq VK^*$ and $\Sigma.\text{Verify}(VK, C', \sigma)$ outputs 0, then $\mathcal{S}$ replies with $\perp$.
- If $VK \neq VK^*$ and $\Sigma.\text{Verify}(VK, C', \sigma)$ outputs 1, then we have $C' = (\mathcal{P}, t, \tilde{P}, C_1, C_2, C_3, \{\kappa_j\}_{R_j \in \tilde{\mathcal{P}}})$ and $h(VK) \neq h(VK^*)$ (otherwise, $\mathcal{A}$ would have found a collision on the hash function $h$, which is considered to be computationally infeasible). The solver $\mathcal{S}$ must simulate the partial decryption values $\kappa_i$ for $R_i \in \mathcal{P}$. If $c_i = 0$, then $\mathcal{S}$ knows $SK_i$ and $\kappa_i$ can be computed as in the description of the protocol. Otherwise, $\mathcal{S}$ chooses $r_i \in \mathbb{Z}_q$ at random and computes

$$\kappa_i = \frac{e\left(C_3, r_i P - \frac{\gamma_i}{h(VK) - h(VK^*)}(bP)\right)}{e\left(C_1, \frac{-\gamma_i \eta}{h(VK) - h(VK^*)}(bP) + r_i[(h(VK) - h(VK^*))P_1 + \eta P]\right)}.$$

It is not difficult to see that this value $\kappa_i$ is a correct partial decryption value for $R_i$, computed with the implicit random value $\tilde{r}_i = r_i - \frac{b\gamma_i}{h(VK) - h(VK^*)}$.

When all the values $\kappa_i$ are computed, $\mathcal{S}$ can recover $\kappa$ and the plaintext $m = C_2 \cdot \kappa$. The solver $\mathcal{S}$ sends $m$ and $\{\kappa_i\}_{R_i \in \mathcal{P}}$ to $\mathcal{A}$.

At some point, $\mathcal{A}$ broadcasts a set $\mathcal{P} = \{R_1, \ldots, R_n\}$, a threshold $t$ such that $1 \leq t \leq n$, and two messages $m_0, m_1 \in \mathbb{G}_2$, such that the number of corrupted users in $\mathcal{P}$ is less than $t$. This means that at least one user $R_u \in \mathcal{P}$ has not been corrupted by $\mathcal{A}$. With probability $1 - \mu$, we have $c_u = 1$ and so $PK_u = \gamma_u(bP)$. In general, we define $\mathcal{P}_0 = \{R_i \in \mathcal{P} : c_i = 0\}$ and $\mathcal{P}_1 = \{R_\ell \in \mathcal{P} : c_\ell = 1\}$. As we have just said, $\mathcal{P}_1$ is not empty with probability at least $1 - \mu$. If this is not the case, $\mathcal{S}$ aborts and outputs a random bit $d \in \{0, 1\}$.

For the challenge ciphertext to be given to $\mathcal{A}$, the solver $\mathcal{S}$ defines $C_1 = cP$ (note that $c$ is unknown to $\mathcal{S}$) and takes $VK^*$ for the verification key. Note that, because of the way in which $Q$ is defined, we have $C_3 = \eta C_1$. To compute

$C_2$, the value $e(P_1, P_2)^c$ must be multiplied with the plaintext. If we define $P_2 = \sum\limits_{R_i \in \mathcal{P}} \lambda_{i0}^{\mathcal{P}} PK_i$, and recalling that $P_1 = aP$, we have

$$e(P_1, P_2)^c = e\Big(aP, \sum_{R_i \in \mathcal{P}_0} \lambda_{i0}^{\mathcal{P}} \gamma_i P\Big)^c \cdot e\Big(aP, \sum_{R_\ell \in \mathcal{P}_1} \lambda_{\ell 0}^{\mathcal{P}} \gamma_\ell (bP)\Big)^c =$$

$$= e(aP, cP)^{\sum\limits_{R_i \in \mathcal{P}_0} \lambda_{i0}^{\mathcal{P}} \gamma_i} \cdot e(P, P)^{abc \sum\limits_{R_\ell \in \mathcal{P}_1} \lambda_{\ell 0}^{\mathcal{P}} \gamma_\ell}.$$

$\mathcal{S}$ chooses a set $\tilde{\mathcal{P}}$ of $n - t$ dummy users such that $\mathcal{P} \cap \tilde{\mathcal{P}} = \emptyset$. Analogously, defining $\tilde{PK}_j = \sum\limits_{R_i \in \mathcal{P}} \lambda_{ij}^{\mathcal{P}} PK_i$ for these users, we have

$$e(\tilde{PK}_j, cP_1) = e(cP, aP)^{\sum\limits_{R_i \in \mathcal{P}_0} \lambda_{ij}^{\mathcal{P}} \gamma_i} \cdot e(P, P)^{abc \sum\limits_{R_\ell \in \mathcal{P}_1} \lambda_{\ell j}^{\mathcal{P}} \gamma_\ell}.$$

$\mathcal{S}$ chooses a random bit $\beta \in \{0, 1\}$ and defines

$$C_2 = m_\beta \cdot \left( e(aP, cP)^{\sum\limits_{R_i \in \mathcal{P}_0} \lambda_{i0}^{\mathcal{P}} \gamma_i} \cdot T^{\sum\limits_{R_\ell \in \mathcal{P}_1} \lambda_{\ell 0}^{\mathcal{P}} \gamma_\ell} \right).$$

And, for every dummy user $R_j \in \tilde{\mathcal{P}}$, $\mathcal{S}$ chooses $r_j \in \mathbb{Z}_q$ at random and defines

$$\kappa_j = \frac{e(C_3, r_j P)}{e(cP, aP)^{\sum\limits_{R_i \in \mathcal{P}_0} \lambda_{ij}^{\mathcal{P}} \gamma_i} \cdot T^{\sum\limits_{R_\ell \in \mathcal{P}_1} \lambda_{\ell j}^{\mathcal{P}} \gamma_\ell} \cdot e(C_1, r_j [h(VK^*)P_1 + Q])}.$$

Note that the resulting $C'^* = (\mathcal{P}, t, \tilde{\mathcal{P}}, C_1, C_2, C_3, \{\kappa_j\}_{R_j \in \tilde{\mathcal{P}}})$ is consistent if and only if $T = e(P, P)^{abc}$. After that, $\mathcal{S}$ runs $\Sigma.\mathsf{Sign}(SK^*, C'^*) \to \sigma^*$. The final challenge ciphertext that is sent to $\mathcal{A}$ is $C^* = (VK^*, C'^*, \sigma^*)$.

At this point, $\mathcal{A}$ is allowed to make new decryption queries, which are replied by $\mathcal{S}$ exactly in the same way as before. After that, $\mathcal{A}$ outputs its guess $\beta'$. If $\beta' = \beta$, then $\mathcal{S}$ outputs $d = 1$ (meaning that it believes that $T = e(P, P)^{abc}$ and so $\mathcal{D} \in \mathcal{D}_{BDH}$). If $\beta' \neq \beta$, then $\mathcal{S}$ outputs $d = 0$ (meaning that it believes that $T$ is a random value in $\mathbb{G}_2$ and so $\mathcal{D} \in \mathcal{D}_{rand}$).

Let us compute the success probability of $\mathcal{S}$. We assume that in the input of the DBDH problem, $\mathcal{D} \in \mathcal{D}_{BDH}$ with probability $1/2$. Let us denote as $\rho$ the probability that $\mathcal{S}$ does not abort in any phase. We have

$$\Pr[\mathcal{S} \text{ succeeds}] = \frac{1}{2}\Pr[\mathcal{S} \text{ succeeds} / \mathcal{D} \in \mathcal{D}_{BDH}] + \frac{1}{2}\Pr[\mathcal{S} \text{ succeeds} / \mathcal{D} \in \mathcal{D}_{rand}] \geq$$

$$\geq \frac{1}{2}\left[ \Pr[\mathcal{S} \text{ does not abort}] \cdot (\frac{1}{2} + \varepsilon) + \Pr[\mathcal{S} \text{ aborts}] \cdot \frac{1}{2} \right] + \frac{1}{2} \cdot \frac{1}{2} \geq$$

$$\geq \frac{1}{4}\rho + \frac{1}{2}\rho\varepsilon + \frac{1}{4}(1 - \rho) + \frac{1}{4} = \frac{1}{2} + \frac{\rho\varepsilon}{2}.$$

Let us denote as $\delta$ the probability that $\mathcal{A}$ makes a decryption query for a valid ciphertext $C = (VK^*, C', \sigma)$ such that $(C', \sigma) \neq (C'^*, \sigma^*)$.

**Lemma 1.** $\delta \leq \varepsilon_\Sigma$.

*Proof.* We are going to prove that a CCA2 attacker $\mathcal{A}$ which makes a valid query $C = (VK^*, C', \sigma)$ to the decryption oracle, such that $(C', \sigma) \neq (C'^*, \sigma^*)$, with probability $\delta$, can be used to construct a forger $\mathcal{F}$ against the one-time signature scheme $\Sigma$, with success probability $\delta$.

When $\mathcal{F}$ receives $VK^*$ as input, he generates **params** and initializes $\mathcal{A}$. Each time $\mathcal{A}$ asks for the creation of a new user $R_i$, the forger $\mathcal{F}$ generates the secret key and public key $(SK_i, PK_i)$ for $R_i$. Later, $\mathcal{F}$ can answer all the corruption and decryption queries made by $\mathcal{A}$, because $\mathcal{F}$ knows all the secret keys. For the challenge ciphertext, $\mathcal{F}$ chooses $VK^*$ as the verification key, and uses his only query to his signing oracle to obtain $\Sigma.\mathsf{Sign}(SK^*, C'^*) \to \sigma^*$.

If at some point $\mathcal{A}$ makes a decryption query for a valid ciphertext $C = (VK^*, C', \sigma)$ verifying $(C', \sigma) \neq (C'^*, \sigma^*)$, then $\mathcal{F}$ aborts and outputs $(C', \sigma)$ as his valid forgery.                                                                                    □

The probability that $\mathcal{S}$ does not abort at any point is $\rho \geq \mu^{q_c}(1-\mu)(1-\delta)$. This value is maximized when $\mu = \frac{q_c}{q_c+1}$, which leads to

$$\rho \geq \left(\frac{1}{1+\frac{1}{q_c}}\right)^{q_c} \cdot \frac{1}{q_c+1} \cdot (1-\delta) \geq \frac{1}{e} \cdot \frac{1-\delta}{q_c+1}.$$

Therefore, the advantage of $\mathcal{S}$ in solving the DBDH problem is

$$\varepsilon' \geq \frac{\rho\varepsilon}{2} \geq \frac{\varepsilon(1-\delta)}{2(q_c+1)e} \geq \frac{\varepsilon(1-\delta)}{6(q_c+1)} \geq \frac{\varepsilon(1-\varepsilon_\Sigma)}{6(q_c+1)}.$$                □

## 5   The Identity-Based Case

The generic transformation of Canetti, Halevi and Katz [11], that we have used as building tool for the construction of our TBE scheme in the previous section, works also to obtain CCA2 secure identity-based cryptosystem from a 2-level hierarchical identity-based cryptosystem with chosen plaintext selective-ID security. Therefore, we should in principle be able to construct an identity-based TBE scheme with maximum security in the standard model, by starting from the 2-level hierarchical scheme in [5]. However, this particular scheme does not seem to properly adapt to the scenario of threshold broadcast encryption.

Nevertheless, it is possible to construct a secure identity-based TBE scheme by following the same idea, but applied to a different scheme. Intuitively, what we need is the Boneh-Franklin identity-based scheme [8] for the first level of identities (i.e. the identities of the receivers) and the Boneh-Boyen identity-based scheme [5] for the second level of identities (corresponding to the verification key $VK$). A consequence of using the Boneh-Franklin scheme is that our scheme will achieve provable CCA2 security in the random oracle model.

Actually, our proposal of identity-based TBE scheme, which results from applying this combination, is very similar to the PKI scheme described and analyzed in Section 4. For this reason, we only sketch the main differences between them:

- The Setup phase is now run by the master entity. It is the same as in the PKI scheme, but now the element $P_1$ is computed as $P_1 = \gamma P$ for some random $\gamma \in \mathbb{Z}_q$ that the master entity keeps secret. An additional hash function $H : \{0,1\}^* \to \mathbb{G}_1$ is chosen and made public.
- The Key Generation phase of the PKI scheme is replaced with a Key Extraction protocol, run by the master entity each time a user with identity $ID_i$ asks for his secret key. The public key of $ID_i$ is easily (and publicly) computable as $PK_i = H(ID_i)$, whereas the corresponding secret key $SK_i = \gamma PK_i$ is computed and delivered by the master entity. Note that in both (PKI and identity-based) schemes the tuples $(P, P_1, PK_i, SK_i)$ are Diffie-Hellman tuples. In particular, in the identity-based scheme, a user can verify that the obtained secret key is consistent, by checking if $e(P, SK_i) = e(P_1, PK_i)$.
- In the security proof, the part of the proof of Theorem 1 where the pairs of keys $(PK_i, SK_i)$ are generated is now the part of the proof where the solver $\mathcal{S}$ answers the queries that the attacker $\mathcal{A}$ makes to the random oracle for $H$. But the result is the same: for some users $(c_i = 0)$ the solver $\mathcal{S}$ will define $H(ID_i) = PK_i = \gamma_i P$ and so $\mathcal{S}$ will know the corresponding $SK_i$, whereas for other users $(c_i = 1)$ the solver $\mathcal{S}$ will define $H(ID_i) = PK_i = \gamma_i(bP)$.

As a result, we obtain an identity-based TBE scheme which is CCA2 secure in the random oracle model, under the Decisional Bilinear Diffie-Hellman Assumption.

## 6   Conclusion

Threshold broadcast encryption (TBE) schemes differ from traditional threshold public key encryption schemes [21,10,6] because the group of receivers and the threshold for decryption are not decided from the beginning, but chosen (ad-hoc) by the entity who encrypts each message. This difference makes TBE schemes more suitable for some applications in real life.

In this work we have designed TBE schemes with shorter ciphertexts than previous proposals, for both PKI-based and identity-based scenarios. The schemes achieve the highest possible level of security (against chosen-ciphertext attacks) assuming that the Decisional Bilinear Diffie-Hellman problem is hard.

Many problems remain open in this area. For example, to design TBE schemes with ciphertexts' length shorter than $\mathcal{O}(n)$ (for PKI or identity-based scenarios) which do not employ bilinear pairings; or to design an identity-based TBE scheme, also with ciphertexts' length shorter than $\mathcal{O}(n)$, which achieves the maximum security in the standard model. Another interesting question to be answered is whether the bound $n - t + \mathcal{O}(1)$ for the ciphertexts' length can be lowered, for fully secure TBE schemes. It is not clear, for example, whether some of the proposed techniques to shorten the ciphertexts' length in standard broadcast encryption schemes [9,13,18] can be extended to our threshold setting.

# Acknowledgments

The work of the two first authors was partially supported by Spanish *Ministry of Education and Science*, under projects SEG2004-04352-C04-01 ("PROPRI-ETAS") and CONSOLIDER CSD2007-00004 ("ARES"). The work of the first author was also supported by the Government of Catalonia under grant 2005 SGR 00446 and by the UNESCO *Chair in Data Privacy*. This author is solely responsible for the view expressed in this paper, which does not necessarily reflect the position of UNESCO nor commits that organization. The work of the two last authors was partially supported by Spanish *Ministry of Education and Science*, under projects TSI2006-02731 and CONSOLIDER MTM2005-24556-E.

# References

1. Abe, M., Cui, Y., Imai, H., Kiltz, E.: Efficient hybrid encryption from ID-based encryption. IACR ePrint (2007), available at http://eprint.iacr.org/2007/023
2. Bellare, M., Boldyreva, A., Micali, S.: Public-key encryption in a multi-user setting: security proofs and improvements. In: Preneel, B. (ed.) EUROCRYPT 2000. LNCS, vol. 1807, pp. 259–274. Springer, Heidelberg (2000)
3. Bellare, M., Goldreich, O.: On defining proofs of knowledge. In: Brickell, E.F. (ed.) CRYPTO 1992. LNCS, vol. 740, pp. 390–420. Springer, Heidelberg (1993)
4. Blakley, G.R.: Safeguarding cryptographic keys. In: Proceedings of the National Computer Conference, American Federation of Information, Processing Societies Proceedings, vol. 48, pp. 313–317 (1979)
5. Boneh, D., Boyen, X.: Efficient selective-ID secure identity-based encryption without random oracles. In: Cachin, C., Camenisch, J.L. (eds.) EUROCRYPT 2004. LNCS, vol. 3027, pp. 223–238. Springer, Heidelberg (2004)
6. Boneh, D., Boyen, X., Halevi, S.: Chosen ciphertext secure public key threshold encryption without random oracles. In: Pointcheval, D. (ed.) CT-RSA 2006. LNCS, vol. 3860, pp. 226–243. Springer, Heidelberg (2006)
7. Boneh, D., Canetti, R., Katz, J., Halevi, S.: Chosen-ciphertext security from identity-based encryption. SIAM Journal on Computing 36(5), 1301–1328 (2007)
8. Boneh, D., Franklin, M.K.: Identity-based encryption from the Weil pairing. SIAM Journal on Computing 32(3), 586–615 (2003)
9. Boneh, D., Gentry, C., Waters, B.: Collusion resistant broadcast encryption with short ciphertexts and private keys. In: Shoup, V. (ed.) CRYPTO 2005. LNCS, vol. 3621, pp. 258–275. Springer, Heidelberg (2005)
10. Canetti, R., Goldwasser, S.: An efficient threshold public key cryptosystem secure against adaptive chosen ciphertext attack. In: Stern, J. (ed.) EUROCRYPT 1999. LNCS, vol. 1592, pp. 90–106. Springer, Heidelberg (1999)
11. Canetti, R., Halevi, S., Katz, J.: Chosen-ciphertext security from identity-based encryption. In: Cachin, C., Camenisch, J.L. (eds.) EUROCRYPT 2004. LNCS, vol. 3027, pp. 207–222. Springer, Heidelberg (2004)
12. Chai, Z., Cao, Z., Zhou, Y.: Efficient ID-based broadcast threshold decryption in ad hoc network. In: Proceedings of IMSCCS 2006, vol. 2, IEEE Computer Society Press, Los Alamitos (2006)
13. Chatterjee, S., Sarkar, P.: Multi-receiver identity-based key encapsulation with shortened ciphertext. In: Barua, R., Lange, T. (eds.) INDOCRYPT 2006. LNCS, vol. 4329, pp. 394–408. Springer, Heidelberg (2006)

14. Daza, V., Herranz, J., Morillo, P., Ràfols, C.: Ad-hoc threshold broadcast encryption with shorter ciphertexts. In: Proceedings of WCAN 2007 (to be published by Electronic Notes in Theoretical Computer Science) (2007)
15. Fiat, A., Naor, M.: Broadcast encryption. In: Stinson, D.R. (ed.) CRYPTO 1993. LNCS, vol. 773, pp. 480–491. Springer, Heidelberg (1994)
16. Ghodosi, H., Pieprzyk, J., Safavi-Naini, R.: Dynamic threshold cryptosystems: a new scheme in group oriented cryptography. In: Proceedings of Pragocrypt 1996, CTU Publishing house, pp. 370–379 (1996)
17. Lim, C.H., Lee, P.J.: Directed signatures and application to threshold cryptosystems. In: Lomas, M. (ed.) Security Protocols. LNCS, vol. 1189, pp. 131–138. Springer, Heidelberg (1997)
18. Sakai, R., Furukawa, J.: Identity-based broadcast encryption. IACR ePrint (2007), available at http://eprint.iacr.org/2007/217
19. Shamir, A.: How to share a secret. Communications of the ACM 22, 612–613 (1979)
20. Shamir, A.: Identity-based cryptosystems and signature schemes. In: Blakely, G.R., Chaum, D. (eds.) CRYPTO 1984. LNCS, vol. 196, pp. 47–53. Springer, Heidelberg (1985)
21. Shoup, V., Gennaro, R.: Securing threshold cryptosystems against chosen ciphertext attack. Journal of Cryptology 15(2), 75–96 (2002)

# Construction of a Hybrid HIBE Protocol Secure Against Adaptive Attacks
## (Without Random Oracle)

Palash Sarkar and Sanjit Chatterjee

Applied Statistics Unit
Indian Statistical Institute
203, B.T. Road, Kolkata
India 700108
{palash,sanjit_t}@isical.ac.in

**Abstract.** We describe a hybrid hierarchical identity based encryption (HIBE) protocol which is secure in the full model without using the random oracle heuristic and whose security is based on the computational hardness of the decisional bilinear Diffie-Hellman (DBDH) problem. The new protocol is obtained by augmenting a previous construction of a HIBE protocol which is secure against chosen plaintext attacks (CPA-secure). The technique for answering decryption queries in the proof is based on earlier work by Boyen-Mei-Waters. Ciphertext validity testing is done indirectly through a symmetric authentication algorithm in a manner similar to the Kurosawa-Desmedt public key encryption protocol. Additionally, we perform symmetric encryption and authentication by a single authenticated encryption algorithm. A net result of all these is that our construction improves upon previously known constructions in the same setting.

## 1 Introduction

Identity based encryption [29,8] is a kind of public key encryption where the public key can be the identity of the receiver. The secret key corresponding to the identity is generated by a private key generator (PKG) and is securely provided to the relevant user. The notion of IBE simplifies the issues of certificate management in public key infrastructure. The PKG issues the private key associated with an identity. The notion of hierarchical IBE (HIBE) [21,19] was introduced to reduce the workload of the PKG. The identity of any entity in a HIBE structure is a tuple $(v_1, \ldots, v_j)$. The private key corresponding to such an identity can be generated by the entity whose identity is $(v_1, \ldots, v_{j-1})$ and which possesses the private key corresponding to this identity. The security model for IBE was extended to that of HIBE in [21,19].

The first construction of an IBE which can be proved to be secure in the full model without the random oracle heuristic was given by Boneh and Boyen in [5]. Later, Waters [31] presented an efficient construction of an IBE which is secure in

W. Susilo, J.K. Liu, and Y. Mu. (Eds.): ProvSec 2007, LNCS 4784, pp. 51–67, 2007.

the same setting. An extension of Waters' construction has been independently described in [13] and [26]. This leads to a controllable trade-off between the size of the public parameters and the efficiency of the protocol (see [13] for details).

A construction of a HIBE secure in the full model without using the random oracle heuristic was suggested in [31]. A recent work [14], describes a HIBE which builds on [31] by reducing the number of public parameters. The constructed HIBE is secure against chosen plaintext attacks (CPA-secure).

**The Problem.** We consider the problem of constructing a HIBE under the following conditions.

- Security is in the full model [8], i.e., the adversary can mount an adaptive chosen ciphertext attack and can choose the challenge identity adaptively.
- The reduction is from the decisional bilinear Diffie-Hellman problem.
- The security proof does not use the random oracle heuristic.

## 1.1   Our Contributions

We describe a hybrid HIBE protocol for the above setting. The new construction is obtained by augmenting the construction in [14]. The idea for this augmentation is based on the technique of [9] and algebraic ideas from the construction of IBE given in [4]. In addition, we make use of two new things. First, we incorporate information about the length of the identity into the ciphertext. Second, we use symmetric key authentication to verify ciphertext well formedness. We also show that the two tasks of symmetric key encryption and authentication can be combined by using an authenticated encryption (AE) protocol.

The idea of using symmetric authentication technique to verify the well formedness of the ciphertext is based on the PKE protocol due to Kurosawa-Desmedt (KD) [25]. To the best of our knowledge, this technique has not been earlier applied to the (H)IBE setting.

We can specialize the HIBE protocol described in this paper to obtain a PKE and an IBE. With some natural simplifications, the PKE turns out to be the key encapsulation mechanism (KEM) proposed by BMW [9] composed with a one-time secure data encapsulation mechanism (DEM). On the other hand, the IBE is different from previous work. Kiltz-Galindo [24] had proposed an IB-KEM. Composed with a suitable symmetric encryption algorithm, this provides an IBE. The decryption algorithm of our IBE is faster than the IBE obtained from the KEM given in [24].

Our construction has a security degradation of approximately $q^h$ (where $q$ is the number of queries and $h$ is the number of levels). This is better than a degradation of $q^{h+1}$ which is what one would obtain by a straightforward application of the known techniques. Another advantage is that by instantiating the AE protocol with a single pass algorithm [27,22,20,12], it is possible to obtain a speed-up by a factor of two for both encryption and decryption of the symmetric part of the hybrid encryption. Also, by using the authentication aspect of the AE protocol for verifying the well formedness of the ciphertext we can avoid a number of pairing based verifications. This leads to a faster decryption algorithm.

We make a few remarks on the proof. Since the new protocol is obtained by augmenting the protocol in [14], the proof of the new protocol is also obtained by augmenting the proof in [14] (which is actually based on the construction and proof in [31]). We do not repeat the aspects of the proof that already appear in [14]. Incorporating the length of the identity in the ciphertext is required to avoid certain attacks as we discuss later. Verifying ciphertext well formedness using symmetric authentication requires us to adapt the proof technique (especially the method of deferred analysis) of [1] to the identity based setting. The combination of different techniques introduces several subtleties in the proof.

## 1.2   Related Work

The construction in [19] is based on the random oracle assumption and does not constitute a solution to the problem considered in this paper. A generic technique [11,7] is known which converts an $(h+1)$-level CPA-secure HIBE protocol into an $h$-level CCA-secure HIBE protocol while preserving the other features (security model, with/without random oracle, hardness assumption) of the original CPA-secure protocol. This technique is based on one-time signatures and requires prepending each identity component by a bit. Applying this technique directly to the protocol in [14] does not provide a protocol which is more efficient than the protocol we describe in this paper.

The BMW paper [9] provided a method of constructing a PKE from an IBE. They also mentioned that the technique can be used for constructing (H)IBE. Later work by Kiltz-Galindo [24] built on the BMW paper and described an efficient CCA-secure IB-KEM. The KG paper suggested a method for extending their IB-KEM to a HIB-KEM. Details were provided in [3]. Our work also uses the BMW technique, but introduces several other ideas to obtain a more efficient (H)IBE compared to previous work.

In an interesting paper, Boneh-Boyen-Goh [6] have shown how to construct a constant size ciphertext (H)IBE based on the weak decisional bilinear Diffie-Hellman exponent problem which is a variant of the DBDH problem. Their protocol is CPA-secure in the selective-ID model. Using the technique of Waters, this protocol can be made CPA-secure in the full model. Further, using the techniques of Boyen-Mei-Waters this can be converted into a CCA-secure protocol. For details of this conversion and also for a protocol secure in a different model see [15]. The work [23] also considers the same problem.

The main difference between the current work and that of [15,23] is that the hardness assumptions are different. This makes a direct comparison difficult. We, however, note that the ciphertext expansion in the later is constant while in the former it increases linearly with the number of components in the identity. This is due to the fact that the assumption used in [15,23] is tailored to ensure constant size ciphertext. On the other hand, the number of public parameters in the current construction is significantly less than the number of public parameters in [15,23]. This is due to the fact that the current protocol is built using the protocol in [14] which significantly reduces the number of public parameters.

**On Security Degradation of HIBE Protocols.** All known HIBE protocols which are secure against adaptive-ID attacks have a security degradation which is exponential in the depth of the HIBE. This is true, even if the random oracle heuristic is used in the security proof. In view of this, all such protocols can be considered to have a valid security bound only for a small number of levels. Currently, the most important open problem in the construction of HIBE protocols is to avoid (or reduce) this exponential security decay.

## 2   Preliminaries

### 2.1   HIBE Protocol

Following [21,19], a hierarchical identity based encryption (HIBE) scheme is specified by four algorithms: Setup, KeyGen, Encrypt and Decrypt. For a HIBE of height $h$ (henceforth denoted as $h$-HIBE) any identity $\mathsf{v}$ is a tuple $(\mathsf{v}_1, \ldots, \mathsf{v}_j)$ where $1 \leq j \leq h$.

- HIBE.Setup: Takes as input a security parameter and outputs $(pk, sk)$, where $pk$ is the public parameter of the PKG and $sk$ is the master secret of the PKG. It also defines the domains of identities, messages and ciphertexts.
- HIBE.KeyGen$(\mathsf{v}, d_{\mathsf{v}|_{j-1}}, pk)$: Takes as input a $j$-level identity $\mathsf{v}$, the secret $d_{\mathsf{v}|_{j-1}}$ corresponding to its $(j-1)$-level prefix and $pk$ and returns as output $d_{\mathsf{v}}$, the secret key corresponding to $\mathsf{v}$. In case $j = 1$, $d_{\mathsf{v}|_{j-1}}$ is equal to $sk$, the master secret of the PKG.
- HIBE.Encrypt$(\mathsf{v}, M, pk)$: Takes as input $\mathsf{v}$, the message $M$ and $pk$, and returns $C$, the ciphertext obtained by encrypting $M$ under $\mathsf{v}$ and $pk$.
- HIBE.Decrypt$(\mathsf{v}, d_{\mathsf{v}}, C, pk)$: Takes as input $\mathsf{v}$, the secret key $d_{\mathsf{v}}$ corresponding to $\mathsf{v}$, a ciphertext $C$ and $pk$. Returns either bad or $M$, the message which is the decryption of $C$.

As usual, for soundness, we require that HIBE.Decrypt$(\mathsf{v}, d_{\mathsf{v}}, C, pk) = M$ must hold for all $\mathsf{v}$, $d_{\mathsf{v}}$, $C$, $pk$, $sk$ and $M$ associated by the above four algorithms.

### 2.2   Security Model for HIBE

Security is defined using an adversarial game. An adversary $\mathcal{A}$ is allowed to query two oracles – a decryption oracle and a key-extraction oracle. At the initiation, it is provided with the public parameters of the PKG. The game has two query phases with a challenge phase in between.

*Query Phase1.* Adversary $\mathcal{A}$ makes a finite number of queries where each query is addressed either to the decryption oracle or to the key-extraction oracle. In a query to the decryption oracle it provides a ciphertext as well as the identity under which it wants the decryption. It gets back the corresponding message or bad if the ciphertext is invalid. Similarly, in a query to the key-extraction oracle, it asks for the private key of the identity it provides and gets back this private key. Further, $\mathcal{A}$ is allowed to make these queries adaptively, i.e., any query may depend on the previous queries as well as their answers. The adversary is not allowed to make any useless queries, i.e., queries for which it can compute the answer itself. For example, the adversary is not allowed to ask for the decryption of a message under an identity if it has already obtained a private key corresponding to the identity.

*Challenge.* At this stage, $\mathcal{A}$ outputs an identity $\mathsf{v}^* = (\mathsf{v}_1^*, \ldots, \mathsf{v}_j^*)$ for $1 \leq j \leq h$, and a pair of messages $M_0$ and $M_1$. There is the natural restriction on the adversary, that it cannot query the key extraction oracle on $\mathsf{v}^*$ or any of its proper prefixes in either of the phases 1 or 2. A random bit $\delta$ is chosen and the adversary is provided with $C^*$ which is an encryption of $M_\delta$ under $\mathsf{v}^*$.

*Query Phase2.* $\mathcal{A}$ now issues additional queries just like Phase 1, with the (obvious) restrictions that it cannot ask the decryption oracle for the decryption of $C^*$ under $\mathsf{v}^*$, nor the key-extraction oracle for the private key of $\mathsf{v}^*$ or any of its prefixes.

*Guess.* $\mathcal{A}$ outputs a guess $\delta'$ of $\delta$.
The advantage of the adversary $\mathcal{A}$ is defined as:

$$\mathsf{Adv}_{\mathcal{A}}^{\mathsf{HIBE}} = |\Pr[(\delta = \delta')] - 1/2|.$$

The quantity $\mathsf{Adv}^{\mathsf{HIBE}}(t, q_{\mathsf{ID}}, q_{\mathsf{C}})$ denotes the maximum of $\mathsf{Adv}_{\mathcal{A}}^{\mathsf{HIBE}}$ where the maximum is taken over all adversaries running in time at most $t$ and making at most $q_{\mathsf{C}}$ queries to the decryption oracle and at most $q_{\mathsf{ID}}$ queries to the key-extraction oracle. A HIBE protocol is said to be $(\epsilon, t, q_{\mathsf{ID}}, q_{\mathsf{C}})$-CCA secure if $\mathsf{Adv}^{\mathsf{HIBE}}(t, q_{\mathsf{ID}}, q_{\mathsf{C}}) \leq \epsilon$.

In the above game, we can disallow the adversary $\mathcal{A}$ from querying the decryption oracle. $\mathsf{Adv}^{\mathsf{HIBE}}(t, q)$ in this context denotes the maximum advantage where the maximum is taken over all adversaries running in time at most $t$ and making at most $q$ queries to the key-extraction oracle. A HIBE protocol is said to be $(t, q, \epsilon)$-CPA secure if $\mathsf{Adv}^{\mathsf{HIBE}}(t, q) \leq \epsilon$.

## 2.3   Cryptographic Bilinear Map

Let $G_1$ and $G_2$ be cyclic groups having the same prime order $p$ and $G_1 = \langle P \rangle$, where we write $G_1$ additively and $G_2$ multiplicatively. A mapping $e : G_1 \times G_1 \to G_2$ is called a cryptographic bilinear map if it satisfies the following properties.

- Bilinearity : $e(aP, bQ) = e(P, Q)^{ab}$ for all $P, Q \in G_1$ and $a, b \in \mathbb{Z}_p$.
- Non-degeneracy : If $G_1 = \langle P \rangle$, then $G_2 = \langle e(P, P) \rangle$.
- Computability : There exists an efficient algorithm to compute $e(P, Q)$ for all $P, Q \in G_1$.

Since $e(aP, bP) = e(P, P)^{ab} = e(bP, aP)$, $e()$ also satisfies the symmetry property. The modified Weil pairing [8] and Tate pairing [2,18] are examples of cryptographic bilinear maps.

Known examples of $e()$ have $G_1$ to be a group of Elliptic Curve (EC) points and $G_2$ to be a subgroup of a multiplicative group of a finite field. Hence, in papers on pairing implementations [2,18], it is customary to write $G_1$ additively and $G_2$ multiplicatively. On the other hand, some "pure" protocol papers such as [5,31] write both $G_1$ and $G_2$ multiplicatively though this is not true of the initial protocol papers [8,19]. Here we follow the first convention as it is closer to the known examples.

## 2.4   Hardness Assumption

The decisional bilinear Diffie-Hellman (DBDH) problem in $\langle G_1, G_2, e \rangle$ [8] is as follows: Given a tuple $\langle P, aP, bP, cP, Z \rangle$, where $Z \in G_2$, decide whether $Z = e(P, P)^{abc}$ (which we denote as $Z$ is real) or $Z$ is random. The advantage of a probabilistic algorithm $\mathcal{B}$, which takes as input a tuple $\langle P, aP, bP, cP, Z \rangle$ and outputs a bit, in solving the DBDH problem is defined as

$$
\begin{aligned}
\mathsf{Adv}_{\mathcal{B}}^{\mathrm{DBDH}} = |\Pr[&\mathcal{B}(P, aP, bP, cP, Z) = 1 | Z \text{ is real}] \\
&-\Pr[\mathcal{B}(P, aP, bP, cP, Z) = 1 | Z \text{ is random}]|
\end{aligned} \tag{1}
$$

where the probability is calculated over the random choices of $a, b, c \in \mathbb{Z}_p$ as well as the random bits used by $\mathcal{B}$. The quantity $\mathsf{Adv}^{\mathrm{DBDH}}(t)$ denotes the maximum of $\mathsf{Adv}_{\mathcal{B}}^{\mathrm{DBDH}}$ where the maximum is taken over all adversaries $\mathcal{B}$ running in time at most $t$. By the $(\epsilon, t)$-DBDH assumption we mean $\mathsf{Adv}^{\mathrm{DBDH}}(t) \leq \epsilon$.

## 2.5   Components (AE, KDF, UOWHF)

We briefly introduce and state the security notions for AE, KDF and UOWHF.

An AE protocol consists of two deterministic algorithms – Encrypt and Decrypt. Both of these use a common secret key $k$. The Encrypt$_k$ algorithm takes as input a nonce IV and a message $M$ and returns $(C, \mathsf{tag})$, where $C$ is the ciphertext corresponding to $M$ (and is usually of the same length as $M$). The Decrypt$_k$ algorithm takes as input IV and a pair $(C, \mathsf{tag})$ and returns either the message $M$ or $\perp$ (indicating invalid ciphertext).

An AE algorithm possesses two security properties – privacy and authenticity. For privacy, the adversarial game is the following. The adversary $\mathcal{A}$ is given access to an oracle which is either the encryption oracle instantiated with a random key $k$ or is an oracle which simply returns random strings of length equal to its input. After interacting with the oracle the adversary ultimately outputs a bit. The advantage of $\mathcal{A}$ is defined to be

$$
|\mathsf{Prob}[\mathcal{A} = 1 | \text{real oracle}] - \mathsf{Prob}[\mathcal{A} = 1 | \text{random oracle}]|.
$$

In the above game, the adversary is assumed to be nonce-respecting, in that it does not repeat a nonce. The requirement that IV is a nonce can be replaced by the requirement that IV is chosen randomly. This leads to an additive quadratic degradation in the advantage.

The security notion defined above is that of pseudorandom permutation. This provides the privacy of an AE protocol. In particular, it implies the following notion of one-time security. The adversary submits two equal length messages $M_0$ and $M_1$. A random $(\mathsf{IV}^*, k^*)$ pair is chosen and a random bit $\delta$ is chosen. The adversary is given $(C^*, \mathsf{tag}^*)$ which is the encryption of $M_\delta$ using $\mathsf{IV}^*$ and $k^*$. The adversary then outputs $\delta'$ and its advantage is

$$\left| \mathsf{Prob}[\delta = \delta'] - \frac{1}{2} \right|.$$

We say that an AE protocol satisfies $(\epsilon, t)$ one-time encryption security if the maximum advantage of any adversary running in time $t$ in the above game is $\epsilon$.

The authenticity property of an AE protocol is defined through the following game. A nonce respecting adversary $\mathcal{A}$ is given access to an encryption oracle instantiated by a secret key $k$. It submits messages to the oracle and receives as output ciphertext-tag pairs. Finally, it outputs a "new" ciphertext-tag pair and a nonce, which can be equal to a previous nonce. The advantage of $\mathcal{A}$ in this game is the probability that the forgery is valid, i.e., it will be accepted as a valid ciphertext.

As before, we can replace the requirement that $\mathsf{IV}$ be a nonce by the requirement that $\mathsf{IV}$ is random without significant loss of security. By an $(\epsilon, t)$-secure authentication of an AE protocol we mean that the maximum advantage of any adversary running in time $t$ in the above game is $\epsilon$.

A KDF is a function $\mathsf{KDF}()$ which takes an input $K$ and produces $(\mathsf{IV}, dk)$ as output. The security notion for KDF is the following. For a randomly chosen $K$, the adversary has to distinguish between $\mathsf{KDF}(K)$ from a randomly chosen $(\mathsf{IV}, dk)$.

A function family $\{H_k\}_{k \in \mathcal{K}}$ is said to be a universal one-way hash family if the following adversarial task is difficult. The adversary outputs an $x$; is then given a randomly chosen $k \in \mathcal{K}$ and has to find $x' \neq x$ such that $H_k(x) = H_k(x')$. We say that the family is $(\epsilon, t)$-secure if the maximum advantage (probability) of an adversary running in time $t$ and winning the above game is $\epsilon$.

## 3   CCA-Secure HIBE Protocol

In this section, we modify the CPA-secure HIBE protocol in [14] to obtain a CCA-secure HIBE protocol. We provide an explicit hybrid protocol. This allows us to improve the decryption efficiency as we explain later. The modification consists of certain additions to the set-up procedure as well as modifications of the encryption and the decryption algorithms. *No changes are required in the key generation algorithm.*

The additions are based on the technique used by Boyen-Mei-Waters [9] and are also based on the IBE construction by Boneh-Boyen [4] (BB-IBE). Some new ideas – incorporating length of the identity into the ciphertext and using symmetric key authentication to verify ciphertext well formedness – are introduced. Also, an AE protocol is used to combine the two tasks of symmetric key encryption and authentication.

*A Useful Notation.* Let $v = (v_1, \ldots, v_l)$, where each $v_i$ is an $(n/l)$-bit string (where $l$ divides $n$) and is considered to be an element of $\mathbb{Z}_{2^{n/l}}$. For $1 \leq k \leq h$ we define,

$$V_k(v) = U'_k + \sum_{i=1}^{l} v_i U_i. \tag{2}$$

The modularity introduced by this notation allows an easier understanding of the protocol, since one does not need to bother about the exact value of $l$. When $v$ is clear from the context, we will write $V_k$ instead of $V_k(v)$.

**Cost of Computing $V_k(v)$.** This consists of computing the individual $v_i U_i$s and then summing the $l$ points. Each $v_i$ is a bit string of length $n/l$. Consequently, the time for computing $V_k(v)$ is approximately equal to the time for computing a scalar multiplication of the form $mP$, where $m$ is an $n$-bit string and $P$ is a point on the curve.

In the protocol, we will be dealing with identities of the form $\mathsf{v} = (\mathsf{v}_1, \ldots, \mathsf{v}_j)$ with $j \in \{1, \ldots, h\}$, $\mathsf{v}_k = (\mathsf{v}_1^{(k)}, \ldots, \mathsf{v}_l^{(k)})$ and $\mathsf{v}_i^{(k)}$ is an $(n/l)$-bit string. In this context, $V_k(\mathsf{v}_k)$ is obtained by replacing $\mathsf{v}_k$ for $v$ in (2).

### 3.1 Construction

The description of the construction is given in Figure 1 and the approximate costs of the different algorithms are given in Table 1. In these costs we do include symmetric encryption or authentication.

The following things should be noted while going through Figure 1.

1. Maximum depth of the HIBE is $h$.
2. Identities are of the form $\mathsf{v} = (\mathsf{v}_1, \ldots, \mathsf{v}_j)$, $j \in \{1, \ldots, h\}$, $\mathsf{v}_k = (\mathsf{v}_1^{(k)}, \ldots, \mathsf{v}_l^{(k)})$ and $\mathsf{v}_i^{(k)}$ is an $(n/l)$-bit string.
3. $\langle G_1, G_2, e \rangle$ is as defined in Section 2.3.
4. The notation $V_k()$ is given in (2).
5. The standard way to avoid the computation of $e(P_1, P_2)$ in HIBE.Encrypt is to replace $P_2$ with $e(P_1, P_2)$ in the public parameters.
6. Key generation is essentially the same as in [31,14].

The bold portions of Figure 1 provide the additional points required over the CPA-secure HIBE construction from [14]. We provide some intuition of how decryption queries are answered. (Key extraction can be answered using the technique from [14] which is built on the work of Waters [31].) First, let us consider what happens if we attempt to simulate decryption queries by key extraction queries. The idea is that we use a key extraction query to derive the private key of the identity which is provided as part of the decryption query. Then this private key is used to decrypt the ciphertext. This idea works fine except for the situation where a decryption query is made on a prefix of the challenge identity. Since, it is not allowed to query the key extraction oracle on

HIBE.SetUp

1. Choose $\alpha$ randomly from $\mathbb{Z}_p$.
2. Set $P_1 = \alpha P$.
3. Choose $P_2, U_1', \ldots, U_h', U_1, \ldots, U_l$ randomly from $G_1$.
4. **Choose W randomly from $G_1$.**
5. **Let $H_s : \{1, \ldots, h\} \times G_1 \to \mathbb{Z}_p$ be chosen from a UOWHF and made public.**
6. Public parameters:
   $P, P_1, P_2, U_1', \ldots, U_h', U_1, \ldots, U_l$ and **W**.
7. Master secret key: $\alpha P_2$.

HIBE.KeyGen: Identity $v = (v_1, \ldots, v_j)$.

1. Choose $r_1, \ldots, r_j$ randomly from $\mathbb{Z}_p$.
2. $d_0 = \alpha P_2 + \sum_{k=1}^{j} r_k V_k(v_k)$.
3. $d_k = r_k P$ for $k = 1, \ldots, j$.
4. Output $d_v = (d_0, d_1, \ldots, d_j)$.

(Key delegation, i.e., generating $d_v$ from
$d_{v|_{j-1}}$ can be done in the standard manner as
shown in [31,14].)

HIBE.Encrypt: Identity $v = (v_1, \ldots, v_j)$; message $M$.

1. Choose $t$ randomly from $\mathbb{Z}_p$.
2. $C_1 = tP$, $B_1 = tV_1(v_1), \ldots, B_j = tV_j(v_j)$.
3. $K = e(P_1, P_2)^t$.
4. $(\mathsf{IV}, dk) = \mathsf{KDF}(K)$.
5. $(\mathsf{cpr}, \mathsf{tag}) = \mathsf{AE.Encrypt}_{dk}(\mathsf{IV}, M)$.
6. $\gamma = \mathbf{H_s(j, C_1)}$; $\mathbf{W_\gamma = W + \gamma P_1}$; $\mathbf{C_2 = tW_\gamma}$.
7. Output $(C_1, \mathbf{C_2}, B_1, \ldots, B_j, \mathsf{cpr}, \mathsf{tag})$.

HIBE.Decrypt: Identity $v = (v_1, \ldots, v_j)$;
ciphertext $(C_1, \mathbf{C_2}, B_1, \ldots, B_j, \mathsf{cpr}, \mathsf{tag})$;
decryption key $d_v = (d_0, d_1, \ldots, d_j)$.

1. $\gamma = \mathbf{H_s(j, C_1)}$; $\mathbf{W_\gamma = W + \gamma P_1}$.
2. **If $e(C_1, W_\gamma) \neq e(P, C_2)$ return $\perp$.**
3. $K = e(d_0, C_1) / \prod_{k=1}^{j} e(B_k, d_k)$.
4. $(\mathsf{IV}, dk) = \mathsf{KDF}(K)$.
5. $M = \mathsf{AE.Decrypt}_{dk}(\mathsf{IV}, C, \mathsf{tag})$.
   (This may abort and return $\perp$.)
6. Output $M$.

**Fig. 1.** CCA-secure HIBE

**Table 1.** Cost of different operations. The variable $j$ refers to the number of components in the input identity tuple. Here $1 \leq j \leq h$, where $h$ is the maximum depth of the HIBE. Cost of symmetric key operations are not shown. [SM]: cost of one scalar multiplication in $G_1$; [P]: cost of one pairing operation; [VP]: cost of one pairing verification of the type $e(Q_1, Q_2) = e(R_1, R_2)$; [e]: cost of one exponentiation in $G_2$; [i]: cost of inversion in $G_2$.

| No. of public parameters | $(3 + h + l)$ elements of $G_1$ and one element of $G_2$ |
|---|---|
| Secret key size | $j + 1$ elements of $G_1$ |
| Cost of key generation | $3j$[SM] |
| Cost of encryption | $(2j + 3)$[SM]+1[e] |
| Cost of decryption | 1[SM]+1[VP]+$(j + 1)$[P]+1[i] |

prefixes of the challenge identity, the above simulation technique will not work. We need an additional mechanism to answer such decryption queries.

The mechanism that we have used is primarily based on the BMW technique. The parameter $W$ along with $P$ and $P_1$ define an instance of a BB-IBE protocol. During encryption, an "identity" $\gamma = H_s(j, C_1)$ for this protocol is generated from the randomizer $C_1 = tP$ and the length $j$ of the identity tuple. Using this identity, a separate encapsulation of the key $e(P_1, P_2)^t$ is made. This encapsulation consists of the element $C_2$ (and $C_1$). In the security proof, if a decryption query is made on the challenge identity, then this encapsulation is used to obtain the private key of $\gamma$ and answer the decryption query.

The use of the function $H()$ is different from its use in [9]. In [9], the function $H()$ maps $G_1$ to $\mathbb{Z}_p$. On the other hand, in the HIBE protocol in Figure 1, $H()$ maps $\{1, \ldots, h\} \times G_1$ to $\mathbb{Z}_p$. Our aim is to include information about the length of the identity into the output of $H()$. Without this information, an encryption for a $(j + 1)$-level identity can be converted to an encryption for its $j$-level prefix by simply dropping the term corresponding to the last component in the identity. (This was pointed out by a reviewer of an earlier version of this work, who, however, did not provide the solution described here.)

The other aspect is that of checking for the well formedness of the ciphertext. A well formed ciphertext requires verifying that $C_1 = tP$, $C_2 = tW_\gamma$ and $B_1 = tV_1(v_1), \ldots, B_j = tV_j(v_j)$. In other words, we need to verify the following.

$$\log_P C_1 = \log_{W_\gamma} C_2 \text{ and } \log_P C_1 = \log_{V_1(v_1)} B_1 = \cdots = \log_{V_j(v_j)} B_j.$$

In Figure 1, the first equality is explicitly verified, whereas the second equality is not. The idea is that if the second equality does not hold, then the key $K$ that will be reconstructed will be improper and indistinguishable from random (to the adversary). Correspondingly, the quantities $(IV, dk)$ will also be indistinguishable from random and symmetric authentication with this pair will fail (otherwise the adversary has broken the authentication of the AE protocol). Thus, instead of using $j$ pairings for verifying the second equality, we use symmetric authentication to reject invalid ciphertext. This leads to a more efficient decryption algorithm. Note that the use of hybrid encryption is very crucial in the current context. This is similar to the Kurosawa-Desmedt PKE, which provides improved efficiency over the Cramer-Shoup protocol for hybrid encryption.

The additional requirements of group elements and operations for attaining CCA-security compared to the protocol in [14] consists of the following.

1. One extra group element in the public parameters.
2. Two additional scalar multiplications during encryption.
3. One additional scalar multiplication and one pairing based verification during decryption.

### 3.2 Security Statement

The security statement for the new protocol is given below.

**Theorem 1.** *The HIBE protocol described in Figure 1 is* $(\epsilon_{hibe}, t, q_{\mathsf{ID}}, q_C)$-CCA *secure assuming that the* $(t', \epsilon_{dbdh})$-*DBDH assumption holds in* $\langle G_1, G_2, e \rangle$; $H_s$ *is an* $(\epsilon_{uowhf}, t)$-*UOWHF;* KDF *is* $(\epsilon_{kdf}, t)$-*secure; and the AE protocol possesses* $(\epsilon_{auth}, t)$-*authorization security and* $(\epsilon_{enc}, t)$ *one-time encryption security; where*

$$\epsilon_{hibe} \leq 2\epsilon_{uowhf} + \frac{\epsilon_{dbdh}}{\lambda} + 4\epsilon_{kdf} + 2\epsilon_{enc} + 2hq_C\epsilon_{auth}. \tag{3}$$

*where* $t' = t + O(\tau q) + \chi(\epsilon_{hibe})$ *and*

$\chi(\epsilon) = O(\tau q + O(\epsilon^{-2}\ln(\epsilon^{-1})\lambda^{-1}\ln(\lambda^{-1})));$
$\tau$ *is the time required for one scalar multiplication in* $G_1$;
$\lambda = 1/(2h(2\sigma(\mu_l + 1))^h)$ *with* $\mu_l = l(2^{n/l} - 1)$, $\sigma = \max(2q, 2^{n/l})$ *and*
$q = q_{\mathsf{ID}} + q_C$.

*We further assume* $2\sigma(1 + \mu_l) < p$.

The proof can be found in the expanded version of this paper [28]. The statement of Theorem 1 is almost the same as that of Theorem 1 in [14] with the following differences.

1. The above theorem states CCA-security where as [14] proves CPA-security.
2. The value of $\lambda$ is equal to $1/(2h(2\sigma(\mu_l+1))^h)$ in the above statement where as it is equal to $1/(2(2\sigma(\mu_l+1))^h)$ in [14], i.e., there is an additional degradation by a factor of $h$.
3. The value of $q$ in the expression for $\sigma$ is the sum of $q_{\mathsf{ID}}$ and $q_C$ whereas in [14] it is only $q_{\mathsf{ID}}$. The reason for having $q_C$ as part of $q$ is that it may be required to simulate decryption queries using key extraction queries.

For $2q \geq 2^{n/l}$ (typically $l$ would be chosen to ensure this), we have

$$\epsilon_{hibe} \leq 2\epsilon_{uowhf} + 2h(4lq2^{n/l})^h\epsilon_{dbdh} + 4\epsilon_{kdf} + 2\epsilon_{enc} + 2hq_C\epsilon_{auth}.$$

The corresponding bound on $\epsilon_{dbdh}$ in [14] is $2(4lq_{\mathsf{ID}}2^{n/l})^h\epsilon_{dbdh}$. Thus, we get an additional security degradation of $\epsilon_{dbdh}$ by a factor of $h$ while attaining CCA-security. Since $h$ is the maximum number of levels in the HIBE, its value is small and the degradation is not significant. Also, $q$ in the present case includes both key extraction and decryption queries.

The statement of Theorem 1 is a little complicated. The complexity is inherited from the corresponding security statement in [14]. These arise from the requirement of tackling key extraction queries and providing challenge ciphertexts. In particular, $\lambda$ is a lower bound on the probability of not abort by the simulator and $O(\epsilon^{-2}\ln(\epsilon^{-1})\lambda^{-1}\ln(\lambda^{-1}))$ is the extra runtime introduced due to the artificial abort requirement. In [14], the security degradation is worked out in more details and much of these also hold for Theorem 1. Hence, we do not repeat the analysis in this paper.

The technique for showing security against chosen plaintext attacks is taken from [14] and is based on the works of Waters [31] and Boneh-Boyen [4]. Since these details are already given in [14], we do not repeat them in the proof of Theorem 1. The proof technique for answering decryption queries is based on the work of Boyen-Mei-Waters [9]. Also relevant is the work of Kiltz-Galindo [24]. The basic idea of using symmetric authentication to verify ciphertext well formedness is taken from the paper by Kurosawa-Desmedt [25]. A proof of the KD protocol using the so called method of "deferred analysis" is given in [1]. This proof is in the PKE setting which we had to adapt to fit the (H)IBE framework.

## 4    Comparison to Previous Work

The construction in Figure 1 can be specialized to obtain CCA-secure PKE and IBE as special cases. We show that when specialized to PKE, the protocol in Figure 1 simplifies to yield the BMW construction. On the other hand, when specialized to IBE, we obtain a more efficient (actually the decryption algorithm is more efficient) IBE protocol compared to the previously best known construction of Kiltz-Galindo [24].

**Public Key Encryption.** In this case there are no identities and no PKG. It is possible to make the following simplifications.

SetUp:
1. The elements $U'_1, \ldots, U'_h, U_1, \ldots, U_l$ are no longer required.
2. The UOWHF $H_s$ can be replaced by an injective embedding from $G_1$ to $\mathbb{Z}_p$.
3. A random $w$ in $\mathbb{Z}_p$ is chosen and $W$ is set to be equal to $wP$.
4. The secret key is set to be equal to $(\alpha P_2, \alpha, w)$.
5. The AE protocol can be replaced with a one-time secure data encapsulation mechanism (DEM).

KeyGen: This is not required at all.

Encrypt:
1. The elements $B_1, \ldots, B_j$ are not required.
2. Encryption with a DEM will not produce a tag.

Decrypt:
1. The purpose of the pairing verification $e(C_1, W_\gamma) = e(P, C_2)$ is to ensure that $C_1 = tP$ and $C_2 = tW_\gamma$, where $W_\gamma = W + \gamma P_1$. With the knowledge of $w$ and $\alpha$, this can be done as follows. Compute $w' = w + \gamma\alpha$ and verify whether $w'C_1 = C_2$. This requires only one scalar multiplication as opposed to one pairing verification.
2. The value of $K$ is reconstructed as $K = e(C_1, \alpha P_2)$.
3. Since the AE protocol is replaced with a DEM, symmetric authentication will not be done.

With these simplifications, the protocol becomes the BMW protocol.

**Identity Based Encryption.** In this case $h = 1$. The protocol in Figure 1 remains unchanged except for one simplification. In a HIBE, the length of the identity tuple can vary from 1 to $h$. For an IBE, the length is always one. Hence, in this case, we can restrict the domain of $H_s$ to be $G_1$. Since, $G_1$ has cardinality $p$, the domain and range of $H_s$ are the same and we can also take $H_s$ to be an injective embedding from $G_1$ to $\mathbb{Z}_p$ as has been done in the BMW construction.

Let us now compare the resulting IBE construction with the previous construction of Kiltz-Galindo [24]. In both cases, the public key portion of the ciphertext is of the form $(C_1, C_2, B_1)$. During decryption, KG protocol verifies that $C_1 = tP$, $C_2 = tW_\gamma$ and $B_1 = tV_1(\mathsf{v}_1)$. This requires two pairing based verifications of the type $e(P, C_2) = e(C_1, W_\gamma)$ and $e(P, B_1) = e(C_1, V_1(\mathsf{v}_1))$. The cost of one such verification is less than the cost of two pairing operations. Recall from Table 1 that by $[VP]$ we denote the cost of one such verification. Also, let $[P]$, $[SM]$, and $[i]$ respectively denote the costs of one pairing operation, one scalar multiplication in $G_1$, and one inversion in $G_2$. The total cost of decryption in the KG protocol with the pairing based verification technique is $1[SM] + 2[VP] + 2[P] + 1[i]$.

**Implicit Rejection.** KG [24] suggests a method of implicit rejection. This provides a KEM which cannot explicitly reject a ciphertext. More precisely, the notion of KEM used by KG [24] is the following. In the adversarial game, the adversary queries the decryption oracle. If the query is valid, then the adversary gets the corresponding secret key, while if the query is invalid, then the adversary gets a random value for the secret key. In particular, the adversary is not told whether the decryption failed.

First, we would like to point out that this is a restricted notion of KEM. The original notion of KEM as conceived by Shoup [30] allows the simulator to inform the adversary whether the decryption failed. We quote from [30, Page 15, Lines 5–6] (the bold font appears in the cited reference).

"if the decryption algorithm **fails**, then this information is given to the adversary"

In view of this, we consider the notion of KEM used by KG to be restricted-KEM. Apart from the difference mentioned above, such a restricted-KEM is not really sufficient for constructing a complete encryption protocol. When combined with a one-time secure DEM (as envisaged by Shoup [30] and later used by many authors), a restricted-KEM provides an encryption protocol which *cannot* reject invalid ciphertexts. Clearly, such an encryption protocol is also more restricted compared to the currently accepted notion. (On the other hand, we do note that the notion of restricted-KEM may be sufficient for some applications.)

In the identity based setting, KG [24] suggests a method of implicit rejection leading to a restricted-KEM. The idea is the following. The pairing based verifications are not done; instead two random elements $r_1$ and $r_2$ are chosen and $K$ is computed as

$$\frac{e(C_1, d_0 + r_1 W_\gamma + r_2 V_1(\mathsf{v}_1))}{e(B_1, d_1 + r_2 P)e(r_1 P, C_2)}.$$

If the ciphertext is proper, then the proper $K$ is computed, while if the ciphertext is improper, then a random $K$ is computed. *Note that an invalid ciphertext is not explicitly rejected and combining such a KEM with a one-time secure DEM will result in a IBE which cannot reject invalid ciphertexts.* The cost of decryption with implicit rejection is $5[SM] + 3[P] + 1[i]$.

In contrast, the cost of verification in our case is $1[SM] + 1[VP] + 2[P] + 1[i]$. The costs of decryption using our algorithm and also that of KG algorithm (for both explicit and implicit rejections) are shown in Table 2. Clearly, the cost of decryption algorithm given in this work is significantly lower than the KG protocol with explicit pairing based verification. Compared to the implicit rejection technique, our cost will be lower when $1[VP] < 1[P] + 4[SM]$. Based on the current status of efficient pairing based algorithms, this seems to be a reasonable condition.

The reason for obtaining this lower cost is that we do not verify $e(P, B_1) = e(C_1, V_1(\mathsf{v}_1))$ either explicitly or implicitly. In other words, we do not verify whether $\log_P C_1 = \log_{V_1(\mathsf{v}_1)} B_1$. If this does not hold, then an incorrect session key will be generated and ultimately the authentication of the AE protocol will fail. In a sense, this is also an implicit verification, but the verification is done using the symmetric component which reduces the total cost of decryption. Also, an invalid ciphertext will always be rejected.

In summary, the IBE version of the protocol in Figure 1 is the currently known most efficient CCA-secure IBE protocol in the full model without the random oracle heuristic and based on the DBDH assumption.

**Hierarchical Identity Based Encryption.** Based on the work by BMW [9], the KG paper [24] sketches a construction of a HIBE. The details are worked out in [3]. Compared to this approach, there are several advantages of our protocol. First, the ciphertext verification procedure in this approach requires the verification of $\log_P C_1 = \log_{V_1(\mathsf{v}_1)} B_1 = \cdots = \log_{V_j(\mathsf{v}_j)} B_j$ either explicitly using pairing based verifications or implicitly (but, without being able to reject invalid ciphertexts) as suggested by Kiltz-Galindo. On the other hand, our approach does not require these verifications. If any of these equalities do not hold, then an improper value of $K$ will be obtained and as a result the authentication of the AE protocol will fail. This significantly reduces the cost of the decryption

**Table 2.** Comparison of decryption algorithms of KG-IBE with our algorithm

| Protocol | Decryption Cost | Reject Invalid Ciphertexts |
|---|---|---|
| KG (explicit rej.) | 1[SM]+2[VP]+2[P]+1[i] | Yes |
| KG (implicit rej.) | 5[SM]+3[P]+1[i] | No |
| This work | 1[SM]+1[VP]+2[P]+1[i] | Yes |

**Table 3.** Comparison of decryption algorithms of KG-HIBE with our algorithm. The quantity $j$ below refers to the number of components in the identity tuple. Here $1 \leq j \leq h$, where $h$ is the maximum depth of the HIBE.

| Protocol | Decryption Cost | Reject Invalid Ciphertexts |
|---|---|---|
| KG (explicit rej.) | 1[SM]+$(j + 1)$[VP]+$(j + 1)$[P]+1[i] | Yes |
| KG (implicit rej.) | $(2j + 1)$[SM]+$(j + 2)$[P]+1[i] | No |
| This work | 1[SM]+1[VP]+$(j + 1)$[P]+1[i] | Yes |

algorithm. Second, we use an AE algorithm to perform simultaneous encryption and authentication which can be twice as fast as separate encryption and authentication. Table 3 shows the costs of decryption algorithms for our method and that of the KG method with explicit and implicit rejection. As mentioned earlier, due to the security degradation being exponential in $h$, the value of $j$ has to be small, at most around 4. Even for small values of $j$, the cost of the new decryption algorithm is smaller than that of the KG-HIBE.

An earlier work [11,7] showed a generic construction for converting an $(h+1)$-level CPA-secure HIBE into an $h$-level CCA-secure HIBE. The construction used one-time signatures, which make it quite inefficient. It was suggested (without details) in [11] that a MAC based construction can be used to remove the inefficiency of the one-time signature based approach. Also, the efficiency of the resulting protocol is less than that of Figure 1. A problem with the approach in [11] is that the identity components of the CCA-secure HIBE are prepended with a bit to obtain identity components of the underlying CPA-secure HIBE. This can cause difficulties in implementation. Typically, the $n$-bit identity will be obtained by hashing an arbitrary length string such as an email address. Suppose, $n = 160$. Hashing gives us a 160-bit identity for the underlying CPA-secure HIBE. Then the length of the identity string for the CCA-secure HIBE is 161. This value of length will not align with byte boundaries and will cause implementation difficulties.

The currently known techniques (both generic and non-generic) for converting a CPA-secure HIBE protocol to a CCA-secure HIBE protocol, starts with an $(h + 1)$-level CPA-secure HIBE and then converts it to an $h$-level CCA-secure HIBE. The security degradation thus correspond to the $(h + 1)$-level HIBE. If we apply this technique to the protocol in [14], then the security degradation for the obtained $h$-level CCA-secure HIBE will be $2(4lq2^{n/l})^{h+1}$. Compared to this, the security degradation given by Theorem 1 is $2h(4lq2^{n/l})^{h}$. In other words, we have managed to reduce the exponent from $(h + 1)$ to $h$ and have introduced a multiplicative factor of $h$. From the viewpoint of concrete security analysis, a typical value of $q$ is $2^{30}$. Assuming this value of $q$, we are able to prevent approximately a 30-bit security degradation compared to previous work.

## 5  Conclusion

In this paper, we have provided a construction of a hybrid HIBE protocol. The protocol is secure against adaptive adversaries (making both key extraction and decryption queries) without using the random oracle hypothesis. Security is reduced from the computational hardness of the DBDH problem. To the best of our knowledge, in this setting, the HIBE protocol described in this paper is the currently known most efficient construction.

## References

1. Abe, M., Gennaro, R., Kurosawa, K., Shoup, V.: Tag-KEM/DEM: A New Framework for Hybrid Encryption and A New Analysis of Kurosawa-Desmedt KEM. In: Cramer [16], pp. 128–146
2. Barreto, P.S.L.M., Kim, H.Y., Lynn, B., Scott, M.: Efficient Algorithms for Pairing-Based Cryptosystems. In: Yung, M. (ed.) CRYPTO 2002. LNCS, vol. 2442, pp. 354–368. Springer, Heidelberg (2002)
3. Birkett, J., Dent, A.W., Neven, G., Schuldt, J.: Identity based key encapsulation with wildcards. In: Cryptology ePrint Archive, Report 2006/377 (2006), http://eprint.iacr.org/
4. Boneh, D., Boyen, X.: Efficient Selective-ID Secure Identity-Based Encryption Without Random Oracles. In: Cachin and Camenisch [10], pp. 223–238
5. Boneh, D., Boyen, X.: Secure Identity Based Encryption Without Random Oracles. In: Franklin [17], pp. 443–459
6. Boneh, D., Boyen, X., Goh, E.-J.: Hierarchical Identity Based Encryption with Constant Size Ciphertext. In: Cramer [16], pp. 440–456, Full version available at Cryptology ePrint Archive; Report 2005/015
7. Boneh, D., Canetti, R., Halevi, S., Katz, J.: Chosen-Ciphertext Security from Identity-Based Encryption. SIAM J. of Computing 36(5), 915–942 (2006)
8. Boneh, D., Franklin, M.K.: Identity-Based Encryption from the Weil Pairing (Earlier version appeared in the proceedings of CRYPTO 2001). SIAM J. Comput. 32(3), 586–615 (2001)
9. Boyen, X., Mei, Q., Waters, B.: Direct Chosen Ciphertext Security from Identity-Based Techniques. In: Atluri, V., Meadows, C., Juels, A. (eds.) ACM Conference on Computer and Communications Security, pp. 320–329. ACM Press, New York (2005)
10. Cachin, C., Camenisch, J. (eds.): EUROCRYPT 2004. LNCS, vol. 3027, pp. 2–6. Springer, Heidelberg (2004)
11. Canetti, R., Halevi, S., Katz, J.: Chosen-Ciphertext Security from Identity-Based Encryption. In: Cachin and Camenisch [10], pp. 207–222.
12. Chakraborty, D., Sarkar, P.: A General Construction of Tweakable Block Ciphers and Different Modes of Operations. In: Lipmaa, H., Yung, M., Lin, D. (eds.) Inscrypt 2006. LNCS, vol. 4318, pp. 88–102. Springer, Heidelberg (2006)

13. Chatterjee, S., Sarkar, P.: Trading Time for Space: Towards an Efficient IBE Scheme with Short(er) Public Parameters in the Standard Model. In: Won, D.H., Kim, S. (eds.) ICISC 2005. LNCS, vol. 3935, pp. 424–440. Springer, Heidelberg (2006)
14. Chatterjee, S., Sarkar, P.: HIBE with Short Public Parameters Without Random Oracle. In: Lai, X., Chen, K. (eds.) ASIACRYPT 2006. LNCS, vol. 4284, pp. 145–160. Springer, Heidelberg (2006), http://eprint.iacr.org/
15. Chatterjee, S., Sarkar, P.: New Constructions of Constant Size Ciphertext HIBE Without Random Oracle. In: Rhee, M.S., Lee, B. (eds.) ICISC 2006. LNCS, vol. 4296, pp. 310–327. Springer, Heidelberg (2006)
16. Cramer, R. (ed.): EUROCRYPT 2005. LNCS, vol. 3494. Springer, Heidelberg (2005)
17. Franklin, M. (ed.): CRYPTO 2004. LNCS, vol. 3152, pp. 15–19. Springer, Heidelberg (2004)
18. Galbraith, S.D., Harrison, K., Soldera, D.: Implementing the Tate Pairing. In: Fieker, C., Kohel, D.R. (eds.) Algorithmic Number Theory. LNCS, vol. 2369, pp. 324–337. Springer, Heidelberg (2002)
19. Gentry, C., Silverberg, A.: Hierarchical ID-Based Cryptography. In: Zheng, Y. (ed.) ASIACRYPT 2002. LNCS, vol. 2501, pp. 548–566. Springer, Heidelberg (2002)
20. Gligor, V.D., Donescu, P.: Fast encryption and authentication: XCBC encryption and XECB authentication modes. In: Matsui, M. (ed.) FSE 2001. LNCS, vol. 2355, pp. 92–108. Springer, Heidelberg (2002)
21. Horwitz, J., Lynn, B.: Toward Hierarchical Identity-Based Encryption. In: Knudsen, L.R. (ed.) EUROCRYPT 2002. LNCS, vol. 2332, pp. 466–481. Springer, Heidelberg (2002)
22. Jutla, C.S.: Encryption Modes with Almost Free Message Integrity. In: Pfitzmann, B. (ed.) EUROCRYPT 2001. LNCS, vol. 2045, pp. 529–544. Springer, Heidelberg (2001)
23. Kiltz, E.: Chosen-ciphertext secure identity-based encryption in the standard model with short ciphertexts. In: Cryptology ePrint Archive, Report 2006/122 (2006), http://eprint.iacr.org/
24. Kiltz, E., Galindo, D.: Direct chosen-ciphertext secure identity-based key encapsulation without random oracles. In: Batten, L.M., Safavi-Naini, R. (eds.) ACISP 2006. LNCS, vol. 4058, pp. 336–347. Springer, Heidelberg (2006), full version available at http://eprint.iacr.org/2006/034
25. Kurosawa, K., Desmedt, Y.: A New Paradigm of Hybrid Encryption Scheme. In: Franklin [17], pp. 426–442
26. Naccache, D.: Secure and Practical Identity-Based Encryption. Cryptology ePrint Archive, Report 2005/369 (2005) http://eprint.iacr.org/
27. Rogaway, P.: Efficient Instantiations of Tweakable Blockciphers and Refinements to Modes OCB and PMAC. In: Lee, P.J. (ed.) ASIACRYPT 2004. LNCS, vol. 3329, pp. 16–31. Springer, Heidelberg (2004)
28. Sarkar, P., Chatterjee, S.: Construction of a hybrid hierarchical identity based encryption protocol secure against adaptive attacks (without random oracle). Cryptology ePrint Archive, Report 2006/362 (2006), http://eprint.iacr.org/
29. Shamir, A.: Identity-Based Cryptosystems and Signature Schemes. In: Blakely, G.R., Chaum, D. (eds.) CRYPTO 1984. LNCS, vol. 196, pp. 47–53. Springer, Heidelberg (1985)
30. Shoup, V.: A proposal for an ISO standard for public key encryption (version 2.1), (December 20, 2001), available from http://www.shoup.net/papers/
31. Waters, B.: Efficient Identity-Based Encryption Without Random Oracles. In: Cramer [16], pp. 114–127

# A CDH-Based Strongly Unforgeable Signature Without Collision Resistant Hash Function

Takahiro Matsuda[1], Nuttapong Attrapadung[2], Goichiro Hanaoka[2],
Kanta Matsuura[1], and Hideki Imai[2,3]

[1] Institute of Industrial Science, The University of Tokyo, Tokyo, Japan
{tmatsuda,kanta}@iis.u-tokyo.ac.jp
[2] Research Center for Information Security, National Institute of Advanced Industrial
Science and Technology, Tokyo, Japan
{n.attrapadung,hanaoka-goichiro,h-imai@}@aist.go.jp
[3] Faculty of Science and Engineering, Chuo University, Tokyo, Japan

**Abstract.** Unforgeability of digital signatures is closely related to the
security of hash functions since hashing messages, such as *hash-and-sign*
paradigm, is necessary in order to sign (arbitrarily) long messages. Recent successful collision finding attacks against practical hash functions
would indicate that constructing practical collision resistant hash functions is difficult to achieve. Thus, it is worth considering to relax the
requirement of collision resistance for hash functions that is used to hash
messages in signature schemes. Currently, the most efficient strongly unforgeable signature scheme in the standard model which is based on the
CDH assumption (in bilinear groups) is the Boneh-Shen-Waters (BSW)
signature proposed in 2006. In their scheme, however, a collision resistant hash function is necessary to prove its security. In this paper, we
construct a signature scheme which has the same properties as the BSW
scheme but does not rely on collision resistant hash functions. Instead,
we use a target collision resistant hash function, which is a strictly weaker
primitive than a collision resistant hash function. Our scheme is, in terms
of the signature size and the computational cost, as efficient as the BSW
scheme.

**Keywords:** digital signature, strong unforgeability, target collision resistant hash function, standard model.

## 1 Introduction

Unforgeability of digital signatures is closely related to the security of hash functions. In particular, signature schemes that utilize the *hash-and-sign* paradigm
[14], where a message of arbitrary length is hashed to fixed length and then
the hashed value is signed, are no more secure if collision resistance of the hash
function is broken. In theory, it is possible to construct an arbitrary-input-length
collision resistant hash function from some concrete assumptions such as the discrete logarithm assumption. In practice, if length of the messages to be signed
is always fixed and short, then a hash function from such theoretical construction would be possible. However, if the length of messages varies arbitrarily or

W. Susilo, J.K. Liu, and Y. Mu. (Eds.): ProvSec 2007, LNCS 4784, pp. 68–84, 2007.

becomes long, hash functions for hashing messages would be, in consideration of computational efficiency, replaced with practical cryptographic hash functions such as MD5 or SHA-1 and assumed that such hash functions have collision resistance. Recent successful results of collision finding attacks against practical cryptographic hash functions (e.g., an attack against SHA-1 by Wang *et al.* [26]) show that it would be no longer easy to construct practical collision resistant hash functions. Thus, if we follow the common practice of using practical hash functions to achieve unforgeability, it is worth considering to relax the requirement of collision resistance for hash functions in signature schemes.

A good substitute for collision resistant hash functions in the hash-and-sign schemes would be *target collision resistant* hash functions (TCRHFs). A TCRHF, firstly introduced by Naor and Yung [21] as a *universal one-way hash function* and later renamed by Bellare and Rogaway [4], is a class of *keyed* hash functions. The important fact is that a TCRHF is proven to be a strictly weaker primitive (hence, easier to construct) than a collision resistant hash function by Simon [23].

Even when we allow arbitrary-length messages in signature schemes, if we use TCRHFs, we also have a general and theoretically secure construction of signature schemes [21]. Its signing process is: choose a random hash-key, hash a message with the key, and sign the concatenation of the hash-key and the hashed value. The signature output from the general construction consists of a signature output from the underlying signing algorithm and the hash-key (we call this general construction the *TCRHF-based hash-and-sign construction*). A obvious but crucial problem of this general construction, however, is that the signature size increases by the hash-key size. Solutions for several concrete schemes were proposed by Mironov [19]. In [19], Mironov constructed modified versions of DSA, PSS-RSS and Cramer-Shoup [13] signatures. Unforgeability of the modified DSA and PSS-RSA are proven in the random oracle model, and the modified Cramer-Shoup signature is proven in the standard model. The sizes of signatures obtained from the modified schemes are the same as the original ones for DSA and PSS-RSA, and shorter by a hash-key than the original one for the Cramer-Shoup scheme. The main idea to obtain the modified schemes is to *reuse* randomness generated in a signing algorithm as a hash-key of a TCRHF. In other words, the randomness plays a double role: used to create a signature itself and also used as a hash-key of the TCRHF that hashes the message to be signed. However, this approach is not generically applicable but scheme-dependent, which means that the ways of reusing randomness and the ways of proving security of the schemes are different from each other.

Such efforts of improving the efficiency of TCRHF-based signature schemes could play an important role when we observe another application of digital signatures. Since we need this observation to show the motivation of our work, we review existing works related to that application, in the following. Typically, "unforgeability" for signature schemes means existential unforgeability against adaptive chosen message attacks [15]. And if we introduce a stronger definition called *strong unforgeability* [1], we can have interesting applications of digital signature schemes: constructions of other cryptographic schemes such as chosen-ciphertext secure public key encryption schemes [12] and group signatures [2,6]. Currently, the most efficient strongly unforgeable signature scheme in the standard model based on the computational Diffie-Hellman (CDH) assumption is due to Boneh, Shen, and Waters [9]. Their scheme was constructed in two steps: first they proposed a transformation which converts unforgeable signature schemes of a specific type into strongly unforgeable one; the concrete scheme is then obtained by applying the transformation to the Waters signature [27], which is currently known as the most efficient unforgeable (but not strongly) signature based on CDH assumption in bilinear groups and is included in the specific type. However, in [9], a collision resistant hash function is used to prove its strong unforgeability (arbitrary-length message signing without applying hash-and-sign paradigm becomes possible because of it, though). There are also several general transformations that convert any unforgeable signatures into strongly unforgeable ones [16,24,25]. However, such general transformations are, though widely applicable, less efficient than the transformation proposed in [9] in terms of the signature size and the computational cost.

*Our Contribution.* In this paper, we propose a strongly unforgeable signature scheme in the standard model which is based on the CDH assumption in bilinear groups and can sign arbitrary-length messages but does not rely on collision resistant hash functions whose input length can be arbitrary. As stated above, there would be several ways to construct a scheme having such properties. (e.g., a straightforward combination of general transformations [16,24,25] and a TCRHF-based hash-and-sign construction that is written above to the Waters scheme). However, our scheme is, in terms of the signature size and the computational cost, more efficient than such general constructions and yet is as efficient as [9]. Our construction is similar to [9], but utilizes TCRHFs. In the construction, we use a technique similar to Mironov [19], that is, a double role of randomness in the signing algorithm. We first construct a transformation that converts unforgeable schemes of a certain type, which is related to the type introduced in [9] but more specific, into strongly unforgeable ones and prove the security of the transformation. Then we show that the Waters signature scheme is included in the type and obtain the proposing scheme using the transformation.

## 2   Preliminaries

In this section, we review the definitions of terms used in this paper.

### 2.1   Digital Signature

A signature scheme $\Sigma$ consists of three (probabilistic) algorithms:

KeyGen : A key generation algorithm that takes $1^\kappa$ (security parameter $\kappa$) as input and outputs a pair of a secret key $sk$ and a public key $pk$.

Sign: A signing algorithm that takes a secret key $sk$ and a message $m \in \mathcal{M}$ as input and outputs a valid signature $\sigma$ on $m$ (where $\mathcal{M}$ is a message space of $\Sigma$).

Verify: A verification algorithm that takes a public key $pk$, a message $m$, and a signature $\sigma$ as input and outputs accept if $\sigma$ is a valid signature on $m$ or reject otherwise.

## 2.2 SEUF-CMA Security

Strong existential unforgeability against adaptive chosen message attacks (SEUF-CMA) [1] is defined using the following SEUF-CMA game between the adversary and the SEUF-CMA challenger:

**Setup.** The challenger runs KeyGen and obtains a secret key $sk$ and a public key $pk$. It then gives $pk$ to the adversary but keeps $sk$ to itself.

**Queries.** The adversary issues signature queries $m_1, m_2, \ldots, m_q$ (at most $q$ times). The challenger responds to each query $m_i$ by running Sign to generate a valid signature $\sigma_i$ on $m_i$ and sends $\sigma_i$ to the adversary. The adversary's query $m_i$ may depend on its previous queries $m_1, \ldots, m_{i-1}$ and the replies $\sigma_1, \ldots, \sigma_{i-1}$.

**Output.** Finally, the adversary outputs a pair $(\hat{m}, \hat{\sigma})$. The adversary wins if $\mathsf{Verify}(pk, \hat{m}, \hat{\sigma}) = \mathtt{accept}$ and $(\hat{m}, \hat{\sigma}) \neq (m_i, \sigma_i)$ for all $i \in \{1, \ldots, q\}$.

**Definition 1.** *We say that a signature scheme $\Sigma$ is $(t, q, \epsilon)$-SEUF-CMA secure if no adversary running in time less than $t$ and making at most $q$ queries can win SEUF-CMA game with probability greater than $\epsilon$. We also say that $\Sigma$ is strongly unforgeable.*

## 2.3 EUF-CMA Security

Same as above, existential unforgeability against adaptive chosen message attacks (EUF-CMA) [15] is defined using the following EUF-CMA game between the adversary and the EUF-CMA challenger:

**Setup and Queries.** Same as in the SEUF-CMA game.

**Output.** Finally, the adversary outputs a pair $(\hat{m}, \hat{\sigma})$. The adversary wins if $\mathsf{Verify}(pk, \hat{m}, \hat{\sigma}) = \mathtt{accept}$ and $\hat{m} \neq m_i$ for all $i \in \{1, \ldots, q\}$.

**Definition 2.** *We say that a signature scheme $\Sigma$ is $(t, q, \epsilon)$-EUF-CMA secure if no adversary running in time less than $t$ and making at most $q$ queries can win the EUF-CMA game with probability greater than $\epsilon$. We also say that $\Sigma$ is (weakly) unforgeable.*

## 2.4 Computational Diffie-Hellman (CDH) Assumption

The computational Diffie-Hellman problem in a cyclic group $\mathbb{G}$ of order $p$ is as follows: given $g, g^a, g^b \in \mathbb{G}$, output $g^{ab} \in \mathbb{G}$, where $g$ is a random generator of $\mathbb{G}$ and $a, b$ are random elements in $\mathbb{Z}_p$.

**Definition 3.** *We say that the $(t, \epsilon)$-CDH assumption holds in $\mathbb{G}$ if no adversary running in time less than $t$ can solve the CDH problem with probability greater than $\epsilon$.*

## 2.5    Discrete Logarithm (DL) Assumption

The discrete logarithm problem in a cyclic group $\mathbb{G}$ of order $p$ is as follows: given $g, g^a \in \mathbb{G}$, output $a \in \mathbb{Z}_p$, where $g$ is a random generator of $\mathbb{G}$ and $a$ is a random element in $\mathbb{Z}_p$.

**Definition 4.** *We say that the $(t, \epsilon)$-DL assumption holds in $\mathbb{G}$ if no adversary running in time less than $t$ can solve the DL problem with probability greater than $\epsilon$.*

## 2.6    Target Collision Resistant Hashing

A target collision resistant hash function (TCRHF), also known as a universal one-way hash function (UOWHF), is a keyed hash function $H : \mathcal{K} \times \mathcal{M}_{in} \to \mathcal{M}_{out}$ keyed by $k \in \mathcal{K}$, where $\mathcal{M}_{in}$ is an input space, $\mathcal{M}_{out}$ is an output space and $\mathcal{K}$ is a hash-key space.

Target collision resistance of a keyed hash function is defined using the following TCR game between the adversary and the TCR challenger:

**Step 1.** The adversary outputs $m_1 \in \mathcal{M}_{in}$.
**Step 2.** The challenger selects random $k \in \mathcal{K}$, and sends this to the adversary.
**Step 3.** The adversary outputs $m_2 \in \mathcal{M}_{in}$. The adversary wins if $H_k(m_1) = H_k(m_2)$ and $m_2 \neq m_1$.

In this game, we call $m_2$ a target collision against $m_1$ under the key $k$.

**Definition 5.** *We say that a keyed hash function is the $(t, \epsilon)$-TCRHF if no adversary running in time less than $t$ can win the TCR game with probability greater than $\epsilon$.*

## 2.7    Bilinear Groups

Let $\mathbb{G}$ and $\mathbb{G}_T$ be cyclic groups of prime order $p$ and let $g$ be a generator of $\mathbb{G}$. We say that $\mathbb{G}$ is a bilinear group if there exists a map $e: \mathbb{G} \times \mathbb{G} \to \mathbb{G}_T$ and a group $\mathbb{G}_T$ that satisfy the following properties:

– Bilinear: for all $u, v \in \mathbb{G}$ and $a, b \in \mathbb{Z}$, $e(u^a, v^b) = e(u, v)^{ab}$.
– Non-degenerate: $e(g, g) \neq 1$.
– Computable: for any $u, v \in \mathbb{G}$, there is an efficient algorithm to compute $e(u, v)$.

# 3    Transformation for Specific Signatures with TCRHF

In PKC 2006, Boneh, Shen, and Waters [9] proposed a SEUF-CMA secure signature scheme, by applying a transformation to the Waters signature scheme [27]. The transformation enables any unforgeable signatures which can be *partitioned* to be a strongly unforgeable ones. We follow this approach. We first recall the definition of *partitioned* signatures by [9] here.

**Definition 6.** *We say that a signature scheme* $\Sigma$ *is* partitioned *if* $\Sigma$ *satisfies the following two properties:*

- **Property 1:** *The signing algorithm* Sign *can be broken into two deterministic algorithms* $S_1$ *and* $S_2$ *so that a signature on a message* $m$ *using a secret key* $sk$ *is computed as follows:*
  1. *Select a random* $r \in \mathcal{R}$.
  2. *Compute* $\sigma_1 = S_1(sk, m, r)$ *and* $\sigma_2 = S_2(sk, r)$.
  3. *Output* $\sigma = (\sigma_1, \sigma_2)$ $\in \mathcal{S}_1 \times \mathcal{S}_2$.
- **Property 2:** *Given* $\sigma_2$ *and* $m \in \mathcal{M}$, *there is at most one* $\sigma_1$ *so that* $(\sigma_1, \sigma_2)$ *is a valid signature on* $m$ *under* $pk$.

*where* $\mathcal{R}$ *is a space of randomness used in* $S_1$ *and* $S_2$, $\mathcal{M}$ *is a message space of* $\Sigma$, *and* $\mathcal{S}_1$ *and* $\mathcal{S}_2$ *are output spaces of* $S_1$ *and* $S_2$ *respectively.*

Then, we introduce a special case of *partitioned* signatures, which we call *simulatable-partitioned*.

**Definition 7.** *We say that signature scheme* $\Sigma$ *is* simulatable-partitioned *if* $\Sigma$ *satisfies the following three properties:*

- **Property 1 and Property2:** *Same as* partitioned *(Definition 6).*
- **Property 3:** *There exist following two algorithms:*
  - KeyGen′ : *a probabilistic algorithm. It takes as input* $1^\kappa$ *(security parameter* $\kappa$), *and outputs* $(sk', pk')$ *with trapdoor* $TD$ *for the algorithm* $S_1'$ *below, where the pair* $(sk', pk')$ *is a valid key pair for* $\Sigma$ *and the distribution of it is the same as* $(sk, pk)$ *output from the original* KeyGen. *This process is denoted:* $(sk', pk', TD) \leftarrow$ KeyGen′$(1^\kappa)$.
  - $S_1'$ : *a deterministic algorithm. It takes as input* $sk$, $\sigma_2$, $m$ *and* $TD$ *output from* KeyGen′ *defined as above, without* $r$, *and outputs* $\sigma_1' \in \mathcal{S}_1$ *such that* Verify$(pk, m, (\sigma_1', \sigma_2)) =$ accept. *This process is denoted:* $\sigma_1' = S_1'(sk, m, \sigma_2, TD)$.

Next, we describe a transformation that converts any *simulatable-partitioned* unforgeable signatures into strongly unforgeable ones. Let $\Sigma = ($KeyGen, Sign, Verify$)$ be a EUF-CMA secure signature scheme which is *simulatable-partitioned*. This means, the signing algorithm Sign can be broken into $S_1$ and $S_2$, and there exist two algorithms KeyGen′ and $S_1'$ which satisfy the property 3 of Definition 7. Let $p$ be a sufficiently large prime and $\mathbb{G}$ be a cyclic group of order $p$. As in [9], we assume that each element of $\mathbb{G}$ has a unique encoding so that the property 2 of *simulatable-partitioned* will hold. Let $H : \mathcal{S}_2 \times \{0,1\}^* \rightarrow \mathbb{Z}_p$, $G : \mathcal{K} \times \mathcal{S}_2 \rightarrow \mathbb{Z}_p$, and $F : \mathcal{K} \times \mathbb{G} \rightarrow \mathcal{M}$ be TCRHFs (the first set of the domain of these hash functions denotes the hash-key space and the second denotes the input space to be hashed). Here, we also assume that the hash-key space of the $H$ can be $\mathcal{S}_2$ (i.e., range of $S_2$), and we can sample random elements in $\mathcal{S}_2$ efficiently.

The description of a new scheme $\Sigma_{new} = ($KeyGen$_{new}$, Sign$_{new}$, Verify$_{new})$ obtained from our transformation is described in Fig. 1

| $\mathsf{KeyGen}_{new}(1^\kappa):$ | $\mathsf{Sign}_{new}(SK, M):$ |
|---|---|
| $(sk, pk) \leftarrow \mathsf{KeyGen}(1^\kappa)$ | $s \leftarrow \mathbb{Z}_p;\ r \leftarrow \mathcal{R};\ \sigma_2 = \mathsf{S}_2(sk, r)$ |
| $g, h_1, h_2 \leftarrow \mathbb{G};\ k \leftarrow \mathcal{K}$ | $t = H_{\sigma_2}(M);\ t' = G_k(\sigma_2);\ m = g^t h_1^s h_2^{t'}$ |
| $SK = (sk),\ PK = (pk, g, h_1, h_2, k)$ | $m' = F_k(m);\ \sigma_1 = \mathsf{S}_1(sk, m', r)$ |
| Output $(SK, PK)$. | Output $\sigma = (\sigma_1, \sigma_2, s)$. |

| $\mathsf{Verify}_{new}(PK, M, \sigma):$ |
|---|
| Parse $\sigma$ as $(\sigma_1, \sigma_2, s)$. |
| $t = H_{\sigma_2}(M);\ t' = G_k(\sigma_2);\ m = g^t h_1^s h_2^{t'};\ m' = F_k(m)$ |
| Output accept if $\mathsf{Verify}(pk, m', (\sigma_1, \sigma_2)) = $ accept. Otherwise output reject. |

**Fig. 1.** Description of $\Sigma_{new}$

*Security.* We prove the strong unforgeability of the new scheme $\Sigma_{new}$ in Appendix.

**Theorem 1.** *The new scheme $\Sigma_{new}$ is $(t, q, \epsilon)$-SEUF-CMA secure if the following conditions are satisfied.*

- *The underlying scheme $\Sigma$ is $(t, q, \epsilon/6)$-EUF-CMA secure and simulatable-partitioned signature scheme.*
- *The $(t, \epsilon/3)$-DL assumption holds in $\mathbb{G}$.*
- *$H$, $G$, and $F$ are $(t, \epsilon/6q)$, $(t, \epsilon/6q)$, and $(t, \epsilon/6q)$-TCRHFs respectively.*

*Idea.* The construction is based on [9]. In our scheme, we use three TCRHFs. The role of the $H$ is to hash the message. The role of $G$ is to ensure that different $\sigma_2$ will be mapped to different elements in $\mathbb{Z}_p$. Thus, an injective mapping can be used (and then we can reduce the number of forgery types in the security proof). The role of $F$ is similar to $G$. So if it is obvious that each element in $\mathbb{G}$ will always be mapped to a different element of $\mathcal{M}$ (i.e., the message space of the underlying signature scheme), then we can replace $F$ with an injective mapping.

Doubling the role of a part of the signature $\sigma_2$, which is a randomness element of the signature as well as a hash-key of $H$, is the technique from [19]. Since $\sigma_2$ is generated each time the underlying Sign is run and is a message-independent random value, $\sigma_2$ can play the same role as a hash-key in the TCRHF-based hash-and-sign construction which we mentioned in Section 1.

As a price of using $\sigma_2$ as a key of $H$, the simulator in the security proof needs to be able to compute valid $\sigma_1$ without knowing inner randomness $r$ when reducing the security to target collision resistance of $H$. That is why we introduce the *simulatable-partitioned* property.

As in the case of [9], generating $\sigma_1$ implies that a signer signs both a original message $M$ input into $\mathsf{Sign}_{new}$ and a randomness element $\sigma_2$. This ensures that any adversary can neither modify the original message nor use other randomness without invaliding the complete signature $(\sigma_1, \sigma_2)$, which would lead to the strong unforgeability. The authors of [9] used a collision resistant hash function to ensure that a hash value of any pair $(M, \sigma_2)$ will differ from each other. In our scheme, we use a combination of a DL-based chameleon hash function [18] and the target collision resistant hash functions $H$ and $G$ for providing similar functionalities to the collision resistant hash function used in [9]. And the chameleon hash function in our scheme is also used to break a circularity: in order to create a message $m'$ for the underlying signing algorithm (i.e. Sign, which takes $m'$ as an input), the simulator has to know in advance the randomness $r$ used to create a part of the signature (i.e., $\sigma_2$, which is output from Sign).

The algorithms KeyGen$'$ and S$_1'$ satisfying the property 3 of *simulatable-partitioned* signatures are needed only for proving security. Thus, it is sufficient to show their existence.

## 4   A Concrete CDH-Based Scheme

In this section, we construct a concrete signature scheme based on CDH. The idea to obtain the SEUF-CMA signature scheme without collision resistant hash function is applying our transformation proposed in Section 3 to the Waters scheme [27] straightforwardly.

The description of the concrete scheme is as follows. Let $p$ be a sufficiently large prime, and $\mathbb{G}$ be a cyclic bilinear group of order $p$. Let $H : \mathbb{G} \times \{0,1\}^* \to \mathbb{Z}_p$, $G : \mathcal{K} \times \mathbb{G} \to \mathbb{Z}_p$, and $F : \mathcal{K} \times \mathbb{G} \to \{0,1\}^n$ be TCRHFs respectively. Let $e : \mathbb{G} \times \mathbb{G} \to \mathbb{G}_1$ denote the bilinear map. We assume that each element of $\mathbb{G}$ has a unique encoding. Note that in the case of the Waters scheme, $\mathcal{S}_2 = \mathbb{G}$. And we also assume that the hash-key space of $H$ can be $\mathbb{G}$ (We can assume that we have $H : \mathcal{K} \times \{0,1\}^* \to \mathbb{Z}_p$, the hash-key space of which is the same as $G$ and $F$, and some bijective mapping between $\mathbb{G}$ and $\mathcal{K}$ that is efficiently bidirectionally computable. When we specify $\mathcal{K} = \mathbb{Z}_p$ for some prime number $p$, a bidirectional mapping between $\mathbb{G}$ of order $p$ on elliptic curves and $\mathbb{Z}_p$ [11] can be used, for example.).

The concrete scheme $\Sigma = $ (KeyGen, Sign, Verify) is described in Fig. 2. We note that the computation of the paring value $e(g_1, g_2)$ used in Verify can be done in KeyGen and be included in $PK$. But we follow the style of description as written in [9].

**Corollary 1.** *The signature scheme in Fig. 2 is $(t, q, \epsilon)$-SEUF-CMA secure if the following conditions are satisfied:*

- *The $(t, \epsilon/48(n+1)q)$-CDH assumption holds in $\mathbb{G}$.*
- *$H$, $G$, and $F$ are $(t, \epsilon/6q)$, $(t, \epsilon/6q)$, and $(t, \epsilon/6q)$-TCRHFs respectively.*

*Proof.* It is already proven in the standard model that the Waters scheme is $(t, q, \epsilon)$-EUF-CMA secure assuming that the $(t, \epsilon/8(n+1)q)$-CDH assumption holds in $\mathbb{G}$. Thus, the Waters scheme is $(t, q, \epsilon/6)$-EUF-CMA secure assuming that the $(t, \epsilon/48(n+1)q)$-CDH assumption holds in $\mathbb{G}$. In this case, the $(t, \epsilon/3)$-DL assumption also holds in $\mathbb{G}$. So, all that is left to do is to make sure that the Waters scheme satisfies a *simulatable-partitioned* property. The following description is the original KeyGen algorithm of the Waters scheme.

| KeyGen($1^\kappa$) : | Sign($SK, M$) : |
|---|---|
| $g \leftarrow \mathbb{G}; \alpha \leftarrow \mathbb{Z}_p; g_1 = g^\alpha$ | $s, r \leftarrow \mathbb{Z}_p; \sigma_2 = g^r$ |
| $g_2, h_1, h_2, u', u_1, \ldots, u_n \leftarrow \mathbb{G}$ | $t = H_{\sigma_2}(M); t' = G_k(\sigma_2)$ |
| $U = (u_1, \ldots, u_n)$ | $m = g^t h_1^s h_2^{t'}; m' = F_k(m)$ |
| $k \leftarrow \mathcal{K}$ | Parse $m'$ as $m'_1 m'_2 \ldots m'_n$ |
| $SK = g_2^\alpha, PK = (g, g_1, g_2, h_1, h_2, u', U, k)$ | (each of $m'_i$ is the $i$-th bit of $m'$). |
| Output ($SK, PK$). | $\sigma_1 = g_2^\alpha \cdot (u' \prod_{i=1}^n u_i^{m'_i})^r$ |
| | Output $\sigma = (\sigma_1, \sigma_2, s)$. |
| Verify($PK, M, \sigma$) : | |

Verify($PK, M, \sigma$) :
Parse $\sigma$ as $(\sigma_1, \sigma_2, s)$.
$t = H_{\sigma_2}(M); t' = G_k(\sigma_2); m = g^t h_1^s h_2^{t'}; m' = F_k(m)$
Parse $m'$ as $m'_1 m'_2 \ldots m'_n$ (each of $m'_i$ is the $i$-th bit of $m'$).
Check $e(\sigma_1, g) \stackrel{?}{=} e(\sigma_2, u' \prod_{i=1}^n u_i^{m'_i}) \cdot e(g_1, g_2)$.
Output accept if this holds. Otherwise output reject.

**Fig. 2.** Proposed Signature Scheme

KeyGen :  1. Select random $g, g_2 \in \mathbb{G}$.
  2. Select random $\alpha \in \mathbb{Z}_p$, and set $g_1 = g^\alpha$.
  3. Select random $u', u_1, u_2, \ldots, u_n \in \mathbb{G}$.
  4. Set $sk = g_2^\alpha$, $pk = (g, g_1, g_2, u', u_1, u_2, \ldots, u_n)$.
  5. Output ($sk, pk$).

Here, we define KeyGen$'$ by the algorithm below which is changed after the step 3 of original KeyGen (step 1 and 2 are the same).

KeyGen$'$ :  1. Select random $g, g_2 \in \mathbb{G}$.
  2. Select random $\alpha \in \mathbb{Z}_p$, and set $g_1 = g^\alpha$.
  3. Select random $\beta', \beta_1, \beta_2, \ldots, \beta_n \in \mathbb{Z}_p$, and then set $u' = g^{\beta'}, u_1 = g^{\beta_1}, u_2 = g^{\beta_2}, \ldots, u_n = g^{\beta_n}$.
  4. Set $sk' = g_2^\alpha$, $pk' = (g, g_1, g_2, u', u_1, u_2, \ldots, u_n)$, $TD = (\beta', \beta_1, \beta_2, \ldots, \beta_n)$.
  5. Output ($sk', pk', TD$).

It is obvious that the distribution of ($sk', pk'$) output from KeyGen$'$ can be the same as the distribution of ($sk, pk$) output from KeyGen.

The Waters signature is shown to be *partitioned* in [9]. The description of $S_1$ and $S_2$ are:

$$\sigma_1 = S_1(sk, m, r) = (sk) \cdot (u' \prod_{i=1}^n u_i^{m_i})^r \quad \in \mathbb{G}$$
$$\sigma_2 = S_2(sk, r) = g^r \quad \in \mathbb{G}$$

where $m_i \in \{0, 1\}$ is the $i$-th bit of $m \in \{0, 1\}^n$, and $u', u_1, \ldots, u_n \in \mathbb{G}$, $r \in \mathbb{Z}_p$, and ($sk$) is an element of $\mathbb{G}$. Here, using $TD$ and $\sigma_2$, we can write $\sigma_1$ as follows:

$$\sigma_1 = (sk) \cdot (u' \prod_{i=1}^n u_i^{m_i})^r = (sk) \cdot (g^{r\beta'} \prod_{i=1}^n (g^{r\beta_i m_i}))$$
$$= (sk) \cdot (g^r)^{\beta' + \sum_{i=1}^n \beta_i m_i} = (sk) \cdot (\sigma_2)^{\beta' + \sum_{i=1}^n \beta_i m_i}$$

This equality means that a valid $\sigma_1$ can be generated only from $sk, m, \sigma_2, TD$, without knowing $r$. Thus, we can define $S'_1(sk, m, \sigma_2, TD)$ by the last equation. Now, we have seen that $S'_1$, KeyGen', and $TD$ satisfy the property 3 of *simulatable-partitioned*. Therefore, the Waters scheme is *simulatable-partitioned*.

In summary, if we assume that the requirements of Corollary 1 all hold, then the requirements of Theorem 1 are satisfied, which means that the scheme in Fig. 2 is SEUF-CMA secure. □

*Asymmetric pairing.* In our scheme in this section, we use a symmetric pairing $e : \mathbb{G} \times \mathbb{G} \rightarrow \mathbb{G}_T$ where $|\mathbb{G}| = |\mathbb{G}_T| = p$. But we note that an asymmetric pairing setting can be used: $e : \mathbb{G}_1 \times \mathbb{G}_2 \rightarrow \mathbb{G}_T$ where $|\mathbb{G}_1| = |\mathbb{G}_2| = |\mathbb{G}_T| = p$, $\mathbb{G}_1 \neq \mathbb{G}_2$. Security then follows from the co-CDH problem [8].

One of the biggest merits to use asymmetric ones is that we can utilize curves due to Barreto and Naehrig [3]. If we use them, the representation of the element of $\mathbb{G}_1$ can be short (e.g., 160-bit), while the representation of the elements of $\mathbb{G}_2$ becomes several times larger than that of $\mathbb{G}_1$. For more details, see [22,17]. If these curves are used, we can shorten the signature size so that both $\sigma_1$ and $\sigma_2$ are included in $\mathbb{G}_1$, while key parameters are almost included in $\mathbb{G}_2$ and become larger. Another approach is to shorten the public key size by choosing the public key parameters from $\mathbb{G}_1$, while the signature elements are included in $\mathbb{G}_2$.

## 5   Comparison

Table 1 compares our proposed scheme and other strongly unforgeable signatures (the Cramer-Shoup (CS) scheme [13], the Boneh-Boyen (BB) scheme [5], and the Boneh-Shen-Waters (BSW) scheme [9]) that are provable in the standard model.

As compared to the BB scheme, the BB scheme is more efficient in the signature size, the signing cost, and the verification cost than ours. However, an advantage of ours is that our scheme is based on CDH, much weaker assumption than the $q$-SDH assumption. And, the message space of the BB scheme is defined only for $\mathbb{Z}_p$. Thus, some hashing operation is necessary if longer messages are signed. Of course hash-and-sign paradigm with a collision resistant hash function or with a TCRHF can be used. If the TCRHF-based hash-and-sign is used, the signature size increases by the hash-key $k$ of a TCRHF (here we denote $H$) and the size of the group (in which the signature elements are included) may also increase for deciding the size of $p$ so that $k||H_k(M)$ belongs to the original message space $\mathbb{Z}_p$.

As compared to the BSW scheme, an advantage of ours is that ours doesn't rely on a collision resistant hash function, and a disadvantage is that our scheme is a bit worse in computation for signing and verification for computing a multiple exponentiation of three bases $g^t h_1^s h_2^{t'}$ (in the BSW scheme, only two bases $g^t h^s$ is needed). However, this difference can be smaller by using the simultaneous exponentiation technique [20].

We cannot directly compare computation costs and the assumptions with CS scheme. However, we can say that the signature size of our scheme is shorter

**Table 1.** Comparison among the strongly unforgeable signature schemes in the standard model. "CRHF" denotes whether an arbitrary-input-length collision resistant hash function is necessary or not in the security proof. "Message space" denotes the input message space assumed for the signing algorithm of the scheme. So if one wants to sign a message from a larger space than this, some hashing operation such as hash-and-sign paradigm is needed. The Waters scheme is not SEUF-CMA secure, but we include for the purpose of reference. $p$ denotes the order of cyclic groups $\mathbb{G}$ and $\mathbb{G}_1$.

| | Assumption | Message space | CRHF | Signature Size | Signing Cost‡† | Verification Cost‡† |
|---|---|---|---|---|---|---|
| CS [13]([19])† | Strong RSA | $\{0,1\}^*$ | no | $161 + 2\lfloor n'\rfloor$ | 2m-exp$_{\mathbb{Z}_{n'}}$ | 2m-exp$_{\mathbb{Z}_{n'}}$ |
| BB [5]‡ | $q$-SDH | $\mathbb{Z}_p$ | no | $2\lvert\mathbb{G}_1\rvert$ | 1exp$_{\mathbb{G}_1}$ | $1P$ + 1m-exp$_{\mathbb{G}_1}$ |
| BSW [9] | CDH | $\{0,1\}^*$ | yes | $2\lvert\mathbb{G}\rvert + \lvert p\rvert$ | 1m-exp$_{\mathbb{G}}$ + 3exp$_{\mathbb{G}}$ | $2P$ + 1m-exp$_{\mathbb{G}}$ + 1exp$_{\mathbb{G}}$ |
| **Ours (§4)** | CDH | $\{0,1\}^*$ | no | $2\lvert\mathbb{G}\rvert + \lvert p\rvert$ | 1m-exp$_{\mathbb{G}}$ + 3exp$_{\mathbb{G}}$ | $2P$ + 1m-exp$_{\mathbb{G}}$ + 1exp$_{\mathbb{G}}$ |
| Waters [27] | CDH | $\{0,1\}^n$ | no | $2\lvert\mathbb{G}\rvert$ | 3exp$_{\mathbb{G}}$ | $2P$ + 1exp$_{\mathbb{G}}$ |

† We assume that the CS scheme [13] is constructed using Mironov's way of using TCRHF, which shorten the signature size [19]. $n'$ denotes the RSA modulus.

‡ In this scheme, we assume that an asymmetric pairing $e : \mathbb{G}_1 \times \mathbb{G}_2 \to \mathbb{G}_T$ is used.

‡† In these columns, $P$ denotes the numbers of paring operation. exp$_{\mathbb{G}}$ denotes the number of single base exponentiations in $\mathbb{G}$, and m-exp$_{\mathbb{G}}$ denotes the number of multiple exponentiations in $\mathbb{G}$. We omit the costs of any other operations. We count so called the "Waters hash" ($u' \prod_{i=1}^{n} u_i^{m_i'}$) as one single base exponentiation. We omit the pairing computation which is independent of message and signature and can be pre-computed in KeyGen of the Waters scheme (thus, the BSW scheme and ours).

considering the currently used RSA modulus size. As for assumptions, the CDH assumption might be a more reasonable assumption than the strong RSA assumption because CDH has a longer history.

# 6   Conclusion

In this paper, we constructed a strongly unforgeable signature scheme based on the CDH assumption in bilinear groups and target collision resistant hash functions. The signature scheme is almost as efficient as [9], while it does not rely on collision resistant hash functions whose input length is arbitrary. Instead, our scheme utilize a target collision resistant hash function, which is a weaker primitive than a collision resistant hash function. Our scheme is not affected by recently emerging collision finding attacks against hash functions. We presented the construction in two steps. First we showed a transformation that converts specific unforgeable signatures into strongly unforgeable signatures and proved its security. And then we applied this transformation to the Waters signature scheme [27]. We also compared our scheme with other strongly unforgeable signature schemes in the standard model and discussed their efficiency.

# References

1. An, J.H., Dodis, Y., Rabin, T.: On the Security of Joint Signature and Encryption. In: Knudsen, L.R. (ed.) EUROCRYPT 2002. LNCS, vol. 2332, pp. 83–107. Springer, Heidelberg (2002)
2. Ateniese, G., Camenisch, J., Joye, M., Tsudik, G., Practical, A.: Provably Secure Coalition-Resistant Group Signature Scheme. In: Bellare, M. (ed.) CRYPTO 2000. LNCS, vol. 1880, pp. 255–270. Springer, Heidelberg (2000)
3. Barreto, P., Naehrig, M.: Pairing-Friendly Elliptic Curves of Prime Order, *Proc. of SAC'05*, LNCS 3897. In: Preneel, B., Tavares, S. (eds.) SAC 2005. LNCS, vol. 3897, pp. 319–331. Springer, Heidelberg (2006)
4. Bellare, M., Rogaway, P.: Collision-Resistant Hashing: Towards Making UOWHFs Practical. In: Kaliski Jr., B.S. (ed.) CRYPTO 1997. LNCS, vol. 1294, pp. 320–335. Springer, Heidelberg (1997)
5. Boneh, D., Boyen, X.: Short Signatures Without Random Oracles. In: Cachin, C., Camenisch, J.L. (eds.) EUROCRYPT 2004. LNCS, vol. 3027, pp. 56–73. Springer, Heidelberg (2004)
6. Boneh, D., Boyen, X., Shacham, H.: Short Group Signatures. In: Franklin, M. (ed.) CRYPTO 2004. LNCS, vol. 3152, pp. 41–55. Springer, Heidelberg (2004)
7. Boneh, D., Lynn, B., Shacham, H.: Short Signatures from the Weil Pairing. In: Boyd, C. (ed.) ASIACRYPT 2001. LNCS, vol. 2248, pp. 514–532. Springer, Heidelberg (2001)
8. Boneh, D., Lynn, B., Shacham, H.: Short Signatures from the Weil Pairing. J. of Cryptology 17(2), 297–319, Full version of [7] (2004)
9. Boneh, D., Shen, E., Waters, B.: Strongly Unforgeable Signatures Based on Computational Diffie-Hellman. In: Yung, M., Dodis, Y., Kiayias, A., Malkin, T.G. (eds.) PKC 2006. LNCS, vol. 3958, pp. 229–240. Springer, Heidelberg (2006)
10. Boyen, X., Mei, Q., Waters, B.: Direct Chosen Ciphertext Security from Identity-Based Techniques. In: Proc. of 12th ACMCCS (2005)
11. Boyen, X., Mei, Q., Waters,B.: Direct Chosen Ciphertext Security from Identity-Based Techniques, Updated version of [10] (2005), available at eprint.iacr.org/2005/288
12. Canetti, R., Halevi, S., Katz, J.: Chosen-Ciphertext Security from Identity-Based Encryption. In: Cachin, C., Camenisch, J.L. (eds.) EUROCRYPT 2004. LNCS, vol. 3027, pp. 207–222. Springer, Heidelberg (2004)
13. Cramer, R., Shoup, V.: Signature Schemes Based on the Strong RSA Assumption. ACM TISSEC 3(3), 161–185 (2000). Extended abstract. In: Proc. of 6th ACMCCS (1999)
14. Damgård, I.: Collision Free Hash Functions and Public Key Signature Schemes. In: Price, W.L., Chaum, D. (eds.) EUROCRYPT 1987. LNCS, vol. 304, pp. 203–216. Springer, Heidelberg (1988)
15. Goldwasser, S., Micali, S., Rivest, R., Digital, A.: Signature Schemes Secure Against Adaptive Chosen-Message Attacks. SIAM J. Computing 17(2), 281–308 (1988)
16. Huang, Q., Wong, D.S., Zhao, Y.: Generic Transformation to Strongly Unforgeable Signatures. In: ACNS 2007. 5th Applied Cryptography and Network Security, vol. 4521, pp. 1–17 (2007)

17. Koblitz, N., Menezes, A.: Pairing-Based Cryptography at High Security Levels. In: Smart, N.P. (ed.) Cryptography and Coding. LNCS, vol. 3796, pp. 13–36. Springer, Heidelberg (2005)
18. Krawczyk, H., Rabin, T.: Chameleon Hashing and Signatures. In: Proc. of NDSS 2000, Internet Society (1998), available at eprint.iacr.org/1998/010
19. Mironov, I.: Collision Resistant No More: Hash-and-Sign Paradigm Revisited. In: Yung, M., Dodis, Y., Kiayias, A., Malkin, T.G. (eds.) PKC 2006. LNCS, vol. 3958, pp. 140–156. Springer, Heidelberg (2006)
20. Menezes, A.J., Oorschot, P.C., Vanstone, S.A.: Handbook of Applied Cryptography. CRC Press, Boca Raton, USA (1996)
21. Naor, M., Yung, M.: Universal One-Way Hash Functions and their Cryptographic Applications. In: Proc. of the Twenty First ACM Symposium on Theory of Computing, pp. 33–43 (1989)
22. Page, D., Smart, N.P., Vercauteren, F.: A comparison of MNT curves and super-singular curves. Applicable Algebra in Engineerings, Communication and Computing(AAECC) 17(5), 379–392 (2006)
23. Simon, D.R.: Finding Collision on One-Way Street: Can Secure Hash Functions Be Based on General Assumptions? In: Nyberg, K. (ed.) EUROCRYPT 1998. LNCS, vol. 1403, pp. 334–345. Springer, Heidelberg (1998)
24. Steinfeld, R., Pieprzyk, J., Wang, H.: How to Strengthen Any Weakly Unforgeable Signature into a Strongly Unforgeable Signature. In: Abe, M. (ed.) CT-RSA 2007. LNCS, vol. 4377, pp. 357–371. Springer, Heidelberg (2006)
25. Teranishi, I., Oyama, T., Ogata, W.: General Conversion for Obtaining Strongly Existentially Unforgeable Signatures. In: Barua, R., Lange, T. (eds.) INDOCRYPT 2006. LNCS, vol. 4329, pp. 191–205. Springer, Heidelberg (2006)
26. Wang, X., Yin, Y.L., Yu, H.: Finding Collisions in the Full SHA-1. In: Shoup, V. (ed.) CRYPTO 2005. LNCS, vol. 3621, pp. 12–36. Springer, Heidelberg (2005)
27. Waters, B.: Efficient Identity-Based Encryption without Random Oracles. In: Cramer, R.J.F. (ed.) EUROCRYPT 2005. LNCS, vol. 3494, pp. 114–127. Springer, Heidelberg (2005)

# Appendix : Proof of Theorem 1

*Proof.* Suppose $\mathcal{A}$ is an adversary that breaks the $(t, q, \epsilon)$-SEUF-CMA security of $\Sigma_{new}$. At the stage *Setup* of the SEUF-CMA game, $\mathcal{A}$ is given a public key $PK = (pk, g, h_1, h_2, k)$. At the stage *Queries*, $\mathcal{A}$ issues a message $M_i$ as the $i$-th query and given a corresponding signature $\sigma_i = (\sigma_{i,1}, \sigma_{i,2}, s_i)$ for all $i \in \{1, \ldots, q\}$. We define $t_i = H_{\sigma_{i,2}}(M_i)$, $t_i' = G_k(\sigma_{i,2})$, $m_i = g^{t_i} h_1^{s_i} h_2^{t_i'}$, and $m_i' = F_k(m_i)$. At the stage *Output*, $\mathcal{A}$ outputs $(\hat{M}, \hat{\sigma} = (\hat{\sigma_1}, \hat{\sigma_2}, \hat{s}))$. We also define $\hat{t} = H_{\hat{\sigma_2}}(\hat{M})$, $\hat{t}' = G_k(\hat{\sigma_2})$, $\hat{m} = g^{\hat{t}} h_1^{\hat{s}} h_2^{\hat{t}'}$, and $\hat{m}' = F_k(\hat{m})$. We classify forgeries output by $\mathcal{A}$ into following six types.

**Type 1.** $\forall i \in \{1, \ldots, q\} : \hat{m}' \neq m_i'$.
**Type 2.** $\exists i \in \{1, \ldots, q\} : \hat{m}' = m_i' \wedge \hat{m} \neq m_i$.
**Type 3.** $\exists i \in \{1, \ldots, q\} : \hat{m}' = m_i' \wedge \hat{m} = m_i \wedge \hat{t}' \neq t_i'$.
**Type 4.** $\exists i \in \{1, \ldots, q\} : \hat{m}' = m_i' \wedge \hat{m} = m_i \wedge \hat{t}' = t_i' \wedge \hat{\sigma_2} \neq \sigma_{i,2}$.
**Type 5.** $\exists i \in \{1, \ldots, q\} : \hat{m}' = m_i' \wedge \hat{m} = m_i \wedge \hat{t}' = t_i' \wedge \hat{\sigma_2} = \sigma_{i,2} \wedge \hat{t} \neq t_i$.
**Type 6.** $\exists i \in \{1, \ldots, q\} : \hat{m}' = m_i' \wedge \hat{m} = m_i \wedge \hat{t}' = t_i' \wedge \hat{\sigma_2} = \sigma_{i,2} \wedge \hat{t} = t_i$.

If $\mathcal{A}$ succeeds in producing a forgery, the forgery output by $\mathcal{A}$ is always included in one of the types above. We will show that the forgery of type 1 can be used to break the EUF-CMA security of the underlying scheme $\Sigma$, type 3 and type 5 to solve the DL problem in $\mathbb{G}$ and type 2, type 4 and type 6 to break TCRHFs. Our simulator can flip a coin at the beginning of the simulation to guess which type of forgery $\mathcal{A}$ will produce, and set up the simulations below appropriately.

Type 1. Suppose $\mathcal{A}$ is a type 1 adversary and can break the $(t, q, \epsilon)$-SEUF-CMA security of $\Sigma_{new}$. We construct a simulator $\mathcal{B}_1$ that can break the $(t, q, \epsilon)$-EUF-CMA security of underlying $\Sigma$. $\mathcal{B}_1$ is first given $pk$, and tries to output a forgery $(\hat{m}', \hat{\sigma} = (\hat{\sigma}_1, \hat{\sigma}_2))$. The description of $\mathcal{B}_1$ is as follows:

**Setup.** $\mathcal{B}_1$ generates $PK$ for $\mathcal{A}$ as follows:
    1. Select random $g \in \mathbb{G}, k \in \mathcal{K}$.
    2. Select random $a, b \in \mathbb{Z}_p^*$ and set $h_1 = g^a, h_2 = g^b$.
    3. Give $PK = (pk, g, h_1, h_2, k)$ to $\mathcal{A}$.
**Queries.** $\mathcal{B}_1$ responds to the query $M_i$ issued by $\mathcal{A}$ as follows:
    1. Select a random $w_i \in \mathbb{Z}_q$ and set $m_i = g^{w_i}$.
    2. Compute $m_i' = F_k(m_i)$.
    3. Issue $m_i'$ as $i$-th query to its own EUF-CMA challenger, and obtain a valid signature $(\sigma_{i,1}, \sigma_{i,2})$ on $m_i'$.
    4. Compute $t_i = H_{\sigma_{i,2}}(M_i)$, $t_i' = G_k(\sigma_{i,2})$.
    5. Compute $s_i = (w_i - t_i - bt_i')/a$.
    6. Return $\sigma_i = (\sigma_{i,1}, \sigma_{i,2}, s_i)$ to $\mathcal{A}$.
**Output.** Finally, $\mathcal{A}$ outputs a type 1 forgery $(\hat{M}, (\hat{\sigma}_1, \hat{\sigma}_2, \hat{s}))$. $\mathcal{B}_1$ computes $\hat{m}'$ according to the procedure of $\mathsf{Verify}_{new}$, then outputs $(\hat{m}', (\hat{\sigma}_1, \hat{\sigma}_2))$.

Note that the description of $\Sigma_{new}$ implies that if $\mathsf{Verify}_{new}(PK, \hat{M}, (\hat{\sigma}_1, \hat{\sigma}_2, \hat{s}))$ $= \mathsf{accept}$, then $\mathsf{Verify}(pk, \hat{m}', (\hat{\sigma}_1, \hat{\sigma}_2)) = \mathsf{accept}$ where $\hat{m}'$ is computed appropriately. Since $\mathcal{A}$ is a type 1 adversary, $\hat{m}' \neq m_i'$ holds for all $i \in \{1, \ldots q\}$. Therefore, whenever $\mathcal{A}$ succeeds in producing a type 1 forgery, $\mathcal{B}_1$ can produce a forgery on a new message $\hat{m}'$ for the underlying signature scheme $\Sigma$ and win the EUF-CMA game.

Type 2. Suppose $\mathcal{A}$ is a type 2 adversary and can break the $(t, q, \epsilon)$-SEUF-CMA security of $\Sigma_{new}$. We construct a simulator $\mathcal{B}_2$ that can break the $(t, \epsilon/q)$-TCRHF $F$. $\mathcal{B}_2$ tries to win the TCRHF game about $F$. The description of $\mathcal{B}_2$ is as follows:

**Setup.** $\mathcal{B}_2$ generates $PK$ for $\mathcal{A}$ as follows:
    1. Select a random index $j \in \{1, \ldots, q\}$.
    2. Run underlying $\mathsf{KeyGen}$ and obtain $sk, pk$.
    3. Select a random $g \in \mathbb{G}$.
    4. Select random $a, b \in \mathbb{Z}_p^*$ and set $h_1 = g^a, h_2 = g^b$.
    5. Select a random $\bar{w} \in \mathbb{Z}_p$ and compute $\bar{m} = g^{\bar{w}}$.
    6. Output $\bar{m}$ for its own TCR challenger and obtain $k \in \mathcal{K}$.
    7. Compute $\bar{m}' = F_k(\bar{m})$
    8. Give $PK = (pk, g, h_1, h_2, k)$ to $\mathcal{A}$, while $SK = sk$ is kept secret.

**Queries.** $\mathcal{B}_2$ responds to the query $M_i$ issued by $\mathcal{A}$ as follows:
- $i \neq j$ : Return $\sigma_i = \mathsf{Sign}_{new}(SK, M_i)$ to $\mathcal{A}$.
- $i = j$ :
  1. Set $m_j = \bar{m}$, $m'_j = \bar{m}'$.
  2. Run underlying $\mathsf{Sign}(sk, m'_j)$ and obtain $(\sigma_{j,1}, \sigma_{j,2})$.
  3. Compute $t_j = H_{\sigma_{j,2}}(M_j)$, $t'_j = G_k(\sigma_{j,2})$.
  4. Compute $s_j = (\bar{w} - t_j - bt'_j)/a$.
  5. Return $\sigma_j = (\sigma_{j,1}, \sigma_{j,2}, s_j)$ to $\mathcal{A}$.

**Output.** Finally, $\mathcal{A}$ outputs a type 2 forgery $(\hat{M}, (\hat{\sigma}_1, \hat{\sigma}_2, \hat{s}))$. $\mathcal{B}_2$ computes $\hat{m}$ from the forgery according to the procedure of $\mathsf{Verify}_{new}$. Then, $\mathcal{B}_2$ outputs $\hat{m}$ if $F_k(\hat{m}) = F_k(m_j) \wedge \hat{m} \neq m_j$ holds, otherwise $\mathcal{B}_2$ reports *failure* and aborts.

Since $\mathcal{A}$ is a type 2 adversary, there exists at least one $i \in \{1, \ldots, q\}$ such that $F_k(\hat{m}) = F_k(m_i) \wedge \hat{m} \neq m_i$ holds (note that $\hat{m}' = m'_i$ implies $F_k(\hat{m}) = F_k(m_i)$). Thus, $\hat{m}$ is a target collision against $m_i$ for $F$ under the key $k$. Probability that $\mathcal{B}_2$ chooses such $i$ as $j$ at the stage *Setup* is at least $1/q$. Therefore, if $\mathcal{A}$ succeeds in producing a type 2 forgery, $\mathcal{B}_2$ can break TCRHF $F$ with probability at least $1/q$.

**Type 3.** Suppose $\mathcal{A}$ is a type 3 adversary and can break the $(t, q, \epsilon)$-SEUF-CMA security of $\Sigma_{new}$. We construct a simulator $\mathcal{B}_3$ that $(t, \epsilon)$-solves the DL problem. $\mathcal{B}_3$ is first given an instance of the DL problem $(g, X)$ and tries to output $\log_g X$. The description of $\mathcal{B}_3$ is as follows:

**Setup.** $\mathcal{B}_3$ generates $PK$ for $\mathcal{A}$ as follows:
1. Set $g$ for element of $PK$.
2. Run underlying $\mathsf{KeyGen}$ and obtain $sk, pk$.
3. Select a random $a \in \mathbb{Z}_p^*$ and set $h_1 = g^a, h_2 = X$.
4. Select a random $k \in \mathcal{K}$.
5. Give $PK = (pk, g, h_1, h_2, k)$ to $\mathcal{A}$ while $SK = sk$ is kept secret.

**Queries.** $\mathcal{B}_3$ responds to the query $M_i$ issued by $\mathcal{A}$ by returning $\sigma_i = \mathsf{Sign}_{new}$ $(SK, M_i)$ to $\mathcal{A}$.

**Output.** Finally, $\mathcal{A}$ outputs a type 3 forgery $(\hat{M}, (\hat{\sigma}_1, \hat{\sigma}_2, \hat{s}))$. $\mathcal{B}_3$ computes $\hat{t}$ and $\hat{t}'$ according to the procedure of $\mathsf{Verify}_{new}$, then computes $\log_g X = (\hat{t} + a\hat{s} - t_i - as_i)/(t'_i - \hat{t}')$ and outputs it as a solution of the DL problem.

Since $\mathcal{A}$ is a type 3 adversary, there exists $i$ such that $\hat{m} = m_i \wedge \hat{t}' \neq t'_i$ holds, and $\mathcal{B}_3$ can know such $i$. Note that $\hat{m} = m_i$ indicates $g^{\hat{t}} h_1^{\hat{s}} h_2^{\hat{t}'} = g^{t_i} h_1^{s_i} h_2^{t'_i}$, which can be written as $g^{\hat{t}+a\hat{s}} X^{\hat{t}'} = g^{t_i+as_i} X^{t'_i}$. From this equality one can compute base $g$ logarithm of $X$. $\hat{t}' \neq t'_i$ ensures $t'_i - \hat{t}' \neq 0$. Therefore, whenever $\mathcal{A}$ succeeds in producing a type 3 forgery, $\mathcal{B}_3$ can solve the DL problem.

**Type 4.** Suppose $\mathcal{A}$ is a type 4 adversary and can break the $(t, q, \epsilon)$-SEUF-CMA security of $\Sigma_{new}$. We construct a simulator $\mathcal{B}_4$ that can break the $(t, \epsilon/q)$-TCRHF $G$. $\mathcal{B}_4$ tries to win the TCR game about $G$. The description of $\mathcal{B}_4$ is as follows:

**Setup.** $\mathcal{B}_4$ generates $PK$ for $\mathcal{A}$ as follows:

1. Select a random index $j \in \{1, \ldots, q\}$.
2. Run underlying KeyGen and obtain $sk, pk$.
3. Select random $g, h_1, h_2 \in \mathbb{G}$.
4. Select a random $\bar{r} \in \mathcal{R}$ and compute $\bar{\sigma}_2 = \mathsf{S}_2(sk, \bar{r})$.
5. Output $\bar{\sigma}_2$ for its own TCR challenger and obtain $k \in \mathcal{K}$.
6. Give $PK = (pk, g, h_1, h_2, k)$ to $\mathcal{A}$, while $SK = sk$ is kept secret.

**Queries.** $\mathcal{B}_4$ responds to the query $M_i$ issued by $\mathcal{A}$ as follows:

- $i \neq j$ : Return $\sigma_i = \mathsf{Sign}_{new}(SK, M_i)$ to $\mathcal{A}$.
- $i = j$ : Compute $\sigma_i = (\sigma_{j,1}, \sigma_{j,2}, s_j)$ the same way as $\mathsf{Sign}_{new}$ using $\bar{r}$ as $r_j$ and $\bar{\sigma}_2$ as $\sigma_{j,2}$, then return it to $\mathcal{A}$.

**Output.** Finally, $\mathcal{A}$ outputs a type 4 forgery $(\hat{M}, (\hat{\sigma}_1, \hat{\sigma}_2, \hat{s}))$. $\mathcal{B}_4$ outputs $\hat{\sigma}_2$ if $G_k(\hat{\sigma}_2) = G_k(\sigma_{j,2}) \wedge \hat{\sigma}_2 \neq \sigma_{j,2}$, otherwise $\mathcal{B}_4$ reports *failure* and aborts.

Since $\mathcal{A}$ is a type 4 adversary, there exists at least one $i \in \{1, \ldots, q\}$ such that $G_k(\hat{\sigma}_2) = G_k(\sigma_{i,2}) \wedge \hat{\sigma}_2 \neq \sigma_{i,2}$ holds (note that $\hat{t}' = t'_j$ implies $G_k(\hat{\sigma}_2) = G_k(\sigma_{i,2})$). Thus, $\hat{\sigma}_2$ is a target collision against $\sigma_{i,2}$ for $G$ under the key $k$. Probability that $\mathcal{B}_4$ chooses such $i$ as $j$ at the stage *Setup* is at least $1/q$. Therefore, if $\mathcal{A}$ succeeds in producing a type 4 forgery, $\mathcal{B}_4$ can break TCRHF $G$ with probability at least $1/q$.

Type 5. Suppose $\mathcal{A}$ is a type 5 adversary and can break the $(t, q, \epsilon)$-SEUF-CMA security of $\Sigma_{new}$. We construct a simulator $\mathcal{B}_5$ that $(t, \epsilon)$-solves the DL problem. $\mathcal{B}_5$ is first given an instance of DL problem $(g, X)$, and tries to find $\log_g X$. The description of $\mathcal{B}_5$ is as follows:

**Setup.** $\mathcal{B}_5$ generates $PK$ for $\mathcal{A}$ as follows:

1. Set $g$ for element of $PK$.
2. Run underlying KeyGen and obtain $sk, pk$.
3. Set $h_1 = X$.
4. Select random $h_2 \in \mathbb{G}, k \in \mathcal{K}$.
5. Give $PK = (pk, g, h_1, h_2, k)$ to $\mathcal{A}$, while $SK = sk$ is kept secret.

**Queries.** $\mathcal{B}_5$ responds to the query $M_i$ issued by $\mathcal{A}$ by returning $\sigma_i = \mathsf{Sign}_{new}$ $(SK, M_i)$ to $\mathcal{A}$.

**Output.** Finally, $\mathcal{A}$ outputs a type 5 forgery $(\hat{M}, (\hat{\sigma}_1, \hat{\sigma}_2, \hat{s}))$. $\mathcal{B}_5$ computes $\hat{t} = H_{\hat{\sigma}_2}(\hat{M})$, and then computes $\log_g X = (\hat{t} - t_i)/(s_i - \hat{s})$ and outputs it as a solution of the DL problem.

Since $\mathcal{A}$ is a type 5 adversary, there exists $i$ such that $\hat{m} = m_i \wedge \hat{t} \neq t_i$, and $\mathcal{B}_5$ can know such $i$. Note that $\hat{m} = m_i$ implies $g^{\hat{t}} X^{\hat{s}} = g^{t_i} X^{s_i}$. In the equality, $s_i - \hat{s} = 0$ never happens since $\hat{s} = s_i \wedge g^{\hat{t}} X^{\hat{s}} = g^{t_i} X^{s_i}$ implies $\hat{t} = t_i$, which means that one can compute base $g$ logarithm of $X$ from the equality. Therefore, whenever $\mathcal{A}$ succeeds in producing a type 5 forgery, $\mathcal{B}_5$ can solve the DL problem.

**Type 6.** Suppose $\mathcal{A}$ is a type 6 adversary and can break the $(t, q, \epsilon)$-SEUF-CMA security of $\Sigma_{new}$. We construct a simulator $\mathcal{B}_6$ that can break the $(t, \epsilon/q)$-TCRHF $H$. $\mathcal{B}_6$ tries to win the TCR game about $H$. The description of $\mathcal{B}_6$ is as follows:

**Setup.** $\mathcal{B}_6$ generates $PK$ for $\mathcal{A}$ as follows:
1. Select a random index $j \in \{1 \ldots q\}$.
2. Run KeyGen$'$ and obtain $sk$, $pk$, $TD$.
3. Select random $g, h_1, h_2 \in \mathbb{G}, k \in \mathcal{K}$.
4. Give $PK = (pk, g, h_1, h_2, k)$ to $\mathcal{A}$, while $SK = sk$ is kept secret.

**Queries.** $\mathcal{B}_6$ responds to the query $M_i$ issued by $\mathcal{A}$ as follows:
- $i \neq j$ : Return $\sigma_i = \mathsf{Sign}_{new}(SK, M_i)$ to $\mathcal{A}$.
- $i = j$ :
   1. Output $M_j$ for its own TCR challenger and obtain $\bar{\sigma}_2 \in \mathcal{S}_2$.
   2. Set $\sigma_{j,2} = \bar{\sigma}_2$.
   3. Compute $t_j = H_{\sigma_{j,2}}(M_j)$, $t'_j = G_k(\sigma_{j,2})$.
   4. Select random $s_j \in \mathbb{Z}_p$.
   5. Compute $m_j = g^{t_j} h_1^{s_j} h_2^{t'_j}$.
   6. Compute $m'_j = F_k(m_j)$.
   7. Compute $\sigma_{j,1} = \mathsf{S}'_1(sk, m'_j, \bar{\sigma}_2, TD)$.
   8. Return $\sigma_j = (\sigma_{j,1}, \sigma_{j,2}, s_j)$ to $\mathcal{A}$.

**Output.** Finally, $\mathcal{A}$ outputs a type 6 forgery $(\hat{M}, (\hat{\sigma}_1, \hat{\sigma}_2, \hat{s}))$. $\mathcal{B}_6$ outputs $\hat{M}$ if $H_{\hat{\sigma}_2}(\hat{M}) = H_{\sigma_{j,2}} \wedge \hat{\sigma}_2 = \sigma_{j,2} \wedge \hat{M} \neq M_j$ holds, otherwise $\mathcal{B}_6$ reports *failure* and aborts.

Note that we need KeyGen$'$ and $\mathsf{S}'_1$ in order to create valid $\sigma_{j,1}$ without knowing $\bar{r}$ that would be used to generate $\sigma_{j,2} = \bar{\sigma}_2$. If $\mathcal{A}$ wins the SEUF-CMA game, $(\hat{M}, \hat{\sigma}_1, \hat{\sigma}_2, \hat{s}) \neq (M_i, \sigma_{i,1}, \sigma_{i,2}, s_i)$ holds for all $i \in \{1 \ldots q\}$. Since $\mathcal{A}$ is a type 6 adversary, there exists at least one $i \in \{1, \ldots, q\}$ such that $\hat{t} = t_i \wedge \hat{\sigma}_2 = \sigma_{i,2} \wedge \hat{s} = s_i$ holds. Note that $\hat{t} = t_i$ implies $H_{\hat{\sigma}_2}(\hat{M}) = H_{\sigma_{i,2}}(M_i)$. Property 2 of *simulatable-partitioned* signature indicates that if $\hat{m}' = m'_i \wedge \hat{\sigma}_2 = \sigma_{i,2}$ holds, then we have $\hat{\sigma}_1 = \sigma_{i,1}$. Put everything together, we have $\exists i \in \{1, \ldots, q\}$ : $\hat{M} \neq M_i \wedge \hat{\sigma}_2 = \sigma_{i,2} \wedge H_{\hat{\sigma}_2}(\hat{M}) = H_{\sigma_{i,2}}(M_i)$. In other words, there exists $i \in \{1, \ldots, q\}$ such that $\hat{M}$ is a target collision against $M_i$ for $H$ under the key $\hat{\sigma} = \sigma_i$. Probability that $\mathcal{B}_6$ chooses such $i$ as $j$ at stage *Setup* is at least $1/q$. Therefore, if $\mathcal{A}$ succeeds in producing a type 6 forgery, $\mathcal{B}_6$ can break TCRHF $H$ with probability at least $1/q$.

In summary, we showed how to construct simulators for all six types of the adversary. Note that simulations for all types of $\mathcal{A}$ are perfect. Type 1 can be used to break EUF-CMA security of underlying $\Sigma$, type 3 and type 5 to solve the DL problem, type 2,4 and 6 to break TCRHF. This completes the proof of Theorem 1. $\qquad\qquad\qquad\qquad\qquad\qquad\qquad\qquad\qquad\qquad\qquad\qquad\qquad\qquad\square$

# Two Notes on the Security of Certificateless Signatures

Rafael Castro* and Ricardo Dahab

UNICAMP, Brazil
rafael.castro@gmail.com, rdahab@ic.unicamp.br
http://www.lca.ic.unicamp.br/

**Abstract.** We discuss two common pitfalls found in proofs of security of various certificateless signature (CLS) schemes. As a result of the first observation, we are able to show that a CLS scheme ([Goy06]), previously thought to be secure, is vulnerable to a key replacement attack. We then proceed to define a class of CLS schemes whose security is provable by standard techniques, leading to a more efficient version of a known CLS scheme ([ARP03]) and a (previously unknown) security proof for another ([LCS05]).

**Keywords:** Certificateless Public-Key Cryptography, Forking Lemma, Signature Schemes.

## 1 Introduction

Certificateless Public-Key Cryptography *(CL-PKC)* was introduced by Al-Riyami and Paterson in [ARP03] as a compromise between ID-Based Cryptography *(ID-PKC)* [Sha85] and traditional PKIs. Its main design goal is to avoid the inherent key escrow of ID-PKC while taming the complexity of running a full-blown PKI. To accomplish this, the responsibility for the generation of the private key is shared by a trusted Key Generation Center *(KGC)* and the user.

The peculiar setting of certificateless signatures *(CLS)* makes proving security of such schemes somewhat tricky. Otherwise widely used techniques must be applied with care when used in this setting. The Oracle Replay Technique [PS00] is a good example of such a technique. It is a very important tool for proving the security of a large class of signature schemes, the so-called *generic* signature schemes, such as Schnorr's [Sch91], that previously had no security proof. Assuming the existence of an adversary capable of generating signature forgeries, two related signatures on the same message are obtained; these forgeries can then be used to solve a hard problem, thus producing a reductionist security proof. The original formulation of the oracle replay technique, however, does not directly apply to the certificateless setting, since it does not cover the possibility of public-key replacement attacks. Nonetheless, most CLS schemes are proved secure using this technique, leaving open the possibility of such attacks. In this

---

* This work was supported by FAPESP grant number 2006/06146-3.

W. Susilo, J.K. Liu, and Y. Mu. (Eds.): ProvSec 2007, LNCS 4784, pp. 85–102, 2007.

work we identify the occurrence of such shortcomings in the security proofs of a few CLS schemes, while also providing improved versions for two of these schemes.

Additionally, we present an attack on the CLS scheme from [Goy06], identifying another common inaccuracy, namely the unjustified assumption that an adversary knows the private key corresponding to the public key used in a forgery.

### 1.1  Organization

In Section 2 we review a few important concepts used throughout this paper. In Sections 3 and 4 we discuss two common pitfalls in the security proofs of CLS schemes, leading us to the main results in this paper. In Section 5 we make a quick summary of the available CLS schemes. Section 6 brings our concluding remarks.

## 2  Preliminaries

### 2.1  Bilinear Maps

Let $\mathbb{G}_1$, $\mathbb{G}_2$ and $\mathbb{G}_T$ be groups such that $|\mathbb{G}_1| = |\mathbb{G}_2| = |\mathbb{G}_T|$. A bilinear map is a map $e : \mathbb{G}_1 \times \mathbb{G}_2 \to \mathbb{G}_T$ that satisfies the following properties.

1. **Bilinearity.** For all $P \in \mathbb{G}_1, Q \in \mathbb{G}_2$ and $a, b \in \mathbb{Z}$, $e(aP, bQ) = e(P, Q)^{ab}$
2. **Non-degeneracy.** Let $Q$ be a generator of $\mathbb{G}_2$ and $\psi()$ an homomorphism from $\mathbb{G}_2$ to $\mathbb{G}_1$. Then $e(\psi(Q), Q) \neq 1$.

Additionally, we want the map $e$ to be efficiently computable. Such a bilinear map is called *admissible*. In the particular case where $\mathbb{G}_1 = \mathbb{G}_2$, the map is called *symmetric*. Examples of bilinear maps widely used in cryptography are the Weil pairing (as in [BF01]) and the Tate pairing.

### 2.2  Security Assumptions and Hard Problems

We base our security reductions on a few important definitions presented below.

**Definition 1. *Decision Diffie-Hellman Problem* (DDHP).** *Given a multiplicative group* $(\mathbb{G}, .)$, *and* $\alpha, \alpha^a, \alpha^b, \alpha^c \in \mathbb{G}$, *decide whether* $c = ab$.

**Definition 2. *Computational Diffie-Hellman Problem* (CDHP).** *Given a multiplicative group* $(\mathbb{G}, .)$, *and* $\alpha, \alpha^a, \alpha^b \in \mathbb{G}$, *compute* $X = \alpha^{ab}$.

**Definition 3. *q-Strong Diffie-Hellman Problem* (q-SDHP).** *Given multiplicative groups* $\mathbb{G}_1, \mathbb{G}_2$, *both with prime order* $p$, *and the* $(q+2)$-*tuple* $(P, Q, \alpha Q, \alpha^2 Q, \ldots, \alpha^q Q)$, *with* $P \in \mathbb{G}_1$ *and* $Q \in \mathbb{G}_2$, *compute the pair* $(c, \frac{1}{c+\alpha}P)$, *for* $c \in \mathbb{Z}_p^*$.

**Definition 4.** *Generalized Computational Diffie-Hellman Problem* **(GCDHP).** *Given a multiplicative group* $(\mathbb{G}, .)$, *and* $\alpha, \alpha^a, \alpha^b \in \mathbb{G}$, *compute* $(\alpha^{abc}, \alpha^c)$.

The GCDHP bears a relation to the Generalized Bilinear Diffie-Hellman Problem *(GBDHP)* used by Al-Riyami & Paterson [ARP03], similar to the one between the CDHP and the Bilinear Diffie-Hellman Problem [BF01]: the GCDHP is a strictly weaker security assumption than the GBDHP.

## 2.3 Certificateless Signature Schemes

The original definition of a CLS scheme was given by Al-Riyami and Paterson in [ARP03]. Since then, alternative formulations have been suggested [Den06]. We use the definition below, from [HWZD06]:

**Definition 5.** *A certificateless public-key signature* (CLS) *scheme consists of the following five polynomial-time algorithms:*

- **Setup.** Run by the KGC to initialize the system. Receives a security parameter $1^k$ and returns a list of system parameters **params** and the master secret key $msk$.
- **PartialKeyGen.** Takes as input **params**, $msk$, and the identity $ID \in \{0,1\}^*$ and outputs the partial private key $D_{ID}$, which is assumed to be sent to the correct user through a secure channel.
- **UserKeysGen.** Takes as input **params** and generates the user's public key $P_{ID}$ and corresponding private key, $S_{ID}$.
- **CL-Sign.** Takes as input **params**, the user's identity $ID$, the pair of secret keys $(D_{ID}, S_{ID})$ and a message $M$. Outputs a correct signature $\sigma$ on $M$.
- **CL-Verify.** Takes as input **params**, $ID$, $P_{ID}$, $M$ and the signature $\sigma$, and outputs ACCEPT if and only if $\sigma$ is a valid signature by user $U_{ID}$, under public key $P_{ID}$, on $M$.

This is a more concise definition that still captures all the features of the original model, as shown in [HWZD06].

## 2.4 Security of Certificateless Signatures

The standard definition of security, as introduced by [GMR88], is *existential unforgeability under adaptively chosen message attack*. Since there is no certification of public keys, in CLS we must always take two types of adversaries into consideration:

- **Type I.** An adversary $\mathcal{A}_I$ that can replace public keys at will, but has no access to the master key $s$.
- **Type II.** An adversary $\mathcal{A}_{II}$ that knows the master key $s$ but is not allowed to replace public keys.

The security of certificateless signatures is thus expressed by two similar games, respectively against $\mathcal{A}_I$ and $\mathcal{A}_{II}$. All our security analysis use the Random Oracle Model and the adversaries have access to the following operations:

- `CreateUser`, `RevealPartialKey`, `RevealSecretValue`, `RevealPublicKey`, `QueryHash`, `ReplacePublicKey`, `Sign`.

If the oracle is required to generate signatures under public keys that were replaced by the adversary (as in [ARP03]), it is called a `StrongSign` oracle. If this requirement is dropped, then we have a `WeakSign` oracle. It is our opinion that, even though a proof using a `StrongSign` oracle may be desirable, as it gives the adversary more power, efficiency should not be sacrificed in order to achieve it. The power an adversary gets from a `StrongSign` oracle has no analogous in a real-world situation.

We can now define the two following games, respectively, for $\mathcal{A}_I$ and $\mathcal{A}_{II}$;

**Definition 6. Game I.** *Let $\mathcal{C}_I$ be the challenger algorithm and $k$ be a security parameter:*

1. *$\mathcal{C}_I$ executes $Setup(1^k)$ and obtains params and the master secret $(msk)$;*
2. *$\mathcal{C}_I$ runs $\mathcal{A}_I$ on $1^k$ and params. During its run, $\mathcal{A}_I$ has access to the following oracles: RevealPublicKey, RevealPartialKey, RevealSecretValue, ReplacePublicKey, QueryHash, Sign;*
3. *$\mathcal{A}_I$ outputs $(ID^*, M^*, \sigma^*)$.*

$\mathcal{A}_I$ wins the game if `CL-Verify`$(params, ID^*, P_{ID^*}, M^*, \sigma^*)$=`ACCEPT` and both conditions below hold:

- `Sign`$(ID^*, M^*)$ was never queried;
- `RevealPartialKey`$(ID^*)$ was also never queried.

**Definition 7. Game II.** *Let $\mathcal{C}_{II}$ be the challenger algorithm and $k$ be a security parameter:*

1. *$\mathcal{C}_{II}$ executes $Setup(1^k)$ and obtains params and the master secret $(msk)$;*
2. *$\mathcal{C}_{II}$ runs $\mathcal{A}_{II}$ on $1^k$, params and msk. During its run, $\mathcal{A}_{II}$ has access to the following oracles: RevealPublicKey, RevealPartialKey, RevealSecretValue, ReplacePublicKey, QueryHash, Sign;*
3. *$\mathcal{A}_{II}$ outputs $(ID^*, M^*, \sigma^*)$.*

$\mathcal{A}_{II}$ wins the game if `CL-Verify`$(params, ID^*, P_{ID^*}, M^*, \sigma^*)$=`ACCEPT` and all conditions below hold:

- `Sign`$(ID^*, M^*)$ was never queried;
- `RevealSecretValue`$(ID^*)$ was never queried;
- `ReplacePublicKey`$(ID^*, .)$ was never queried.

For a longer discussion on CLS security models, we refer the reader to [HWZD07]. Throughout the rest of this paper we will mostly be concerned with Type-I adversaries because it is the attack model that is most peculiar to CLS and where most of the problems arise.

# 3    First Pitfall - A Problem with Security Models

In this section we identify a common misconception on the security model of certificateless schemes, one which usually leads to vulnerabilities in these schemes. We use the scheme from [Goy06] to make this claim concrete, presenting a sketch of the original security proof, pointing our objections, and then proposing an attack, to our knowledge the first attack on this scheme, that takes direct advantage of this misconception on the security model. We would like to point out that this misconception is found in many security proofs, such as the ones in [HSMZ05][YHG06] [DW07] [CPHL07], and is not specific to the scheme from [Goy06]. We merely use this latter scheme to make our presentation more concrete.

## 3.1    The Goya-Terada Certificateless Signature Scheme

This very efficient CLS scheme is based on the IBS scheme by Barreto et al. [BLMQ05] and needs only one pairing calculation for signature verification. The scheme is defined as below:

- **Setup**
    1. Generate $(\mathbb{G}_1, \mathbb{G}_2, \mathbb{G}_T, e)$ where $|\mathbb{G}_1| = |\mathbb{G}_2| = |\mathbb{G}_T| = p$ and $e : \mathbb{G}_1 \times \mathbb{G}_2 \to \mathbb{G}_T$ is an admissible pairing;
    2. choose generators $P \in \mathbb{G}_1$ and $Q \in \mathbb{G}_2$ such that $P = \psi(Q)$, where $\psi()$ is a homomorphism from $\mathbb{G}_2$ to $\mathbb{G}_1$;
    3. compute $g = e(P, Q)$;
    4. randomly select the `master-key` $s \xleftarrow{R} \mathbb{Z}_p^*$ and compute $Q_{pub} = sQ$;
    5. choose hash functions $H_1 : \{0,1\}^* \to \mathbb{Z}_p^*$ and $H_2 : \{0,1\}^* \times \{0,1\}^* \times \mathbb{G}_T \times \mathbb{G}_T \to \mathbb{Z}_p^*$.
- **PartialKeyGen.** Compute the partial key $D_A = \frac{1}{H_1(ID_A)+s}P$.
- **UserKeysGen.** Pick a random $t_A \in \mathbb{Z}_p^*$ and compute $N_A = g^{t_A}$. $N_A$ is the user's public key and $t_A$ is the user's secret key.
- **CL-Sign.** Pick a random $r \in \mathbb{Z}_p^*$; compute $U = g^r \in \mathbb{G}_T$; compute $h = H_2(M, ID_A, N_A, U) \in \mathbb{Z}_p^*$, and $S = (r + ht_A)D_A \in \mathbb{G}_1$. The signature is $\sigma = (S, h)$.
- **CL-Verify.** Compute $U' = e[S, H_1(ID_A)Q + Q_{pub}](N_A)^{-h}$; accept if and only if
$$h = H_2(M, ID_A, N_A, U').$$

## 3.2    Security Argument Against Type-I Adversaries

We present a sketch of the original proof[1] of security against Type-I adversaries. For gaps in our presentation, we refer the reader to Barreto et al.'s IBS paper [BLMQ05], whose security is closely related to Goya-Terada's.

---

[1] We base our presentation on the security reduction presented, in Portuguese, in the MSc. thesis of one of the authors. Their CLS scheme is also presented in [TGO], but with a different security reduction.

As in most proofs of security for CLS schemes, we assume an adversary $\mathcal{A}_I$ that can generate a forgery for a given ID, in an adaptively chosen-message attack. The main security lemma is

**Lemma 1.** *Let $\mathcal{A}_I$ be a Type-I Adversary that breaks Goya-Terada in time $T_1$ and with non-negligible probability $\epsilon_1$ under a given-ID attack. Let $q_S$ and $q_{H_1}$ be the maximum number of queries to, respectively, the* Sign *and* IdentityHash *oracles. Assume that $\epsilon_1 \geq (10(q_S + 1)(q_S + q_{H_1}))/2^k$. Then, the q-SDHP can be solved within running time $T_1' \leq (120686 q_{H_1} T_1)/(\epsilon_1(1 - \frac{1}{2^k}))$, where $k$ is a security parameter.*

We construct a challenger algorithm $\mathcal{C}_I$ that uses $\mathcal{A}_I$ to break the q-SDHP. The input to $\mathcal{C}_I$ is $(P, Q, \alpha Q, \alpha^2 Q, \ldots, \alpha^q Q)$ and it should output a pair $(c, \frac{1}{c+\alpha}P)$.

The system setup phase is identical to the one in the IBS scheme, obtaining $q-1$ pairs of the form $(w_i, \frac{1}{\alpha+w_i}P)$, and $Q_{pub} = \alpha Q$. $\mathcal{C}_I$ runs $\mathcal{A}_I$ with a randomly chosen $ID^*$ as target identity. Oracle queries are simulated in an intuitive way, using the computed pairs $(w_i, \frac{1}{\alpha+w_i}P)$ to answer ID-Hash and RevealPartialKey queries $(H_1(ID_i) = w_i, D_{ID_i} = \frac{1}{\alpha+w_i}P)$, unless $ID^*$ is queried, in which case a random answer $w^*$ different from the precomputed pairs is chsoen and $(H_1(ID^*) = w^*, D_{ID^*} = \perp)$.

If $\mathcal{C}_I$ does not abort during the simulation, $\mathcal{A}_I$ outputs a forgery $\gamma_1 = (S_1, h_1)$. The replay technique (Lemma 8) is used to obtain a second, related forgery $\gamma_2 = (S_2, h_2)$, such that:

$$e(S_1, Q_{ID^*})(N^*)^{-h_1} = e(S_2, Q_{ID^*})(N^*)^{-h_2},$$
$$e(S_1, Q_{ID^*})e(S_2, Q_{ID^*})^{-1} = (N^*)^{h_1}(N^*)^{-h_2},$$
$$e(S_1 - S_2, Q_{ID^*}) = e(P, Q)^{t^*(h_1 - h_2)},$$
$$e([t^*(h_1 - h_2)]^{-1}(S_1 - S_2), H_1(ID^*)Q + Q_{pub}) = e(P, Q),$$

and

$$Y = (h_1 - h_2)^{-1}(S_1 - S_2) = t^*(1/(\alpha + w^*))P,$$

which is *almost* the result we are looking for, were it not for the $t^*$ factor, absent from the proof in [BLMQ05]. This is the private key corresponding to the public key $N^*$ under which the signature was forged, which was potentially replaced by the adversary. Now, the authors of [Goy06] assume that the value $t^*$ can be recovered from the adversary; then, it is a simple matter of computing $t^{*-1}Y$, and proceeding with the technique from [BLMQ05] to finish the reduction. The whole structure of this security argument is very sound and compelling, except for this dangerous assumption.

### 3.3   An Attack on the Scheme

The gap in the security argument above directly leads to an attack on the scheme. An adversary can perform the following steps to forge signatures on arbitrary messages:

- Given the target identity $ID_A$:
  1. choose a random $t_A \in \mathbb{Z}_q^*$ and compute
  $$N_A = (e(P, Q_{pub})g^{H_1(ID_A)})^{t_A} = (g^s g^{H_1(ID_A)})^{t_A} = g^{t_A(s+H_1(ID_A))};$$
  2. replace $ID_A$'s public key with $N_A$.
- Now, to a sign message $M$:
  1. choose a random $r \in \mathbb{Z}_q^*$ and compute $U = N_A^r$;
  2. compute $h = H(M, ID_A, N_A, U)$;
  3. compute $S = (r + h)t_A P$;
  4. output the forgery $\gamma = (S, h)$.

So, $\gamma$ is a valid forgery on message $M$ because it is accepted by the verification procedure:

$$
\begin{aligned}
U' &= e[S, H_1(ID_A)Q + Q_{pub}](N_A)^{-h} \\
&= e[(r+h)t_A P, (H_1(ID_A) + s)Q]g^{t_A(H_1(ID_A)+s)(-h)} \\
&= g^{(r+h)t_A(H_1(ID_A)+s)}g^{-ht_A(H_1(ID_A)+s)} \\
&= g^{rt_A(H_1(ID)+s)} \\
&= U.
\end{aligned}
$$

Therefore, $h = H_2(M, ID_A, N_A, U')$.

Notice that the adversary performing this attack is unable to compute a "correct" private key corresponding to the public key he published. Therefore, the assumption that one can recover the private key's value from the adversary is an unreal requirement that has, nonetheless, been used in other security proofs of CLS schemes such as [HSMZ05] [YHG06] [DW07] [CPHL07]. We do not claim that all these are insecure[2], we merely claim that their security results should not be trusted as is.

## 4    Second Pitfall - On the Use of the Oracle Replay Technique

In this section we discuss the use of the oracle replay technique on CLS schemes. This proof technique is mainly based on a result from [PS00] that is widely known as the *Forking Lemma*:

**Definition 8.** *Forking Lemma. Let $S$ be a generic signature scheme. Let $A$ be a probabilistic polynomial-time Turing machine, with only public data as input. Let $Q$ and $R$ be, respectively, the number of queries made by $A$ to the random oracle and to $S$'s signing oracle. Assume that, within a time bound $\tau$, $A$ produces, with probability $\epsilon \geq \frac{10(R+1)(R+Q)}{2^k}$, a valid signature $(m, U, h, V)$. If the triples $(U, h, V)$ can be simulated without knowing the secret key, with an indistinguishable distribution probability, then there is another machine which has control*

---

[2] In fact, later on we prove the security of (a slight modification of) the scheme from [HSMZ05].

*over the machine obtained from $\mathcal{A}$ replacing interaction with the signer by simulation, and which produces two valid signatures $(m, U, h, V)$ and $(m, U, h', V')$ such that $h \neq h'$, within time $\tau' \leq \frac{120686QT}{\epsilon}$.*

This definition is based on the notion of a *generic* signature scheme, against which the adversary $\mathcal{A}$ generates a forgery. Generic signature schemes are defined as follows:

**Definition 9.** *A signature scheme $\mathcal{S}$ is said to be generic if, given the input message $M$, it produces triples $(\sigma_1, h, \sigma_2)$, where:*

1. *$\sigma_1$ takes its value randomly within a large set;*
2. *$h$ is the hash value of $m$, $\sigma_1$;*
3. *$\sigma_2$ depends only on $\sigma_1$, $m$ and $h$.*

Well-known examples of generic signature schemes are Schnorr [Sch91], and signature schemes derived from the Fiat-Shamir heuristic [FS87]. The problem lies in directly applying the Forking Lemma to CLS schemes. Clearly, the possibility of key replacement is not covered by the original model and is an exploitable vulnerability. Nevertheless, many CLS schemes, such as [YHG06] [HSMZ05] [Goy06], use the replay technique to prove their security, without explicitly justifying its use in their particular context.

### 4.1   Forking Lemma and CLS

In order to define a certificateless version of the Forking Lemma, we first have to define what is the certificateless equivalent of a generic signature scheme:

**Definition 10.** *CL-Generic Signature Schemes. A certificateless signature scheme $\mathcal{S}$ is said to be CL-generic if, given the input message $M$, it produces triples $(\sigma_1, h, \sigma_2)$, where:*

1. *$\sigma_1$ takes its value randomly within a large set;*
2. *$h$ is the hash value of at least $m$, $\sigma_1$ and the user's public key $P_{ID}$;*
3. *$\sigma_2$ depends only on $\sigma_1$, $m$ and $h$.*

Note that, $h$ or $\sigma_1$ could eventually be omitted, if they can be correctly recovered from the other two components. The schemes from [HSMZ05] and [Goy06] are CL-generic, while the ones from [ARP03], [YHG06] are not. Notably, the latter scheme had a security proof which used the replay technique, but was, nevertheless, broken in [ZF06].

The reasoning behind this definition is the fact that, by making the message-hash depend on the public key, we thwart any attempt by the adversary of first "guessing" a signature and then computing a public key that will make the verification process accept that signature.

A little more formally, we note that a typical (greatly simplified) successful execution of the replay technique goes as follows:

1. The forger $\mathcal{F}$ is run, making various oracle queries, and outputs a forgery $\gamma = \langle m, \sigma_1, h, \sigma_2 \rangle$;
2. then $\mathcal{F}$ is run again, with the same random tape, receiving the same answer to all oracle queries up to the point when it queries $H(m, \sigma_1)$: that is when the execution is "forked" and a different oracle answer $h'$ is given;
3. $\mathcal{F}$ outputs a forgery $\gamma' = \langle m, \sigma_1', h', \sigma_2' \rangle$.

Note that the value of $\sigma_1$ in both executions must be the same, as $\mathcal{F}$ is run with the same random tape. If the fork is successful, the two related forgeries $\gamma$ and $\gamma'$ are such that $\sigma_1 = \sigma_1'$ but $\sigma_2 \neq \sigma_2'$.

By guaranteeing that the public key is in that hash query, we can be sure that any public-key replacements have already taken place at that moment, and that $P_{ID^*} = P_{ID^*}'$.

This somewhat informal argument supports our claim that the Forking Lemma is also valid for CL-generic signature schemes: a formal proof of this fact would be almost identical to the original proof in [PS00].

The next section brings an example of the use of this definition.

## 4.2   Al-Riyami and Paterson's CLS Scheme

In [ARP03], Al-Riyami and Paterson proposed the first CLS scheme. They did not provide any security proof for this scheme and, in fact, it was later [HSMZ05] proved insecure. We analyze the corrections proposed to this scheme and put forth a new, more efficient, version of the scheme.

Let us begin by presenting the original scheme:

**The Scheme**

- **Setup.**
    1. Choose two groups $\mathbb{G}_1$ and $\mathbb{G}_2$ of prime order $p$, an admissible pairing $e : \mathbb{G}_1 \times \mathbb{G}_1 \to \mathbb{G}_2$ and a generator $P \in \mathbb{G}_1$;
    2. randomly select the master secret $s \in \mathbb{Z}_p^*$ and set $P_{pub} = sP$;
    3. select hash functions $H_1 : \{0,1\}^* \to \mathbb{G}_1^*$ and $H_2 : \{0,1\}^* \times \mathbb{G}_2 \to \mathbb{Z}_p^*$;
    4. params is $\langle \mathbb{G}_1, \mathbb{G}_2, e, P, P_{pub}, H_1, H_2 \rangle$.
- **PartialKeyGen.**
    1. Compute $Q_A = H(ID_A) \in \mathbb{G}_1^*$;
    2. output the partial private key $D_A = sQ_A \in \mathbb{G}_1^*$.
- **UserKeysGen.**
    1. Randomly select $t_A \in \mathbb{Z}_p^*$;
    2. compute the public key $N_A = \langle X_A, Y_A \rangle$, where $X_A = t_A P$ and $Y_A = t_A P_{pub} = t_A sP$.
- **CL-Sign.**
    1. Randomly choose $r \in \mathbb{Z}_p^*$ and compute $u = e(rP, P) \in \mathbb{G}_2$;
    2. set $h = H_2(M, u) \in \mathbb{Z}_q^*$;
    3. compute $S = ht_A D_A + rP \in \mathbb{G}_1$;
    4. output the signature $\sigma = \langle S, h \rangle$.
- **CL-Verify.**
    1. Check if $e(X_A, P_{pub}) = e(Y_A, P)$. Else, abort and return reject;
    2. compute $u' = e(S, P)e(Q_A, -Y_A)^h$;
    3. if $h = H_2(M, u')$ return accept. Else, return reject.

**Security Problems.** In the original paper, no proof of security was given for this scheme. We could easily devise a security argument using the oracle replay technique, but since this scheme is not CL-generic, it would be invalid. In [HSMZ05] a vulnerability against Type-I adversaries is shown. The proposed attack exploits the fact that, even though the validity of the public key is checked in step 1 of the verification procedure, there is no real assurance that the secret value $t_A$ was indeed used in the computation of $S$. This allows a Type-I attacker to guess a random "signature" and then compute the proper public key that will make it valid. The attack proceeds as follows:

1. Select a random $S \in \mathbb{G}_1$;
2. compute $u' = e(S, P)(Q_A, -P_{pub})$;
3. compute $h = H_2(M, u')$;
4. let $t_A = h^{-1} \pmod{q}$;
5. compute $X_A = t_A P$ and $Y_A = t_A P_{pub}$;
6. replace the user's public key with $N_A = \langle X_A, Y_A \rangle$;
7. output $\sigma = \langle S, h \rangle$ as $A$'s signature on $M$.

This signature is clearly accepted by the verification procedure, as $N_A$ is a valid public key, and

$$e(S, P)(Q_A, -Y_A)^h = e(S, P)e(Q_A, -h^{-1}P_{pub})^h = e(S, P)e(Q_A, -P_{pub}) = u'.$$

**Making It Secure.** With the above attack in mind, again in [HSMZ05], the authors proposed a new version of the Al-Riyami/Paterson scheme that is secure against Type-I adversaries. They argue that hashing the value $e(t_A D_A, P)$ together with the message is enough to prevent Type-I attacks, and they give a full security proof of this claim (using the replay technique). We make two observations concerning this correction:

1. even though no justification was given for the use of the Forking Lemma in this context, we claim that it is valid because this version of the scheme is CL-generic;
2. thus, hashing the public key $N_A$ with the message is as secure as hashing $e(t_A D_A, P)$ (while avoiding a pairing computation).

These observations lead to the following **CL-Sign** and **CL-Verify** procedures:

- **CL-Sign.**
    1. Randomly choose $r \in \mathbb{Z}_p^*$ and compute $u = e(rP, P) \in \mathbb{G}_2$;
    2. Set $\boxed{h = H_2(M, u, N_A) \in \mathbb{Z}_p^*}$;
    3. Compute $S = ht_A D_A + rP \in \mathbb{G}_1$;
    4. Output the signature $\sigma = \langle S, h \rangle$.
- **CL-Verify.**
    1. Check if $e(X_A, P_{pub}) = e(Y_A, P)$. Else, abort and return reject;
    2. Compute $u' = e(S, P)e(Q_A, -Y_A)^h$;
    3. If $\boxed{h = H_2(M, u', N_A)}$ return accept. Else, return reject.

We claim this is enough to thwart Type-I attacks. Intuitively, the same argument given in [HSMZ05] is valid: since the public key is used in the computation of $h$, the adversary cannot compute it *after* choosing $S$, $r$ and $h$. More precisely, the fact that this scheme is now CL-generic allows us to build a proof based on the oracle replay technique. The complete proof (analogous to the one in [HSMZ05]) is given in the appendix.

**Lemma 2.** *Let $\mathcal{A}_I$ be a Type-I Adversary that breaks our scheme in time $T_1$ and with non-negligible probability $\epsilon_1$ under a given-ID attack. Let $q_S$ and $q_{H_2}$ be the maximum number of queries to, respectively, the* $\mathtt{Sign}$ *and* $\mathtt{IdentityHash}$ *oracles. Assume that $\epsilon_1 \geq (10(q_S + 1)(q_S + q_{H_2}))/2^k$. Then, the GCDHP can be solved within running time $T_1' \leq (120686 q_{H_1} T_1)/(\epsilon_1(1 - \frac{1}{2^k}))$, where $k$ is a security parameter.*

*Proof.* In the appendix.

Since both schemes from [ARP03] and [HSMZ05] are secure against Type-II attacks, it is intuitive that our scheme is too. In fact, the proof given in [HSMZ05] is easily adaptable to our scheme, as shown in the appendix.

**Lemma 3.** *Let $\mathcal{A}_{II}$ be a Type-II Adversary that breaks our scheme in time $T_2$ and with non-negligible probability $\epsilon_2$ under a given-ID attack. Let $q_S$ and $q_{H_2}$ be the maximum number of queries to, respectively, the* $\mathtt{Sign}$ *and* $\mathtt{IdentityHash}$ *oracles. Assume that $\epsilon_2 \geq (10(q_S + 1)(q_S + q_{H_2}))/2^k$. Then, the CDHP can be solved within running time $T_2' \leq (120686 q_{H_2} T_2)/(\epsilon_2(1 - \frac{1}{2^k}))$, where $k$ is a security parameter.*

*Proof.* In the appendix.

This leads us to our main security claim.

**Theorem 1.** *Our scheme is unforgeable in the random oracle model if both the GBDHP and the CDHP are hard in $\mathbb{G}_1$.*

*Proof.* In the appendix.

**A Related CLS Scheme.** In [LCS05] a CLS scheme is presented but no security proof is given. It has many similarities with the original Al-Riyami/Paterson, such as not being CL-generic and having a public-key sanity check ($e(X_A, P_{pub}) \overset{?}{=} e(Y_A, P)$) in the signature verification procedure. However, no attack has been shown on this scheme. We make no claims regarding the security of the scheme as is, but we claim that if the scheme is turned into CL-generic (by placing the public-key in the message hash), a proof of security analogous to the above can be easily devised.

## 5   A Summary of CL-Signature Schemes

In table 1 we present all (as far as our knowledge goes) certificateless signature schemes proposed in the literature. We express the cost of each protocol by the

**Table 1.** Rough performance comparison of certificateless signature schemes

| Scheme | Signing Cost | Verification Cost | Status |
|---|---|---|---|
| Al-Riyami & Paterson [ARP03] | 1 | 4 | *Broken* |
| Al-Riyami & Paterson 2 [HSMZ05] | 2 | 5 | **OK** |
| Al-Riyami & Paterson 3 (Our Version) | 1 | 4 | **OK** |
| Gorantla & Saxena [GS05] | 0 | 2 | *Broken* |
| Li, Chen & Sun [LCS05] | 0 | 4 | **OK** [3] |
| Yap, Heng & Goi [YHG06] | 0 | 2 | *Broken* |
| Zhang et al. [ZWXF06] | 0 | 4 | **OK** |
| Goya & Terada [Goy06] | 0 | 1 | *Broken* |
| Liu, Au & Susilo [LAS06] [4] | 0 | 6 | **OK** |
| Du & Wen [DW07] | 0 | 1 | *Unknown*[5] |
| Choi et al. - 1 [CPHL07] | 0 | 1 | *Unknown*[5] |
| Choi et al. - 2 [CPHL07] | 0 | 2 | *Unknown*[5] |

number of pairing computations that must be done in the signing and verification procedures. Note that this performance comparison is very rough, as we do not take into account less costly but still not negligible operations such as hashing to points on the curve or multiplying the results of pairings. In addition to the schemes in table 1, the security mediated scheme from [YCHG07] can also be transformed into an efficient CLS that does not depend on pairings.

# 6  Conclusion

In this paper we analyzed two common inaccuracies found in several security proofs of certificateless signature (CLS) schemes. We exploited one of these inaccuracies, namely the assumption that an adversary is able to compute a private key matching a replaced public key, to show that the scheme from [Goy06] is insecure against Type-I adversaries.

The second inaccuracy refers to the use of the Forking Lemma in security proofs of CLS schemes. By redefining the scope of application of the Forking Lemma in the CL realm, we produced new, provably secure, versions of the schemes in [ARP03] and [LCS05]. Also, we were able to clarify the reasons for which the scheme in [YHG06] was broken, while having been previously proved secure.

# Acknowledgements

We would like to thank the anonymous referees for many constructive suggestions on this text.

---

[3] This scheme can be proven secure by using the results in this paper.

[4] This is the only CLS scheme proven secure in the Standard Model, suffering from the performance penalties that usually accompany such schemes.

[5] These recently proposed schemes have security proofs with the misconception discussed in section 3. So, even though no attack has been proposed on them, we consider their security unknown as of yet.

# References

[ARP03]    Sattam, S.: Al-Riyami and Kenneth G. Paterson. Certificateless public key
           cryptography. In: Laih, C.-S. (ed.) ASIACRYPT 2003. LNCS, vol. 2894,
           pp. 452–473. Springer, Heidelberg (2003)
[BF01]     Boneh, D., Franklin, M.K.: Dan Boneh and Matthew K. Franklin. Identity-
           based encryption from the Weil pairing. In: Kilian, J. (ed.) CRYPTO 2001.
           LNCS, vol. 2139, pp. 213–229. Springer, Heidelberg (2001)
[BLMQ05]   Barreto, P.S.L.M., Libert, B., McCullagh, N., Quisquater, J.-J.: Efficient
           and provably-secure identity-based signatures and signcryption from bi-
           linear maps. In: Roy, B. (ed.) ASIACRYPT 2005. LNCS, vol. 3788, pp.
           515–532. Springer, Heidelberg (2005)
[CC03]     Cha, J.C., Cheon, J.H.: An identity-based signature from gap diffie-
           hellman groups. In: Desmedt, Y.G. (ed.) PKC 2003. LNCS, vol. 2567,
           pp. 18–30. Springer, Heidelberg (2002)
[CPHL07]   Choi, K.Y., Park, J.H., Hwang, J.Y., Lee, D.H.: Efficient certificateless
           signature schemes. In: Katz, Yung: [KY07], pages 443–458.
[Den06]    Dent, W.A.: A survey of certificateless encryption schemes and security
           models. Cryptology ePrint Archive, Report 2006/211 (2006)
[DW07]     Du, H., Wen, Q.: Efficient and provably-secure certificateless short sig-
           nature scheme from bilinear pairings. Cryptology ePrint Archive, Report
           2007/250 (2007), http://eprint.iacr.org/
[FS87]     Fiat, A., Shamir, A.: How to prove yourself: Practical solutions to identi-
           fication and signature problems. In: Odlyzko, A.M. (ed.) CRYPTO 1986.
           LNCS, vol. 263, pp. 186–194. Springer, Heidelberg (1987)
[GMR88]    Goldwasser, S., Micali, S., Rivest, R.L.: A digital signature scheme se-
           cure against adaptive chosen-message attacks. SIAM Journal on Comput-
           ing 17(2), 281–308 (1988)
[Goy06]    Goya, G.H.: Proposta de esquemas de criptografia e de assinatura sob
           modelo de criptografia de cha pública sem certificado. Master's thesis,
           USP (2006)
[GS05]     Gorantla, M.C., Saxena, A.: An efficient certificateless signature scheme.
           In: Hao, Y., Liu, J., Wang, Y.-P., Cheung, Y.-m., Yin, H., Jiao, L., Ma,
           J., Jiao, Y.-C. (eds.) CIS 2005. LNCS (LNAI), vol. 3802, pp. 110–116.
           Springer, Heidelberg (2005)
[HSMZ05]   Huang, X., Susilo, W., Mu, Y., Zhang, F.: On the security of certificateless
           signature schemes from asiacrypt 2003. In: Desmedt, Y., Wang, H., Mu, Y.,
           Li, Y. (eds.) CANS 2005. LNCS, vol. 3810, pp. 13–25. Springer, Heidelberg
           (2005)
[HWZD06]   Hu, B.C., Wong, D.S., Zhang, Z., Deng, X.: Key replacement attack
           against a generic construction of certificateless signature. In: Batten,
           L.M., Safavi-Naini, R. (eds.) ACISP 2006. LNCS, vol. 4058, pp. 235–246.
           Springer, Heidelberg (2006)
[HWZD07]   Hu, B.C., Wong, D.S., Zhang, Z., Deng, X.: Certificateless signature: a
           new security model and an improved generic construction. Des. Codes
           Cryptography 42(2), 109–126 (2007)
[KY07]     Katz, J., Yung, M.: Applied Cryptography and Network Security. In:
           ACNS 2007. Proceedings 5th International Conference, Zhuhai, China,
           June 5-8, 2007. LNCS, vol. 4521, Springer, Heidelberg (2007)

[LAS06]    Liu, J.K., Au, M.H., Susilo, W.: Self-generated-certificate public key cryptography and certificateless signature / encryption scheme in the standard model. Cryptology ePrint Archive, Report, /373, 2006. (2006), http://eprint.iacr.org/

[LCS05]    Li, X., Chen, K., Sun, L.: Certificateless signature and proxy signature schemes from bilinear pairings. Lithuanian Mathematical Journal 45(1), 76–83 (2005)

[PS00]    Pointcheval, D., Stern, J.: Security arguments for digital signatures and blind signatures. Journal of Cryptology: the journal of the International Association for Cryptologic Research 13(3), 361–396 (2000)

[Sch91]    Schnorr, C.P.: Efficient signature generation for smart cards. Journal of Cryptology 4(3), 239–252 (1991)

[Sha85]    Shamir, A.: Identity-based cryptosystems and signature schemes. In: Blakely, G.R., Chaum, D. (eds.) CRYPTO 1984. LNCS, vol. 196, pp. 47–53. Springer, Heidelberg (1985)

[TGO]    Terada, R., Goya, D.H., Okamoto, E.: A certificateless signature scheme based on bilinear pairing functions. In: SCIS 2007. Symposium on Cryptography and Information Security, Japan (2007)

[YCHG07]    Yap, W.-S., Chow, S.S.M., Heng, S.-H., Goi, B.-M.: Security mediated certificateless signatures. In: Katz, Yung (eds.) [KY 07], pp. 459–477 (2007)

[YHG06]    Yap, W.-S., Heng, S.-H., Goi, B.-M.: An efficient certificateless signature scheme. In: Zhou, X., Sokolsky, O., Yan, L., Jung, E.-S., Shao, Z., Mu, Y., Lee, D.C., Kim, D., Jeong, Y.-S., Xu, C.-Z. (eds.) Emerging Directions in Embedded and Ubiquitous Computing. LNCS, vol. 4097, pp. 322–331. Springer, Heidelberg (2006)

[ZF06]    Zhang, Z., Feng, D.: Key replacement attack on a certificateless signature scheme. Cryptology ePrint Archive, Report 2006/453 (2006), http://eprint.iacr.org/

[ZWXF06]    Zhang, Z., Wong, D.S., Xu, J., Feng, D.: Certificateless public-key signature: Security model and efficient construction. In: Zhou, J., Yung, M., Bao, F. (eds.) ACNS 2006. LNCS, vol. 3989, pp. 293–308. Springer, Heidelberg (2006)

# A    Proof of Security of Al-Riyami/Paterson-3

Notice that the proofs presented are closely related to the proofs in [HSMZ05]. The biggest difference is that we do not assume we can recover the secret key from the adversary in Type-I attacks, following the recommendations from Section 3. First, we prove two lemmas concerning the security of the schemes under a *Given-ID* attack. Then, we can use the lemma from [CC03] to reduce Chosen-ID security to Given-ID security, thus proving the full security of the scheme.

**Lemma 2.** *Let $\mathcal{A}_I$ be a Type-I Adversary that breaks our scheme in time $T_1$ and with non-negligible probability $\epsilon_1$. Let $q_S$ and $q_{H_2}$ be the maximum number of queries to, respectively, the* Sign *and* IdentityHash *oracles. Assume that $\epsilon_1 \geq (10(q_S+1)(q_S+q_{H_2}))/2^k$. Then, the GCDHP can be solved within running time $T_1' \leq (120686 q_{H_2} T_1)/(\epsilon_1(1 - \frac{1}{2^k}))$, where $k$ is a security parameter.*

*Proof.* We construct a challenger algorithm $\mathcal{C}_I$ that, on input $(P, aP, bP) \in \mathbb{G}_1^3$, uses $\mathcal{A}_I$ to solve the GCDHP. On the setup phase, $\mathcal{C}_I$ sets $P$ as the generator of the group and sets $P_{pub} \leftarrow aP$. $\mathcal{C}_I$ then randomly chooses the target identity $ID^*$ and runs $\mathcal{A}_I$, answering oracle queries as follows:

**ID-Hash Query$[H_1(ID_i)]$.**
1. Test whether $ID_i = ID^*$:
    - if $ID_i = ID^*$ then $Q_i = H_1(ID_i) = bP$, and $y_i = \perp$;
    - else, generate a random $y_i$ and make $Q_i = H_1(ID_i) = y_i P$.
2. make $P_i = x_i = \perp$ and save the tuple $(ID_i, Q_i, P_i, y_i, x_i)$;
3. finally, return $Q_i$.

**Partial Key Extraction$(ID_i)$.**
1. Find the tuple $(ID_i, Q_i, P_i, y_i, x_i)$;
    - if it does not exist, or $y_i = \perp$, then $\mathcal{C}_I$ aborts.
2. otherwise answer with $D_{ID_i} = y_i P_{pub} = y_i(aP)$.
Note that $\mathcal{A}_I$ is not allowed to request the partial key for $ID^*$.

**Secret Value Extraction$(ID_i)$.**
1. Find the tuple $(ID_i, Q_i, P_i, y_i, x_i)$;
    - if it does not exist, then $\mathcal{C}_I$ aborts.
2. if the public key has been replaced, then $\mathcal{C}_I$ aborts;
3. if $x_i = \perp$ (no secret value has been created yet), pick $x_i \xleftarrow{R} \mathbb{Z}_p$;
4. return $x_i$.

**Public Key Extraction$(ID_i)$.**
1. Find the tuple $(ID_i, Q_i, P_i, y_i, x_i)$;
    - if it does not exist, $y_i = \perp$ or $P_{ID_i}$ has been replaced, abort.
2. if $x_i = \perp$, execute `Secret Value Extraction` to generate a secret value;
3. answer with $P_{ID_i} = \langle x_i P, x_i P_{pub} \rangle$.

**Public Key Replacement$(ID_i, P_i')$.**
1. Find the tuple $(ID_i, Q_i, P_i, x_i)$;
    - if it does not exist, $\mathcal{C}_I$ aborts.
2. otherwise $\mathcal{C}_I$ sets $x_i = \perp$ and $P_i = P_i'$.

**Message-Hash Query$[H_2(M_j, R_j, P_{ID_j})]$.**
1. If $H_2(M_j, R_j, P_{ID_j})$ is not yet defined:
    - pick $h_j \xleftarrow{R} \mathbb{Z}_p$
    - set $H_2(M_j, R_j, P_{ID_j}) = h_j$.
2. Return $H_2(M_j, R_j, P_{ID_j})$.

**Sign Query$(ID_i, M_j)$.**
1. Find the tuple $(ID_i, Q_i, \langle X_i, Y_i \rangle, y_i)$;
    - If it does not exist, $\mathcal{C}_I$ aborts.
2. pick $S_i \xleftarrow{R} \mathbb{G}_1$ and $h_j \xleftarrow{R} \mathbb{Z}_q^*$;

3. compute $R_i = e(S_i, P)e(H_1(ID_i), -Y_i)^{h_j}$
4. if $H_2(M_j, R_t, Y_i)$ is defined, abort; else, set $H_2(M_j, R_t, Y_i) = h_j$;
5. return the signature $\sigma = (S_i, h_j)$.

Notice that the secret value of the user is not used by the Sign oracle, making it a StrongSign oracle.

If $C_I$ does not abort, $A_I$ will output a valid forgery $\gamma = \langle ID^*, m, S, h \rangle$ with probability $\epsilon_1$. The probability of $C_I$ aborting is $\frac{1}{2^k}$. Using the oracle replay technique we obtain two valid signatures $\sigma_1 = \langle ID^*, m, S_1, h_1 \rangle$ and $\sigma_2 = \langle ID^*, m, S_2, h_2 \rangle$ within time $T_1' \leq \frac{120686 q_{H_1} T_1}{\epsilon_1(1-\frac{1}{2^k})}$. Since they are both valid for the same value of $U$, we have that

$$U = e(S_1, P)e(H_1(ID^*), -Y^*)^{h_1} = e(S_2, P)e(H_1(ID^*), -Y^*)^{h_2}$$
$$e(S_1, P)e(bP, -x^* aP)^{h_1} = e(S_2, P)e(bP, -x^* aP)^{h_2}$$
$$e(S_1 - S_2, P) = e(bP, -x^* aP)^{h_2 - h_1}$$
$$e(S_1 - S_2, P) = e(-(h_2 - h_1)x^* abP, P)$$

Let $W = (h_2 - h_1)(S_1 - S_2) = x^* abP$. Remembering that $X_i = x^* P$, we have that $(X_i, W)$ is a valid answer for our GCDHP instance. □

**Lemma 3.** *Let $A_{II}$ be a Type-II Adversary that breaks our scheme in time $T_2$ and with non-negligible probability $\epsilon_2$. Let $q_S$ and $q_{H_2}$ be the maximum number of queries to, respectively, the Sign and IdentityHash oracles. Assume that $\epsilon_2 \geq (10(q_S + 1)(q_S + q_{H_2}))/2^k$. Then, the CDHP can be solved within running time $T_2' \leq (120686 q_{H_2} T_2)/(\epsilon_2(1 - \frac{1}{2^k}))$, where $k$ is a security parameter.*

*Proof.* We construct a challenger algorithm $C_{II}$ that, on input $(P, aP, bP) \in \mathbb{G}_1^3$, uses $A_{II}$ to solve the CDHP. On the setup phase, $C_{II}$ sets $P$ as the generator of the group and chooses $s \xleftarrow{R} \mathbb{Z}_p^*$, setting $P_{pub} \leftarrow sP$. $C_{II}$ then randomly chooses the target identity $ID^*$ and runs $A_{II}$, answering oracle queries as follows:

**ID-Hash Query$[H_1(ID_i)]$.**
1. Test whether $ID_i = ID^*$:
   - if $ID_i = ID^*$ then $Q_i = H_1(ID_i) = aP$, and $y_i = \bot$;
   - else, generate a random $y_i$ and make $Q_i = H_1(ID_i) = y_i P$.
2. make $P_i = x_i = \bot$ and save the tuple $(ID_i, Q_i, P_i, y_i, x_i)$;
3. finally, return $Q_i$.

**Partial Key Extraction$(ID_i)$.**
1. Find the tuple $(ID_i, Q_i, P_i, y_i, x_i)$;
   - if it does not exist, or $y_i = \bot$, then $C_{II}$ aborts.
2. otherwise answer with $D_{ID_i} = sQ_i$.
Note that $A_{II}$ is able to compute these by himself.

**Secret Value Extraction$(ID_i)$.**
1. If $ID_i = ID^*$, then $C_{II}$ aborts.
2. find the tuple $(ID_i, Q_i, P_i, y_i, x_i)$;
   - if it does not exist, then $C_{II}$ aborts.

3. if the public key has been replaced, then $\mathcal{C}_{II}$ aborts;
4. if $x_i = \bot$ (no secret value has been created yet), pick $x_i \xleftarrow{R} \mathbb{Z}_p$;
5. return $x_i$.

**Public Key Extraction($ID_i$).**
1. Find the tuple $(ID_i, Q_i, P_i, y_i, x_i)$;
    - if it does not exist, $y_i = \bot$ or $P_{ID_i}$ has been replaced, abort.
2. if $ID_i = ID^*$, then
    - return $P_{ID_i} = \langle bP, s(bP) \rangle$
3. Else, if $x_i = \bot$, execute **Secret Value Extraction** to generate a secret value;
4. return $P_{ID_i} = \langle x_i P, x_i P_{pub} \rangle$.

**Public Key Replacement($ID_i$,$P_i'$).**
1. If $ID_i = ID^*$, $\mathcal{C}_{II}$ aborts.
2. Find the tuple $(ID_i, Q_i, P_i, x_i)$;
    - if it does not exist, $\mathcal{C}_{II}$ aborts.
3. otherwise $\mathcal{C}_{II}$ sets $x_i = \bot$ and $P_i = P_i'$.

**Message-Hash Query[$H_2(M_j,R_j,P_{ID_j})$].**
1. If $H_2(M_j, R_j, P_{ID_j})$ is not yet defined:
    - pick $h_j \xleftarrow{R} \mathbb{Z}_p^*$
    - set $H_2(M_j, R_j, P_{ID_j}) = h_j$.
2. Return $H_2(M_j, R_j, P_{ID_j})$.

**Sign Query($ID_i$,$M_j$).**
1. Find the tuple $(ID_i, Q_i, \langle X_i, Y_i \rangle, y_i)$;
    - If it does not exist, $\mathcal{C}_{II}$ aborts.
2. pick $S_j \xleftarrow{R} \mathbb{G}_1$ and $h_j \xleftarrow{R} \mathbb{Z}_p^*$;
3. compute $R_j = e(S_j, P)e(H_1(ID_i), -Y_i)^{h_j}$
4. if $H_2(M_j, R_j, Y_i)$ is defined, abort; else, set $H_2(M_j, R_j, Y_i) = h_j$;
5. return the signature $\sigma = (S_j, h_j)$.

Note that the secret value of the user is not used by the **Sign** oracle, making it a **StrongSign** oracle. If $\mathcal{C}_{II}$ does not abort, $\mathcal{A}_{II}$ will output a valid forgery $\gamma = \langle ID^*, m, S, h \rangle$ with probability $\epsilon_2$. The probability of $\mathcal{C}_{II}$ aborting is $\frac{1}{2^k}$. Using the oracle replay technique we obtain two valid signatures $\sigma_1 = \langle ID^*, m, S_1, h_1 \rangle$ and $\sigma_2 = \langle ID^*, m, S_2, h_2 \rangle$ within time $T_2' \leq \frac{120686 q_{H_1} T_2}{\epsilon_2(1 - \frac{1}{2^k})}$. Since they are both valid (for the same value of $U$), we have that

$$U = e(S_1, P)e(H_1(ID^*), -Y^*)^{h_1} = e(S_2, P)e(H_1(ID^*), -Y^*)^{h_2}$$
$$e(S_1, P)e(aP, -s^*bP)^{h_1} = e(S_2, P)e(aP, -sbP)^{h_2}$$
$$e(S_1 - S_2, P) = e(aP, -sbP)^{h_2 - h_1}$$
$$e(S_1 - S_2, P) = e(-(h_2 - h_1)sabP, P)$$

Let $W = (h_2 - h_1)(S_1 - S_2)s^{-1} = abP$. Then $W$ is the answer of our CDHP instance.    □

From [CC03] we use the following lemma:

**Lemma 4 (CL-Version).** *Let $\mathcal{A}$ be an adversary that makes at most $q_H$ id-hash queries and $(T, \epsilon)$-breaks an CL-PKS scheme. Let $ID^*$ be a randomly chosen target ID.*

*There is an adversary $\mathcal{A}'$ that $(T', \epsilon')$-breaks the scheme for the identity $ID^*$ for*

$$T \leq T', \qquad \epsilon' \geq \frac{\epsilon(1 - \frac{1}{2^k})}{q_H}.$$

Theorem 4.2 is a corollary of lemmas 2, 3 and 4.

# A Provably Secure Ring Signature Scheme in Certificateless Cryptography⋆

Lei Zhang[1], Futai Zhang[1], and Wei Wu[2]

[1]College of Mathematics and Computer Science
Nanjing Normal University, P.R. China
[2]Centre for Computer and Information Security Research
School of Computer Science & Software Engineering
University of Wollongong, Australia
lei_zhangzl@126.com, zhangfutai@njnu.edu.cn,
weiwu81@gmail.com

**Abstract.** Ring signature is a kind of group-oriented signature. It allows a member of a group to sign messages on behalf of the group without revealing his/her identity. Certificateless public key cryptography was first introduced by Al-Riyami and Paterson in Asiacrypt 2003. In certificateless cryptography, it does not require the use of certificates to guarantee the authenticity of users' public keys. Meanwhile, certificateless cryptography does not have the key escrow problem, which seems to be inherent in the Identity-based cryptography. In this paper, we introduce the notion of ring signature into certificateless public key cryptography and propose a concrete certificateless ring signature scheme. The security models of certificateless ring signature are also formalized. Our new scheme is provably secure in the random oracle model, with the assumption that the Computational Diffie-Hellman problem is hard.

**Keywords:** Ring Signature, Certificateless Cryptography, Provable Security, Random Oracle model.

## 1 Introduction

In Asiacrypt 2001, Rivest, Shamir and Tauman [26] introduced the concept of ring signature, which makes it possible to specify a set of possible signers without revealing which member actually produced the signature. As pointed in [26], ring signatures provide an elegant way to leak authoritative secrets in an anonymous way, to sign casual email in a special way that can only be verified by its intended recipient, anonymous membership authentication for ad hoc groups [6], etc. In addition, ring signatures can also be served as the building block of concurrent signatures and solve some other problems in multiparty computations.

Certificateless public key cryptography (CL-PKC) is a new paradigm proposed by Al-Riyami and Paterson [2]. It enjoys the implicit certification property of

---

⋆ Project supported by the nature science foundation of China (No. 60673070), the nature science foundation of Jiangsu province (No. BK2006217).

W. Susilo, J.K. Liu, and Y. Mu (Eds.): ProvSec 2007, LNCS 4784, pp. 103–121, 2007.

identity based public key cryptography (ID-PKC) [27] while without suffering from its inherent key escrow problem. Different from ID-PKC, a third party which we call Key Generation Center (KGC) in CL-PKC does not have access to a user's private key. Instead, the KGC supplies a user with a partial private key, which derives from the user's identity. Then the user combines the partial private key with some secret information chosen by himself to generate his actual private key. The corresponding public key is computed from the system's public parameters and the secret information chosen by the user, and is published by the user himself. Like ID-PKC, CL-PKC does not use public key certificates. The KGC does not access the full private key of a user, hence, certificateless cryptography does not suffer from the key escrow problem.

In this paper, we integrate the concept of ring signatures with certificateless cryptography to give the notion of certificateless ring signatures (CL-Ring), and investigate secure and efficient construction of CL-Ring schemes.

**Motivations.** Certificateless cryptography have some advantages over traditional PKC and ID-PKC in some aspects. As a useful primitive, ring signatures have been studied in traditional PKC and ID-PKC for more than five years. Even in a theoretic point of view, ring signatures should be studied in CL-PKC to rich the theories and techniques of CL-PKC. In practice, to generate a ring signature on behalf of a group in traditional PKC, the signer must first verify all the certificates of the group members, otherwise his anonymity is jeopardized and the ring signature will be rejected if he uses invalid certificates of some group members. Given a ring signature, the verifier must perform the same verification as well before checking the validity of the ring signature. These verifications inevitably lead to the inefficiency of the whole scheme since the computational cost increases linearly with the group size. Although Identity-based ring signatures eliminate such costly verifications, they suffer from a security drawback induced by the inherent key escrow problem of ID-PKC. Namely, a malicious PKG can always issue valid ring signatures on behalf of any group. As CL-PKC does not use public key certificates, and in the meantime, it removes the key escrow problem of ID-PKC, we think it supplies an appropriate environment for implementing ring signatures. So it is necessary to extend the notion and security model of ring signatures to CL-PKC. Compared with ring signature schemes in traditional PKC, in a CL-Ring scheme, both the signer and the verifier can avoid the costly verification of group members' certificates. On the other hand, in contrast to ID-based ring signatures, the KGC can no longer forge a ring signature on behalf of a group without being detected.

In application aspects, like ring signatures in traditional PKC and ID-PKC, certificateless ring signatures can also be used in leaking authoritative secrets in an anonymous way, anonymous membership authentication for ad hoc groups [6], reports to the authorities embezzlement and corruption, certificateless designated signatures and concurrent signatures, etc.

**Our Contributions.** In this paper, we introduce the notion of ring signature into certificateless cryptography and propose a concrete certificateless ring signature scheme.

Firstly, we provide the security models of certificateless ring signatures. Two types of adversaries: Type I adversary $\mathcal{A}_I$ and Type II adversary $\mathcal{A}_{II}$ are formally defined. The above two adversaries in our definition are "super adversaries" as defined in [19]. That is, the adversary can get valid ring signatures of the group whose public keys have been replaced, without supplying the secret values that are used to generate those public keys. In addition, our models also capture the group-changing attack [24] in the notion of ring signatures.

Next, we present a concrete construction of certificateless ring signatures. The new scheme uses the bilinear maps on elliptic curves. Its signing phase requires 2 pairings and its verification phase requires 3 pairings. We prove its security in the random oracle model, with the assumption that Computational Diffie-Hellman problem is intractable.

**Related Works.** Following the prior work of Rivest, Shamir and Tauman [26], a number of constructions of ring signature in traditional PKC and ID-PKC have been presented. Abe, Ohkubo, and Suzuki [1] provided a construction applicable for several categories of public keys (e.g., integer factoring based and discrete-log based). A simple ring signature using bilinear maps was given in [5]. Herranz and Saez [15] generalized the forking lemma to the ring signatures. In [31], Zhang and Kim extended the concept to Identity-Based ring signature (IDRS) schemes. Later Herranz and Saez [16], Chow et al. [9], Chow and D. Wong [12] presented some efficient IDRS schemes respectively. In [10] Chow el al. gave a solid and inspiring survey of Identity-Based ring signatures from a number of perspectives. Some ring signature schemes with constant-size were also presented in [13,25]. Threshold ring signatures were studied by Bresson et al. [6] and Wong et al. [28]. Other variations of basic ring signatures such as linkable ring signature [23], blind ring signatures [7] were also introduced.

In terms of security models for provably secure ring signature schemes, there are three models commonly used. They provide different security levels. The first and the weakest model was introduced by Rivest et al. [26]. Later Abe et al. [1] proposed a very strong model. Finally, Liu and Wong [24] presented a model whose security level is considered to be lying in between the two foregoing models. We mainly use the ideas of constructing IDRS schemes in [16], and the security models of ring signatures in [24] in this paper.

CL-PKC has got fruitful achievements since its introduction in [2]. Al-Riyami and Paterson presented [2] the first certificateless signature (CLS) scheme. Since then, several CLS schemes [14,18,20,21,29,30,32] were proposed. In [20], Huang et al. defined the security model of CLS schemes. Zhang et al. [32] improved the security model of CLS schemes, and presented a secure CLS scheme. Generic ways to construct CLS schemes were investigated in [30], [18]. In [21], a certificateless proxy signature scheme was proposed. A generic construction of CLE secure in the standard model was given in [8], while [22] gave a specific construction of CLE and the first CLS scheme secure in the standard model. These constructions and their security proofs gave us some inspiration to our present work on certificateless ring signature. Very recently, an independent work about certificateless ring signature was done by Chow and Yap [11]. The security of their scheme is based on the hardness of the $k$-CAA problem and Modified Inverse Computational Diffie-Hellman problem and is proved in a weak model that requires a type I adversary to submit the secret values corresponding to the replaced public keys to the challenger in the sign queries. The computional cost of their scheme involves a large amount of paring operations which linearly increase with the number of group members. So far as we know, there is no certificateless ring signature (CL-Ring) scheme whose security is based on some classical assumptions.

**Organization.** The rest of the paper is organized as follows. In the next section, we review some preliminaries which are required in this paper. Section 3 defines the security models in the notion of certificateless ring signatures. A concrete construction of certificateless ring signature is proposed in Section 4. Its security proofs are given in Section 5. Finally, Section 6 comes our conclusion.

## 2 Preliminaries

In this section, we will review some fundamental backgrounds required in this paper.

### 2.1 Bilinear Maps and Computational Problems

Let $G_1$ be an additive group of prime order $q$ and $G_2$ be a multiplicative group of the same order. A mapping $e : G_1 \times G_1 \longrightarrow G_2$ is called a bilinear mapping if it satisfies the following properties:

1. Bilinear: $e(aP, bQ) = e(P, Q)^{ab}$ for all $P, Q \in G_1, a, b \in Z_q^*$.
2. Non-degeneracy: There exists $P, Q \in G_1$ such that $e(P, Q) \neq 1$.
3. Computable: There exists an efficient algorithm to compute $e(P, Q)$ for any $P, Q \in G_1$.

**Discrete Logarithm (DL) Problem.** *Given a generator $P$ of a cyclic additive group $G$ with order $q$, and $Q \in G^*$ to find an integer $a \in Z_q^*$ such that $Q = aP$.*

**Computational Diffie-Hellman (CDH) Problem.** *Given a generator $P$ of a cyclic additive group $G$ with order $q$, and given $(aP, bP)$ for unknown $a, b \in Z_q^*$; to compute $abP$.*

### 2.2 The Concept of Certificateless Ring Signature Schemes

A CL-Ring scheme is defined by seven algorithms: Setup, Partial-Private-Key-Extract, Set-Secret-Value, Set-Private-Key, Set-Public-Key, Ring-Sign and Verify. The description of each algorithm is as follows.

- Setup: This algorithm takes as input a security parameter $\ell$ to produce a masterkey and a list of system parameters param.
- Partial-Private-Key-Extract: This algorithm takes as input a user's identity $ID$, a parameter list param and a masterkey to produce the user's partial private key $D_{ID}$.

- Set-Secret-Value: This algorithm takes as input a parameter list param and a user's identity $ID$ to produce the user's secret value $x$.
- Set-Private-Key: This algorithm takes as input a parameter list param, a user's identity $ID$, the user's partial private key $D_{ID}$ and secret value $x$ to produce a private signing key $S_{ID}$ for this user.
- Set-Public-Key: This algorithm takes as input a parameter list param, a user's identity $ID$ and secret value $x_{ID}$ to produce a public key $P_{ID}$ for the user.
- Ring-Sign: This algorithm takes as input a message $M \in \mathcal{M}$, $\mathcal{M}$ is the message space, a set of $n$ group members whose identities form the set $L_{ID} = \{ID_1, ..., ID_n\}$ and their corresponding public keys form the set $L_{PK} = \{P_{ID_1}, ..., P_{ID_n}\}$, a parameter list param and a signer's signing key $S_{ID_s}$ to produce a ring signature $\sigma$. Here $S_{ID_s}$ is the $s$-th group member's private key.
- Verify: This algorithm takes as input a message $M$, a ring signature $\sigma$, a parameter list param, the set $L_{ID}$ of the group members' identities and the set $L_{PK}$ of the corresponding public keys of the group members to output $True$ if the signature is correct, or $False$ otherwise.

## 3  Security Models of Certificateless Ring Signature Schemes

Due to the lack of certification in CL-PKC, it is conceivable that the adversary can replace anyone's public key of his choice. This key replacement attack is also called *Type I adversary* in [2]. Obviously, a secure signature scheme in CL-PKC must has the property that it is infeasible for *Type I adversary* to create a valid signature under the false public key chosen by the adversary himself. An assumption that must be made is that KGC does not mount a public key replacement attack to a target user since he is armed with this user's partial private key. However, KGC might engage in other adversarial activities: eavesdropping on signatures and making signing queries, which is also known as *Type II Adversary*. In this way, the level of trust is similar to the trust in a CA in a traditional PKI.

Combining the security notions of certificateless public key cryptography and security models of ring signature schemes in traditional PKC and ID-PKC, we define the security of a CL-Ring scheme via the following two games between a challenger $\mathcal{C}$ and an adversary $\mathcal{A}_I$ or $\mathcal{A}_{II}$.

### Game 1: Unforgeability of CL-Ring Against Type I Adversary $\mathcal{A}_I$

*Setup*: $\mathcal{C}$ runs the Setup algorithm, takes as input a security parameter $\ell$ to obtain a masterkey and the system parameters param. $\mathcal{C}$ then sends param to the adversary $\mathcal{A}_I$ while keeping the masterkey as secret. In addition, $\mathcal{C}$ will maintain three lists $L_1, L_2, L_3$ where

- $L_1$ is used to record the identities which have been chosen by $\mathcal{A}_I$ in the Partial-Private-Key Queries.

- $L_2$ is used to record the identities whose public keys have been replaced by $\mathcal{A}_I$.
- $L_3$ is used to record the identities which have been chosen by $\mathcal{A}_I$ in the Private-Key Queries.

All these three lists $L_1, L_2, L_3$ are the empty set $\emptyset$ at the beginning of the game.

*Training*: The adversary $\mathcal{A}_I$ can adaptively issue a polynomially bounded number of queries as defined below:

- Partial-Private-Key Queries $PPK(ID)$: $\mathcal{A}_I$ can request the partial private key of any user whose identity is $ID$. In respond,
  1. $\mathcal{C}$ first resets $L_1 = L_1 \cup \{ID\}$.
  2. $\mathcal{C}$ then runs the algorithm Partial-Private-Key-Extract and outputs the partial private key $D_{ID}$ as answer.
- Public-Key Queries $PK(ID)$: $\mathcal{A}_I$ can request the public key of a user whose identity is $ID$. In respond,
  1. $\mathcal{C}$ first runs the algorithm Set-Secret-Value and obtains the secret value $x_{ID}$.
  2. $\mathcal{C}$ then runs the algorithm Set-Public-Key and obtains the public key $P_{ID}$. $\mathcal{C}$ outputs the public key $P_{ID}$ as answer.
- Public-Key-Replacement Queries $PKR(ID, P'_{ID})$: For any user whose identity is $ID$, $\mathcal{A}_I$ can choose a new public key $P'_{ID}$. $\mathcal{A}_I$ then sets $P'_{ID}$ as the new public key of this user and submits $(ID, P'_{ID})$ to $\mathcal{C}$. On receiving a query $PKR(ID, P'_{ID})$, $\mathcal{C}$ resets $L_2 = L_2 \cup \{ID\}$ and updates the public key of this user to the new value $P'_{ID}$.
- Private-Key Queries $PrK(ID)$: $\mathcal{A}_I$ can request the private key of a user whose identity is $ID$. In respond,
  1. $\mathcal{C}$ first checks the set $L_2$. If $ID \in L_2$ (that is, the public key of the user $ID$ has been replaced), $\mathcal{C}$ will return the symbol $\perp$ which means $\mathcal{C}$ cannot output the private key of an identity whose public key has been replaced.
  2. Otherwise, $ID \notin L_2$ and $\mathcal{C}$ resets $L_3 = L_3 \cup \{ID\}$. $\mathcal{C}$ then runs the algorithm Set-Private-Key and outputs the private key $S_{ID}$ as answer.
- Ring-Sign Queries $RS(M, L_{ID}, L_{PK})$: $\mathcal{A}_I$ can request the ring signature of a message $M$ on behalf of a group whose identities are listed in the set $L_{ID}$ and the corresponding public keys are in the set $L_{PK}$. In respond, $\mathcal{C}$ outputs a ring signature $\sigma$ for the message $M$. It is required that the algorithm Verify will output $True$ for the input $(M, \sigma, \text{param}, L_{ID}, L_{PK})$.

*Forgery*: Finally, $\mathcal{A}_I$ outputs a tuple $(M^*, \sigma^*, L^*_{ID}, L^*_{PK})$ as the forgery. We say $\mathcal{A}_I$ wins the game if the forgery satisfies all the following requirements:

1. The algorithm Verify outputs $True$ for the input $(M^*, \sigma^*, \text{param}, L^*_{ID}, L^*_{PK})$.
2. $L^*_{ID} \cap L_1 \cap L_2 = \emptyset$ and $L^*_{ID} \cap L_3 = \emptyset$.
3. $(M^*, L^*_{ID}, L^*_{PK})$ has never been queried during the Ring-Sign Queries.

**Game 2: Unforgeability of CL-Ring Against Type II Adversary $\mathcal{A}_{II}$**

*Setup*: $\mathcal{C}$ runs the Setup algorithm, takes as input a security parameter $\ell$ to obtain the system parameter list param and also the system's masterkey. $\mathcal{C}$ then sends param and masterkey to the adversary $\mathcal{A}_{II}$. $\mathcal{C}$ will maintain two lists $L_1, L_2$ where

- $L_1$ is used to record the identities whose public keys have been replaced by $\mathcal{A}_{II}$.
- $L_2$ is used to record the identities which have been chosen by $\mathcal{A}_{II}$ in the Private-Key Queries.

Both two lists $L_1, L_2$ are empty at the beginning of the game.

*Training*: As defined in **Game 1**, the type II adversary $\mathcal{A}_{II}$ can issue a polynomially bounded number of Public Key Queries, Private-Key Queries, Public-Key-Replacement Queries and Ring-Sign Queries. $\mathcal{C}$ will answer those queries in the same way as in **Game 1**. Note that $\mathcal{A}_{II}$ does not need to issue Partial-Private-Key queries because he has already known the system's masterkey.

*Forgery*: Finally, $\mathcal{A}_{II}$ outputs a tuple $(M^*, \sigma^*, L_{ID}^*, L_{PK}^*)$ as the forgery. We say $\mathcal{A}_{II}$ wins the game if the forgery satisfies all the following requirements:

1. The algorithm Verify outputs $True$ for the input $(M^*, \sigma^*, \text{param}, L_{ID}^*, L_{PK}^*)$.
2. $L_{ID}^* \cap L_1 = \emptyset$ and $L_{ID}^* \cap L_2 = \emptyset$.
3. $(M^*, L_{ID}^*, L_{PK}^*)$ has never been queried during the Ring-Sign Queries.

**Definition 1.** *A CL-Ring scheme is existentially unforgeable under adaptively chosen-message attack iff the success probability of any polynomially bounded adversary in the above two games is negligible.*

**Definition 2.** *A CL-Ring scheme is said to have the unconditional signer anonymity if for any group of n users whose identities form the set $L_{ID}$ and their corresponding public keys form the set $L_{PK}$, any message M and any ring signature $\sigma = Ring\text{-}Sign(M, L_{ID}, L_{PK}, S_{ID_s})$, any verifier $\mathcal{V}$ (even the verifier knows the private keys of all the group members) cannot identify the actual signer with probability better than a random guess. That is, $\mathcal{V}$ can only output the actual signer with probability no better than $\frac{1}{n}$ ($\frac{1}{n-1}$ when $\mathcal{V}$ is in the signers' ring).*

# 4   A Concrete Certificateless Ring Signatures Scheme

In this section, we will give the concrete construction of a certificateless ring signature scheme. In our scheme, we employ some ideas of the certificateless signature scheme in [32], the ID-based signature scheme in [17], and the ID-based ring signature scheme in [16].

## 4.1   Description of Our CL-Ring Scheme

Our CL-Ring scheme consists of the following algorithms:

- Setup: Given a security parameter $\ell$, the algorithm works as follows.
    1. Specify $G_1, G_2, e$, as described in Section 2.1.
    2. Arbitrarily choose a generator $P \in G_1$ and set $g = e(P, P)$.
    3. Choose a random masterkey $\kappa \in Z_q^*$ and set $P_0 = \kappa P$.
    4. Choose cryptographic hash functions $H_1 : \{0,1\}^* \longrightarrow G_1$, $H_2 : \{0,1\}^* \longrightarrow Z_q^*$ and $H_3 : \{0,1\}^* \longrightarrow G_1$.

    The system parameters param$=(G_1, G_2, e, P, g, P_0, H_1, H_2, H_3)$. The message space is $\mathcal{M} = \{0,1\}^*$.
- Partial-Private-Key-Extract: This algorithm accepts param, masterkey and a user's identity $ID_i \in \{0,1\}^*$ to output the user's partial private key $D_i = \kappa Q_i$. Where $Q_i = H_1(ID_i)$.
- Set-Secret-Value: Given param, this algorithm selects a random $x_i \in Z_q^*$ as the user's (whose identity is $ID_i$) secret value.
- Set-Private-Key: This algorithm takes as input param, a user's identity $ID_i$, the user's partial private key $D_i$ and the user's secret value $x_i \in Z_q^*$. The output of the algorithm is the user's private key $S_i = (x_i, D_i)$.
- Set-Public-Key: This algorithm accepts param, a user's identity $ID_i$ and his secret value $x_i \in Z_q^*$ to produce the user's public key $P_i = x_i P$.
- Ring-Sign: Suppose there's a group of $n$ users whose identities form the set $L_{ID} = \{ID_1, ..., ID_n\}$, and their corresponding public keys form the set $L_{PK} = \{P_1, ..., P_n\}$. To sign a message $M \in \mathcal{M}$ on behalf of the group, the actual signer, indexed by $s$ using the private key $S_s = (x_s, D_s)$, performs the following steps.
    1. For each $i \in \{1, ..., n\}\backslash\{s\}$, select $r_i \in Z_q^*$ uniformly at random, compute $y_i = g^{r_i}$.
    2. Compute $h_i = H_2(M||L_{ID}||L_{PK}||y_i)$ for all $i \in \{1, ..., n\}\backslash\{s\}$.
    3. Choose random $r_s \in Z_q^*$, compute $U = H_3(M||L_{ID}||L_{PK})$, $y_s = g^{r_s} e(-P_0, \sum_{i \neq s} h_i Q_i) e(-U, \sum_{i \neq s} h_i P_i)$. If $y_s = 1_{G_2}$ or $y_s = y_i$ for some $i \neq s$, then redo this step.
    4. Compute $h_s = H_2(M||L_{ID}||L_{PK}||y_s)$.
    5. Compute $V = (\sum_{i=1}^n r_i)P + h_s(D_s + x_s U)$.
    6. Output the ring signature on $M$ as $\sigma = \{(y_1, ..., y_n), V\}$.
- Verify: To verify a ring signature $\sigma = \{(y_1, ..., y_n), V\}$ on a message $M$ with identities in $L_{ID}$ and corresponding public keys in $L_{PK}$, the verifier performs the following steps.
    1. Compute $h_i = H_2(M||L_{ID}||L_{PK}||y_i)$ for all $i \in \{1, ..., n\}$, compute $U = H_3(M||L_{ID}||L_{PK})$.
    2. Verify $e(V, P) \overset{?}{=} y_1 \cdot ... \cdot y_n e(\sum_{i=1}^n h_i Q_i, P_0) e(\sum_{i=1}^n h_i P_i, U)$ holds with equality.
    3. Accept the ring signature as valid and output $True$ if the above equation holds, otherwise, output $False$.

## 4.2  Efficiency

We only consider the costly operations including the pairing operation (Pairing), scalar multiplication in $G_1$ ($G_1$ SM), exponentiation in $G_2$ ($G_2$ E) and MapTo-Point hash operation [4] (Hash). The numbers of these operations in our scheme are shown in Table 1.

**Table 1.** Table 1. Efficiency

|        | Pairing | $G_1$ SM | $G_2$ E | Hash |
|--------|---------|----------|---------|------|
| Sign   | 2       | $2n+3$   | $n$     | $n+1$ |
| Verify | 3       | $2n$     | 0       | $n+1$ |
| Total  | 5       | $4n+3$   | $n$     | $2n+2$ |

Pairing operation is relatively time consuming. Our CL-Ring scheme only requires 5 pairing operations which is independent of the group size. Note that we use symmetric bilinear maps in our construction only for simplicity, asymmetric ones can be applied with no doubt.

# 5  Analysis of the Proposed CL-Ring Scheme

In this section, we will analyze our proposed scheme in detail.

## 5.1  Correctness

The correctness of the proposed scheme can be easily verified with the following:

$$e(V, P) = e((\sum_{i=1}^{n} r_i)P + h_s(D_s + x_s U), P)$$

$$= e((\sum_{i=1}^{n} r_i)P, P)e(h_s(D_s + x_s U), P)$$

$$= y_1 \cdot ... \cdot y_n e(\sum_{i \neq s} h_i Q_i, P_0)e(\sum_{i \neq s} h_i P_i, U)e(h_s D_s, P)e(h_s x_s U, P)$$

$$= y_1 \cdot ... \cdot y_n e(\sum_{i \neq s} h_i Q_i, P_0)e(\sum_{i \neq s} h_i P_i, U)e(h_s Q_s, P_0)e(h_s P_s, U)$$

$$= y_1 \cdot ... \cdot y_n e(\sum_{i=1}^{n} h_i Q_i, P_0)e(\sum_{i=1}^{n} h_i P_i, U)$$

## 5.2  Unconditional Anonymity

Let $\sigma = \{(y_1, ..., y_n), V\}$ be a valid ring signature of a message $M$ on behalf of a group of $n$ members specified by identities in $L_{ID}$ and public keys in $L_{PK}$. Since all the $r_i, i \in \{0, ..., n\}\backslash\{s\}$ are randomly generated, hence all $y_i, i \in \{0, ..., n\}\backslash\{s\}$ are also uniformly distributed. The randomness of $r_s$ chosen by the signer implies $y_s = g^{r_s}e(-P_0, \sum_{i\neq s} h_iQ_i)e(-U, \sum_{i\neq s} h_iP_i)$ is also uniformly distributed. So $(y_1, ..., y_n)$ in the signature reveals no information about the signer.

It remains to consider whether $V = (\sum_{i=1}^{n} r_i)P + h_s(D_s + x_sU)$ leaks information about the actual signer. From the construction of $V$, it is obvious to see that $D_s + x_sU = h_s^{-1}(V - (\sum_{i=1}^{n} r_i)P)$. To identify whether $ID_s$ is the identity of the actual signer, the only way is to check $e(Q_s, P_0)e(P_s, U) \overset{?}{=} e(D_s + x_sU, P)$. Namely, $e(Q_s, P_0)e(P_s, U) \overset{?}{=} e(h_s^{-1}(V - (\sum_{i=1}^{n} r_i)P), P)$. If $ID_s$ is the identity of the actual signer, it should hold $y_s = g^{r_s}e(-P_0, \sum_{i\neq s} h_iQ_i)e(-U, \sum_{i\neq s} h_iP_i)$. It remains to check

$$e(Q_s, P_0)e(P_s, U) \overset{?}{=} \left(\frac{e(V, P)}{y_1 \cdot ... \cdot y_n e(P_0, \sum_{i\neq s} h_sQ_s)e(U, \sum_{i\neq j} h_sP_i)}\right)^{h_s^{-1}}$$

However, we have for each $j \in \{1, 2, ..., n\}$

$$\left(\frac{e(V, P)}{y_1 \cdot ... \cdot y_n e(P_0, \sum_{i\neq j} h_iQ_i)e(U, \sum_{i\neq j} h_iP_i)}\right)^{h_j^{-1}}$$
$$= \left(\frac{e(\sum_{i=1}^{n} r_i)P + h_s(D_s + x_sU), P)}{y_1 \cdot ... \cdot y_n e(P_0, \sum_{i\neq s} h_iQ_i)e(U, \sum_{i\neq s} h_iP_i)e(h_sQ_s, P_0)e(h_sP_s, U)w}\right)^{h_j^{-1}}$$
$$= \left(\frac{e((\sum_{i=1}^{n} r_i)P, P)}{e((\sum_{i\neq s} r_i)P, P)y_s e(P_0, \sum_{i\neq s} h_iQ_i)e(U, \sum_{i\neq s} h_iP_i)w}\right)^{h_j^{-1}}$$
$$= w^{-h_j^{-1}} = e(Q_j, P_0)e(P_j, U)$$

where $w = e(-h_jQ_j, P_0)e(-h_jP_j, U)$, and $ID_s$ is the identity of the actual signer. This fact shows that $V$ in the signature does not leak any information about the identity of the actual signer. And hence, the unconditional anonymity of our CL-Ring scheme is proved.

As mentioned in [11], for real anonymity, the signer should obtain the "correct" copy of the public key that each member in the diversion group is using. Otherwise, one can always repudiate being the signer of a certain ring signature by demonstrating the ability to give a normal signature with the knowledge of the private key that corresponding to a different public key. For how to guarantee the correctness of the group members' public keys, please refer to [11].

## 5.3   Unforgeability

Assuming that the CDH problem is hard, we now show the unforgeability of our CL-Ring scheme.

**Theorem 1.** *In the random oracle model [3], if $\mathcal{A}_I$ can win Game 1, with an advantage $\epsilon \geq 7P_n^{q_{H_1}}/2^\ell$ within a time span $t$ for a security parameter $\ell$; and asking at most $q_K$ Partial-Private-Key queries, at most $q_P$ Public-Key queries, at* most $q_{Pr}$ Private-Key queries, at most $q_{H_1}$ $H_1$ queries, at most $q_{H_2}$ $H_2$ queries, at most $q_{H_3}$ $H_3$ queries, $q_S$ Ring-Sign queries. Then the CDH problem in $G_1$ can be solved within time $2(t+q_{H_1}T_1+q_{H_2}T_2+q_{H_3}T_3+q_KT_K+q_PT_P+q_{Pr}T_{Pr}+q_ST_S)$ and with probability $\geq ((\frac{q_K+q_{Pr}}{q_K+q_{Pr}+n})^{q_K+q_{Pr}+n}(\frac{n}{q_K+q_{Pr}+n})^n\epsilon)^2/66P_n^{q_{H_1}}$, where $n$ is the group scale, $P_n^{q_{H_1}}$ is defined as the number of $n$-permutations of $q_{H_1}$ elements i.e. $P_n^{q_{H_1}} = q_{H_1}\cdot...\cdot(q_{H_1}-n+2)\cdot(q_{H_1}-n+1)$, $T_1$ (resp. $T_2, T_3, T_K, T_P, T_{Pr}$ and $T_S$) is the time cost of an $H_1$ (resp. $H_2, H_3$, Partial-Private-Key, Public-Key, Private-Key and Ring-Sign) query.

*Proof.* Let $\mathcal{C}$ be a CDH attacker, $\mathcal{A}_I$ be a type I adversary of our CL-Ring scheme who interacts with $\mathcal{C}$ following Game 1 and can forge a valid ring signature. Suppose $\mathcal{C}$ receives a random instance $(P, aP, bP)$ of the CDH problem in $G_1$. We show how $\mathcal{C}$ can use $\mathcal{A}_I$ to solve the CDH problem, i.e. to compute $abP$.

*Setup:* $\mathcal{C}$ first sets $P_0 = aP$ and selects param=$(G_1, G_2, e, P, g, P_0, H_1, H_2, H_3)$, then sends param to $\mathcal{A}_I$. We take hash functions $H_1, H_2$ and $H_3$ as random oracles.

*Training:* $\mathcal{A}_I$ can ask $\mathcal{C}$ $H_1, H_2, H_3$, Partial-Private-Key, Public-Key, Private-Key, Public-Key-Replacement and Ring-Sign queries. In order to maintain consistency and avoid conflict, $\mathcal{C}$ keeps four lists $\mathbf{H_1}$, $\mathbf{H_2}$, $\mathbf{H_3}$, and $\mathbf{K}$ to store the answers used, where $\mathbf{H_1}$ includes items of the form $(ID, \alpha, Q_{ID}, c)$, $\mathbf{H_2}$ includes items of the form $(M, L_{ID}, L_{PK}, y, h)$, $\mathbf{H_3}$ includes items of the form $(M, L_{ID}, L_{PK}, \beta, U, c'')$, and $\mathbf{K}$ includes items of the form $(ID, x, D_{ID}, P_{ID}, c')$. All of these four lists are initially empty. $\mathcal{C}$ also maintains three lists $L_1, L_2, L_3$, the functions of these three lists are the same as mentioned in Game 1 in Section 3.

$H_1$ *Queries:* On receiving a query $H_1(ID)$, $\mathcal{C}$ does as follows.

1. If there exists an item $(ID, \alpha, Q_{ID}, c)$ in $\mathbf{H_1}$, then $\mathcal{C}$ returns $Q_{ID}$ as answer.
2. Otherwise, $\mathcal{C}$ first flips a coin $c \in \{0,1\}$ that yields 0 with probability $\delta$ and 1 with probability $1 - \delta$ ($\delta$ will be determined later), then picks a random element $\alpha$ (has not been used before) in $Z_q^*$. If $c = 0$, $\mathcal{C}$ computes $Q_{ID} = H_1(ID) = \alpha P$; if $c = 1$, it computes $Q_{ID} = H_1(ID) = \alpha bP$. $\mathcal{C}$ then adds $(ID, \alpha, Q_{ID}, c)$ to $\mathbf{H_1}$ and returns $Q_{ID}$ as answer.

$H_2$ *Queries:* On receiving a query $H_2(M||L_{ID}||L_{PK}||y)$, $\mathcal{C}$ first checks if there exists an item $(M, L_{ID}, L_{PK}, y, h)$ in $\mathbf{H_2}$, if so, returns $h$ as answer. Otherwise, $\mathcal{C}$ picks a random $h \in Z_q^*$ which has not been used in the answers of the former $H_2$ Queries, then returns $h$ as answer and adds $(M, L_{ID}, L_{PK}, y, h)$ to $\mathbf{H_2}$.

$H_3$ *Queries:* On receiving a query $H_3(M||L_{ID}||L_{PK})$, $\mathcal{C}$ first checks if there exists an item $(M, L_{ID}, L_{PK}, \beta, U, c'')$ in $\mathbf{H_3}$, if so, returns $U$ as answer. Otherwise, $\mathcal{C}$ first flips a coin $c'' \in \{0,1\}$ that yields 0 with probability $\delta$ and 1 with probability $1 - \delta$ then picks a random $\beta \in Z_q^*$ which has not been used in the answers of the former $H_3$ Queries. If $c'' = 0$, compute $U = \beta P$; while $c'' = 1$, compute $U = \beta bP$. In both cases, $\mathcal{C}$ will add $(M, L_{ID}, L_{PK}, \beta, U, c'')$ to $\mathbf{H_3}$ and return $U$ as answer.

*Partial-Private-Key Queries*: Whenever $C$ receives a query $PPK(ID)$

1. If there exists an item $(ID, x, D_{ID}, P_{ID}, c')$ in $\mathbf{K}$, $C$ does the following:
   (a) If $D_{ID} \neq \perp$, $C$ returns $D_{ID}$ as answer.
   (b) Else, if there exists an item $(ID, \alpha, Q_{ID}, c)$ in $\mathbf{H_1}$, $C$ sets $L_1 = L_1 \cup \{ID\}$, $D_{ID} = \alpha P_0$ and returns $D_{ID}$ as answer when $c = 0$; while $c = 1$, $C$ aborts.
   (c) Otherwise, $C$ first makes an $H_1(ID)$ query to obtain an item $(ID, \alpha, Q_{ID}, c)$. If $c = 1$, $C$ aborts; while $c = 0$, $C$ sets $L_1 = L_1 \cup \{ID\}$, $D_{ID} = \alpha P_0$ and returns $D_{ID}$ as answer.
2. Otherwise $C$ does the following:
   (a) If there exists an item $(ID, \alpha, Q_{ID}, c)$ in $\mathbf{H_1}$, $C$ sets $L_1 = L_1 \cup \{ID\}$, computes $D_{ID} = \alpha P_0$, sets $x = \perp$, $P_{ID} = \perp$, adds $(ID, x, D_{ID}, P_{ID}, c')$ to $\mathbf{K}$ and returns $D_{ID}$ as answer when $c = 0$; while $c = 1$, $C$ aborts.
   (b) Otherwise, $C$ first makes an $H_1(ID)$ query to obtain an item $(ID, \alpha, Q_{ID}, c)$ in $\mathbf{H_1}$, then proceeds as in (a).

*Public-Key Queries*: Whenever $C$ receives a query $PK(ID)$

1. If there exists an item $(ID, x, D_{ID}, P_{ID}, c')$ in $\mathbf{K}$, $C$ does the following:
   (a) If $P_{ID} \neq \perp$, $C$ returns $P_{ID}$ as answer;
   (b) Otherwise, $C$ first flips a coin $c' \in \{0,1\}$ that yields 0 with probability $\delta$ and 1 with probability $1 - \delta$, then picks a random $x \in Z_q^*$. If $c' = 0$, $C$ sets $P_{ID} = xP$; if $c = 1$, it computes $P_{ID} = xaP$. $C$ then updates $(ID, x, D_{ID}, P_{ID}, c')$ with new values and returns $P_{ID}$ as answer.
2. Otherwise, $C$ first flips a coin $c' \in \{0,1\}$ that yields 0 with probability $\delta$ and 1 with probability $1 - \delta$, then picks a random $x \in Z_q^*$. If $c' = 0$, $C$ sets $P_{ID} = xP$; otherwise, it computes $P_{ID} = xaP$. $C$ then sets $D_{ID} = \perp$, returns $P_{ID}$ as answer and adds $(ID, x, D_{ID}, P_{ID}, c')$ to $\mathbf{K}$.

*Public-Key-Replacement Queries*: On receiving a query $PKR(ID, P'_{ID})$ ($C$ sets $L_2 = L_2 \cup \{ID\}$), $C$ first makes a $PPK(ID)$ query to obtain an item $(ID, x, D_{ID}, P_{ID}, c')$, then sets $x = \perp$, $P_{ID} = P'_{ID}$, and updates the item $(ID, x, D_{ID}, P_{ID}, c')$ in $\mathbf{K}$ to record this replacement.

*Private-Key Queries*: Whenever receives a query $PrK(ID)$, if $ID \in L_2$, $C$ returns $\perp$, otherwise

1. When there exists an item $(ID, x, D_{ID}, P_{ID}, c')$ in $\mathbf{K}$
   (a) If $x = \perp$, $C$ first makes a $PK(ID)$ query. If $c' \neq 1$, $C$ sets $L_3 = L_3 \cup \{ID\}$, returns $(x, D_{ID})$ as answer; otherwise $C$ aborts.
   (b) Else if $D_{ID} = \perp$, $C$ first makes a $PPK(ID)$ query, if $C$ does not abort and $c' \neq 1$, $C$ sets $L_3 = L_3 \cup \{ID\}$ and returns $(x, D_{ID})$ as answer. Otherwise $C$ aborts.
   (c) Otherwise, when $c' = 1$ $C$ aborts, while $c' = 0$ $C$ sets $L_3 = L_3 \cup \{ID\}$ and returns $(x, D_{ID})$ as answer.
2. Otherwise, $C$ first makes $PK(ID)$ and $PPK(ID)$ queries. If $C$ does not abort and $c' \neq 1$, then sets $L_3 = L_3 \cup \{ID\}$, returns $(x, D_{ID})$ as answer and adds $(ID, x, D_{ID}, P_{ID}, c')$ to $\mathbf{K}$; otherwise, $C$ aborts.

*Ring-Sign Queries*: $\mathcal{A}_I$ chooses a group of $n$ users whose identities form the set $L_{ID} = \{ID_1, ..., ID_n\}$ and their corresponding public keys form the set $L_{PK} = \{P_1, ..., P_n\}$, and may ask a ring signature on a message $M$ of this group. On receiving a Ring-Sign query $RS(M, L_{ID}, L_{PK})$, $\mathcal{C}$ creates a ring signature as follows:

1. Choose a random index $s \in \{1, ..., n\}$.
2. For all $i \in \{1, ..., n\}\backslash\{s\}$, choose $r_i \in Z_q^*$ uniformly at random, compute $y_i = g^{r_i}$.
3. For all $i \in \{1, ..., n\}\backslash\{s\}$, compute $h_i = H_2(M||L_{ID}||L_{PK}||y_i)$.
4. Choose $h_s \in Z_q^*, V \in G_1$ at random.
5. Compute $y_s = e(V - (\sum_{i \neq s} r_i)P, P)e(\sum_{i=1}^n h_i Q_i, -P_0)e(\sum_{i=1}^n h_i P_i, -U)$, where $U = H_3(M|| L_{ID}||L_{PK})$, $Q_i = H_1(ID_i)$. If $y_s = 1_{G_2}$ or $y_s = y_i$ for some $i \neq s$, then goto step 4.
6. Set $H_2(M||L_{ID}||L_{PK}||y_s) = h_s$.
7. Return $(M, L_{ID}, L_{PK}, \sigma = ((y_1, ..., y_n), V))$ as answer.

*Forgery*: Finally, $\mathcal{A}_I$ outputs a tuple $(M^*, L_{ID}^* = \{ID_1^*, ..., ID_n^*\}, L_{PK}^* = \{P_1^*, ..., P_n^*\}, \sigma^* = ((y_1^*, ..., y_n^*), V^*))$ which means $\sigma^*$ is a ring signature on message $M^*$ on behalf of the group specified by identities in $L_{ID}^*$ and the corresponding public keys in $L_{PK}^*$. It is required that $\mathcal{C}$ does not know the private key of any member in this group, $L_{ID}^* \cap ((L_1 \cap L_2) \cup L_3) = \emptyset$ and the ring signature $\sigma^*$ on message $M^*$ on behalf of the group must be valid (**Event 1**). Now, applying the 'ring forking lemma' [16], if $\mathcal{A}_I$ succeeds in outputting a valid ring signature $\sigma^*$ with probability $\epsilon \geq 7P_n^{q_{H_1}}/2^\ell$ in a time span $t$ in the above interaction, then within time $2t$ and probability $\geq \epsilon^2/66P_n^{q_{H_1}}$, $\mathcal{C}$ can get two valid ring signatures $(M^*, L_{ID}^*, L_{PK}^*, \sigma^* = ((y_1^*, ..., y_n^*), V^*))$ and $(M^*, L_{ID}^*, L_{PK}^*, \sigma'^* = ((y_1^*, ..., y_n^*), V'^*))$. From these two valid ring signatures, $\mathcal{C}$ obtains

$$e(V^*, P) = y_1^* \cdot ... \cdot y_n^* e(\sum_{i=1}^n h_i^* P_i^*, U^*)e(\sum_{i=1}^n h_i^* Q_i^*, P_0)$$

and

$$e(V'^*, P) = y_1^* \cdot ... \cdot y_n^* e(\sum_{i=1}^n h_i'^* P_i^*, U^*)e(\sum_{i=1}^n h_i'^* Q_i^*, P_0)$$

Where $U^* = H_3(M^*||L_{ID}^*||L_{PK}^*)$, $Q_i^* = H_1(ID_i^*)$, $h_i^* = H_2(M^*, L_{ID}^*, L_{PK}^*, y_i^*)$, $h_i'^* = H_2'(M^*, L_{ID}^*, L_{PK}^*, y_i^*)$, and for some $s \in \{1, ..., n\}$, $h_s^* \neq h_s'^*$, while for $i \in \{1, ..., n\}\backslash\{s\}$, $h_i^* = h_i'^*$. From the above two equations we have

$$e(V^* - V'^*, P) = e((h_s^* - h_s'^*)P_s^*, U^*)e((h_s^* - h_s'^*)Q_s^*, P_0)$$

At this stage, $\mathcal{C}$ may find the item $(M^*, L_{ID}^*, L_{PK}^*, \beta^*, U^*, c''^*)$ from $\mathbf{H_3}$, $(ID_s^*, \alpha_s^*, Q_s^*, c_s^*)$ from $\mathbf{H_1}$, $(ID_s^*, x_s^*, D_s^*, P_s^*, c_s'^*)$ from $\mathbf{K}$. There are three cases in which $\mathcal{C}$ can successfully solve the CDH problem.

- **Case 1:** $c_s^* = 1, c''^* = 0$, this means $Q_s^* = \alpha_s^* bP, U^* = \beta^* P$. In this case, $e(V^* - V'^*, P) = e((h_s^* - h_s'^*)(\beta^* P_s^* + \alpha_s^* abP), P)$. So, $\mathcal{C}$ can get $abP = \alpha_s^{*-1}((h - h')^{-1}(V^* - V'^*) - \beta^* P_s^*)$.

- **Case 2:** $c_s'^* = 1, c''^* = 1, c_s^* = 0, x_s^* \neq \perp$, and $P_s^* = x_s^* aP, U^* = \beta^* bP, Q_s^* = \alpha_s^* P$, $\mathcal{C}$ can get $abP = (x_s^* \beta^*)^{-1}((h - h')^{-1}(V^* - V'^*) - \alpha_s^* P_0)$.
- **Case 3:** $c_s'^* = 1, c''^* = 1, c_s^* = 1, x_s^* \neq \perp$, and $P_s^* = x_s^* aP, U^* = \beta^* bP, Q_s^* = \alpha_s^* bP$, $\mathcal{C}$ can get $abP = (x_s^* \beta^* + \alpha_s^*)^{-1}(h - h')^{-1}(V^* - V'^*)$ (Note the probability that $x_s^* \beta^* + \alpha_s^* = 0$ is negligible).

*Probability of Success*: Now we determine the value of $\delta$ and consider the probability for $\mathcal{C}$ to successfully solve the given CDH problem. The probability that $\mathcal{C}$ does not abort in all the $q_K$ *Partial-Private-Key Queries* and $q_{Pr}$ *Private-Key Queries* is at least $\delta^{q_K + q_{Pr}}$. The probability that the forged ring signature is helpful for $\mathcal{C}$ to solve the CDH problem is $Pr[(\mathbf{Case1} \vee \mathbf{Case2} \vee \mathbf{Case3}) \wedge \mathbf{Event\ 1}] \leq (1 - \delta)^n$. So the combined probability is $\delta^{q_K + q_{Pr}}(1 - \delta)^n$. We can find the value of $\delta$ that maximize this probability is $\frac{q_K + q_{Pr}}{q_K + q_{Pr} + n}$ and the maximized probability is $(\frac{q_K + q_{Pr}}{q_K + q_{Pr} + n})^{q_K + q_{Pr}}(\frac{n}{q_K + q_{Pr} + n})^n$.

Based on the bound from the ring forking lemma [16], if $\mathcal{A}_I$ succeeds in time $\leq t$ with probability $\epsilon \geq 7P_n^{q_{H_1}}/2^\ell$, then the CDH problem in $G_1$ can be solved by $\mathcal{C}$ within time $2(t + q_{H_1}T_1 + q_{H_2}T_2 + q_{H_3}T_3 + q_K T_K + q_P T_P + q_{Pr}T_{Pr} + q_S T_S)$ and with probability $\geq ((\frac{q_K + q_{Pr}}{q_K + q_{Pr} + n})^{q_K + q_{Pr}} \cdot (\frac{n}{q_K + q_{Pr} + n})^n \epsilon)^2/66P_n^{q_{H_1}}$.

**Theorem 2.** *In the random oracle model, if $\mathcal{A}_{II}$ can win the Game 2, with an advantage $\epsilon \geq 7P_n^{q_{H_1}}/2^\ell$ within a time span $t$ for a security parameter $\ell$; and asking at most $q_P$ Public-Key queries, at most $q_K$ Private-Key queries, at most $q_{H_1}$ $H_1$ queries, at most $q_{H_2}$ $H_2$ queries, at most $q_{H_3}$ $H_3$ queries, at most $q_S$ Ring-Sign queries. Then the CDH problem in $G_1$ can be solved within time $2(t + q_{H_1}T_1 + q_{H_2}T_2 + q_{H_3}T_3 + q_K T_{Pr} + q_P T_P + q_S T_S)$ and with probability $\geq ((\frac{q_K}{q_K + n})^{q_K + n}(\frac{n}{q_K + n})^n \epsilon)^2/66P_n^{q_{H_1}}$.*

*Proof.* Let $\mathcal{A}_{II}$ be our type II adversary, $\mathcal{C}$ be a CDH attacker who receives a random instance $(P, aP, bP)$ and has to compute the value of $abP$.

*Setup:* $\mathcal{C}$ generates the KGC's masterkey $\kappa \in Z_q^*$ and the system parameters param=$(G_1, G_2, e, P, g, P_0, H_1, H_2, H_3)$. When the simulation is started, $\mathcal{A}_{II}$ is provided with param and the masterkey $\kappa$.

*Training:* $\mathcal{A}_{II}$ can ask $\mathcal{C}$ $H_1, H_2, H_3$, Public-Key, Private-Key, and Ring-Sign queries. Since $\mathcal{A}_{II}$ has access to the masterkey $\kappa$, he can do Partial-Private-Key-Extract himself. $\mathcal{C}$ also maintains four lists, namely $\mathbf{H_1}$ contains items of the form $(ID, Q_{ID})$, $\mathbf{H_2}$ contains items of the form $(M, L_{ID}, L_{PK}, y, h)$, $\mathbf{H_3}$ contains items of the form $(M, L_{ID}, L_{PK}, \beta, U)$ and $\mathbf{K}$ contains items of the form $(ID, x, P_{ID})$ to store the answers used. All of these four lists are initially empty. $\mathcal{C}$ also maintains two lists $L_1, L_2$, the functions of these two lists are the same as mentioned in Game 2 in Section 3.

*$H_1$ Queries:* On receiving a query $H_1(ID)$. If $(ID, Q_{ID})$ exists in $\mathbf{H_1}$, $\mathcal{C}$ returns $Q_{ID}$ as answer. Otherwise, $\mathcal{C}$ picks a random $Q_{ID} \in G_1^*$ which has not been used in the former $H_1$ *Queries*, then returns $Q_{ID}$ as answer and adds $(ID, Q_{ID})$ to $\mathbf{H_1}$.

$H_2$ *Queries*: On receiving a query $H_2(M||L_{ID}||L_{PK}||y)$, $\mathcal{C}$ first checks whether there exists an item $(M, L_{ID}, L_{PK}, y, h)$ in $\mathbf{H_2}$, if so, returns $h$ as answer. Otherwise, $\mathcal{C}$ picks a random $h \in Z_q^*$ which has not been used in the former $H_2$ *Queries*, then returns $h$ as answer and adds $(M, L_{ID}, L_{PK}, y, h)$ to $\mathbf{H_2}$.

$H_3$ *Queries*: Whenever receives a query $H_3(M||L_{ID}||L_{PK})$, $\mathcal{C}$ first checks whether there exists an item $(M, L_{ID}, L_{PK}, \beta, U)$ in $\mathbf{H_3}$, if so, returns $U$ as answer. Otherwise, $\mathcal{C}$ picks a random $\beta \in Z_q^*$ which has not been used in the former $H_3$ *Queries*, computes $U = \beta aP$, then adds $(M, L_{ID}, L_{PK}, \beta, U)$ to $\mathbf{H_3}$ and returns $U$ as answer.

*Public-Key Queries*: On receiving a query $PK(ID)$

1. If there is an item $(ID, x, P_{ID}, c)$ exists in $\mathbf{K}$, then $\mathcal{C}$ returns $P_{ID}$ as answer.
2. Otherwise, $\mathcal{C}$ first flips a coin $c \in \{0, 1\}$ that yields 0 with probability $\delta$ and 1 with probability $1 - \delta$, then picks a random $x \in Z_q^*$. If $c = 0$, $\mathcal{C}$ sets $P_{ID} = xP$, returns $P_{ID}$ as answer and adds $(ID, x, P_{ID}, c)$ to $\mathbf{K}$. If $c = 1$, $\mathcal{C}$ sets $P_{ID} = xbP$, returns $P_{ID}$ as answer and adds $(ID, x, P_{ID}, c)$ to $\mathbf{K}$.

*Public-Key-Replacement Queries*: On receiving a query $PKR(ID, P'_{ID})$, $\mathcal{C}$ sets $L_1 = L_1 \cup \{ID\}$, and makes a $PPK(ID)$ query to obtain an item $(ID, x, P_{ID}, c)$, then sets $x = \bot$, $P_{ID} = P'_{ID}$, and updates the item $(ID, x, P_{ID}, c)$ in $\mathbf{K}$ to record this replacement.

*Private-Key Queries*: On receiving a query $PrK(ID)$, if $ID \in L_1$, $\mathcal{C}$ returns $\bot$, otherwise

1. If there is an item $(ID, x, P_{ID}, c)$ in $\mathbf{K}$, and $c = 0$ $\mathcal{C}$ sets $L_2 = L_2 \cup \{ID\}$, returns $(x, D_{ID})$ as answer (where $D_{ID} = \kappa H_1(ID)$ is the partial private key of the user whose identity is $ID$); while $c = 1$, $\mathcal{C}$ aborts.
2. Otherwise, $\mathcal{C}$ first makes a $PK(ID)$ query to obtain an item $(ID, x, P_{ID}, c)$ in $\mathbf{K}$. If $c = 0$, $\mathcal{C}$ sets $L_2 = L_2 \cup \{ID\}$, returns $(x, D_{ID})$ as answer; while $c = 1$, $\mathcal{C}$ aborts.

*Ring-Sign Queries*: $\mathcal{A}_{II}$ chooses a group of $n$ users whose identities form the set $L_{ID} = \{ID_1, ..., ID_n\}$ and their corresponding public keys form the set $L_{PK} = \{P_1, ..., P_n\}$. On receiving a Ring-Sign query $RS(M, L_{ID}, L_{PK})$, $\mathcal{C}$ creates a ring signature as follows:

1. Choose a random index $s \in \{1, ..., n\}$;
2. For all $i \in \{1, ..., n\} \backslash \{s\}$, choose $r_i \in Z_q^*$ uniformly at random, compute $y_i = g^{r_i}$.
3. For all $i \in \{1, ..., n\} \backslash \{s\}$, set $h_i = H_2(M||L_{ID}||L_{PK}||y_i)$.
4. Randomly choose $h_s \in Z_q^*, V \in G_1$.
5. Compute $y_s = e(V - (\sum_{i \neq s} r_i)P, P)e(\sum_{i=1}^n h_i Q_i, -P_0)e(\sum_{i=1}^n h_i P_i, -U)$, where $U = H_3(M|| L_{ID}||L_{PK})$, $Q_i = H_1(ID_i)$. If $y_s = 1_{G_2}$ or $y_s = y_i$ for some $i \neq s$, then goto step 4.
6. Set $H_2(M||L_{ID}||L_{PK}||y_s) = h_s$.
7. Return $(M, L_{ID}, L_{PK}, \sigma = ((y_1, ..., y_n), V))$ as answer.

*Forgery:* Finally, $\mathcal{A}_{II}$ outputs a tuple $(M^*, L^*_{ID} = \{ID^*_1, ..., ID^*_n\}, L^*_{PK} = \{P^*_1, ..., P^*_n\}, \sigma^* = ((y^*_1, ..., y^*_n), V^*))$ which implies that $\sigma^*$ is a ring signature on message $M^*$ on behalf of the group specified by identities in $L^*_{ID}$ and the corresponding public keys in $L^*_{PK}$. It is required that $(M^*, \sigma^*)$ is a valid message and ring signature pair, $L^*_{ID} \cap (L_1 \cup L_2) = \emptyset$ and $\mathcal{C}$ does not know the private key of any member in the group specified by $L^*_{ID}$ and $L^*_{PK}$ (**Event 1**). Now, Applying the 'ring forking lemma' [16], $\mathcal{C}$ gets two valid ring signatures $(M^*, L^*_{ID}, L^*_{PK}, \sigma^* = ((y^*_1, ..., y^*_n), V^*))$ and $(M^*, L^*_{ID}, L^*_{PK}, \sigma'^* = ((y^*_1, ..., y^*_n), V'^*))$. From these two ring signatures, $\mathcal{C}$ obtains

$$e(V^*, P) = y^*_1 \cdot ... \cdot y^*_n e(\sum_{i=1}^{n} h^*_i P^*_i, U^*) e(\sum_{i=1}^{n} h^*_i Q^*_i, P_0)$$

and

$$e(V'^*, P) = y^*_1 \cdot ... \cdot y^*_n e(\sum_{i=1}^{n} h'^*_i P^*_i, U^*) e(\sum_{i=1}^{n} h'^*_i Q^*_i, P_0)$$

where $U^* = H_3(M^* \| L^*_{ID} \| L^*_{PK})$, $Q^*_i = H(ID^*_i)$, $h^*_i = H_2(M^*, L^*_{ID}, L^*_{PK}, y^*_i)$ and $h'^*_i = H'_2(M^*, L^*_{ID}, L^*_{PK}, y^*_i)$. The hash functions $H_2$ and $H'_2$ satisfy: for some $s \in \{1, ..., n\}$, $h^*_s \neq h'^*_s$, while $i \in \{1, ..., n\} \setminus \{s\}$, $h^*_i = h'^*_i$. From the above two equations we have

$$e(V^* - V'^*, P) = e((h^*_s - h'^*_s)P^*_s, U^*) e((h^*_s - h'^*_s)Q^*_s, P_0)$$

At this point, $\mathcal{C}$ may find the item $(M^*, L^*_{ID}, L^*_{PK}, \beta^*, U^*)$ from $\mathbf{H_3}$, $(ID^*_s, Q^*_s)$ from $\mathbf{H_1}$ and $(ID^*_s, x^*_s, P^*_s, c^*)$ from $\mathbf{K}$. Since $U^* = \beta^* aP$, $P^*_s = x^*_s bP$, $\mathcal{C}$ has the following

$$e(V^* - V'^*, P) = e((h^*_s - h'^*_s)(x^*_s \beta^* abP + \kappa Q^*_s), P)$$

This implies

$$V^* - V'^* = (h^*_s - h'^*_s)(x^*_s \beta^* abP + \kappa Q^*_s)$$

Hence, $\mathcal{C}$ can obtain $abP = (x^*_s \beta^*)^{-1}((h^*_s - h'^*_s)^{-1}(V^* - V'^*) - \kappa Q^*_s)$.

*Probability of Success:* Now we determine the value of $\delta$ and consider the probability for $\mathcal{C}$ to successfully solve the given CDH problem. The probability that $\mathcal{C}$ does not abort in all the $q_K$ *Private-Key Queries* is $\delta^{q_K}$. The probability that $\mathcal{A}_{II}$ forged a valid ring signature which $\mathcal{C}$ does not know any private key of the group members' involved in the ring signature is $(1-\delta)^n$. So the combined probability $(Pr[\textbf{Event 1}])$ is $\delta^{q_K}(1-\delta)^n$. We can find the value of $\delta$ that maximize this probability is $\frac{q_K}{q_K+n}$ and the maximized probability is $(\frac{q_K}{q_K+n})^{q_K}(\frac{n}{q_K+n})^n$.

Based on the bound from the ring forking lemma [16], if $\mathcal{A}_{II}$ succeeds in time $\leq t$ with probability $\epsilon \geq 7P_n^{q_{H_1}}/2^\ell$, then the CDH problem in $G_1$ can be solved by $\mathcal{C}$ within time $2(t + q_{H_1}T_1 + q_{H_2}T_2 + q_{H_3}T_3 + q_K T_{Pr} + q_P T_P + q_S T_S)$ and with probability $\geq ((\frac{q_K}{q_K+n})^{q_K}(\frac{n}{q_K+n})^n \epsilon)^2/66P_n^{q_{H_1}}$.

# 6   Conclusion

The notion and security models of certificateless ring signatures are formalized. The models capture the essence of the possible adversaries in the notion of certificateless system and ring signatures. A concrete construction of certificateless ring signature scheme from the bilinear maps is presented. The unforgeability of our CL-Ring scheme is proved in the random oracle model based on the hardness of Computational Diffie-Hellman problem. Our CL-Ring scheme is computationally efficient in that it just needs 5 pairing operations in its signing and verification phases. We note that CL-Ring schemes may be more efficient than ring signature schemes in traditional PKC since they avoid the costly computation for the verification of the public key certificates of the group members. And no key escrow in CL-PKC makes it impossible for the KGC to forge any valid ring signatures.

## Acknowledgement

The authors would like to express their gratitude to Prof. Damien Vergnaud for his fruitful discussion and suggestion on our paper. We would also like to thank the anonymous referees of Provable Security 2007 for the suggestions to improve this paper.

## References

1. Abe, M., Ohkubo, M., Suzuki, K.: 1-out-of-n signatures from a variety of keys. In: Zheng, Y. (ed.) ASIACRYPT 2002. LNCS, vol. 2501, pp. 415–432. Springer, Heidelberg (2002)
2. Al-Riyami, S., Paterson, K.: Certificateless public key cryptography. In: Laih, C.-S. (ed.) ASIACRYPT 2003. LNCS, vol. 2894, pp. 452–473. Springer, Heidelberg (2003)
3. Bellare, M., Rogaway, P.: Random oracles are practical: A paradigm for designing efficient protocols. In: ACM CCCS 1993, pp. 62–73. ACM Press, New York (1993)
4. Boneh, D., Lynn, B., Shacham, H.: Short signatures from the weil pairing. In: Boyd, C. (ed.) ASIACRYPT 2001. LNCS, vol. 2248, pp. 514–532. Springer, Heidelberg (2001)
5. Boneh, D., Gentry, C., Lynn, B., Shacham, H.: Aggregate and verifiably encrypted signatures from bilinear maps. In: Biham, E. (ed.) Advances in Cryptology – EUROCRPYT 2003. LNCS, vol. 2656, pp. 416–432. Springer, Heidelberg (2003)
6. Bresson, E., Stern, J., Szydlo, M.: Threshold ring signature and applications to ad-hoc groups. In: Yung, M. (ed.) CRYPTO 2002. LNCS, vol. 2442, pp. 465–480. Springer, Heidelberg (2002)
7. Chan, T., Fung, K., Liu, J., Wei, V.: Blind spontaneous anonymous groupsignatures for ad hoc groups. In: Castelluccia, C., Hartenstein, H., Paar, C., Westhoff, D. (eds.) ESAS 2004. LNCS, vol. 3313, pp. 82–84. Springer, Heidelberg (2005)
8. Chow, S., Boyd, C., Nieto, J.: Security-mediated certificateless cryptography. In: Yung, M., Dodis, Y., Kiayias, A., Malkin, T.G. (eds.) PKC 2006. LNCS, vol. 3958, pp. 508–524. Springer, Heidelberg (2006)

9. Chow, S., Yiu, S., Hui, L.: Efficient identity based ring signature. In: Ioannidis, J., Keromytis, A.D., Yung, M. (eds.) ACNS 2005. LNCS, vol. 3531, pp. 499–512. Springer, Heidelberg (2005)

10. Chow, S., Lui, R., Hui, L., Yiu, S.: Identity based ring signature: why, how and what next. In: Chadwick, D., Zhao, G. (eds.) EuroPKI 2005. LNCS, vol. 3545, pp. 144–161. Springer, Heidelberg (2005)

11. Chow, S., Yap, W.: Certificateless Ring Signatures. Cryptology ePrint Archive, Report 2007/236

12. Chow, S., Wong, D.: Anonymous Identification and Designated-Verifiers Signatures from Insecure Batch Verification. In: EuroPKI 2007. LNCS, vol. 4582, pp. 203–219. Springer, Heidelberg (2007)

13. Dodis, Y., Kiayias, A., Nicolosi, A., Shoup, V.: Anonymous identification in ad hoc groups. In: Cachin, C., Camenisch, J.L. (eds.) EUROCRYPT 2004. LNCS, vol. 3027, pp. 609–626. Springer, Heidelberg (2004)

14. Gorantla, M., Saxena, A.: An efficient certificateless signature scheme. In: Hao, Y., Liu, J., Wang, Y.-P., Cheung, Y.-m., Yin, H., Jiao, L., Ma, J., Jiao, Y.-C. (eds.) CIS 2005. LNCS (LNAI), vol. 3802, pp. 110–116. Springer, Heidelberg (2005)

15. Herranz, J., Saez, G.: Forking lemmas for ring signature schemes. In: Johansson, T., Maitra, S. (eds.) INDOCRYPT 2003. LNCS, vol. 2904, pp. 266–279. Springer, Heidelberg (2003)

16. Herranz, J., Saez, G.: New identity-based ring signature schemes. In: Lopez, J., Qing, S., Okamoto, E. (eds.) ICICS 2004. LNCS, vol. 3269, pp. 27–39. Springer, Heidelberg (2004)

17. Hess, F.: Efficient Identity Based Signature Schemes Based on Pairings. In: Nyberg, K., Heys, H.M. (eds.) SAC 2002. LNCS, vol. 2595, pp. 310–324. Springer, Heidelberg (2003)

18. Hu, B., Wong, D., Zhang, Z., Deng, X.: Key replacement attack against a generic construction of certificateless signature. In: Batten, L.M., Safavi-Naini, R. (eds.) ACISP 2006. LNCS, vol. 4058, pp. 235–346. Springer, Heidelberg (2006)

19. Huang, X., Mu, Y., Susilo, W., Wong, D., Wu, W.: Certificateless signature revisited. In: ACISP 2007. LNCS, pp. 308–322. Springer, Heidelberg (2007)

20. Huang, X., Susilo, W., Mu, Y., Zhang, F.: On the security of a certificateless signature scheme. In: Desmedt, Y.G., Wang, H., Mu, Y., Li, Y. (eds.) CANS 2005. LNCS, vol. 3810, pp. 13–25. Springer, Heidelberg (2005)

21. Li, X., Chen, K., Sun, L.: Certificateless signature and proxy signature schemes from bilinear pairings. Lithuanian Mathematical Journal 45, 76–83 (2005)

22. Liu, J., Au, M., Susilo, W.: Self-Generated-Certificate Public Key Cryptography and Certificateless Signature/Encryption Scheme in the Standard Model. In: ASIACCS 2007. 2007 ACM Symposium on InformAtion, Computer and Communications Security (2007)

23. Liu, J., Wei, V., Wong, D.: Linkable spontaneous anonymous group signature for ad hoc groups. In: Wang, H., Pieprzyk, J., Varadharajan, V. (eds.) ACISP 2004. LNCS, vol. 3108, pp. 325–335. Springer, Heidelberg (2004)

24. Liu, J., Wong, D.: On the security models of (threshold) ring signature schemes. In: Park, C.-s., Chee, S. (eds.) ICISC 2004. LNCS, vol. 3506, pp. 204–217. Springer, Heidelberg (2005)

25. Nguyen, L.: Accumulators from bilinear pairings and applications. In: Menezes, A.J. (ed.) CT-RSA 2005. LNCS, vol. 3376, pp. 275–292. Springer, Heidelberg (2005)

26. Rivest, R., Shamir, A., Tauman, Y.: How to leak a secret. In: Boyd, C. (ed.) ASIACRYPT 2001. LNCS, vol. 2248, pp. 552–565. Springer, Heidelberg (2001)

27. Shamir, A.: Identity based cryptosystems and signature schemes. In: Blakely, G.R., Chaum, D. (eds.) CRYPTO 1984. LNCS, vol. 196, pp. 47–53. Springer, Heidelberg (1985)
28. Wong, D., Fung, K., Liu, J., Wei, V.: On the RSCode construction of ring signature schemes and a threshold setting of RST. In: Qing, S., Gollmann, D., Zhou, J. (eds.) ICICS 2003. LNCS, vol. 2836, pp. 34–46. Springer, Heidelberg (2003)
29. Yap, W., Heng, S., Goi1, B.: An efficient certificateless signature scheme. In: Zhou, X., Sokolsky, O., Yan, L., Jung, E.-S., Shao, Z., Mu, Y., Lee, D.C., Kim, D., Jeong, Y.-S., Xu, C.-Z. (eds.) Emerging Directions in Embedded and Ubiquitous Computing. LNCS, vol. 4097, pp. 322–331. Springer, Heidelberg (2006)
30. Yum, D., Lee, P.: Generic construction of certificateless signature. In: Wang, H., Pieprzyk, J., Varadharajan, V. (eds.) ACISP 2004. LNCS, vol. 3108, pp. 200–211. Springer, Heidelberg (2004)
31. Zhang, F., Kim, K.: ID-Based blind signature and ring signature from pairings. In: Zheng, Y. (ed.) ASIACRYPT 2002. LNCS, vol. 2501, pp. 533–547. Springer, Heidelberg (2002)
32. Zhang, Z., Wong, D., Xu, J., Feng, D.: Certificateless public-key signature: security model and efficient construction. In: Zhou, J., Yung, M., Bao, F. (eds.) ACNS 2006. LNCS, vol. 3989, pp. 293–308. Springer, Heidelberg (2006)

# Complex Zero-Knowledge Proofs of Knowledge Are Easy to Use

Sébastien Canard, Iwen Coisel, and Jacques Traoré

Orange Labs, 42 rue des Coutures, 14000 Caen, France
{sebastien.canard,iwen.coisel,jacques.traore}@orange-ftgroup.com

**Abstract.** Since 1985 and their introduction by Goldwasser, Micali and Rackoff, followed in 1988 by Feige, Fiat and Shamir, zero-knowledge proofs of knowledge have become a central tool in modern cryptography. Many articles use them as building blocks to construct more complex protocols, for which security is often hard to prove. The aim of this paper is to simplify analysis of many of these protocols, by providing the cryptographers with a theorem which will save them from stating explicit security proofs. Kiayias, Tsiounis and Yung made a first step in this direction at Eurocrypt'04, but they only addressed the case of so-called "triangular set of discrete-log relations". By generalizing their result to any set of discrete-log relations, we greatly extend the range of protocols it can be applied to.

## 1 Introduction

The main purpose of authentication is to know who is who. More precisely, Alice wants to be convinced that the entity she communicates with is the right one. When using cryptography, this is often achieved by proving knowledge of a particular secret without (provably) revealing it. In 1985, Goldwasser, Micali and Rackoff [19] introduced the concept of zero-knowledge interactive proofs (ZKIP). The idea of using it for purposes of authentication came one year later in the article by Fiat and Shamir [15], followed in 1988 by Feige, Fiat and Shamir [14], who introduced the zero-knowledge proofs of knowledge (ZKPK).

In modern cryptography, these protocols are not only used for authentication but also as building blocks to achieve more complex purposes, such as for example guaranteeing the anonymity of a user [1,5,9] or committing to a secret value without being able to change one's mind [16]. In these schemes, users typically have to compute some public data relying on secret and random values, then prove that these public data are well-formed by using these building blocks. The security of the global construction relies both on the computed data and protocols they are involved in, which consequently have to be proven as being ZKPK.

The aim of this paper is to simplify analysis of many of these protocols, by providing the cryptographers with a theorem which will save them from stating explicit security proofs. Kiayias, Tsiounis and Yung made a first step in this direction at Eurocrypt'04, but they only addressed the case of so-called "triangular set of

W. Susilo, J.K. Liu, and Y. Mu. (Eds.): ProvSec 2007, LNCS 4784, pp. 122–137, 2007.
© Springer-Verlag Berlin Heidelberg 2007

discrete-log relations". By generalizing their result to any set of discrete-log relations, we greatly extend the range of protocols it can be applied to.

## 1.1 Related Work

Many ZKPK have been proposed since the article of Feige et al. in 1988 [14]. When based on discrete logarithms, they are often built over a cyclic group $\mathcal{G} = \langle g \rangle$ either of known prime order $q$ (after Schnorr's article [22]) or of unknown order (but in the same range of magnitude as the order of G). In this paper, we will only consider discrete-logarithm based ZKPK in groups of unknown order, since this is the most difficult case. In this setting, the building block is the GPS authentication scheme [18], which allows to prove knowledge of a discrete logarithm in such groups.

The construction of complex cryptographic tools such as group signature schemes, credential schemes or e-cash systems, always requires more than a single proof of knowledge of a single discrete logarithm. Rather, it involves several secret values and several (discrete-log based) relations between these values. The GPS scheme has therefore to be extended in order to obtain first new building blocks as e.g. a proof of knowledge of a representation [16,13], that involves two secret values and one relation, a proof of equality of two known representations [11,7], which requires four secret values and two relations, or the proof that a committed value lies in an interval [4,7,10,3], that necessitates several secret values and relations. Then, these various building blocks are used to construct still more elaborate protocols, the security of which must be demonstrated in detail for each of them, though the proofs are very similar to each other. As a consequence, it would be very useful to design a "general proof" which could apply to a wide range of such protocols, saving the designers from proving them secure.

Kiayias, Tsiounis and Yung [20] use such complex protocols in their construction of traceable signatures and, as an independent interest of the paper, make a first step towards designing such a general proof. They introduce the notion of *Discrete-Log Relation Set* (DLRS), that is a set of relations involving objects (as public keys and parameters) and free variables (as secret elements). For each free variable, there is a corresponding secret known by a prover $\mathcal{P}$. Then they propose a generic 3-move honest verifier zero-knowledge proof that allows $\mathcal{P}$ to prove the knowledge of these values. They also show that their construction is a ZKPK in the particular case of a triangular discrete-log relation set, that is when each relation introduces at most one new free variable w.r.t. the previous ones. They thus solve the above problem only in part, since their security proof only addresses a particular case. The aim of our paper is to solve this problem in general, for any discrete-log relation set.

## 1.2 Our Contribution

In this paper, we prove the soundness of any discrete-log relation set (DLRS), as defined by Kiayas, Tsiounis and Yung [20], i.e. when G is a (large) subgroup of the multiplicative group of the ring of integers modulo a composite integer. We do not address the zero-knowledge property, since it happens that it can be derived from [20] in a straight-forward manner. Unlike in [20], we do not have any restrictions on the kind of DLRS we use.

All security proofs for a ZKPK in a group of unknown order use the trick of either solving the Flexible RSA problem or retrieving all secret values involved in the proof[1]. Another contribution of this paper is that, to the best of our knowledge, our proof is the first one where the instance of the Flexible RSA problem is clearly defined.

### 1.3    Organization of the Paper

We first give some preliminaries in the next section. Section 3 introduces the first results on DLRS. It also gives evidence that the model of Kiayias *et al.* does not cover all kind of DLRS. We then give our new theorem and its proof in Section 4, then conclude in Section 5.

## 2    Preliminaries

In the following, $G$ will be typically a group $QR(n)$ of quadratic residues modulo $n$, where $n$ is a safe RSA modulus, as defined in the next subsection. By definition, the group $G$ is a group of possibly unknown order but where the size of the group order, denoted by $l_G$, is known.

### 2.1    Mathematical Background

A prime $p$ is a safe prime when $p = 2p'+1$ and $p'$ is a prime. A safe RSA modulus $n$ is an integer which is the product of two distinct safe primes $p = 2p' + 1$ and $q = 2q' + 1$, that is $n = pq$. The following technical lemma (see e.g. [17]) will be useful.

**Lemma 1.** *Let $n = pq$, where $p < q$, $p = 2p' + 1$, $q = 2q' + 1$, and $p$, $q$, $p'$, $q'$ are all prime numbers. Then,*

1. *The order of elements in $\mathbb{Z}_n^*$ is in $\{1, 2, p', q', 2p', 2q', p'q', 2p'q'\}$.*
2. *Given an element $w \in \mathbb{Z}_n^* \setminus \{-1, 1\}$ such that $\operatorname{ord}(w) < p'q'$, then either $\gcd(w - 1, n)$ or $\gcd(w + 1, n)$ is a prime factor of $n$.*

As a consequence of the above lemma, any value found by a party that does not know (and cannot compute) the factorization of $n$ must be of order at least $p'q'$ in $\mathbb{Z}_n^*$ (except for $-1$ and $1$).

**Lemma 2.** *Let $n = pq$, where $p < q$, $p = 2p' + 1$, $q = 2q' + 1$, and $p$, $q$, $p'$, $q'$ are all prime numbers.*
    *If $\nu^2 = 1$ and $\nu \in QR(n)$ then $\nu = 1$.*

---

[1] This is not the case for group of prime order.

*Proof.* As a safe modulus, $n$ is also a Blum number (a product of two primes equal to $3 \bmod 4$). As a consequence, any element of $QR(n)$ has exactly one square root in $QR(n)$. Since 1 is in $QR(n)$, 1 is the only square root of 1 in $QR(n)$.

## 2.2 Number Theoretic Assumption

The security of discrete-logarithm based zero-knowledge proofs of knowledge in groups of unknown order relies on the Flexible RSA assumption (independently introduced by Barić and Pfitzmann [2] and by Fujisaki and Okamoto [16], also known as Strong RSA). This assumption can be stated as follows, restricted to safe modulus, as it is the case in our paper.

**Assumption 1 (Flexible RSA).** *Given a safe RSA modulus $n$ and $\Gamma \in QR(n)$, it is infeasible to find $u \in \mathbb{Z}_n^*$ and $e \in \mathbb{Z}_{>1}$ such that $u^e = \Gamma \pmod{n}$, in time polynomial in $\lceil \log p'q' \rceil$ with a non-negligible probability.*

## 2.3 Zero-Knowledge Proofs of Knowledge

The notion of interactive zero-knowledge proof of knowledge has been formalized by Feige, Fiat and Shamir [14]. As in [20], we only consider honest verifier zero-knowledge since this is always the considered setting in studied complex constructions. Let us give the following (informal) definition.

**Definition 1.** *An interactive protocol between a prover $\mathcal{P}$ and a verifier $\mathcal{V}$, that takes on input $\mathcal{Y}$, is a zero-knowledge proof of knowledge of a secret $x$ if the three following properties are verified.*

- *Completeness: given an honest prover $\mathcal{P}$ and an honest verifier $\mathcal{V}$, the protocol succeeds with overwhelming probability.*
- *Soundness: given a dishonest prover $\tilde{\mathcal{P}}$ that is accepted by a verifier $\mathcal{V}$ with non-negligible probability, it is possible to construct a probabilistic polynomial time Turing machine $\mathcal{M}$ that can find $x$ by interacting with $\tilde{\mathcal{P}}$.*
- *(Honest verifier) zero-knowledge: it exists a probabilistic polynomial-time Turing machine that takes on input $\mathcal{Y}$ and which can simulate the communications between an honest prover $\mathcal{P}$ and an honest verifier $\mathcal{V}$ such that these simulated communications are indistinguishable from those between a real prover $\mathcal{P}$ and a real honest verifier $\mathcal{V}$.*

# 3    First Result on DLRS

Discrete-log relation sets (DLRS) were introduced by Kiayias *et al.* [20], and are useful when constructing complex proofs of knowledge for protocols operating over any group, even of unknown order. These constructions are quite useful in many complex cryptographic protocols [16,1,5,9].

### 3.1 Introduction of the Concept of DLRS

The following definition of a DLRS has been proposed in [20]:

**Definition 2.** *(see [20]) Let $G$ be a finite group. A discrete-log relation set $R$ with $z$ relations over $r$ variables and $m$ objects is a set of relations defined over the objects $A_1, \dots, A_m \in G$ and the free variables $\alpha_1, \dots, \alpha_r$ with the following specifications:*

1. *the $i$-th relation in the set $R$ is specified by a tuple $\langle a_1^i, \dots, a_m^i \rangle$ so that each $a_j^i$ is selected to be one of the free variables $\{\alpha_1 \dots, \alpha_r\}$ or an element of $\mathbb{Z}$. The relation is to be interpreted as $\prod_{j=1}^{m} A_j^{a_j^i} = 1$.*
2. *every free variable $\alpha_\omega$ is assumed to take values in a finite integer range $]2^{l_\omega} - 2^{\mu_\omega}, 2^{l_\omega} + 2^{\mu_\omega}[$ where $l_\omega, \mu_\omega \geq 0$.*

*We will write $R(\alpha_1, \dots, \alpha_r)$ to denote the conjunction of all relations $\prod_{j=1}^{m} A_j^{a_j^i} = 1$ that are included in $R$.*

*Notation.* The following notation will be used for the rest of the article. For the $i$-th relation, we define for each free variable $\alpha_\omega$ ($\omega \in \{1, \dots, r\}$) the set $\mathcal{J}_{\omega,i} \subseteq \{1, \dots, m\}$ of the variable's locations in the tuple $\langle a_1^i, \dots, a_m^i \rangle$. If a free variable $\alpha_\omega$ is not contained in the relation $i$, the set $\mathcal{J}_{\omega,i}$ is empty. We also set $\mathcal{J}_i = \bigcup_{\omega=1}^{r} \mathcal{J}_{\omega,i}$. Note that $j \notin \mathcal{J}_i$ means $a_j^i \in \mathbb{Z}$. Finally, for all $\omega = 1, \dots, r$, let us denote $\tilde{A}_{\omega,i} = \prod_{j \in \mathcal{J}_{\omega,i}} A_j$. Naturally, if $\mathcal{J}_{\omega,i} = \phi$ then $\tilde{A}_{\omega,i} = 1$. Consequently, the $i$-th relation verifies the following relation.

$$\prod_{j=1}^{m} A_j^{a_j^i} = 1 \Leftrightarrow \prod_{\omega=1}^{r} \tilde{A}_{\omega,i}^{\alpha_\omega} \prod_{j \notin \mathcal{J}_i} A_j^{a_j^i} = 1$$

| $\mathcal{P}$ | | $\mathcal{V}$ |
|---|---|---|
| $\forall \omega \in \{1, \cdots, r\}, r_\omega \in_R \pm\{0,1\}^{\epsilon(\mu_\omega + k)}$<br>$\forall i \in \{1, \cdots, z\}, t_i = \prod_{\omega=1}^{r} \tilde{A}_{\omega,i}^{r_\omega}$ | | |
| | $t = \{t_i\}$ $\longrightarrow$ | $c \in_R \{0,1\}^k$ |
| | $\longleftarrow$ $c$ | |
| $\forall \omega \in \{1, \cdots, r\}, s_\omega = r_\omega - c(x_\omega - 2^{l_\omega})$ | | |
| | $s = \{s_\omega\}$ $\longrightarrow$ | |
| | | $\forall i \in \{1, \cdots, z\}$, $\prod_{\omega=1}^{r} \tilde{A}_{\omega,i}^{s_\omega} \stackrel{?}{=} t_i \left( \prod_{j \notin \mathcal{J}_i} A_j^{a_j^i} \prod_{\omega=1}^{r} \tilde{A}_{\omega,i}^{2^{l_\omega}} \right)^c$<br>$\forall \omega \in \{1, \dots, r\}, s_\omega \stackrel{?}{\in} \pm\{0,1\}^{\epsilon(\mu_\omega + k)+1}$ |

**Fig. 1.** Discrete-log Relation Set $R$

Using these notations, a 3-move honest verifier zero-knowledge proof allows a prover that knows witnesses $x_1, \ldots, x_r$ such that $\forall \omega, x_\omega \in ]2^{l_\omega} - 2^{\epsilon(\mu_\omega + k)+2}, 2^{l_\omega} + 2^{\epsilon(\mu_\omega+k)+2}[$ and $R(x_1, \ldots, x_r) = 1$ to prove knowledge of these values, is presented in [20] and shown in Figure 1, where $\epsilon$ and $k$ are both security parameters such that $\epsilon > 1$ and $k \in \mathbb{N}$.

*Remark 1.* Note that the proof of knowledge of Figure 1 only proves that a witness $x \in ]2^l - 2^\mu, 2^l + 2^\mu[$ lies in $]2^l - 2^{\epsilon(\mu+k)+2}, 2^l + 2^{\epsilon(\mu+k)+2}[$. If needed, Boudot presents in [4] a scheme that provides a perfect proof but with less efficiency. If the interval is small, it is also possible to use a bit-by-bit solution, such as in [3,8].

## 3.2   The Result of Kiayias, Tsiounis and Yung

In [20], the authors present a particular case of our result. They prove the security of the construction of DLRS $R$ presented in Figure 1 w.r.t. Definition 1 (see Section 2.3) in the case the relation $R$ is *triangular*, and when $G$ is the group $QR(n)$ of quadratic residue modulo $n$ where $n$ is a safe RSA modulus. In the following, $G$ will also be this group. In the next section, we will prove the security of this construction in the general case. A triangular DLRS is introduced in [20] by the following definition.

**Definition 3.** *(see [20]) A discrete-log relation set $R$ is* triangular *if for each relation $i$ containing the $b + 1$ free variables $\alpha_\omega, \alpha_{\omega_1}, \ldots, \alpha_{\omega_b}$ it holds that $\{\alpha_{\omega_1}, \ldots, \alpha_{\omega_b}\}$ is a subset of the union of all the free variables involved in relations $1, \ldots, i - 1$.*

In this context, Kiayias *et al.* prove that the construction in Figure 1 is secure, i.e. for any triangular discrete-log relation set $R$ the 3-move protocol of figure 1 is complete, sound and honest-verifier zero-knowledge.

## 3.3   On the Use of Kiayias, Tsiounis and Yung Result

If a complex proof of knowledge can be represented by a triangular discrete-log relation set, the construction of [20] is suitable. This is for example the case in the group signature scheme proposed by Ateniese et al. [1], where the DLRS is composed of the 9 objects $T_1, T_2, T_3, A, a_0, a, y, g, h$, the 4 free-variables $\alpha, \beta, \gamma, \delta$ such that the 4 relations $a_0 = T_1^\alpha/(a^\beta y^\gamma) \wedge T_2 = g^\delta \wedge 1 = T_2^\alpha/g^\gamma \wedge T_3 = g^\alpha h^\delta)$ are verified in order to produce a signature.

But, in some cases, their approach cannot be applied. For example, the construction of [5] uses a DLRS with 8 objects $(C, C_1, C_2, C_3, g, h, 1/g, 1/h)$ and 11 variables $(\alpha, \beta, \gamma, \delta, \eta, \zeta, \phi, \psi, \theta, \sigma, \nu)$ verifying the following conjunction of the 7 relations

$$C = g^\alpha h^\phi \wedge g = \left(\frac{C}{g}\right)^\gamma h^\psi \wedge g = (gC)^\sigma h^\nu \wedge C_3 = g^\zeta h^\eta$$

$$\wedge C_1 = g^\alpha h^\theta \wedge v = C_2^\alpha \left(\frac{1}{h}\right)^\beta \wedge 1 = C_3^\alpha \left(\frac{1}{h}\right)^\delta \left(\frac{1}{g}\right)^\beta.$$

This DLRS clearly cannot be represented by a triangular discrete-log relation set.

This is also the case for [9] and more simply if Alice wants to commit to the value $x$ using the Fujisaki-Okamoto construction [16], and that she knows the commited value. The latter can be done by computing $PK(\alpha, \beta : C = g^\alpha h^\beta)$, that is a DLRS $R$ of 1 relation over 2 variables and 3 objects.

Consequently, there is sometimes more than one new free-variable at each new relation. More generally speaking, when a discrete-log relation set $R$ is not triangular, then for each relation $i$ containing the free variables $\alpha_{\tilde{\omega}_1}, \ldots, \alpha_{\tilde{\omega}_d}, \alpha_{\omega_1}, \ldots, \alpha_{\omega_b}$ it holds that the free variables $\alpha_{\omega_1}, \ldots, \alpha_{\omega_b}$ were contained in the union of all the free variables involved in relations $1, \ldots, i-1$. But that does not imply that the construction proposed in Figure 1 does not suit the general case. What lacks is a security proof for this construction in the general setting: the result of Kiayias $et\ al.$ [20] cannot be used as it is in the general case.

# 4   Generalization of the DLRS Theorem

In the general setting, the proof of completeness and honest-verifier zero-knowledge are not different to the one described in [20]. They will consequently not be treated in this paper. On the contrary, the proof of soundness of [20] must be deeply modified to suit the model considering any kind of DLRS, not only the triangular ones. This adaptation is the actual contribution of this paper.

An interactive protocol between a prover $\mathcal{P}$ and a verifier $\mathcal{V}$ verifies the soundness property if a dishonest prover $\tilde{\mathcal{P}}$ can not be accepted by a verifier $\mathcal{V}$ with non-negligible probability. Generally, a probabilistic polynomial time Turing machine $\mathcal{M}$ that can find $x$ by interacting with $\tilde{\mathcal{P}}$ is constructed to prove this property.

## 4.1   Our Result in a Nutshell

In this section, we briefly present our proof of soundness for all kinds of DLRS. The global structure of our proof is described in Figure 2.

In the first step, we assume that there exists $\tilde{\mathcal{P}}$ able to produce, with non-negligible probability, valid proofs of knowledge without knowing the secret values $X = \{x_1, \ldots, x_s\}$. Our aim is to construct a p.p.t. Turing machine $\mathcal{M}$ which, for each equation, is able to solve a given instance of the Flexible RSA problem (FRSA).

We first give an instance $(n, \Gamma)$ of the Flexible RSA problem to $\mathcal{M}$. $\mathcal{M}$ generates a random DLRS R, function of this instance. We then ask $\tilde{\mathcal{P}}$ to produce a valid proof of knowledge until we obtain two valid conversations $\langle t, c, s \rangle, \langle t, c^*, s^* \rangle$, where $c \neq c^*, t = \{t_1, \ldots, t_z\}, s = \{s_1, \ldots, s_r\}, s^* = \{s_1^*, \ldots, s_r^*\}$. We also denote $\tilde{s}_i = s_i - s_i^*$ for all $i$, $\tilde{S} = \{\tilde{s}_1, \ldots, \tilde{s}_r\}$ and $\tilde{c} = c - c^*$.

From these relations, $\mathcal{M}$ then computes for each of the $z$ relations an independent equation only depending on $c$, $c^*$, $s$ and $s^*$. Each couple $(s_i, s_i^*)$ is related to a free variable, and thus to a secret. Our aim is then to retrieve the value of all secrets.

In a similar way to [20], the machine $\mathcal{M}$ always operates as follows.

1. For each of the $z$ relations, it first pushes aside the couples $(s_i, s_i^*)$ for which the secret has already been retrieved. This step is not done for the first relation.
2. It then calculates the number of secrets that are unknown in the relation. Depending on it, there are three cases.
   (a) There is only one unknown secret. This is the case that has been studied in [20]. In fact, if, for each relation, there is only one unknown secret, the DLRS is then triangular. The conclusion is that either we can compute all secret or we can solve the instance $(n, \Gamma)$ of the Flexible RSA problem.
   (b) There are two unknown secrets. This case corresponds to the ZKPK of a representation. In a group of unknown order, the case has been studied in [13], using the Root assumption. We thus adapt it by using the Flexible RSA assumption. The conclusion is that either we can compute all secrets or we can solve the instance $(n, \Gamma)$ of the Flexible RSA problem.
   (c) The general case (up to three but the cases 1 and 2 can also be seen as particular cases) is the one we study in this paper. The relation can thus be denoted as $\tilde{A}_1^{\tilde{s}_1} \ldots \tilde{A}_d^{\tilde{s}_d} = \Psi_i^{\tilde{c}}$. $\tilde{A}_1, \ldots, \tilde{A}_d$ correspond to the objects defined after the DLRS definition (see Section 3) and $\Psi_i$ is the product of a constant element and possibly some objects $\tilde{\mathcal{A}}_j$ raised to the power of secret values already compute. $\tilde{c}, \tilde{S}$ are dependant of $c, c^*, S, S^*$.
   We then study two cases. In the first one, $\mathcal{M}$ retrieves all secrets involved in this relation. The second case is also divided into two possible cases.
       i. $\mathcal{M}$ can solve the instance $(n, \Gamma)$ of the FRSA problem.
       ii. We prove that the second case only happens with probability less than $1/2$.
   If $\mathcal{M}$ is able to find all the secret values, $\tilde{\mathcal{P}}$ can also do it. So, under the assumption that $\tilde{\mathcal{P}}$ does not know these values, we conclude that $\mathcal{M}$ solves the given instance of the Flexible RSA problem.

In all papers where there is a ZKPK in the group of unknown order $QR(n)$, such as in the paper of Kiayias, Tsiounis and Yung [20] but also e.g. in [1,6], a p.p.t. Turing machine $\mathcal{M}$ is constructed so as to solve with a non-negligible probability an instance of the Flexible RSA problem. However, this instance is never specified so that it could possibly be an easy instance of the problem.

More precisely, the solved instance corresponds to the modular multiplication of public parameters (the $A_i$'s) but nothing is said about the difficulty of solving the Flexible RSA on one $A_i$ nor on the modular multiplication of some of them. It seems better, and that's what we do in our proof, to introduce a challenger $\mathcal{C}$ which gives to $\mathcal{M}$ a random instance of the Flexible RSA problem at the beginning of the proof.

Nevertheless, as we will see in our proof, $\mathcal{M}$ will need to interact possibly with several dishonest provers $\tilde{\mathcal{P}}$, depending on the objects $A_1, \ldots, A_m$ the machine $\mathcal{M}$ has to use to solve the Flexible RSA instance. The number $z$ of relations and the number $r$ of free variables can be unchanged between all the interactions. This consequently implies the use of an attacker $\tilde{\mathcal{P}}$ being able to break the soundness of a DLRS for a polynomial number of tuples $A_1, \ldots, A_m$.

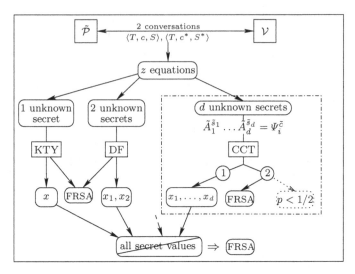

**Fig. 2.** Sketch of proof

## 4.2   The New Theorem

We can then introduce our new theorem and prove the security of the construction in Figure 1 in the case of any discrete-log relation set.

**Theorem 1.** *Let $G = QR(n)$ where $n(= (2p' + 1)(2q' + 1))$ is safe. For any discrete-log relation set $R$ the 3-move protocol of Figure 1 is a honest-verifier zero-knowledge proof of knowledge that can be used by a first party (prover) knowing a witness for $R$ to prove knowledge of the witness to a second party (verifier).*

*Proof.* We have to prove that the protocol of Figure 1 verifies the three properties of completeness, soundness and honest verifier zero-knowledge. The proof of completeness and honest verifier zero-knowledge can be found in [20]. They will not be treated in this proof. The proof of soundness of [20] must be modified to suit our model (all kinds of DLRS, not only the triangular ones).

   Assume it exists a dishonest prover $\tilde{\mathcal{P}}$ attacking the soundness of the protocol presented in Figure 1. It means that $\tilde{\mathcal{P}}$ is able to produce valid conversations for this protocol with non-negligible probability, and without knowing all the involved secrets. We define a p.p.t. Turing machine $\mathcal{M}$ which solves a given instance of the Flexible RSA problem, using $\tilde{\mathcal{P}}$ as an oracle. Let $\mathcal{C}$ be the challenger who gives the instance $(n, \Gamma)$ of the Flexible RSA problem to $\mathcal{M}$. The Turing machine $\mathcal{M}$:

- takes on input the instance $(n, \Gamma)$ of the FRSA problem given by $\mathcal{C}$,
- generates a random DLRS $R$,
- interacts with $\tilde{\mathcal{P}}$,
- solves the given instance using $\tilde{\mathcal{P}}$'s outputs.

In order to define $R$, $\mathcal{M}$ randomly chooses integers $\gamma_\omega \in \{1, \ldots, n^2\}$ and computes $A_\omega = \Gamma^{\gamma_\omega}$, for $\omega \in \{1, \ldots, m\}$. Under the factorisation assumption, the order of $\Gamma$ is $\phi(n)/4$ and consequently, the $A_\omega$ are distributed over $QR(n)$. $\mathcal{M}$ sends $R$ to the dishonest prover $\tilde{\mathcal{P}}$. Let $\langle t_1, \ldots, t_z, c, s_1, \ldots, s_r \rangle$ and $\langle t_1, \ldots, t_z, c^*, s_1^*, \ldots, s_r^* \rangle$, with $c \neq c^*$, be two accepted protocols for R between $\tilde{\mathcal{P}}$ and an (honest) verifier. As these protocols are valid, both following relations are true for all $i \in \{1, \ldots, z\}$:

$$\prod_{\omega=1}^{r} \tilde{A}_{\omega,i}^{s_\omega} = t_i \left( \prod_{j \notin \mathcal{J}_i} A_j^{a_j^i} \prod_{\omega=1}^{r} \tilde{A}_{\omega,i}^{2^{l_\omega}} \right)^c \quad \text{and} \quad \prod_{\omega=1}^{r} \tilde{A}_{\omega,i}^{s_\omega^*} = t_i \left( \prod_{j \notin \mathcal{J}_i} A_j^{a_j^i} \prod_{\omega=1}^{r} \tilde{A}_{\omega,i}^{2^{l_\omega}} \right)^{c^*}$$

$$\Rightarrow \prod_{\omega=1}^{r} \tilde{A}_{\omega,i}^{s_\omega - s_\omega^*} = \left( \prod_{j \notin \mathcal{J}_i} A_j^{a_j^i} \prod_{\omega=1}^{r} \tilde{A}_{\omega,i}^{2^{l_\omega}} \right)^{c-c^*}. \tag{1}$$

The proof consists now in proving that using relations (1) for all $i \in \{1, \ldots, z\}$, $\mathcal{M}$ is able to solve the given instance of the Flexible RSA problem. First, we introduce the notations we will use in the following of the proof. For $\omega \in \{1, \ldots, r\}$: $\tilde{s}_\omega := s_\omega - s_\omega^*$, and $\tilde{c} := c - c^*$. We also introduce the sets of distinct integers $\Omega_i = \{\omega_{i,1}, \ldots, \omega_{i,d}\}$, for each relation $i$ (i.e. for $i$ from 1 to $z$), such that the free variables $\alpha_{\omega_{i,1}}, \ldots, \alpha_{\omega_{i,d}}$ are the ones involved in the $i$-th relation. Using these notations, for $i \in \{1, \ldots, z\}$, the relation (1) can be written:

$$\prod_{\omega \in \Omega_i} \tilde{A}_{\omega,i}^{\tilde{s}_\omega} = \left( \prod_{j \notin \mathcal{J}_i} A_j^{a_j^i} \prod_{\omega \in \Omega_i} \tilde{A}_{\omega,i}^{2^{l_\omega}} \right)^{\tilde{c}}. \tag{2}$$

**Relation 1.** Considering the first relation, there are two cases:

- $\tilde{c}$ divides all the integers $\tilde{s}_\omega$
  The particular case where $d = 1$ (as in [20]) is included in the general case. So we restrict our proof to the general case, where $d \geq 1$. It holds that the first relationship in $R$ involves $d$ free variables denoted by $\alpha_\omega$ for $\omega \in \Omega_1 = \{\omega_{1,1}, \ldots, \omega_{1,d}\}$. In this case, we have the following relation, where $\tilde{A}_\omega$ stands for $\tilde{A}_{\omega,1}$:

$$\prod_{\omega \in \Omega_1} \tilde{A}_\omega^{\tilde{s}_\omega} = \left( \prod_{\omega \in \Omega_1} \tilde{A}_\omega^{2^{l_\omega}} \prod_{j \notin \mathcal{J}_1} A_j^{a_j^1} \right)^{\tilde{c}}.$$

As $\tilde{c}$ divides $\tilde{s}_\omega$, for all $\omega \in \Omega_1$, the previous relation becomes (see remark below):

$$\prod_{\omega \in \Omega_1} \tilde{A}_\omega^{-\frac{\tilde{s}_\omega}{\tilde{c}} + 2^{l_\omega}} \prod_{j \notin \mathcal{J}_1} A_j^{a_j^1} = 1. \tag{3}$$

*Remark 2.* In fact, we have the following equivalence :

$$\prod_{\omega \in \Omega_1} \tilde{A}_\omega^{\tilde{s}_\omega} = \left( \prod_{\omega \in \Omega_1} \tilde{A}_\omega^{2^{l_\omega}} \prod_{j \notin \mathcal{J}_1} A_j^{a_j^1} \right)^{\tilde{c}} \Leftrightarrow \prod_{\omega \in \Omega_1} \tilde{A}_\omega^{\frac{\tilde{s}_\omega}{\tilde{c}}} = \nu \prod_{\omega \in \Omega_1} \tilde{A}_\omega^{2^{l_\omega}} \prod_{j \notin \mathcal{J}_1} A_j^{a_j^1},$$

with $\nu^c = 1$. Indeed, by definition $\tilde{c} < 2^k$ and thus $\tilde{c} < min(p, q)$. By Lemma 1, we can then affirm that the order of $\nu$ can only be equal to 1 or 2 and by lemma 2, that $\nu$ can only be equal to 1. We will not repeat this remark later, even when it holds.

The equality 3 implies that we have constructed the $d$ witnesses for each $\omega$-th variable $\tilde{x}_\omega = \frac{\tilde{s}_\omega}{\tilde{c}} + 2^{l_\omega} = \frac{s_\omega - s_\omega^*}{c - c^*} + 2^{l_\omega}$ where $\omega \in \Omega_1$.
We verify that these values are in the right interval. For $\omega \in \Omega_1$, $\tilde{s}_\omega \in \pm\{0,1\}^{\epsilon(\mu_\omega + k) + 2}$ (since $s_\omega, s_\omega^* \in \pm\{0,1\}^{\epsilon(\mu_\omega + k) + 1}$, it implies that $s_\omega^* - s_\omega \in \pm\{0,1\}^{\epsilon(\mu_\omega + k) + 2}$) it follows that $\frac{\tilde{s}_\omega}{\tilde{c}} \in \pm\{0,1\}^{\epsilon(\mu_\omega + k) + 2}$ and as a result $\tilde{x}_\omega \in ]2^{l_\omega} - 2^{\epsilon(\mu_\omega + k) + 2}, 2^{l_\omega} + 2^{\epsilon(\mu_\omega + k) + 2}[$. Consequently, $\mathcal{M}$ finds the secrets $\{\tilde{x}_\omega\}$ *for* $\omega \in \Omega_1$ in polynomial time, $\mathcal{P}$ can also find it. So we can assume that $\mathcal{P}$ already knows it.
- It exists at least one integer $\omega \in \Omega_1$ such that $\tilde{c}$ does not divide $\tilde{s}_\omega$.
Now, we prove that $\mathcal{M}$ solves the given instance $(n, \Gamma)$ of the FRSA problem on $G$. Let

$$T_1 = \left( \prod_{\omega \in \Omega_1} \tilde{A}_\omega^{2^{l_\omega}} \prod_{j \notin \mathcal{J}_1} A_j^{a_j^1} \right).$$

For all $j$ in $\{1, \ldots, d\}$, $A_j = \Gamma^{\gamma_j}$, and for all $\omega \in \Omega_1$, we have $\tilde{A}_\omega = \prod_{j \in \mathcal{J}_{\omega,1}} A_j = \prod_{j \in \mathcal{J}_{\omega,1}} \Gamma^{\gamma_j} = \Gamma^{\sum_{j \in \mathcal{J}_{\omega,1}} \gamma_j}$. We define $\theta_\omega = \sum_{j \in \mathcal{J}_{\omega,1}} \gamma_j$ (mod $n^2$) for all $\omega \in \Omega_1$. Consequently, with those notations relation (2) becomes:

$$\prod_{\omega \in \Omega_1} \left( \Gamma^{\sum_{j \in \mathcal{J}_{\omega,1}} \gamma_j} \right)^{\tilde{s}_\omega} = T_1^{\tilde{c}} \quad \Leftrightarrow \quad \Gamma^{\sum_{\omega \in \Omega_1} \theta_\omega \tilde{s}_\omega} = T_1^{\tilde{c}}. \tag{4}$$

Without loss of generality, we assume that integers $\tilde{s}_{1,1}, \ldots, \tilde{s}_{1,d_1}$ are divisible by $\tilde{c}$, as opposed to integers $\tilde{s}_{1,d_1+1}, \ldots, \tilde{s}_{1,d_2}$, with $1 \le d_1 < d_2 = d$. If $d_2 = 1$, because we assumed that $\tilde{c}$ does not divide all the $\tilde{s}_\omega$, then $d_1 = 0$. Then there are two cases:
1. If $\tilde{c}$ does not divide $\sum_{\omega \in \Omega_1} \theta_\omega \tilde{s}_\omega$, $\mathcal{M}$ can solve the given instance of the Flexible RSA problem as follows. Let $\delta$ be the greatest common divisor of $\tilde{c}$ and $\sum_{\omega \in \Omega_1} \theta_\omega \tilde{s}_\omega$. There exist $\alpha$ and $\beta$ in $\mathbb{Z}$ such that $\alpha\tilde{c} + \beta\left(\sum_{\omega \in \Omega_1} \theta_\omega \tilde{s}_\omega\right) = \delta$. It follows that

$$\Gamma = \Gamma^{\left(\alpha\tilde{c} + \beta(\sum_{\omega \in \Omega_1} \theta_\omega \tilde{s}_\omega)\right)/\delta} = (\Gamma^\alpha T_1^\beta)^{\tilde{c}/\delta}.$$

By assumption, $\delta < \tilde{c}$ and so, we can set $e = \tilde{c}/\delta$ and $u = \Gamma^\alpha T_1^\beta$, which is a solution of the Flexible RSA problem on $G$ relatively to the instance $(n, \Gamma)$.

*Remark 3.* This part of the proof works with any values of the integer $d_1 < d_2$.

2. If $\tilde{c}$ divides $\sum_{\omega \in \Omega_1} \theta_\omega \tilde{s}_\omega$, we prove that, as $\tilde{\mathcal{P}}$ does not have complete information about the $\theta_\omega$'s, this case only happens with probability less or equal to $1/2$. Consequently, case (1) happens with probability greater than $1/2$ and the probability to break the Flexible RSA assumption is greater than $1/2$. The strategy consists in choosing the $\theta_\omega$'s until we get back on case (1). This quickly happens in a bounded time with non-negligible probability.

   Let $f$ be a prime factor of $\tilde{c}$ and $e$ an integer such that:
   - $f^e$ is the greatest power of $f$ that divides $\tilde{c}$,
   - at least one of the $\tilde{s}_\omega$ is non-zero modulo $f^e$.

   This value must exist since $\tilde{c}$ does not divide at least one of the $\tilde{s}_\omega$, even if $d_2 = 1$. For all $\omega \in \Omega_1$, we define $b_\omega = \theta_\omega \pmod{\mathrm{ord}(G)}$ and $h_\omega$ such that $\theta_\omega = b_\omega + h_\omega \, \mathrm{ord}(G)$. Note that the $\tilde{A}_{\omega,1}$'s represent all the information the machine $\tilde{\mathcal{P}}$ knows about the $\theta_\omega$'s and the $b_\omega$'s are uniquely determined from the $\tilde{A}_{\omega,1}$'s, whereas the $h_\omega$'s are completely unknown. As $f^e$ divides $\sum_{\omega \in \Omega_1} \theta_\omega \tilde{s}_\omega$ (since $\tilde{c}$ does), it follows that

$$\sum_{\omega \in \Omega_1} \theta_\omega \tilde{s}_\omega = 0 \pmod{f^e} \quad \text{and} \quad \sum_{j=1}^{d_2} \theta_{\omega_{1,j}} \tilde{s}_{\omega_{1,j}} = 0 \pmod{f^e}.$$

We know that for $j$ from 1 to $d_1$, $\tilde{s}_{\omega_{1,j}} \equiv 0 \pmod{f^e}$ as they are divisible by $\tilde{c}$, consequently, $\sum_{j=1}^{d_1} \theta_{\omega_{1,j}} \tilde{s}_{\omega_{1,j}} \equiv 0 \pmod{f^e}$.

$$\sum_{j=d_1+1}^{d_2} b_{\omega_{1,j}} \tilde{s}_{\omega_{1,j}} + \mathrm{ord}(G) \sum_{j=d_1+1}^{d_2} h_{\omega_{1,j}} \tilde{s}_{\omega_{1,j}} = 0 \pmod{f^e}. \qquad (5)$$

Since $f^e \leq 2^k \leq min(p', q')$, we have $|G| \neq 0 \pmod{f}$. $\tilde{\mathcal{P}}$ does not know anything about the $h_\omega$'s except that they follow the uniform distribution and that they satisfy equation (5). Let $\tilde{\omega}$ be one of the indexes such that $\tilde{s}_{\tilde{\omega}}$ is not divisible by $f^e$. If $d_2 = 1$, it is evident that $\tilde{\omega} = 1$. If we fix the $h_\omega$'s for $\omega \in \Omega_1/\{\tilde{\omega}\}$, then the number of solutions modulo $f^e$ of the equation (5) is at most $gcd(|G|\tilde{s}_{\tilde{\omega}}, f^e)$. This number is necessarily a power of $f$, since $f^e$ does not divide $|G|\tilde{s}_{\tilde{\omega}}$, and at most $f^{e-1}$. Since for all $\omega \in \Omega_1$, $\theta_\omega$ has been chosen from a large interval, the distribution of $b_\omega$ is statistically indistinguishable from the uniform distribution on $\mathbb{Z}_{p'q'}$. Moreover the distribution of $h_\omega$ is statistically indistinguishable from the uniform distribution on $\{0, \ldots, M\}$, where $M = \lfloor n^2/p'q' \rfloor$. Thus, there are nearly $M^{d_2}$ possible tuples $\langle h_1, \ldots, h_{d_2} \rangle$ uniformly distributed [12]. Let $w \in \mathbb{R}$ such that $M = wf^e$. The number of solutions of the equation is at most $[wf^{e-1}]M^{d_2-1}$, hence the probability that the $h_\omega$'s verify the equation is at most

$$\frac{[wf^{e-1}]M^{d_2-1}}{M^{d_2}} \leq \frac{wf^{e-1}}{M} \leq \frac{wf^{e-1}}{wf^e} \leq \frac{1}{f} \leq \frac{1}{2}.$$

We can then solve the instance of the Flexible RSA problem with non-negligible probability.

If $\tilde{\mathcal{P}}$ outputs integers $\tilde{c}, \tilde{s}_1, \ldots, \tilde{s}_r$ such that relation (4) is verified and at least one of the $\tilde{s}_\omega$ is not divisible by $\tilde{c}$, for $\omega \in \Omega_1$, then $\mathcal{M}$ solves the given instance of the Flexible RSA problem.

**Relation $i$.** Now, we assume that we have processed all the relations with index less than $i$ and $\mathcal{M}$ did not already solve the instance of the FRSA problem. We process the $i$-th relation which involves variables $\alpha_\omega$, for all $\omega \in \Omega_i (= \{\omega_{i,1}, \ldots, \omega_{i,d}\})$. As we have processed all the relations with index less than $i$, some of these variables are already known. We split $\Omega_i$ in two sets of integers $\Omega_{i,1} = \{\omega_{i,1}, \ldots, \omega_{i,d_2}\}$ and $\Omega_{i,2} = \{\omega_{i,d_2+1}, \ldots, \omega_{i,d}\}$ so that the variables $\alpha_\omega$, for $\omega \in \Omega_{i,2}$ are already contained in previous relations. We assume that these variables are known by $\mathcal{M}$ and then by $\tilde{\mathcal{P}}$. By an inductive argument, we construct witnesses for the free-variables $\tilde{x}_\omega = \frac{-\tilde{s}_\omega}{\tilde{c}} + 2^{l_\omega} = \frac{s_\omega^* - s_\omega}{c - c^*} + 2^{l_\omega}$, and $\tilde{c}$ divides $\tilde{s}_\omega$, for all $\omega \in \Omega_{i,2}$. There are again two cases:

- $\tilde{c}$ divides $\tilde{s}_\omega$, for all $\omega \in \Omega_{i,1}$

  First, we study the particular case where $d_2 = 1$ (see also [20]): the $i$-th relation in R involves variables $\alpha_{\omega_{i,1}}, \ldots, \alpha_{\omega_{i,d}}$, where $\alpha_{\omega_{i,1}}$ is the only one for which the witness associated is not yet constructed. Using relation (2), the $i$-th relation becomes, where $\tilde{A}_\omega$ stands for $\tilde{A}_{\omega,i}$:

$$\tilde{A}_{\omega_{i,1}}^{\tilde{s}_{\omega_{i,1}}} \prod_{\omega \in \Omega_{i,2}} \tilde{A}_\omega^{\tilde{s}_\omega} = \left( \tilde{A}_{\omega_{i,1}}^{2^{l_{\omega_{i,1}}}} \prod_{\omega \in \Omega_{i,2}} \tilde{A}_\omega^{2^{l_\omega}} \prod_{j \notin \mathcal{J}_i} A_j^{a_j^i} \right)^{\tilde{c}}$$

$$\tilde{A}_{\omega_{i,1}}^{\tilde{s}_{\omega_{i,1}}} = \left( \tilde{A}_{\omega_{i,1}}^{2^{l_{\omega_{i,1}}}} \prod_{\omega \in \Omega_{i,2}} \tilde{A}_\omega^{\tilde{x}_\omega} \prod_{j \notin \mathcal{J}_i} A_j^{a_j^i} \right)^{\tilde{c}}.$$

  As $\tilde{c}$ divides $s_{\omega_{i,1}}$ we obtain the    following relation :

$$\tilde{A}_{\omega_{i,1}}^{\frac{-\tilde{s}_{\omega_{i,1}} + 2^{l_{\omega_{i,1}}}}{\tilde{c}}} \prod_{\omega \in \Omega_{i,2}} \tilde{A}_\omega^{\tilde{x}_\omega} \prod_{j \notin \mathcal{J}_i} A_j^{a_j^i} = 1.$$

The above equality implies that we have constructed the witness for the variables $\tilde{x}_{\omega_{i,1}} = \frac{-\tilde{s}_{\omega_{i,1}}}{\tilde{c}} + 2^{l_{\omega_{i,1}}} = \frac{s_{\omega_{i,1}}^* - s_{\omega_{i,1}}}{c - c^*} + 2^{l_{\omega_{i,1}}}$. As previously, it is possible to show that this witness is in the right interval, i.e. $\tilde{x}_{\omega_{i,1}} \in ]2^{l_{\omega_{i,1}}} - 2^{\epsilon(\mu_{\omega_{i,1}}+k)+2}, 2^{l_{\omega_{i,1}}} + 2^{\epsilon(\mu_{\omega_{i,1}}+k)+2}[$. We can also assume in this case that $\tilde{\mathcal{P}}$ already knows this witness.

Now, we study the general case where $d_2 \neq 1$: the $i$-th relation in R involves variables $\alpha_{\omega_1}, \ldots, \alpha_{\omega_d}$ so that variables $\alpha_{\omega_{d_2+1}}, \ldots, \alpha_{\omega_d}$ were already contained in previous relations. So the associated witnesses are known by $\tilde{\mathcal{P}}$.

Using relation (2), the $i$-th relation becomes:

$$\prod_{\omega \in \Omega_{i,1}} \tilde{A}_{\omega}^{\tilde{s}_{\omega}} \prod_{\omega \in \Omega_{i,2}} \tilde{A}_{\omega}^{\tilde{s}_{\omega}} = \left( \prod_{\omega \in \Omega_{i,1}} \tilde{A}_{\omega}^{2^{l_{\omega}}} \prod_{\omega \in \Omega_{i,2}} \tilde{A}_{\omega}^{2^{l_{\omega}}} \prod_{j \notin \mathcal{J}_i} A_j^{a_j^i} \right)^{\tilde{c}} \tag{6}$$

$$\prod_{\omega \in \Omega_{i,1}} \tilde{A}_{\omega}^{\tilde{s}_{\omega}} = \left( \prod_{\omega \in \Omega_{i,1}} \tilde{A}_{\omega}^{2^{l_{\omega}}} \prod_{\omega \in \Omega_{i,2}} \tilde{A}_{\omega}^{\tilde{x}_{\omega}} \prod_{j \notin \mathcal{J}_i} A_j^{a_j^i} \right)^{\tilde{c}}. \tag{7}$$

As $\tilde{c}$ divides $s_{\omega}$ for all $\omega \in \Omega_{i,1}$ we obtain the following relation:

$$\prod_{\omega \in \Omega_{i,1}} \tilde{A}_{\omega}^{\frac{-\tilde{s}_{\omega}+2^{l_{\omega}}}{\tilde{c}}} \prod_{\omega \in \Omega_{i,2}} \tilde{A}_{\omega}^{x_{\omega}} \prod_{j \notin \mathcal{J}_i} A_j^{a_j^i} = 1.$$

The above equality implies that we have constructed $d_2$ witnesses for each $\omega$-th variable $\tilde{x}_{\omega} = \frac{-\tilde{s}_{\omega}}{\tilde{c}} + 2^{l_{\omega}} = \frac{s_{\omega}^* - s_{\omega}}{c - c^*} + 2^{l_{\omega}}$, for all $\omega \in \Omega_{i,1}$. As previously, it is possible to show that these witnesses are in the right intervals, i.e. $\tilde{x}_{\omega} \in ]2^{l_{\omega}} - 2^{\epsilon(\mu_{\omega}+k)+2}, 2^{l_{\omega}} + 2^{\epsilon(\mu_{\omega}+k)+2}[$, for all $\omega \in \Omega_{i,1}$. We can also assume in this case that $\tilde{\mathcal{P}}$ already knows those witnesses.

- It exists at least one integer $\omega \in \Omega_{i,1}$ such that $\tilde{c}$ does not divide $\tilde{s}_{\omega}$. Like in part (4.2), we have to prove that $\mathcal{M}$ can solve the given instance $(n, \Gamma)$ of the Flexible RSA problem on G. As in the previous part, the relation (7) is true. Let $T_i = \left( \prod_{\omega \in \Omega_{i,1}} \tilde{A}_{\omega}^{2^{l_{\omega}}} \prod_{\omega \in \Omega_{i,2}} \tilde{A}_{\omega}^{\tilde{x}_{\omega}} \prod_{j \notin \mathcal{J}_i} A_j^{a_j^i} \right)$. As in part (4.2), we have, for all $\omega \in \Omega_{i,1}$, $\tilde{A}_{\omega} = \Gamma^{\sum_{j \in \mathcal{J}_{\omega,i}} \gamma_j}$, and we define $\theta_{\omega} = \sum_{j \in \mathcal{J}_{\omega,i}} \gamma_j$, for all $\omega \in \Omega_{i,1}$. With those notations, relation (7) becomes $\Gamma^{\sum_{\omega \in \Omega_{i,1}} \theta_{\omega} \tilde{s}_{\omega}} = T_i^{\tilde{c}}$. This relation has exactly the same form than relation (4). Then, it is possible to conclude similarly that $\mathcal{M}$ solves the given instance of the Flexible RSA problem on G with a non-negligible probability.

In conclusion, $\mathcal{M}$ will not be able to solve the given instance $(n, \Gamma)$ of the Flexible RSA problem only if $\tilde{c}$ divides all integers $\tilde{s}_1, \ldots, \tilde{s}_r$. But in this case, it is necessary that $\tilde{\mathcal{P}}$ knows all the witnesses involved in the protocol, which is infeasible by assumption. Consequently, $\mathcal{M}$ necessarily solves the given instance $(n, \Gamma)$ if it obtains as input two valid conversations from $\tilde{\mathcal{P}}$. Since the machine $\mathcal{M}$ interacts a polynomial number of times with $\tilde{\mathcal{P}}$ which runs in polynomial time, $\mathcal{M}$ solves the random instance of the Flexible RSA problem in polynomial time. Thus, under the Flexible RSA assumption, $\tilde{\mathcal{P}}$ cannot product valid conversations for the protocol of Figure 1, then the soundness of the DLRS is proved.

## 5   Conclusion

We have proved that many complex discrete-logarithm protocols in groups of unknown order are ZKPK under the Flexible RSA assumption. A result by

Kiayias, Tsiounis and Yung appears as a particular case of our construction. It is possible to extend the work done in this paper to signature schemes using the Fiat-Shamir heuristic [15]. The security of the construction can then be proven by using the result of [21].

There is still some work to do since complex cryptographic constructions can also use ZKPK of secret values verifying some different properties not studied in this paper such as *e.g.* the proof of the "or" statement and the proof of equality of two discrete logarithms in different groups.

## Acknowledgements

We are grateful to Marc Girault for his suggestions of improvement, and to anonymous referees for their valuable comments. This work has been partially financially supported by the European Commission through the IST Program under Contract IST-2002-507932 ECRYPT.

## References

1. Ateniese, G., Camenisch, J., Joye, M., Tsudik, G.: A Practical and Provably Secure Coalition-Resistant Group Signature Scheme. In: Bellare, M. (ed.) CRYPTO 2000. LNCS, vol. 1880, pp. 255–270. Springer, Heidelberg (2000)
2. Barić, N., Pfitzmann, B.: Collision-Free Accumulators and Fail-Stop Signature Schemes Without Trees. In: Fumy, W. (ed.) EUROCRYPT 1997. LNCS, vol. 1233, pp. 480–484. Springer, Heidelberg (1997)
3. Bellare, M., Goldwasser, S.: Verifiable Partial Key Escrow. In: ACM CCS 1997, pp. 78–91. ACM Press, New York (1997)
4. Boudot, F.: Efficient Proofs that a Committed Number Lies in an Interval. In: Preneel, B. (ed.) EUROCRYPT 2000. LNCS, vol. 1807, pp. 431–444. Springer, Heidelberg (2000)
5. Camenisch, J., Lysyanskaya, A.: Dynamic Accumulators and Application to Efficient Revocation of Anonymous Credentials. In: Yung, M. (ed.) CRYPTO 2002. LNCS, vol. 2442, pp. 61–76. Springer, Heidelberg (2002)
6. Camenisch, J., Michels, M.: A Group Signature Scheme Based on an RSA-Variant. In: Ohta, K., Pei, D. (eds.) ASIACRYPT 1998. LNCS, vol. 1514, pp. 160–174. Springer, Heidelberg (1998)
7. Camenisch, J., Michels, M.: Proving in Zero-Knowledge that a Number is the Product of Two Safe Primes. In: Stern, J. (ed.) EUROCRYPT 1999. LNCS, vol. 1592, pp. 107–122. Springer, Heidelberg (1999)
8. Canard, S., Gouget, A., Hufschmitt, E.: A Handy Muti-Coupon System. In: Jakobsson, M., Yung, M., Zhou, J. (eds.) ACNS 2004. LNCS, vol. 3089, pp. 66–81. Springer, Heidelberg (2004)
9. Canard, S., Traoré, J.: On Fair E-cash Systems based on Group Signature Schemes. In: Safavi-Naini, R., Seberry, J. (eds.) ACISP 2003. LNCS, vol. 2727, pp. 237–248. Springer, Heidelberg (2003)
10. Chan, A.H., Frankel, Y., Tsiounis, Y.: Easy Come - Easy Go Divisible Cash. In: Nyberg, K. (ed.) EUROCRYPT 1998. LNCS, vol. 1403, pp. 561–575. Springer, Heidelberg (1998)

11. Chaum, D., Pedersen, T.: Transferred Cash Grows in Size. In: Rueppel, R.A. (ed.) EUROCRYPT 1992. LNCS, vol. 658, pp. 390–407. Springer, Heidelberg (1993)
12. Cramer, R., Shoup, V.: Signature Schemes Based on the Strong RSA Assumption. ACM TISSEC 3(3), 161–185 (2000)
13. Damgå, I.: rd and E. Fujisaki, A Statistically-Hiding Integer Commitment Scheme Based on Groups with Hidden Order. In: Zheng, Y. (ed.) ASIACRYPT 2002. LNCS, vol. 2501, pp. 143–159. Springer, Heidelberg (2002)
14. Feige, U., Fiat, A., Shamir, A.: Zero-knowledge Proofs of Identity. Journal of Cryptology 1(2), 77–94 (1988)
15. Fiat, A., Shamir, A.: How to Prove Yourself: Practical Solutions to Identification and Signature Problems. In: Odlyzko, A.M. (ed.) CRYPTO 1986. LNCS, vol. 263, pp. 186–194. Springer, Heidelberg (1987)
16. Fujisaki, E., Okamoto, T.: Statistical Zero-Knowledge Protocols Solution to Identification and Signature Problems. In: Kaliski Jr., B.S. (ed.) CRYPTO 1997. LNCS, vol. 1294, pp. 16–30. Springer, Heidelberg (1997)
17. Gennaro, R., Rabin, T., Krawczyk, H.: RSA-Based Undeniable Signatures. Journal of Cryptology 13(4), 397–416 (2000)
18. Girault, M., Poupard, G., Stern, J.: On the Fly Authentication and Signature Schemes Based on Groups of Unknown Order. Journal of Cryptology 19(4), 463–487 (2006)
19. Goldwasser, S., Micali, S., Rackoff, C.W.: The Knowledge Complexity of Interactive Proof Systems. SIAM Journal of Computing 18(1), 186–208 (1989)
20. Kiayias, A., Tsiounis, Y., Yung, M.: Traceable Signatures. In: Cachin, C., Camenisch, J.L. (eds.) EUROCRYPT 2004. LNCS, vol. 3027, pp. 571–589. Springer, Heidelberg (2004), http://eprint.iacr.org/
21. Pointcheval, D., Stern, J.: Security Arguments for Digital Signatures and Blind Signatures. Journal of Cryptology 13(3), 361–396 (2000)
22. Schnorr, C.P.: Efficient Signature Generation for Smart Cards. Journal of Cryptology 4(3), 239–252 (1991)

# Does Secure Time-Stamping Imply Collision-Free Hash Functions?

Ahto Buldas[1,2,3,*] and Aivo Jürgenson[2,4]

[1] Cybernetica, Akadeemia tee 21, 12618 Tallinn, Estonia
[2] Tallinn University of Technology, Raja 15, 12618 Tallinn, Estonia
Aivo.Jurgenson@eesti.ee
[3] University of Tartu, Liivi 2, 50409 Tartu, Estonia
Ahto.Buldas@ut.ee
[4] Elion Enterprises Ltd, Endla 16, 15033 Tallinn, Estonia

**Abstract.** We prove that there are no black-box reductions from Collision-Free Hash Functions to secure time-stamping schemes, which means that in principle secure time-stamping schemes may exist even if there exist no collision-resistant hash functions. We show that there is an oracle relative to which there exist secure time-stamping schemes but no hash function is collision-free. The oracle we use is not new — a similar idea was already used by Simon in 1998 to show that collision-free hash functions cannot be constructed from one-way permutations in a black-box way. Our oracle contains a random hash function family $f$ and a universal collision-finder $A$. We show that hash-tree time-stamping schemes that use $f$ as a hash function remain secure even in the presence of $A$. From more practical view, our result is an implicit confirmation that collision-finding attacks against hash functions will tell us quite little about the security of hash-tree time-stamping schemes and that we need more dedicated research about back-dating attacks against practical hash functions.

## 1 Introduction

Cryptographic hash functions transform a message $X$ of an arbitrary length into a digest $h(X)$ of a fixed length. They have several applications, such as electronic signatures, fast Message Authentication Codes (MACs), secure registries, time-stamping schemes, etc. Though the range of hash function applications is growing rapidly, not much is known either about suitable design criteria or about how to formalize the security conditions for hash functions demanded by applications.

Security proofs of applications often assume the *collision-freedom* of hash functions and this gives an impression as if such a strong security requirement was necessary. Recent success in finding collisions for practical hash functions (MD4,MD5, RIPEMD, SHA-0) by Wang et al. [13,14,16] and later improvements [11,15] forced us to revisit the security proofs in order to clarify for which practical implementations the collisions are a real threat.

This paper focuses on one particular application of cryptographic hash functions – time-stamping. For a long time it was believed that collision-freedom is a necessary

---

* Partially supported by Estonian SF grant no. 6944, and by EU FP6-15964: "AEOLUS".

W. Susilo, J.K. Liu, and Y. Mu. (Eds.): ProvSec 2007, LNCS 4784, pp. 138–150, 2007.

and sufficient condition for the security of hash-tree based time-stamping schemes. In 2004, it was shown by Buldas and Saarepera [3] that collision-freedom is probably *insufficient* to prove that unbounded hash-tree time-stamping schemes [1,5] (without explicit restrictions to the length of hash-chains) are secure. Buldas and Laur [2] then showed that collision-freeness (and even one-wayness) is also *unnecessary*—once there are hash functions that are secure for time-stamping, then there also exist hash functions which are secure for time-stamping but are not even one-way (and hence, not collision-resistant). This result shows that breaking a particular hash function in terms of collisions (even if they are meaningful textual documents) does not necessarily mean that this particular hash function is insecure for time-stamping.

In this paper we go even further. We show that collision-free hash functions cannot be constructed from secure time-stamping schemes in a black-box way. This means that even if one finds a universal collision-finder that "breaks" all known hash functions, there may still exist hash functions that remain secure for time-stamping. We show that there is an oracle relative to which there exist secure time-stamping schemes but no hash function is collision-free. The oracle we use is not new — a similar construction was already used by Simon [12] to show that collision-free hash functions cannot be constructed from one-way permutations in a black-box way. Our oracle contains a random hash function family $f: \{0,1\}^{2k} \rightarrow \{0,1\}^k$ and a universal collision-finder $A$. To prove the main result of this paper we will show that hash-tree time-stamping schemes with the random hash function $f$ remain secure in the presence of the universal collision-finding oracle $A$.

From the practical point of view, our result is another confirmation that collision-finding attacks against hash functions will tell us quite little about the security of time-stamping schemes that use these "broken" hash functions. Therefore, to study the security of hash-based time-stamping schemes, it is insufficient to study the feasibility of collision-finding attacks. Instead, we need dedicated research on practical back-dating attacks. To our knowledge, there is only one work published on this issue [8].

The paper is organized as follows. Section 2 gives necessary notations and definitions. Section 3 outlines the basics of secure hash-based time-stamping schemes. In Section 4, for the self-consistency of this paper, we provide the reader with basic definitions and results about oracle separation. In Section 5, we define the separating oracles and prove the main result of this work.

## 2 Preliminaries and Notation

By $x \leftarrow \mathcal{D}$ we mean that $x$ is chosen randomly according to a distribution $\mathcal{D}$. If A is a probabilistic function or a Turing machine, then $x \leftarrow A(y)$ means that $x$ is chosen according to the output distribution of A on an input $y$. By $\mathcal{U}_n$ we denote the uniform distribution on $\{0,1\}^n$. If $\mathcal{D}_1, \ldots, \mathcal{D}_m$ are distributions and $F(x_1, \ldots, x_m)$ is a predicate, then $\Pr[x_1 \leftarrow \mathcal{D}_1, \ldots, x_m \leftarrow \mathcal{D}_m : F(x_1, \ldots, x_m)]$ denotes the probability that $F(x_1, \ldots, x_m)$ is true after the ordered assignment of $x_1, \ldots, x_m$. For functions $f, g: \mathbb{N} \rightarrow \mathbb{R}$, we write $f(k) = O(g(k))$ if there are $c, k_0 \in \mathbb{R}$, so that $f(k) \leq cg(k)$ ($\forall k > k_0$). We write $f(k) = \omega(g(k))$ if $\lim_{k \to \infty} \frac{g(k)}{f(k)} = 0$. If $f(k) = k^{-\omega(1)}$, then $f$ is *negligible*. A Turing machine M is *polynomial-time* (*poly-time*) if it runs in time

$k^{O(1)}$, where $k$ denotes the input size. Let FP be the class of all probabilistic functions $f: \{0,1\}^* \to \{0,1\}^*$ computable by a poly-time M.

By an *oracle Turing machine* we mean an incompletely specified Turing machine $S$ that comprises calls to *oracles*. The description can be completed by defining the oracle as a function $\mathcal{O}: \{0,1\}^* \to \{0,1\}^*$. In this case, the machine is denoted by $S^{\mathcal{O}}$. The function $y \leftarrow \mathcal{O}(x)$ is not necessarily computable but may still have assigned a conditional running time $t(x)$, which does not reflect the actual amount of computations needed to produce $y$ from $x$. The running time of $S^{\mathcal{O}}$ comprises the conditional running time of oracle calls – each call $\mathcal{O}(x)$ takes $t(x)$ steps. An oracle $\mathcal{O}$ is *poly-time* if $t(x) = |x|^{O(1)}$, where $|x|$ denotes the bit-length of $x$. We say that $S$ is a *poly-time oracle machine* if $S^{\mathcal{O}}$ runs in poly-time, whenever $\mathcal{O}$ is poly-time.

A *primitive* $\mathcal{P}$ is a class of (not necessarily computable by ordinary Turing machines) functions intended to perform a security related task (e.g. data confidentiality, integrity etc.). Each primitive $\mathcal{P}$ is characterized by the success $\delta(k)$ of an adversary A. An instance $f$ of a primitive $\mathcal{P}$ is *secure* if every poly-time adversary can break $f$ only with a negligible success. Let $\mathcal{O}$ be an oracle. We say that $f$ is *secure relative to* $\mathcal{O}$ if every poly-time oracle adversary $A^{\mathcal{O}}$ can break $f$ only with negligible success.

A distribution family $\{\mathcal{D}_k\}_{k \in \mathbb{N}}$ is *poly-sampleable* if there is $D \in$ FP with output distribution $D(1^k) \equiv \mathcal{D}_k$. Let $\mathcal{F} = \{\mathcal{F}_k\}_{k \in \mathbb{N}}$ be a poly-sampleable distribution family such that every $h \leftarrow \mathcal{F}_k$ is a function $h: \{0,1\}^{\ell(k)} \to \{0,1\}^k$, where $\ell(k) = k^{O(1)}$ and $\ell(k) > k$ for every $k \geq 0$. We say that $\mathcal{F}$ is *collision-free* if for every $A \in$ FP:

$$\Pr\left[h \leftarrow \mathcal{F}_k, (x, x') \leftarrow A(1^k, h): x \neq x', h(x) = h(x')\right] = k^{-\omega(1)} .$$

If for every $k$ there exists $h_k$ so that $\Pr[h \leftarrow \mathcal{F}_k: h = h_k] = 1$, then we have a fixed family of functions, i.e. for each $k$ we have a single unkeyed hash function, e.g. SHA-1.

## 3    Secure Time-Stamping

A time-stamping procedure consists of the following general steps:

– Client sends a request $x \in \{0,1\}^k$ to Server.
– Server binds $x$ with a time value $t$ and sends Client a time-certificate $c$.

Time-stamping protocols process requests in batches $\mathcal{X}_1, \mathcal{X}_2, \mathcal{X}_3 \ldots$ that we call *rounds*. The rounds correspond to time periods of fixed duration (one hour, one day, etc.) After the $t$-th period, a short commitment $r_t = \mathrm{Com}(\mathcal{X}_t)$ of the corresponding batch $\mathcal{X}_t$ is published. A request $x \in \mathcal{X}_t$ precedes another request $x' \in \mathcal{X}_{t'}$ if $t < t'$. The requests of the same batch are considered simultaneous. For such a scheme to be efficient there must be an efficient way to prove inclusions $x \in \mathcal{X}_t$, i.e. there is a verification algorithm Ver that on input a request $x$, a certificate $c$ and a commitment $r_t$ returns true if $x \in \mathcal{X}_t$. On the one hand, it should be easy to create certificates for the members $x \in \mathcal{X}_t$, i.e. there has to be an efficient certificate generation algorithm Cert that outputs a certificate $c = \mathrm{Cert}(x, \mathcal{X}_t)$. On the other hand, for the security of this scheme it must be infeasible to create such proofs for non-members $y \notin \mathcal{X}_t$, i.e. it is infeasible to find a certificate $c'$ such that $\mathrm{Ver}(y, c', r_t) = \mathsf{true}$.

**Definition 1.** *By a time-stamping scheme we mean a triple* (Com, Cert, Ver) *of efficient algorithms, where:*

- Com *is a commitment algorithm, which on input a set* $X$ *of requests outputs a commitment* $r =$ Com($X$).
- *(Compression property) for every* $k > 0$, $m > 0$ *and for any set* $X = \{x_1, \ldots, x_m\}$, *where* $x_i \in \{0, 1\}^k$, *the output* Com($X$) *belongs to* $\{0, 1\}^k$. *Hence, the commitment procedure is able to compress* $mk$-*bit strings into* $k$-*bit commitments.*
- Cert *is a certificate generation algorithm, which on input a set* $X$ *and an element* $x \in X$ *generates a certificate* $c =$ Cert($X$, $x$).
- Ver *is a verification algorithm, which on input a request* $x$, *a certificate* $c$ *and a commitment* $r$ *outputs* yes *or* no, *depending on whether* $x$ *is a member of* $X$ *(the set that corresponds to the commitment* $r$). *It is assumed that for every set* $X$ *of requests and every member-request* $x \in X$ *the following correctness condition holds:*

$$\mathsf{Ver}(x, \mathsf{Cert}(x, X), \mathsf{Com}(X)) = \mathsf{yes} \ . \tag{1}$$

The compression property is crucial for the results of this paper being interesting. If non-compressing commitment procedures were allowed, it would be pretty straightforward to show that collision-resistant hash functions cannot be constructed from time-stamping schemes. We will return to this question later when we introduce the notion of security.

### 3.1 Security Condition for Time-Stamping Schemes

Different security definitions exist for time-stamping schemes [3,2,5]. In this paper, we use the strongest definition [2], which though applying to so-called *hash-tree time-stamping schemes*, can be easily generalized to all time-stamping schemes. The security condition of [2] is inspired by the following attack-scenario with a malicious Server:

(1) Server computes a commitment $r$ and publishes it. Note that Server is assumed to be malicious, so there are no guarantees that $r$ is created by applying Com to a set $X$ of requests.
(2) Alice, an inventor, creates a description $\mathcal{D}_A \in \{0, 1\}^*$ of her invention and protects it somehow, possibly by filing a patent or obtaining a time stamp.
(3) Some time later, the invention $\mathcal{D}_A$ is disclosed to the public and Server tries to steal it by showing that the invention was known to Server long before Alice time-stamped it. He creates a slightly modified version $\mathcal{D}'_A$ of $A$, i.e. changes the in-vertor's name, modifies the creation time, and possibly rewords the document in a suitable way.
(4) Finally, Server back-dates a hash value $x = H(\mathcal{D}'_A)$ of the modified invention document, by finding a certificate $c$, so that $\mathsf{Ver}(x, c, r) = \mathsf{yes}$.

To formalize such a scenario, a two-staged adversary $A = (A_1, A_2)$ is used. The first stage $A_1$ *computes* $r$ (and an advice string $a$) after which the second stage $A_2$ finds a new $x$ (which is assumed to be a random variable with a sufficient amount of entropy) and a certificate $c$ such that $\mathsf{Ver}(x, c, r) = \mathsf{yes}$. Note that $x$ must be unpredictable because otherwise $x$ could have been pre-computed by $A_1$ and hence there would be nothing wrong in proving that $x$ existed before $r$ was computed and published.

Hence, for defining the security of time-stamping schemes, the class of possible adversaries is restricted. We have to consider only those adversaries that produce unpredictable $x$. Let FPU be the class of all two-staged probabilistic poly-time adversaries $(A_1, A_2)$, such that the output component $x$ is unpredictable, even if the output of $A_1$ is known to the predictor, i.e. for every poly-time predictor $\Pi$:

$$\Pr\left[(r,a) \leftarrow A_1(1^k), x' \leftarrow \Pi(r,a), (x,c) \leftarrow A_2(r,a): x' = x\right] = k^{-\omega(1)} \ . \tag{2}$$

The internal random coins of $A_2$ and $\Pi$ are not explicitly shown in (2), i.e. are not included into $a$. Otherwise, $\Pi \equiv A_2$ would contradict the definition.

Note also that it is reasonable to assume that the advice string $a$ contains all internal random coins of $A_1$ (see [2] for more details) and we will use this assumption later in the proof of our main theorem. However, as we will show, the separation result still remains valid without this assumption.

**Definition 2.** *A time-stamping scheme is secure if for every* $(A_1, A_2) \in$ FPU:

$$\Pr\left[(r,a) \leftarrow A_1(1^k), (x,c) \leftarrow A_2(r,a): \mathsf{Ver}(x,c,r) = \mathsf{yes}\right] = k^{-\omega(1)} \ . \tag{3}$$

**Remark on the Compression Property.** If the compression property was not assumed in Def. 1, then we would have a trivial provably secure time-stamping scheme $T_0$. Define $\mathsf{Com}(\mathcal{X}) = \mathcal{X}$, $\mathsf{Cert}(\mathcal{X}, x) = \lfloor\rfloor$, and $\mathsf{Ver}(x,c,r) = \mathsf{yes}$ iff $x \in r$. Clearly, $T_0$ cannot be broken by any adversary with any amount of computational resources. If we have a black-box cryptographic reduction that constructs collision-free hash functions $H^T$ based on arbitrary time-stamping scheme $T$, then also $H^{T_0}$ must be a collision-free hash function. However, collision-free hash functions can never be secure against arbitrary computational power—collisions always exist and can be found with exhaustive search. Therefore, even if such a construction exists, it must be very inefficient. So, without assuming the compression property, our separation result would not be very interesting.

## 3.2   Hash Tree Time-Stamping Schemes

The commitments $r_t$ are computed as the root hash values of Merkle hash trees [9]. For the self-consistency of this paper, we outline the basic facts about hash-chains and how they are used in time-stamping. We use the notation and definitions introduced in [2]. By $\lfloor\rfloor$ we mean the empty string. If $x = x_1 \| x_2 \in \{0,1\}^{2k}$ and $x_1, x_2 \in \{0,1\}^k$, then by $y \in x$ we mean the inclusion $y \in \{x_1, x_2\}$ (i.e. $y$ is one of the two halves of $x$).

**Definition 3 (Hash-Chain).** *Let* $h: \{0,1\}^{2k} \rightarrow \{0,1\}^k$ *be a twice-compressing hash function. By an* $h$-chain *from* $x \in \{0,1\}^k$ *to* $r \in \{0,1\}^k$ *we mean a (possibly empty) sequence* $c = (c_1, \ldots, c_\ell)$ *of pairs* $c_i \in \{0,1\}^{2k}$, *such that the next two conditions hold:*

*(1) if* $c = \lfloor\rfloor$ *then* $x = r$; *and*
*(2) if* $c \neq \lfloor\rfloor$ *then* $x \in c_1$, $r = h(c_\ell)$, *and* $h(c_i) \in c_{i+1}$ *for every* $i \in \{1, \ldots, \ell - 1\}$.

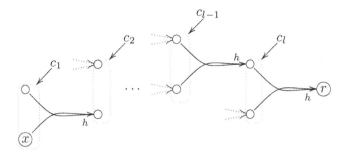

**Fig. 1.** Representation of a hash-chain

*We denote by $\mathsf{Chain}_h(x,c) = r$ the proposition that $c$ is an $h$-chain from $x$ to $r$. Note that $\mathsf{Chain}_h(x, \|) = x$ for every $x \in \{0,1\}^k$. An illustration of this definition is given in Fig. 1.*

**Hash-tree time-stamping schemes** use Merkle trees to compute the commitments $r_t$ for batches $X_t$. The commitment $\mathsf{Com}(X_t)$ of a batch $X_t = \{x_1, \ldots, x_N\}$ is $r_t = T^h(x_1, \ldots, x_N) \in \{0,1\}^k$, where $T^h$ is a tree-shaped hashing scheme. A certificate for $x \in X_t$ is a hash chain $c$ such that $\mathsf{Chain}_h(x,c) = r_t$. The verification procedure $\mathsf{Ver}(x, c, r_t)$ returns yes whenever $\mathsf{Chain}_h(x,c) = r_t$. In this paper, we denote the hash-tree time-stamping scheme by $T^h$.

# 4 Black-Box Reductions and Separation Techniques

When constructing a cryptographic primitive $\mathcal{P}$ out of another primitive $\mathcal{Q}$ one mostly uses *black-box reductions*, i.e. $\mathcal{P}$ is constructed by using $\mathcal{Q}$ as a subroutine without paying any attention to its implementation. One may also say that $\mathcal{Q}$ is used as a *black box*. In security proofs for $\mathcal{P}$ an adversary for $\mathcal{Q}$ is constructed by using an arbitrarily chosen adversary for $\mathcal{P}$ as a subroutine. Black-box reductions between cryptographic primitives were first defined informally by Impagliazzo and Rudich [7]. A somewhat more formal definition was later given by Gertner et al. [4].

## 4.1 Fully Black-Box Reductions

**Definition 4.** *Black-box reduction (or fully black-box reduction) from primitive $\mathcal{P}$ to primitive $\mathcal{Q}$ consists of two poly-time oracle machines* P *and* S, *satisfying the following two conditions:*

- *$\forall f$ (any function) implementing $\mathcal{Q}$, $P^f$ implements $\mathcal{P}$; and*
- *$\forall A \forall f$ (any functions) $f$ A breaks $P^f$ (as $\mathcal{P}$), then $S^{A,f}$ breaks $f$ (as $\mathcal{Q}$).*

There are several forms of black-box reductions. For a detailed discussion on black-box reductions, see [10]. Almost all reductions used in cryptography are indeed black-box reductions.

To show that no general reduction from $\mathcal{P}$ to $\mathcal{Q}$ exists requires proving that no efficient instances of $\mathcal{Q}$ exist, which is unreachable for the current state of the art. It is however still possible to show that *no black-box reduction from $\mathcal{P}$ to $\mathcal{Q}$ exists*. This of course does not completely eliminate the existence of general reductions but still indicates the hardness of constructing a reduction by showing that the traditional techniques certainly will fail. The first such statement in cryptography was proved by Impagliazzo and Rudich [7]. They built an oracle relative to which a key agreement does not exist but one-way permutations do, which shows the impossibility of black-box reductions of a key agreement to one-way permutations. There are many other such results known in cryptography [12,6,4]. Many of these separation results actually proved the non-existence of the so-called *semi black-box reductions*, but as reported by Hsiao and Reyzin [6], showing the non-existence of fully black-box reductions is much more simple. In this paper, we use their separation technique, which can be formalized as follows:

**Theorem 1 (Hsiao,Reyzin).** *If there are two oracles A and f such that*

*(1) there is a poly-time oracle machine $\mathsf{T}^f$ that implements $\mathcal{Q}$;*
*(2) for every poly-time oracle machine $\mathsf{P}^f$ that implements $\mathcal{P}$, there is a poly-time oracle machine $\mathsf{D}^{A,f}$ that breaks $\mathsf{P}^f$;*
*(3) there is no poly-time oracle machine S such that $\mathsf{S}^{A,f}$ breaks $\mathsf{T}^f$;*

*then there exist no black-box reductions from $\mathcal{P}$ to $\mathcal{Q}$.*

Compared to the separation of Simon [12], this result is weaker and applies only to fully black-box reductions. However, in practice this weaker result is not so weak at all because almost all efficient reductions in cryptography are fully black-box.

## 4.2 Semi Black-Box Reductions

So called *semi black-box* reductions differ from *black-box* reduction in the way we construct an adversary for breaking the original primitive $f$ based on an adversary A that breaks the constructed primitive $P^f$. In black-box reductions there was a uniform algorithm S for this task, whereas in semi black-box reductions there is no such algorithm:

**Definition 5.** *Semi black-box reduction from primitive $\mathcal{P}$ to primitive $\mathcal{Q}$ is a poly-time oracle machine* P, *satisfying the following two conditions:*

– *$\forall f$ (any function) implementing $\mathcal{Q}$, $\mathsf{P}^f$ implements $\mathcal{P}$; and*
– *$\forall A$ (a poly-time oracle-machine) $\exists B$ (a poly-time oracle machine), so that $\forall f$ (any function), if $A^f$ breaks $\mathsf{P}^f$ (as $\mathcal{P}$), then $B^f$ breaks $f$ (as $\mathcal{Q}$).*

To show the impossibility of semi-black-box reductions, we would have to prove that for every poly-time oracle machine $P^{A,f}$ that implements $\mathcal{P}$, there is a poly-time oracle machine $D^{A,f}$ that efficiently breaks $P^{A,f}$. So, $A$ should be able to break constructions in which it participates itself. Needless to say that separation results with such a self-reference are not very easy to follow and in this work we make no attempts to establish such separation.

## 5 Separating Collision-Free Hash Functions from Time-Stamping

### 5.1 Choice of $A$ and $f$

Let $\mathcal{F}^{2-1} = \{\mathcal{F}_k^{2-1}\}_{k \in \mathbb{N}}$ be a function family, where $\{\mathcal{F}_k^{2-1}\}_{k \in \mathbb{N}}$ is the set of all functions $f_k$ of type $\{0,1\}^{2k} \to \{0,1\}^k$. Let $f$ be an oracle which contains a random function family $\mathcal{F}^{2-1}$, where $f_k \leftarrow \mathcal{F}_k^{2-1}$. Oracle $f$ answers to a query $(k, x)$ (where $x \in \{0,1\}^{2k}$) with $f(k, x) = f_k(x)$. We assume that all $f$-queries are of unit cost. We will later omit $k$ and write $f(x)$ instead of $f(k, x)$ if the value of $k$ is clear from the context.

Let $A$ be another oracle which uses the same function family $\{f_k\}$ and also a countably infinite random string $\omega \leftarrow \{0,1\}^\infty$ for the internal coin-tosses of $A$. Oracle $A$ is a universal collision-finder that takes as input a description $"F^f"$ of a function $F^f \colon \{0,1\}^m \to \{0,1\}^\ell$ that may comprise $f$-calls. We assume that the description explicitly includes $m$ and $\ell$ and is represented in the form of an $f$-circuit, i.e. a boolean circuit which in addition to ordinary boolean gates also comprises $f$-gates (possibly, with various $m$ and $\ell$). The circuit description helps to make the running time of oracle calls independent of inputs and the choices of $f$ and $A$. We also assume that for every description $"F^f"$ there is a canonical ordering of $f$-queries, which does not necessarily coincide with the order in which the queries are made in real computations. Note that it is very hard to imagine a description language where such an ordering is not possible.

The behavior of $A$ is defined as follows:

> **Definition of** $A$: $A("F^f")$ picks $X \leftarrow \{0,1\}^m$, chooses $X' \leftarrow F^{-1}(F(X))$ and returns $(X, X')$. For these random choices, dedicated sections of the random string $\omega$ are used. $A("F^f")$ also returns the pairs of $(y, f(y))$, which will be known during the computation of $F^f(X)$ and $F^f(X')$. The conditional running time of $A("F^f")$ is defined to be twice the number of gates in the description of $F^f$.

The random variables $X$ and $X'$ are both uniformly distributed, but depend on each other. Like in [12], the identical distribution of $X$ and $X'$ is a crucial detail in the proof of the separation theorem. Clearly not all collision-finding oracles are suitable for separation as we will see later in Sec. 6.

For our purposes it is safe to assume that the oracle calls are never repeated (i.e. $A$ is never called twice with the same arguments) and hence we need no more than $2m$ random bits for each function description $F^f \colon \{0,1\}^m \to \{0,1\}^\ell$. We will also assume that the random bits used by different $A$-queries are independent. We will show that:

(1) *Relative to $f$ and $A$ there are no collision-resistant function families.* This is clear because for every poly-time oracle machine $P^f$ that implements a function family $p_k \colon \{0,1\}^{m(k)} \to \{0,1\}^{\ell(k)}$ there is a poly-time oracle machine $D^A$ which on input $1^k$ generates a finite circuit $"F_k^f"$ for computing $p_k$ (i.e. restricts the input domain, unrolls the loops, etc.) and outputs a collision $(x, x') \leftarrow A("F_k^f")$. Even though $A$ can break only finite-domain hash functions $F \colon \{0,1\}^m \to \{0,1\}^\ell$, we can use $A$ for breaking infinite domain hash functions as well. Indeed, if $F \colon \{0,1\}^\infty \to \{0,1\}^\ell$ is poly-time, then we can represent $F$ as a uniform polynomial-size circuit family and then use $A$ for a particular member-circuit.

(2) *The standard Merkle-tree time-stamping scheme* $\mathsf{T}^f$ *is secure relative to $f$ and $A$. We show that no poly-time oracle machine $\mathsf{S}^{A,f}$ can break $\mathsf{T}^f$ better than with negligible probability.*

From Thm. 1 it then follows that there exist no black-box reductions of collision-free hash functions to secure time-stamping schemes.

## 5.2   Separation Theorem

**Theorem 2.** *For every poly-time oracle machine* $\mathsf{S}^{A,f} = (\mathsf{S}_1^{A,f}, \mathsf{S}_2^{A,f})$ *which is unpredictable in terms of (2):*

$$\delta_S(k) = \mathsf{Pr}\left[(r,a)\leftarrow\mathsf{S}_1^{A,f}(1^k),(x,c)\leftarrow\mathsf{S}_2^{A,f}(r,a)\colon\mathsf{Chain}_f(x,c){=}r\right]=k^{-\omega(1)} \ . \quad (4)$$

*Recall that* $\mathsf{Chain}_f(x,c) = r$ *is equivalent to* $\mathsf{Ver}(x,c,r) =$ yes *in our particular case.*

*Proof.* Let $\mathsf{S}^{A,f} = (\mathsf{S}_1^{A,f}, \mathsf{S}_2^{A,f})$ be an adversary which is unpredictable in terms of (2). As a result of a successful attack a hash-chain $c = (c_1,\dots,c_m)$ is found, where $x \in c_1$ and $f_k(c_m) = r$.

In any stage of the attack let $\mathcal{R}$ denote the set of all pairs $(x,f_k(x)) \in \{0,1\}^{2k} \times \{0,1\}^k$ that are known to $\mathsf{S}^{A,f}$. This knowledge may only be originated from $f$- and $A$-calls and hence $\mathcal{R}$ can be created by the following rules:

– After an $f$-call, $y \leftarrow f_k(x)$, the pair $(x,f_k(x))$ is added to $\mathcal{R}$.
– After an $A$-call, $(X,X') \leftarrow A(\text{"}F^f\text{"})$, all pairs of $(x,f_k(x))$, which will be known from the computation of $F^f(X)$ and $F^f(X')$, are added to $\mathcal{R}$.

Let $\mathcal{R}^1$ denote the set of all known pairs after the stop of $\mathsf{S}_1^{A,f}(1^k)$ and let $\mathcal{R}^2$ be the set of known pairs added to $\mathcal{R}$ after the stop of $\mathsf{S}_2^{A,f}(r,a)$, i.e. $\mathcal{R} = \mathcal{R}^1 \cup \mathcal{R}^2$ (see Fig. 2).

We assume without loss of generality that after a successful attack $\mathsf{S}_2^{A,f}$ "knows" all the internal computations of $c$, i.e. $(c_i,f_k(c_i)) \in \mathcal{R}$ for all $i = 1,\dots,m$. Indeed, even if $\mathsf{S}_2^{A,f}$ returns $x$ and $c$ without actually using any oracle calls, we can always construct a new adversary that verifies $c$ the internal $f$- and $A$-calls of $c$. The success probability of the new adversary is not smaller than that of the original adversary.

Let $\mathcal{X}^1$ be the set that consists of $r$ and all $x \in \{0,1\}^k$ for which there is a pair $(c,f(c)) \in \mathcal{R}^1$ and $x \in c$, i.e. $\mathcal{X}^1 = \{x | \exists c\colon x \in c, (c,f(c)) \in \mathcal{R}^1\} \cup \{r\}$. First, we prove that the probability $\mathsf{Pr}\left[x \in \mathcal{X}^1\right]$ (after the attack scenario (4)) is negligible. Indeed, otherwise it would be possible to construct a predictor $\mathsf{\Pi}^{A,f}(r,a)$ from $\mathsf{S}_1^{A,f}$. The predictor will extract the random string $\omega_1$ of $\mathsf{S}_1^{A,f}$ from the advice $a$. After that it will simulate the run of $\mathsf{S}_1$ using $A$- and $f$-calls and will re-produce $\mathcal{R}^1$ and $\mathcal{X}^1$. The predictor will output a random $x'$ from $\mathcal{X}^1$. Predictor $\mathsf{\Pi}^{A,f}$ would succeed with probability $(1/|\mathcal{X}^1|) \cdot \mathsf{Pr}\left[x \in \mathcal{X}^1\right]$. As $\mathsf{S}^{A,f} = (\mathsf{S}_1^{A,f}, \mathsf{S}_2^{A,f})$ is assumed to be unpredictable in terms of (2), we have $\mathsf{Pr}\left[x \in \mathcal{X}^1\right] = k^{-\omega(1)}$.

Note that even if $\omega_1$ cannot be extracted from $a$, a suitable predictor can still be constructed from $\mathsf{S}_2^{A,f}$. Indeed, if $\mathsf{Pr}\left[x \in \mathcal{X}^1\right] \neq k^{-\omega(1)}$, then due to the polynomial size of $\mathcal{X}^1$ there is an element $x_0 \in \mathcal{X}^1$ so that $\alpha(k) := \mathsf{Pr}\left[x = x_0\right] \neq k^{-\omega(1)}$, and

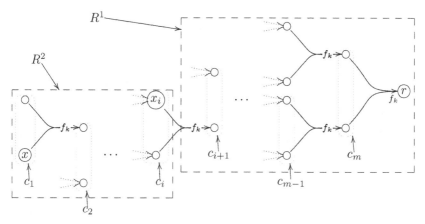

**Fig. 2.** Hash-chain $c = (c_1, \ldots, c_m)$ and the sets $\mathcal{R}^1$ and $\mathcal{R}^2$ after a successful run of $\mathsf{S}^{A,f}$

therefore the probability that the same $x$ is produced by two independent executions of $\mathsf{S}_2^{A,f}(r, a)$ (with fixed $r$ and $a$) is at least $\alpha^2(k) \neq k^{-\omega(1)}$. Therefore, a predictor $\Pi^{A,f}(r, a)$ that simply executes $(x, c) \leftarrow \mathsf{S}_2^{A,f}(r, a)$ and outputs $x$ will succeed with non-negligible probability.

Hence, $x \notin \mathcal{X}^1$ with probability $1 - k^{-\omega(1)}$. So, for the attack to be successful with non-negligible probability, the second stage $\mathsf{S}_2^{A,f}$ should be able to find a pair $c_i$ such that $f(c_i) \in \mathcal{X}^1$ but there is $x_i \in c_i$ so that $x_i \notin \mathcal{X}^1$. To show that this is possible only with negligible probability, we will analyze the work of $\mathsf{S}_2^{A,f}$.

Let $Q_j$ denote the $j$-th oracle query ($A$-query or $f$-query) made by $\mathsf{S}_2^{A,f}(r, a)$ and $\Delta_j$ denote the event that:

1) During $Q_j$ a pair $(y, f(y))$ has been found such that $f(y) \in \mathcal{X}^1$ but there is $x' \in y$ such that $x' \notin \mathcal{X}^1$. We call such a pair $(y, f(y))$ a *hit*.
2) No hits occured during the previous calls $Q_1, \ldots, Q_{j-1}$.

Let the probability of getting a hit at step $j$ be $\delta_j = \Pr[\Delta_j]$. If $Q_j$ is an $f$-query, then we note the probability of having the first hit at step $j$ by $\delta_j^f$ and in the case of an $A$-query we denote this probability by $\delta_j^A$. The total probability of success $\delta_S(k)$ can then be estimated with the following sum over all oracle queries:

$$\delta_S(k) \leq \underbrace{\sum \delta_j^f}_{f\text{-queries}} + \underbrace{\sum \delta_j^A}_{A\text{-queries}} .$$

If $Q_j$ is an $f$-query, then obviously $\delta_j^f = \Pr[\Delta_j] \leq \frac{|\mathcal{X}^1|}{2^k}$, because $f$ is a random function. Recall also that the running time of each $f$-query is 1.

If $Q_j$ is an $A$-query (say $A("F^{f}"))$[1], then we estimate $\Pr[\Delta_j]$ as follows. We will denote by $\Delta_j(F^f(X))$ and $\Delta_j(F^f(X'))$ the events of having a hit in $F^f(X)$ and in $F^f(X')$, respectively. As $X$ and $X'$ are identically distributed, the events $\Delta_j(F^f(X))$

---

[1] The choice of $F^f$ varies in the $A$-queries made by $\mathsf{S}^{A,f}$.

and $\Delta_j(F^f(X'))$ are equally probable, no matter that the generation of $X'$ (after $X$ is fixed) requires "super-human" knowledge about $F^f$. Therefore,

$$\Pr\left[\Delta_j\right] \leq \Pr\left[\Delta_j(F^f(X))\right] + \Pr\left[\Delta_j(F^f(X'))\right] = 2 \cdot \Pr\left[\Delta_j(F^f(X))\right] \ .$$

Let $c_f("F^f")$ denote the number of $f$-gates in "$F^f$". By assumption, we have a natural order in which the $f$-calls are performed inside the computation of $F^f(X)$. If a hit occurs during this computation at all, then one of the $f$-calls must certainly be *the first hit*, which as we already estimated, occurs with probability $\frac{|\mathcal{X}^1|}{2^k}$. Thereby, for $A$-queries we have

$$\Pr\left[\Delta_j\right] \leq 2 \cdot \Pr\left[\Delta_j(F^f(X))\right] \leq 2 \cdot c_f("F^f") \cdot \frac{|\mathcal{X}^1|}{2^k} \ ,$$

and the total success probability of S can be estimated as follows:

$$\delta_S(k) \leq \sum_{f\text{-queries}} \frac{|\mathcal{X}^1|}{2^k} + \sum_{A\text{-queries } A("F_j^f")} 2 \cdot c_f("F_j^f") \cdot \frac{|\mathcal{X}^1|}{2^k}$$

$$= \frac{|\mathcal{X}^1|}{2^k}\left( \sum_{f\text{-queries}} 1 + \sum_{A\text{-queries } A("F_j^f")} 2 \cdot c_f("F_j^f") \right) \leq \frac{|\mathcal{X}^1|}{2^k} \cdot t_S(k)$$

$$= \frac{k^{O(1)}}{2^k} \cdot k^{O(1)} = k^{-\omega(1)} \ ,$$

where $t_S(k)$ is the total running time of S. The last inequality follows from the observation that $t_S(k)$ cannot be smaller than the time spent for oracle calls. □

## 6   Remark on a Poor Choice of $A$

Like in [12], the particular choice of the $A$-oracle is very important. For example, if one chooses $A$ so that given a description of "$F^f$" it returns a uniformly chosen collision from the set $\{(X, X'): F^f(X) = F^f(X')\}$ of all collisions (including the trivial ones with $X = X'$), then such $A$ can be abused to break the hash-based time-stamping system $\mathsf{T}^f$. The adversary $\mathsf{S}^{A,f} = (\mathsf{S}_1^{A,f}, \mathsf{S}_2^{A,f})$ is defined as follows:

1) $\mathsf{S}_1^{A,f}(1^k)$ assigns $a = 0^{2k}$ computes $r = f(a)$ and outputs $(r, a)$.
2) $\mathsf{S}_2^{A,f}(r, a)$ picks $z \leftarrow \{0,1\}^{4k-1}$, builds a description "$F_{r,z,k}^f$" of a function of type $F_{r,z,k}^f: \{0,1\}^{4k} \rightarrow \{0,1\}^{4k-1}$, which is defined as follows:

$$F_{r,z,k}^f(x) = \begin{cases} z & \text{if } f(x_{\{1...2k\}}) = r \\ x_{\{1...4k-1\}} & \text{if } f(x_{\{1...2k\}}) \neq r \ , \end{cases}$$

$\mathsf{S}_2^{A,f}(r, a)$ then calls $(X, X') \leftarrow A("F_{r,z,k}^f")$ and returns $(X_{\{1...k\}}, X_{\{1...2k\}})$.

The success probability of $\mathsf{S}^{A,f}$ relies on finding collisions for $F^f$ by $A$. There are two types of collisions of $F^f$:

(1) **First type.** The collisions $(x, x')$ where $F^f(x) = F^f(x') = z$. This happens when $f(x_{\{1...2k\}}) = f(x'_{\{1...2k\}}) = r$. There are at least $2^{2k}$ $F$-preimages of $z$ because $F^f_{r,z,k}(0^{2k}\|y) = z$ for every $y \in \{0,1\}^{2k}$. The number of first type collisions is thereby at least $2^{2k} \cdot 2^{2k} - 2^{2k} = 2^{4k} - 2^{2k}$. Let the exact number of pre-images of $z$ be $2^{2k} + C$ for some $C \geq 0$. Hence, the exact number of collisions of the first type is $(2^{2k} + C)(2^{2k} + C - 1)$.

(2) **Second type.** The collisions $(x, x')$ where $F^f(x) = F^f(x') \neq z$. For any $z' \neq z$ there are only two $F$-preimages: $z'\|0$ and $z'\|1$. Thus, there are at most $2^{4k} - 2^{2k} - C$ collisions of the second type.

If $S_2$ produces a collision of the first type, then by definition $F^f_{r,z,k} = z$. Hence, for $x = X_{\{1...k\}}$ and $c = X_{\{1...2k\}}$ we have $F_f(x, c) = r$ and S successfully back-dates $x$. So, for $k > 0$ we get the success probability of $S^{A,f}$

$$
\begin{aligned}
\delta_S(k) &\geq \frac{(2^{2k} + C)(2^{2k} + C - 1)}{(2^{2k} + C)(2^{2k} + C - 1) + 2^{4k} - 2^{2k} - C} \\
&= \frac{(2^{2k} + C)(2^{2k} + C - 1)}{2 \cdot (2^{2k} + C)(2^{2k} + C - 1) - 2C \cdot 2^{2k} - C^2} \geq \frac{1}{2} \ .
\end{aligned}
$$

The adversary $S^{A,f}$ is unpredictable in terms of (2) because of the use of $z$ by $A_2$ and the assumption that random coins for different function descriptions are independent. This means that the output of $A_2$ has at least $k$ bits of Rényi entropy. Therefore, $S^{A,f}$ breaks the time-stamping scheme $T^f$ with success $\frac{1}{2}$.

## 7  Conclusions and Open Questions

Probably, our separation result can be generalized in order to show that there are no semi-black-box reductions from collision-free hash functions to secure time-stamping schemes.

It would also be interesting to study the relations between one-way functions and time-stamping schemes. If we can construct time-stamping schemes from one-way functions (or equivalently, from universal one-way hash functions) this would mean that the result of this paper is a direct consequence from the work of Simon [12]. Indeed, if there was a construction of a collision-free hash function from a time-stamping scheme, then by composing two reductions we would obtain a black-box construction of a collision-free hash function from a one-way function, which is impossible by [12].

A very intriguing open question is whether there is an oracle relative to which every function is invertible (not one-way) but still secure time-stamping schemes exist—this would be an extension of the result of Buldas and Laur [2] who showed that secure hash-tree time-stamping schemes can be built based on hash functions that are not one-way. If such an oracle does not exist, the question is, can we construct one-way functions from black-box time-stamping schemes? So far, neither of these two possibilities is either proven or has informal confirmations.

# References

1. Bayer, D., Haber, S., Stornetta, W.-S.: Improving the efficiency and reliability of digital time-stamping. In: Sequences II: Methods in Communication, Security, and Computer Science, pp. 329–334. Springer, New York (1993)
2. Buldas, A., Laur, S.: Do broken hash functions affect the security of time-stamping schemes? In: Zhou, J., Yung, M., Bao, F. (eds.) ACNS 2006. LNCS, vol. 3989, pp. 50–65. Springer, Heidelberg (2006)
3. Buldas, A., Saarepera, M.: On Provably Secure Time-Stamping Schemes. In: Lee, P.J. (ed.) ASIACRYPT 2004. LNCS, vol. 3329, pp. 500–514. Springer, Heidelberg (2004)
4. Gertner, Y., Kannan, S., Malkin, T., Reingold, O., Viswanathan, M.: The relationship between public key encryption and oblivious transfer. In: 41st Annual Symposium on Foundations of Computer Science, Redondo Beach, California, pp. 325–335 (November 2000)
5. Haber, S., Stornetta, W.-S.: Secure Names for Bit-Strings. In: on Computer and Communications Security, pp. 28–35 (1997)
6. Hsiao, C.-Y., Reyzin, L.: Finding Collisions on a Public Road, or Do Secure Hash Functions Need Secret Coins? In: Franklin, M. (ed.) CRYPTO 2004. LNCS, vol. 3152, pp. 92–105. Springer, Heidelberg (2004)
7. Impagliazzo, R., Rudich, S.: Limits on the provable consequences of one-way permutations. In: Proc. of the Twenty First Annual ACM Symposium on Theory of Computing, pp. 44–61. ACM Press, New York (1989)
8. Kelsey, J., Konho, T.: Herding hash functions and the Nostradamus attack. In: IACR e-print archive, p. 281 (2006)
9. Merkle, R.C.: Protocols for public-key cryptosystems. In: Proceedings of the 1980 IEEE Symposium on Security and Privacy, pp. 122–134. IEEE Computer Society Press, Los Alamitos (1980)
10. Reingold, O., Trevisan, L., Vadhan, S.: Notions of reducibility between cryptographic primitives. In: Naor, M. (ed.) TCC 2004. LNCS, vol. 2951, pp. 1–20. Springer, Heidelberg (2004)
11. Rijmen, V., Oswald, E.: Update on SHA-1. In: Menezes, A.J. (ed.) CT-RSA 2005. LNCS, vol. 3376, pp. 58–71. Springer, Heidelberg (2005)
12. Simon, D.: Finding Collisions on a One-Way Street: Can Secure Hash Functions Be Based on General Assumptions? In: Nyberg, K. (ed.) EUROCRYPT 1998. LNCS, vol. 1403, pp. 334–345. Springer, Heidelberg (1998)
13. Wang, X., Lai, X., Feng, D., Chen, H., Yu, X.: Cryptanalysis of the Hash Functions MD4 and RIPEMD. In: Cramer, R.J.F. (ed.) EUROCRYPT 2005. LNCS, vol. 3494, pp. 1–18. Springer, Heidelberg (2005)
14. Wang, X., Yu, H.: How to Break MD5 and Other Hash Functions. In: Cramer, R.J.F. (ed.) EUROCRYPT 2005. LNCS, vol. 3494, pp. 19–35. Springer, Heidelberg (2005)
15. Wang, X., Yin, Y.L., Yu, H.: Finding Collisions in the Full SHA-1. In: Shoup, V. (ed.) CRYPTO 2005. LNCS, vol. 3621, pp. 17–36. Springer, Heidelberg (2005)
16. Wang, X., Yu, H., Yin, Y.L.: Efficient Collision Search Attacks on SHA-0. In: Shoup, V. (ed.) CRYPTO 2005. LNCS, vol. 3621, pp. 1–16. Springer, Heidelberg (2005)

# Formal Proof of Provable Security by Game-Playing in a Proof Assistant

Reynald Affeldt[1], Miki Tanaka[2], and Nicolas Marti[3]

[1] Research Center for Information Security,
National Institute of Advanced Industrial Science and Technology
`reynald.affeldt@aist.go.jp`
[2] Information Security Research Center,
National Institute of Information and Communications Technology
[3] Department of Computer Science, University of Tokyo

**Abstract.** Game-playing is an approach to write security proofs that are easy to verify. In this approach, security definitions and intractable problems are written as programs called games and reductionist security proofs are sequences of game transformations. This bias towards programming languages suggests the implementation of a tool based on compiler techniques (syntactic program transformations) to build security proofs, but it also raises the question of the soundness of such a tool. In this paper, we advocate the formalization of game-playing in a proof assistant as a tool to build security proofs. In a proof assistant, starting from just the formal definition of a probabilistic programming language, all the properties required in game-based security proofs can be proved internally as lemmas whose soundness is ensured by proof theory. Concretely, we show how to formalize the game-playing framework of Bellare and Rogaway in the Coq proof assistant, how to prove formally reusable lemmas such as the fundamental lemma of game-playing, and how to use them to formally prove the PRP/PRF Switching Lemma.

## 1 Introduction

Game-playing is an approach to write security proofs that are easy to verify. In this approach, security definitions and intractable problems are written as programs called games and reductionist security proofs are sequences of game transformations [6,7,8].

The bias of game-playing towards programming languages suggests the implementation of a tool based on compiler techniques to build security proofs [9], but it also raises the question of the soundness of such a tool. To make our point clearer, let us consider CryptoVerif [13], a pioneer implementation of game-playing that has been applied to several standard cryptographic schemes taken from the literature [4,5]. To perform game transformations, CryptoVerif implements techniques of compiler optimization (constant propagation, dead-code elimination, etc.). The latter program transformations sometimes rely on high-level program equivalences that are only proved on paper and introduced in

W. Susilo, J.K. Liu, and Y. Mu. (Eds.): ProvSec 2007, LNCS 4784, pp. 151–168, 2007.

CryptoVerif as axioms (see Appendix B of [13]). This can be seen as an important limitation of CryptoVerif because it endangers its soundness.

In this paper, we advocate the formalization of game-playing in a proof assistant as a tool to build security proofs. In a proof assistant, starting from just the formal definition of a probabilistic programming language, all the properties required in game-based security proofs can be proved internally as lemmas whose soundness is ensured by proof theory: no game transformation needs to be proved out of the box. Concretely, we show how to formalize the game-playing framework of Bellare and Rogaway [7] in the Coq proof assistant [1], how to prove formally reusable lemmas such as the fundamental lemma of game-playing, and how to use these lemmas to formally prove the PRP/PRF Switching Lemma. To our knowledge, this is the first formalization of game-playing with a random oracle and a working fundamental lemma used in a complete use-case.

*About the Coq Proof Assistant.* The Coq proof assistant [1] is an implementation of proof theory developed at INRIA in France since 1984. It provides a higher-order logic (i.e., even predicates can be quantified) to state mathematical properties and a functional programming language to build proofs. This setting stems from the Curry-Howard isomorphism [2], through which logical formulas are considered as types of functional programs that are themselves considered as proofs. This makes up for a very small and well-understood proof-checking mechanism that justifies the reliability of proof assistants. Proof assistants are now reasonably mature tools and, in particular, the Coq proof assistant recently made it possible for several important achievements such as the formalization of the four color theorem or the certification of a C compiler.

*Notations in this Paper.* All the definitions and lemmas in this paper are written in the Coq syntax. This syntax uses only ASCII characters; the mathematical notations are just to ease reading (for example, we write $\forall$ instead of the Coq `forall` construct, $\wedge$ instead of /\, etc.). We display Coq code as it appears in our formalization. To improve understanding, we sometimes put comments (between (* and *)) or hide non-relevant parts (using "..."). In our experience, using the Coq syntax in this way is the best way to present a formalization because it avoids ambiguities while being accessible to readers with little familiarity with formal methods or functional programming languages. There are some Coq-specific constructs, but we introduce them gently in the first sections. We concentrate on the main points of the formalization (basic definitions and statements of lemmas) and do not enter the details of formal proofs; for technical inquiries, the complete Coq development is available online [16].

The rest of this paper is organized as follows. In Sect. 2, we explain how we formalize the notions of distribution and probability in Coq. In Sect. 3, we explain how we formalize random oracles and a probabilistic programming language to write games. In Sect. 4, we formalize a version of the fundamental lemma of game-playing, the most important tool for game-playing. In Sect. 5, we apply our formalization of the game-playing framework to the proof of the PRP/PRF Switching Lemma. We review related work in Sect. 6 and conclude in Sect. 7.

## 2    Formalization of Probabilities

In this section, we explain how we formalize the notion of distribution of states and the notion of probability. We consider a probability space made of *deterministic states* and we call *probabilistic state* a distribution of deterministic states. As far as the formalization of distributions is concerned, we do not commit ourselves to any particular kind of states (this makes our formalization more reusable). In type parlance, we just assume that all deterministic states belong to some type A and pursue formalization using this type. In Coq, types themselves have types, and we declare the type A to belong to the predefined type Set of data structures. This is achieved by the declaration Variable A : Set.

In later sections, we instantiate the type A with a concrete notion of deterministic state. For example, let us assume that deterministic states are *stores*, i.e., sets of pairs of variables and values. We can use the standard Coq natural numbers (type nat of type Set) to formalize variables and values, and Coq lists (type list of type Set) to formalize stores. Variables are defined to be naturals using the definition Definition var := nat. Stores are defined to be lists of pairs of variables and naturals by Definition store := list (var * nat). Since lists belong to Set, so do stores, and therefore we can substitute A for store to obtain a formalization of distributions of stores.

### 2.1    Formalization of Distributions

A distribution of deterministic states is a map from deterministic states to real numbers, such that the real numbers associated with a given deterministic state represent the weight of this state in the map. Given the Coq reals (type R) and our type A of deterministic states, we define distributions to be lists of appropriate type: Definition distrib := list (R * A).

There is little point in having distributions with deterministic states associated with negative or null reals. The Coq way to enforce this is to introduce a logical predicate to sort out devious distributions. Like there is the predefined type Set for data structures, there is the predefined type Prop for logical predicates. Logical predicates in Coq are just definitions with type Prop. A logical predicate that holds only for distributions with strictly positive reals (hereafter, *coefficients*) has to go recursively through the underlying list to check the sign of coefficients. Such recursive definitions are introduced by the keyword Fixpoint:

```
(* A distribution d has positive coefficients... *)
Fixpoint coeff_pos (d : distrib) : Prop :=
  match d with
    (* if its head and its tail have positive coefficients... *)
    | (p, _) :: tl => 0 < p /\ coeff_pos tl
    (* or if it is empty.*)
    | nil => True
  end.
```

In our formalization, we do not insist on having the sum of coefficients of distributions equal to 1, as it is customary with probabilities. We made this choice

for convenience because of if-then-else constructs in the language of games. Even
if we insisted on normalizing probabilities, as soon as the control-flow enters a
branch, the distribution is partitioned, and the sum of coefficients in each branch
cannot be guaranteed to be equal to the sum of coefficients before the branch
(this observation is made in [12]). We therefore express probabilities with respect
to the sum of coefficients of the very first distribution. Sums of coefficients are
computed with the following recursive function:

```
Fixpoint sum (d : distrib) : R :=
  match d with (p, _) :: tl => p + sum tl | nil => 0 end.
```

## 2.2   Probability of Events

We identify events with boolean functions over deterministic states, that is to
say `Definition event := A → bool`. The probability that an event holds in
a distribution is equal to the sum of the coefficients associated with the deterministic states in which this event holds. To sort out relevant deterministic
states, we use a function `filter` that selects only those states such that the event
e holds (++ is the notation for the Coq function that appends lists):

```
Fixpoint filter (e : event) (d : distrib) : distrib :=
  match d with
  | (p, a) :: tl => (if e a then (p, a) :: nil else nil) ++ filter e tl
  | nil => nil
  end.
```

The probability `Pr` that an event e holds in a distribution d immediately follows
from the definition of `sum` and `filter`:

```
Definition Pr (e : event) (d : distrib) : R := sum (filter e d).
```

Equipped with above definitions of distributions, events and probabilities, we can
define concrete events (using Coq standard boolean functions `orb`, `andb`, `negb`,
etc.) and prove formally well-known facts in probability theory:

```
(* standard definitions *)
Definition union (e1 e2 : event) (a : A) : event := orb (e1 a) (e2 a).
  (* Notation: _ ∪ _ *)
Definition inter (e1 e2 : event) (a : A) : event := andb (e1 a) (e2 a).
  (* Notation: _ ∩ _ *)
Definition cplt (e : event) (a : A) : event := negb (e a).
  (* Notation: ‾ *)
...
(* well-known facts *)
Lemma Pr_union_inter : ∀ d e1 e2,
  Pr (e1 ∪ e2) d = Pr e1 d + Pr e2 d - Pr (e1 ∩ e2) d.
Lemma Pr_distributivity : ∀ d e1 e2 e3,
  Pr (e1 ∩ (e2 ∪ e3)) d = Pr ((e1 ∩ e2) ∪ (e1 ∩ e3)) d.
Lemma Pr_cplt: ∀ d e,  Pr ‾e d = sum d - Pr e d.
...
```

## 2.3    Transformations of Distributions

Our formalization of distributions also features functions that transform distributions according to operations such as random sampling. Let us consider a concrete example of what these transformations are supposed to achieve. We take stores of variables (as defined at the beginning of this section) for deterministic states. Let us assume that we are given the probabilistic state $(p_0, x = 0), (p_1, x = 1)$ and that we perform a random sampling with probability $0 < p < 1$ of the variable $y$ from the set $\{0, 1\}$. The effect of this random sampling is to multiply the original distribution by the number of possible outcomes of the random sampling (here: $y = 0$ or $y = 1$), each distribution being scaled by the adequate probability (here: $p$ and $1 - p$), as depicted informally in Fig. 1.

$$\boxed{(p_0, x = 0), (p_1, x = 1)}$$

$$\boxed{(p \cdot p_0, x = 0 \wedge y = 0), (p \cdot p_1, x = 1 \wedge y = 0)} \quad \boxed{((1-p) \cdot p_0, x = 0 \wedge y = 1), ((1-p) \cdot p_1, x = 1 \wedge y = 1)}$$

**Fig. 1.** Effect on a distribution of the random sampling $y \xleftarrow{p} \{0, 1\}$

The function `fork` below implements the most general form of transformation illustrated above. It takes as input a distribution `d` and a list `l` of real scaling factors and functions that transform deterministic states:

```
Fixpoint fork (l : list (R * (A → A))) (d : distrib) : distrib :=
  match l with
  | (k, f) :: tl => map f (scale k d) ++ fork tl d
  | nil => nil
  end.
```

(The function `map` applies a function to each deterministic state of a distribution, the function `scale` multiplies each coefficient by the same real; Coq code omitted to save space.) For example, the transformation depicted in Fig. 1 is performed by the function call `fork ((p, update y 0)::(1-p, update y 1)::nil)` where `update` is a function that updates stores.

# 3    Formalization of a Probabilistic Language for Games

## 3.1    Random Oracle

A *random oracle* is a data structure used in security proofs to represent a pseudorandom function or a hash function. Concretely, it is a map from a set of bitstrings to uniformly and independently sampled bitstrings. From a programming language perspective, a random oracle can be thought of as a hash table with random values, as depicted in Fig. 2. Indeed, like a hash table, insertion of new records (key-value pairs) and retrieval of the value associated with a key are the most important operations. In security proofs, it is also important to be able to look for already allocated keys or values, to talk about the $i$th inserted record, to know the number of records, etc. The most reusable way to formalize such a rich data structure is via an *abstract datatype*, i.e., a type that is known to enjoy some properties but whose formalization is hidden. In Coq, abstract datatypes are formalized with *modules*. Here follows the type of a module for an abstract datatype t that enjoys the properties of a random oracle:

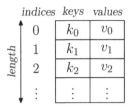

**Fig. 2.** A simple random oracle

```
Module Type ORACLE.
 Parameter t : Set.
 Parameter empty : t.
 Definition key := nat.
 Definition value := nat.

 (* access functions *)
 Parameter length : t → nat.
 Parameter insert : key → value → t → t.
 Parameter nth_key : nat → t → (*default*) key → key.
 Parameter nth_value : nat → t → (*default*) value → value.
 Parameter find_key : key → t → nat.
 Parameter find_value : value → t → nat.
 ...
 (* properties *)
 Parameter insert_new_len : ∀ o k v,
   find_key k o = 0 → length (insert k v o) = length o + 1.
 ...
End ORACLE.
```

In the following, we use a module `oracle` of type `ORACLE` such that `oracle.t` is the type of our random oracles. Each time we need to manipulate an oracle, we can use functions such as `oracle.length` and we know that they satisfy properties such as `oracle.insert_new_len`. Observe that we use naturals instead of bitstrings but we are careful to keep track of cardinality information; in the future, we plan to use instead the module for machine integers from [14] so that we can handle more faithfully security proofs that make a precise usage of bitstrings (such as the security proof of PSS [5]). For the time being, we have just specified the `oracle` module. A random oracle with one value per key can be implemented on the model of the finite map from [11]; however, most security proofs require random oracles with several values per key, so that we defer to future work the formalization of a module that accommodates such generality.

## 3.2   Execution State

The random oracle from Sect. 3.1 is only one part of the execution state of games. The other part is the store of variables as we defined in Sect. 2. A deterministic state `dstate` is therefore a pair of a store and an oracle. It is possible to access a deterministic state to lookup for the value of a variable, or to update the value of a variable (using functions `lookup` and `update` respectively):

```
Definition dstate := store * oracle.t.
Definition lookup (v:var) (d:dstate) : nat := ...
Definition update (v:var) (n:nat) (d:dstate) : dstate := ...
```

Finally, a *probabilistic state* is a distribution (as defined in Sect. 2) of deterministic states: `Definition pstate := distrib dstate.`

### 3.3 Programming Language

Our probabilistic programming language is an imperative language with random sampling and function calls built after [7].

The expressions `expr` of our programming language contain variables, integer constants, and a C-like negation operator (this can be easily extended but is sufficient for our purpose in this paper):

```
Inductive expr : Set :=
    var_e : var → expr | int_e : nat → expr | neg_e : expr → expr.
```

An expression is a datatype so it belongs to `Set`; since an expression can be made up of other expressions, the `expr` type is introduced by the keyword `Inductive`. Everytime the `Inductive` keyword is used, Coq generates an induction principle for the datatype that allows for proof by induction. An expression `e` can be evaluated in a deterministic state `ds` using the function `eval`:

```
Fixpoint eval (e:expr) (ds:dstate) : nat := ...
```

We now define the commands of our programming language. Random sampling is available through two commands: `x <-$- n` (notation for `sample_n x n`) uniformly samples a natural from the interval $[0, n-1]$, and `x <-b- p` (notation for `sample_b x p`) samples a boolean (in fact, a natural among 0 and 1) with probability $0 < p < 1$. For the random oracle, there are two commands to access it: `insert k v` adds a new record `(k,v)`, `find_value x e` tests for the occurrence of the value `e` and sets the variable `x` accordingly. It is possible to put together atomic commands using control-flow commands: `c1;c2` (notation for `seq c1 c2`) represents a sequence of commands, `ifte b c1 c2` represents an if-then-else with condition `b` (an expression) and two branches `c1` and `c2`. Other commands' names are self-explanatory:

```
Definition fun_id := nat.
Inductive cmd : Set :=
| skip : cmd
| assign : var → expr → cmd            (* Notation: _ <- _ *)
| sample_n : var → nat → cmd           (* Notation: _ <-$- _ *)
| sample_b : var → R → cmd             (* Notation: _ <-b- _ *)
| find_value : var → expr → cmd
| insert : expr → expr → cmd
| ifte : expr → cmd → cmd → cmd
| seq : cmd → cmd → cmd                 (* Notation: _ ; _ *)
| call : fun_id → cmd.
```

Like expressions, commands are just another datatype belonging to Set and the Inductive keyword provides us with an induction principle to reason about the syntax of games.

So far we have only defined the syntax of games without giving them meaning. Now we define their semantics. We do that by formalizing an operational semantics [3] with the logical predicate _||-_--_-->_ (notation for (exec _ _ _ _)) between (1) an environment (a set of function ids and commands), (2) a starting probabilistic state, (3) a command, and (4) a resulting probabilistic state:

```
Definition prog := list (fun_id * cmd).
Inductive exec (prg : prog) : pstate → cmd → pstate → Prop := ...
```

Because this is a logical predicate it belongs to type Prop. It is also defined using the Inductive keyword so that Coq provides an induction principle to reason by induction on the execution of games; this induction principle is used pervasively in our formal proofs. Let us illustrate the exec predicate with the operational semantics of random sampling commands (the complete predicate can be found in Appendix A). The constructor exec_sample_b formalizes the semantics of (possibly non-uniform) boolean sampling:

```
| exec_sample_b : ∀ x p st, 0 < p < 1 →
  prg ||- st -- x <-b- p -->
                    fork ((p, update x 1)::(1-p, update x 0)::nil) st
```

Starting from a probabilistic state st, the command x <-b- n yields a probabilistic state fork ((p, update x 1)::(1-p, update x 0)::nil) st. This transformation actually corresponds to the situation depicted in Fig. 1, Sect. 2.3, where the function fork has been explained. The constructor exec_sample_n formalizes the semantics of uniform random sampling:

```
| exec_sample_n: ∀ x n st, n > 0 →
  prg ||- st -- x <-$- n --> fork (sample_n_fork_distrib 0 n n x) st
```

Starting from a probabilistic state st, the command x <-$- n yields a probabilistic state fork (sample_n_fork_distrib 0 n n x) st. The function application sample_n_fork_distrib produces an appropriate list of scaling factors and state transformations: (1/n, update x 0)::(1/n, update x 1)::···::(1/n, update x (n-1)). It is defined by recursion on the size of the sample space:

```
Fixpoint sample_n_fork_distrib
  (min span card:nat) (v:var) : list (R * (dstate -> dstate)) :=
    match span with
    | 0 => nil
    | S span' => (1/INR card, fun x => update v (min + span') x) ::
                  sample_n_fork_distrib min span' card v
    end.
```

(The constructor S is the successor function of naturals; the function INR injects naturals into reals; the construct fun x => ... corresponds to an anonymous function, i.e., it is equivalent to Definition *anonymous_function* x := ...)

*Loop Constructs.* In security proofs, the computational power of the adversary is always bounded. As a consequence, we do not need any general form of while-loops and we can get along with macros for looping constructs. For example, the function below represents $i$ copies of some parameterized loop body:

```
Fixpoint loop (i : nat) (c : nat → cmd) : cmd :=
  match n with
    | 0 => skip
    | S j => loop j c; c j
  end.
```

### 3.4  Properties of the Probabilistic Language of Games

Using the probabilistic programming language defined above, we have formally proved in Coq several reusable lemmas to reason about games. The most important of these lemmas is the fundamental lemma of game-playing that is explained in Sect. 4. There are many other useful lemmas. The most important of them are those that capture the properties of random sampling, answering questions such as: "What is the probability that two random variables are equal?" Such a question arises for example when comparing the value stored in a random oracle with a newly sampled value.

For illustration, let us consider the case of two uniformly sampled values. In Coq, lemmas are proved interactively in a special mode entered in via the keyword Lemma. The lemma corresponding to the question above consists of two hypotheses. First, we are given an execution step of a game: it goes from state st to state st' by performing a uniform random sampling whose outcome is stored in variable x (this is *hypo 1* below). Second, we are given a function f that retrieves values from the oracle and we know that in state st these values are uniformaly distributed with probability p (this is *hypo 2* below). The conclusion of the lemma states that the probability that the value of x is equal to the value retrieved by f is also p:

```
Lemma exec_sample_n_twice_Pr : ∀ x n st st' prg,
  (* hypo 1 *) prg ||- st -- x <-$- n --> st' →
  ∀ (f:oracle.t → nat) p,
  (* hypo 2 *) (∀ m, m < n →
    Pr (fun s => beq_nat m (f (get_oracle s))) st = p * sum st) →
  (* conclusion *)
  Pr (fun s => beq_nat (lookup x s) (f (get_oracle s))) st' = p * sum st'
```

(get_oracle is a function that extracts the oracle from a deterministic state; beq_nat tests natural numbers for equality and returns a Coq boolean.)

## 4  The Fundamental Lemma of Game-Playing

In game-playing, each game represents a sequence of interactions with the adversary, and a security proof consists of a sequence of game transformations. During game-transformation steps, we keep track of the bounds incurred in probability changes in order to derive a bound on the probability that the adversary wins. This is often achieved by application of the "fundamental lemma of game-playing" [6,7,8].

## 4.1 Probabilistic Account

Assume one wants to know the difference `Rabs(Pr e d1 - Pr e d2)` of probabilities of some event `e` in two different probability distributions `d1` and `d2` (`Rabs` is the absolute value in Coq). One way to bound this value is to analyze the event `e` with respect to some other event `f` so that the event `e` can be partitioned into events `e ∩ f` and `e ∩ f̄`. Then one has `Pr e d1 = Pr (e ∩ f) d1 + Pr (e ∩ f̄) d1`, and similarly for `d2`.

The lemma below is a version of the fundamental lemma of game-playing with only distributions (games will be added in the next section). It states that, under the hypothesis `Pr (e ∩ f̄) d1 = Pr (e ∩ f̄) d2` (i), we have a simple bound[1]:

```
Lemma abstract_fundamental_lemma : ∀ d1 d2 e f r, 0 ≤ r →
  sum d1 = sum d2 → coeff_pos d1 → coeff_pos d2 →
    Pr f d1 = Pr f d2 = r → Pr (e ∩ f̄) d1 = Pr (e ∩ f̄) d2 →
      Rabs(Pr e d1 - Pr e d2) ≤ r.
```

The hypotheses `sum d1 = sum d2`, `coeff_pos d1` and `coeff_pos d2` come from how we formalize distributions, see Sect. 2.1. This lemma is proved in Coq as follows: first use the equality (i) to eliminate the terms with `f̄`, then the difference becomes `Rabs(Pr (e ∩ f) d1 - Pr (e ∩ f) d2)`, which is easily seen to be bounded by the probability `r` that `f` occurs.

## 4.2 Identical-Until-Bad Games

The lemma of the previous section does not say anything about games, but it can actually be used to transform one game to another if they are "identical-until-bad", a syntactic property that can be automatically verified in Coq for the probabilistic language we introduced earlier.

The property "identical-until-bad" [7] assumes the existence of a special variable conventionally called `bad` that can be set only once. Two games are "identical-until-bad" when they have the same syntax tree except for those subtrees following the command `bad <- 1`. We formalize the property "identical-until-bad" using the logical predicates `no_assign_cmd` and `no_assign` that check for variable assignments; this is not the most general formalization but it is sufficient for our purpose in this paper. For example, assume that we have three commands `c1`, `c2`, `c2'` such that `no_assign_cmd bad` holds, and a program `prg` such that `no_assign bad` holds. Then the following two programs are "identical-until-bad":

```
prg ||- ⌴ -- ifte b          prg ||- ⌴ -- ifte b
      c1                            c1
      (bad <- int_e 1; c2) --> ⌴    (bad <- int_e 1; c2') --> ⌴
```

---

[1] This lemma can actually be generalized to use two pairs of different events `e1`, `e2` and `f1`, `f2` in two different probability distributions `d1` and `d2` and with a bound equal to the maximum of `Pr f1 d1` and `Pr f2 d2`.

The following example shows "identical-until-bad" games containing a loop; here, commands c1, c2, c2', c3, and all c0 i for $0 \le i < q$ satisfy no_assign_cmd bad, and the program prg satisfies no_assign bad:

```
prg ||- ␣ -- loop q (fun i =>        prg ||- ␣ -- loop q (fun i =>
       c0 i;                                c0 i;
       ifte b                               ifte b
         c1                                   c1
         (bad <- int_e 1; c2);                (bad <- int_e 1; c2');
       c3) --> ␣                            c3) --> ␣
```

## 4.3   Fundamental Lemma of Game-Playing: Formal Statement

In this section, we show how to formally state and prove the fundamental lemma of game-playing. For this purpose, we use the lemma of Sect. 4.1 and the property "identical-until-bad" of Sect. 4.2. The relation between the abstract fundamental lemma and the property "identical-until-bad" is the event "the variable bad is set to one". We identify the event e in Sect. 4.1 with the event that the adversary wins, and the event f with the event sets bad 1 where sets is defined as follows:

```
Definition sets (v:var) (n:nat) : event dstate :=
  fun s => beq_nat (lookup v s) n.
```

Keeping this relation in mind, we can now state the fundamental lemma of game-playing. First, we take two "identical-until-bad" games. As seen in Sect. 4.2, this boils down to automatically check some no_assign bad and no_assign_cmd bad logical predicates. For concreteness, let us consider the two games of the Switching Lemma. Second, we take two initial distributions st and st' such that:

$$\text{Permutation (filter } (\overline{\text{sets bad 1}}) \text{ st) (filter } (\overline{\text{sets bad 1}}) \text{ st')} \qquad \text{(ii)}$$

With these hypotheses, the following fundamental lemma of game-playing can be proved formally in Coq (no_assign_cmd_list is a variant of the no_assign_cmd predicate):

```
Lemma fundamental_lemma :
  ∀ prg (c0:nat → cmd) b bad c1 c2 c2' c3 e q st st' end end',
  no_assign_cmd_list bad c1 c2 c2' c3 → (∀ i, no_assign_cmd bad (c0 i)) →
  no_assign bad prg → coeff_pos st → coeff_pos st' → sum st = sum st' →
  Permutation (filter (sets bad 1) st) (filter (sets bad 1) st') →
  prg ||- st  --
    loop q (fun i => c0 i; ifte b c1 (bad <- int_e 1; c2 ); c3) --> end →
  prg ||- st' --
    loop q (fun i => c0 i; ifte b c1 (bad <- int_e 1; c2'); c3) --> end' →
  Rabs (Pr e end - Pr e end') <= Pr (sets bad 1) end.
```

A detailed account of the proof of this lemma can be found in Appendix B. The next section shows how it can be concretely applied.

# 5   The PRP/PRF Switching Lemma

The PRP/PRF Switching Lemma is used in security proofs of cryptographic schemes based on block ciphers. Although block ciphers are assumed to behave as pseudorandom permutations (PRP), it is easier to consider them as pseudorandom functions (PRF) in security proofs. The Switching Lemma quantifies in terms of probabilities the difference induced by this approximation. As explained in [7], it is non-trivial to prove this lemma correctly; here follows a formal proof.

## 5.1   Formal Statement

The proof of the Switching Lemma in game-playing assumes an adversary A that does q queries to two games G0 and G1 that represent respectively a pseudorandom function and a pseudorandom permutation:

```
Definition G0' bad (A:nat→nat) i :=    Definition G1' bad (A:nat→nat) i:=
x <- int_e (A i) ;                     x <- int_e (A i) ;
y <-$- n ;                             y <-$- n ;
find_value z (var_e y) ;               find_value z (var_e y) ;
ifte (var_e z)                         ifte (var_e z)
  (bad <- int_e 1)                       (bad <- int_e 1; any)
  skip;                                  skip;
insert (var_e x) (var_e y).            insert (var_e x) (var_e y).


Definition G0 bad q (A:nat→nat) :=     Definition G1 bad q (A:nat→nat) :=
loop q (G0' bad A).                    loop q (G1' bad A).
```

The bad variable is set when the function built is not a permutation. The difference between the two games is that, when bad is set, G1 performs a command any. This command can be anything that does not modify bad; in practice, any samples y again in a way such that it does build a permutation. We do not need to be specific about what any does because it is irrelevant to the proof.

The Switching Lemma is formally stated as follows. Starting with a valid distribution st such that bad is not set, the execution of games G0 and G1 leads to two distributions st' and st'' such that the difference of the probabilities that an event e occurs is bounded by $\frac{q(q-1)}{2n}$ (where $n$ is the cardinal of the random sampling):

```
Lemma switching : ∀ q, q ≠ 0 → ∀ A, (∀ x y, x ≠ y → A x ≠ A y) →
  ∀ st, coeff_pos st → sum st > 0 → plength 0 st →
  Pr (sets bad 1) st = 0 →
  ∀ st', nil ||- st -- G0 bad q A --> st' →
  ∀ st'', nil ||- st -- G1 bad q A --> st'' →
  ∀ e, Rabs (Pr e st'' - Pr e st') ≤ INR(q*(q-1))/INR(2*n) * sum st'.
```

## 5.2   Formal Proof

The proof of the Switching Lemma consists of the successive application of the two following lemmas switching_part1 and switching_part2:

```
Lemma switching_part1 : ∀ q, ∀ A, (∀ x y, x ≠ y → A x ≠ A y) →
  ∀ st, coeff_pos st →
  ∀ st', nil ||- st -- G0 bad q A --> st' →
  ∀ st'', nil ||- st -- G1 bad q A --> st'' →
  ∀ e, Rabs (Pr e st'' - Pr e st') ≤ Pr (sets bad 1) st'.
```

The proof of `switching_part1` is by application of the fundamental lemma of game playing seen in Sect. 4.

The goal of the second part of the Switching Lemma is to upper-bound the probability that the variable `bad` is set in game `G0`. This is a proof by induction on the number of requests of the adversary but it requires a generalization to be handled gracefully. We introduce *probabilistic predicates* for the purpose of generalization. In the same way that events (defined in Sect. 2) are predicates for deterministic states `dstate`, probabilistic predicates are predicates for probabilistic states `pstate`. Technically, a probabilistic predicate is a Coq function of type `pstate` → `Prop`. For example, the property that all the random oracles of a probabilistic state have the same length is captured by the predicate `plength`:

```
Definition plength (len:nat) (ps:pstate) : Prop :=
  ∀ p ds, (p, ds) ∈ st → oracle.length (get_oracle ds) = len.
```

Similarly, the property that the $i$th key of all the random oracles of a probabilistic state is $k$ is captured by the predicate `pnth_key` and the property that the $i$th value of all the random oracles of a probabilistic state is uniformly distributed with probability $\frac{1}{n}$ is captured by the predicate `pnth_value_uniform`:

```
Definition pnth_key (i k:nat) (ps:pstate) :=
  ∀ p ds, (p, ds) ∈ ps → oracle.nth_key' i (get_oracle ds) = Some k.
```

```
Definition pnth_value_uniform (i n:nat) (st:pstate) :=
  ∀ m, m < n →
    Pr (fun s => beq_nat m (oracle.nth_value i (get_oracle s) 0)) st =
    1/INR n * sum st.
```

Using probabilistic predicates, the second part of the Switching Lemma is stated as follows:

```
Lemma switching_part2 : ∀ q, q ≠ 0 → ∀ A, (∀ x y, x ≠ y → A x ≠ A y) →
  ∀ st, coeff_pos st → sum st > 0 → plength 0 st →
  Pr (sets bad 1) st = 0 →
  ∀ st', nil ||- st -- G0 bad q A --> st' →
  plength q st' ∧
  (∀ k, k < q → pnth_key k (A k) st' ∧ pnth_value_uniform k n st') ∧
  Pr (sets bad 1) st' ≤ INR(q*(q-1))/INR(2*n) * sum st'.
```

Intuitively, probabilistic predicates `plength`, `pnth_key`, and `pnth_value_uniform` capture how the random oracle is transformed from one loop iteration to the other: at any point of execution, the length of the oracle is equal to the number of queries so far, the keys of the oracle correspond to the queries so far, and associated values are all uniformly distributed. In the following, we briefly skim through the formal proof.

The proof is by induction on the number `q` of adversary queries, like the proof by induction of the Gauss formula for the sum of consecutive integers. In the inductive case, we are led to quantify the difference between the probabilities that bad is set before and after an iteration of the loop:

```
Pr (sets bad 1) st' ≤ Pr (sets bad 1) st + INR(q+1)/INR n * sum st'
```

This is equivalent to upper-bounding the probability that the randomly sampled y already appears in the values of the random oracle:

```
Pr (fun s => beq_nat (eval (neg_e (var_e z)) s) 0) st
                                  ≤ INR(q+1)/INR n * sum st
```

The probability of the occurence of a value in the values of the random oracle can be upper-bounded by the sum of the probabilities that it is equal to each value, using the general-purpose lemma below:

```
Lemma Pr_iter_orb : ∀ st len e, coeff_pos st → plength len st →
 Pr (fun s => (eval e s) ∈ (oracle.values (get_oracle s))) st ≤
  Sum 0 len (fun x => Pr (fun s =>
    beq_nat (eval e s) (oracle.nth_value x (get_oracle s) 0)) st).
```

(Sum 0 len f is a Coq function for $\sum_{x=0}^{len-1} f(x)$.) By the lemma from Sect. 3.4, we know that the probability that the randomly sampled y is equal to a (randomly sampled) value of the random oracle is $\frac{1}{n}$:

```
∀ i, i < q+1 → Pr (fun s =>
  beq_nat (lookup y s) (oracle.nth_value i (get_oracle s) 0)) st =
    1/INR n * sum st
```

Because this probability is a constant, the sum inherited from the previous lemma is equal to INR(q+1)/INR n * sum st. Using the inductive hypothesis, this completes the proof of the PRP/PRF Switching Lemma.

# 6    Related Work

CryptoVerif is a tool to automate proofs of cryptographic protocols in the computational model. In particular, it has been applied to security proofs written as sequences of games [13]. In CryptoVerif, games are written in a process calculus and game transformations are captured by probabilistic bisimulation relations. The validity of game transformations sometimes require non-trivial manual proofs (see Appendix B of [13]). Though our formalization of the game-playing framework is not as rich as CryptoVerif, our Coq-centric approach provides a way to avoid manual proofs.

Our probabilistic programming language with probabilities and probabilistic predicates is reminiscent of probabilistic Hoare logic. The latter has been used to build the IND-CPA security proof of the ElGamal encryption scheme [12]. Though manual, this proof is so detailed that we think it is close to being formalized. Our formalization of the game-playing framework is not strictly speaking a formalization of probabilistic Hoare logic, but it gives a good idea of the effort it would require and, more importantly, how to extend it with random oracles (which is not done in [12]).

There exist other formalizations of security proofs in the Coq proof assistant. An early work makes use of the Generic Model and of the Random Oracle Model but without game-playing [10]. In this formalization, an adversary is defined as an inductive set of possible actions and this allows for reasoning about its chances to resolve a challenge. Yet, no use-case has been completely formalized that demonstrates the effectiveness of this approach. A recent work formalizes the IND-CPA security proof of the ElGamal encryption scheme by game-playing in the standard model [15]. In this formalization, games are encoded directly as Coq functions; the absence of syntax seems to simplify formal reasoning but it is likely to hinder automation of game transformations, which are syntactic in nature. Besides this issue, we regard this work as complementary to ours: it provides an IND-CPA security proof using a formalization of cyclic groups that can be easily integrated in our formalization.

# 7    Conclusion

In this paper, we explained a formalization of the game-playing framework of Bellare and Rogaway in the Coq proof assistant. Our formalization features a probabilistic language to write games and several reusable lemmas to carry out security proofs, including in particular an instance of the fundamental lemma of game-playing. We have illustrated the usefulness of our formalization by proving the PRP/PRF Switching Lemma. The complete Coq development is available online [16]. To our knowledge this is the first formalization of game-playing with a random oracle and a working fundamental lemma used in a complete use-case.

*Future Work.* For the time being, the fundamental lemma of game-playing as it appears in Sect. 4 can only be applied to a restricted set of games. Of course, we can easily formalize variants on the same model, but ideally it should be generalized so as to encompass any pair of "identical-until-bad" games [7].

We already have a good idea of how to extend our formalization of the game-playing framework to carry out the security proof of the Full-domain Hash signature scheme from [8]. This will require a formalization of random oracles with several values per key and, more importantly, introduce concurrency issues arising from the parallel execution of several oracles.

*Acknowledgments.* The first and second authors acknowledge partial support from, respectively, the Grant-in-Aid of Special Coordination Funds for Promoting Science and Technology, and the Grant-in-Aid for Young Scientists (B)(Grant number 187602935003), both by the Ministry of Education, Culture, Sports, Science and Technology, Japan (MEXT).

# References

1. The LogiCal Project, INRIA. The Coq proof assistant: `http://coq.inria.fr`
2. Thompson, S.: Type Theory and Functional Programming. Addison-Wesley, Reading (1991)

3. Winskel, G.: The Formal Semantics of Programming Languages. MIT Press, Cambridge (1993)
4. Bellare, M., Rogaway, P.: Random Oracle are Practical: A Paradigm for Designing Efficient Protocols. In: CCS 1993. 1st ACM Conference on Computer and Communications Security, pp. 62–73. ACM Press, New York
5. Bellare, M., Rogaway, P.: The Exact Security of Digital Signatures—How to Sign with RSA and Rabin. In: Maurer, U.M. (ed.) EUROCRYPT 1996. LNCS, vol. 1070, pp. 399–416. Springer, Heidelberg (1996)
6. Shoup, V.: Sequence of Games: A Tool for Taming Complexity in Security Proofs. Manuscript (2004) (Revised 2006), available at
http://www.shoup.net/papers/games.pdf
7. Bellare, M., Rogaway, P.: Code-Based Game-Playing Proofs and the Security of Triple Encryption. In: Vaudenay, S. (ed.) EUROCRYPT 2006. LNCS, vol. 4004, pp. 409–426. Springer, Heidelberg (2006)
8. Pointcheval, D.: Provable Security for Public Key Schemes. In: Contemporary Cryptology, Advanced Courses in Mathematics CRM Barcelona, pp. 133–189. Birkhäuser Publishers (2005)
9. Halevi, S.: A plausible approach to computer-aided cryptographic proofs. Cryptology ePrint Archive: Report (2005)/181
10. Tarento, S.: Machine-Checked Security Proofs of Cryptographic Signature Schemes. In: di Vimercati, S.d.C., Syverson, P.F., Gollmann, D. (eds.) ESORICS 2005. LNCS, vol. 3679, pp. 140–158. Springer, Heidelberg (2005)
11. Marti, N., Affeldt, R., Yonezawa, A.: Formal Verification of the Heap Manager of an Operating System using Separation Logic. In: Liu, Z., He, J. (eds.) ICFEM 2006. LNCS, vol. 4260, pp. 400–419. Springer, Heidelberg (2006)
12. Corin, R., den Hartog, J.: A Probabilistic Hoare-style Logic for Game-Based Cryptographic Proofs. In: Bugliesi, M., Preneel, B., Sassone, V., Wegener, I. (eds.) ICALP 2006. LNCS, vol. 4052, pp. 252–263. Springer, Heidelberg (2006)
13. Blanchet, B., Pointcheval, D.: Automated Security Proofs with Sequences of Games. In: CRYPTO 2006. LNCS, vol. 4117, pp. 537–554. Springer (2006) Extended version: Cryptology ePrint Archive: Report (2006)/069
14. Affeldt, R., Marti, N.: An Approach to Formal Verification of Arithmetic Functions in Assembly. In: 11th Annual Asian Computing Science Conference (ASIAN 2006), Focusing on Secure Software and Related Issues, Lecture Notes in Computer Science. Springer (to appear, 2007)
15. Nowak, D.: A Framework for Game-Based Security Proofs. Cryptology ePrint Archive: Report (2007)/199
16. Affeldt, R., Tanaka, M., Marti, N.: Formal Proof of Provable Security by Game-playing in a Proof Assistant. Coq scripts, available at
http://staff.aist.go.jp/reynald.affeldt/secprf/provsec2007

# A     Formalization Excerpt: Operational Semantics

```
Inductive exec (prg : prog) : pstate → cmd → pstate → Prop :=
| exec_skip : ∀ st, prg ||- st -- skip --> st

| exec_assign : ∀ x e st,
  prg ||- st -- x <- e -->
    fork ((1, fun s => update x (eval e s) s)::nil) st
```

```
| exec_sample_b : ∀ x p st, 0 < p < 1 →
  prg ||- st -- x <-b- p -->
    fork ((p, update x 1)::(1-p, update x 0)::nil ) st

| exec_find_value : ∀ x st e,
  prg ||- st -- find_value x e -->
    fork ((1, fun s =>
      update x (oracle.find_value (eval e s) (get_oracle s)) s)::nil) st

| exec_sample_n: ∀ x n st, n > 0 →
  prg ||- st -- x <-$- n --> fork (sample_n_fork_distrib 0 n n x) st

| exec_ifte : ∀ e c d st st_true st_false stc std,
  st_true = filter (fun s => beq_nat (eval (neg_e e) s) 0) st →
    st_false = filter (fun s => beq_nat (eval e s) 0) st →
      prg ||- st_true -- c --> stc →
        prg ||- st_false -- d --> std →
          prg ||- st -- ifte e c d --> stc ++ std

| exec_seq : ∀ st st'' st' c d,
  prg ||- st -- c --> st'' →
    prg ||- st'' -- d --> st' →
      prg ||- st -- c ; d --> st'

| exec_insert : ∀ st e e',
  prg ||- st -- insert e e' -->
    fork ((1, fun s => (get_store s,
      oracle.insert (eval e s) (eval e' s) (get_oracle s)))::nil) st

| exec_call : ∀ st st' callee c,
  get_fun_cmd prg callee = Some c →
    prg ||- st -- c --> st' →
      prg ||- st -- call callee --> st'
where "prg ||- st -- c --> st'" := (exec prg st c st').
```

## B   Proof Sketch for the Lemma of Sect. 4.3

In order to prove the fundamental lemma of game-playing, we need the following two lemmas identical_until_bad and after_bad_is_set that relate the condition (ii) and the executions of "identical-until-bad" commands. The lemma identical_until_bad states that, given two games that are "identical-until-bad" (defined with no_assign_cmd bad and no_assign bad predicates), the condition(ii) is preserved by the execution of the games:

```
Lemma identical_until_bad :
  ∀ prg (c0:nat → cmd) b bad c1 c2 c2' c3 q st st' end end',
  no_assign_cmd_list bad c1 c2 c2' c3 → (∀ i, no_assign_cmd bad (c0 i)) →
  no_assign bad prg → coeff_pos st → coeff_pos st' →
  Permutation (filter (sets bad 1) st) (filter (sets bad 1) st') →
  prg ||- st --
    loop q (fun i => c0 i; ifte b c1 (bad <- int_e 1; c2); c3) --> end →
  prg ||- st' --
    loop q (fun i => c0 i; ifte b c1 (bad <- int_e 1; c2'); c3) --> end' →
  Permutation (filter (sets bad 1) end) (filter (sets bad 1) end').
```

Concerning the lemma `after_bad_is_set`, note that when both (ii) and `sum st` = `sum st'` hold, the two initial distributions of the execution have the same probabilities for the `sets bad 1` event. The lemma states that this property is also preserved after the execution of "identical-until-bad" games:

```
Lemma after_bad_is_set :
 ∀ prg (c0:nat → cmd) b bad c1 c2 c2' c3 q st st' end end',
 no_assign_cmd_list bad c1 c2 c2' c3 → (∀ i, no_assign_cmd bad (c0 i)) →
 no_assign bad prg → coeff_pos st' → coeff_pos st' → sum st = sum st' →
 Permutation (filter (sets bad 1) st) (filter (sets bad 1) st') →
 prg ||- st --
   loop q (fun i => c0 i; ifte b c1 (bad <- int_e 1; c2); c3) --> end →
 prg ||- st' --
   loop q (fun i => c0 i; ifte b c1 (bad <- int_e 1; c2'); c3) --> end' →
 Pr (sets bad 1) end = Pr (sets bad 1) end'.
```

The proof of the fundamental lemma of game-playing proceeds along the lines of the proof of the abstract fundamental lemma of Sect. 4.1. First, we prove `Pr (sets bad 1) end = Pr (sets bad 1) end'` by direct application of the lemma `after_bad_is_set`. Second, using the lemma `identical_until_bad` we prove

$$\text{Pr (f} \cap \overline{\text{(sets bad 1)}}\text{) end = Pr (f} \cap \overline{\text{(sets bad 1)}}\text{) end'}$$

which is equivalent to the condition (i) in Sect. 4.1. We use this equality to eliminate the terms with complement. Then the difference becomes

$$\text{Rabs (Pr (f} \cap \text{(sets bad 1)) end - Pr (f} \cap \text{(sets bad 1)) end')}$$

and the rest of the argument is exactly the same as the case of abstract fundamental lemma.

# Security of a Leakage-Resilient Protocol for Key Establishment and Mutual Authentication
## (Extended Abstract)

Raphael C.-W. Phan[1], Kim-Kwang Raymond Choo[2,*], and Swee-Huay Heng[3]

[1] Laboratoire de sécurité et de cryptographie, EPFL, Lausanne, Switzerland
raphael.phan@epfl.ch
[2] Canberra, Australia
raymond.choo.au@gmail.com
[3] Centre for Cryptography and Information Security (CCIS),
Faculty of Information Science and Technology, Multimedia University, Malaysia
shheng@mmu.edu.my

**Abstract.** We revisit Shin *et al.*'s leakage-resilient password-based authenticated key establishment protocol (LR-AKEP) and the security model used to prove the security of LR-AKEP. By refining the **Leak** oracle in the security model, we show that LR-AKE (1) can, in fact, achieve a stronger notion of leakage-resilience than initially claimed and (2) also achieve an additional feature of traceability, not previously mentioned.

**Keywords:** Key establishment, mutual athentication, leakage-resilient.

## 1 Introduction

Authenticated Key Establishment protocols (AKEPs) allow two parties to share a secret key based on long-term secrets associated with individual entities (typically passwords). Passwords are strings easily memorized by humans and thus of low entropy. Such protocols are especially popular in computationally restricted devices and those requiring interaction with human users. For example, in practical applications, the secrets derived from passwords are stored in some devices (e.g., a table containing hashed values of passwords kept by a trusted server). A fundamental security threat for password-based AKEPs is, unsurprisingly, dictionary attacks due to low entropy of password-based AKEPs.

We revisit the leakage-resilient password-based AKEPs (LR-AKEPs), first proposed by Shin, Kobara and Imai [7] and subsequently extended in [4,8,9,10]. LR-AKEPs, designed to maintain the secrecy of the long-term password even in the case when stored secrets (i.e., functions of the password) are leaked, can be broadly categorised into two families: the Diffie–Hellman-based LR-AKEPs [7,8,9] and the RSA-based LR-AKEPs [4,10].

---

* The views and opinions expressed in this paper are those of the author and do not reflect those of any organisation with which the author may be affiliated. This research was undertaken in the author's personal capacity.

W. Susilo, J.K. Liu, and Y. Mu. (Eds.): ProvSec 2007, LNCS 4784, pp. 169–177, 2007.
© Springer-Verlag Berlin Heidelberg 2007

Widely used security models for AKEPs (including password-based AKEPs) include the indistinguishability-based models of Bellare, Pointcheval, and Rogaway [1] model (hereafter referred to as the BPR2000 model) and Canetti and Krawczyk [2][1]. In the BPR2000 model, leakages of established secret session keys and long-term secrets (e.g., private key or password) are considered by allowing the adversary to have access to the Reveal oracle and the Corrupt oracle respectively. To model leakage-resilience, Shin et al. [7] introduced an additional Leak oracle that allows the adversary to learn the stored secrets of unrelated sessions.

The focus of this paper is on the Diffie–Hellman-based LR-AKEP published in ASIACRYPT 2003 [7] (hereafter referred to as "the LR-AKE protocol"). A distinct difference between the LR-AKE protocol and latter extensions [8,9] is that only one secret is stored on the client in the latter schemes.

We regard our contributions in this paper to be three-fold:

1. **Revised security model:** We refine the original model used by Shin et al. to prove the security of the LR-AKE protocol by splitting the Leak oracle into LeakC and LeakS oracles[2]. By so doing, we are able to define *how many* leakages occur on the server side.
2. **Stronger notion of leakage-resilience than that defined by Shin et al.:** Shin et al. proved that the LR-AKE protocol is secure when the leaks do not originate from both the client and servers simultaneously. We demonstrate that the LR-AKE protocol can, in fact, provide an *almost* perfect security level.
3. **Notion of traceability not previously mentioned by Shin et al.:** We demonstrate that the LR-AKE protocol can provide traceability, which allows us to identify the compromised client or server devices when leakages occur.

## 2    Revisiting the Leakage-Resilient AKE Protocol of ASIACRYPT 2003

The notation used throughout this paper is as described in Table 1.

The LR-AKE protocol, described in Fig. 1, can be considered a two-party password-based AKE involving a client-server pair where the server is one out of $n - 1$ possible servers. The client, $C$, remembers a chosen password, $pw$, and stores $n - 1$ secret values, $h_i$ $(i = 1, \ldots, n - 1)$, derived from $pw$ in $C$'s device. A partial secret value, $h^{p(i) \cdot \lambda_i}$ for $1 \leq i \leq n - 1$ (not a share) of $pw$, is registered with each of the $n - 1$ servers. This will enable $C$ to establish a session key with any of these servers in subsequent sessions. The underlined values in Fig. 1 represent the stored secrets of the respective client and server. Note that

---

[1] Interested reader is referred to [3] for a comparison and a discussion of existing security models for AKEPs.

[2] The definitions of oracles A1 through A4 in Section 4 of [9] implicitly split the Leak oracle, thereby distinguishing whether the leakage occurs at the client or at the server.

**Table 1.** Summary of notations

| | |
|---|---|
| $C$ | The client with identity $ID_C$ |
| $S_i$ | The $i^{th}$ server with identity $ID_{S_i}$, $(1 \leq i \leq n-1)$ |
| $G$ | Finite cyclic group of large prime order $q$ |
| $g, h$ | Generators of $G$ |
| $r_i$ | A random value in $(\mathbb{Z}/q\mathbb{Z})^*$ |
| $pw$ | The password chosen by the client |
| $p(\cdot)$ | Random polynomial of degree $n-1$ with coefficients also randomly chosen in $(\mathbb{Z}/q\mathbb{Z})^*$; defined as $p(x) = \Sigma_{j=0}^{n-1}\alpha_j \cdot x^j \mod q$ for which $\alpha_0 = pw$ |
| $h^{p(i).\lambda_i}$ | The secret value registered by client with server $S_i$, where $p(i)$ is a share of $(n,n)$-threshold secret sharing and $\lambda_i$ is a Lagrange coefficient. Note that $h^{-p(i).\lambda_i} = h_i \cdot h^{-pw}$, which allows for both client and server to compute the same MAC keys $km_c$ and $km_s$, respectively. |
| $h_i$ | Client's stored secret corresponding to server $S_i$; equals $h^{\Sigma_{l=1, l \neq i}^{n} p(l).\lambda_l}$ |
| $Tag_c, Tag_s, Tag_{sk}$ | Pre-determined distinct values, e.g., $Tag_c = (ID_C\|\|ID_S\|\|00)$, $Tag_s = (ID_C\|\|ID_S\|\|01)$ and $Tag_{sk} = (ID_C\|\|ID_S\|\|11)$ |
| $MAC_k(\cdot)$ | A MAC generation function with $k$ as its keying material |

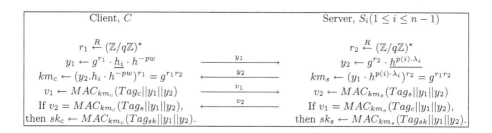

**Fig. 1.** Original LR-AKE protocol of Shin, Kobara, and Imai [7]

we only present sufficient details to understand this paper and we refer interested reader to [7] for further details.

Shin *et al.* proved the LR-AKE protocol secure against off-line dictionary attacks even if the stored secrets are leaked from *either* the client or up to all $n-1$ servers, but not from *both* client and $n-1$ servers simultaneously [7, Theorem 1].

## 3   Refining the Oracle for Leakage Resilience

We now revisit the BPR2000 model used by Shin *et al.* to prove the security of the LR-AKE protocol.

PROTOCOL PARTICIPANTS. Let $ID \stackrel{\text{def}}{=} Clients \cup Servers$ be a non-empty set of protocol participants, or *principals*. We assume $Servers$ consists of $n-1$ servers, $\{S_1, \ldots, S_{n-1}\}$ and at any time a client $C \in Clients$ is interacting with a server $S_i \in Servers$ to establish an LR-AKE session.

PROTOCOL EXECUTION. The adversary, $\mathcal{A}$, controls the communications between the protocol participants by interacting with the set of oracles, $\Pi^i_{U_u, U_v}$, where $\Pi^i_{U_u, U_v}$ is defined to be the $i^{\text{th}}$ instantiation of a protocol participant, $U_u$, in a specific protocol run and $U_v$ is the principal with whom $U_u$ wishes to establish a secret key. $\mathcal{A}$ controls the communication channels via the queries to the targeted oracles. A description of the oracle types is presented as follows. Note that we had split the Leak oracle into LeakC and LeakS oracles as this will allow us to distinguish whether the leakage occurs at the client or at the server.

Send($U_u, U_v, i, m$) **query.** This query to an oracle, $\Pi^i_{U_u, U_v}$, computes a response according to the protocol specification and decision on whether to accept or reject yet, and returns them to the adversary $\mathcal{A}$. If $\Pi^i_{U_u, U_v}$ has either accepted with some session key or terminated, this will be made known to $\mathcal{A}$. Note that if $m = *$, then this will result in the instantiation of the oracle $\Pi^i_{U_u, U_v}$ if such an oracle has not been created previously.

Reveal($U_u, U_v, i$) **query.** Any oracle, $\Pi^i_{U_u, U_v}$, upon receiving such a query and if $\Pi^i_{U_u, U_v}$ has accepted and holds some session key, will send this session key back to $\mathcal{A}$. The Reveal query is designed to capture this notion.

Corrupt($U_u$) **query.** This query captures unknown key share attacks and insider attacks. This query allows $\mathcal{A}$ to corrupt the principal $U_u$ at will, and thereby learn the complete internal state of the corrupted principal. Notice that a Corrupt query does not result in the release of the session keys since $\mathcal{A}$ already has the ability to obtain session keys through Reveal queries.

LeakC($\ell, \jmath$) **query.** This query allows $\mathcal{A}$ to learn $\ell$ $(1 \le \ell \le n-1)$ stored secrets $h_\iota$ of the client oracle and the corresponding indices $\iota$ (for $\iota \in \{1, \ldots, n-1\}, \iota \ne \jmath$) of the leaked secrets.

LeakS($t, \iota$) **query.** This query to a server oracle, $U_v$, returns the corresponding stored secrets $h^{p(\jmath) \cdot \lambda_\jmath}$ of any $t$ $(1 \le t \le n-1)$ servers and their corresponding indices $\jmath$ (for $\jmath \in \{1, \ldots, n-1\}, \jmath \ne \iota$) of these leaked servers.

PROTOCOL SECURITY. Security of the LR-AKE protocol [7] is defined in two stages.

1. Proving that the protocol is secure even when the stored secrets are leaked.
2. The standard indistinguishability-based security proof (of the established session key) as required by the BPR2000 model [1].

A revised security proof for the LR-AKE protocol, presented in Appendix A, demonstrates that the LR-AKE protocol described in Fig. 1 provides both key establishment and mutual authentication.

# 4  Strengthened Notions of Leakage Resilience and Traceability

Shin *et al.* [7,9] state that one cannot achieve security when there are leakages from both the client and server(s) side (see **Fact 2**), the situation in which they call perfect security (see **Goal 1**).

Goal 1: **Perfect Security [7,9].** *Any AKE protocol with 'perfect security' remains secure against leakages from client **and** server(s), **simultaneously**.*

Fact 2. **Impossibility of Perfect Security [7,9].** *Any AKE protocol cannot achieve (strong) security against leakage from **both** a client and servers simultaneously. If an adversary obtains stored secrets from both a client and servers at the same time, s/he can perfectly simulate the protocol using the leaked secrets. Thus s/he can try the password candidates off-line in parallel.*

Shin *et al.* then argue that the next highest achievable goal is the security of the password against offline dictionary attacks even in the situation when there are "leakages" from *either* the client *or* the server(s) (see Goal 2 below).

Goal 2: **Strong Security [7,9].** *In absence of 'perfect security', [7,9] claim that the next highest goal is to achieve so-called 'strong security', i.e. security against the "leakages" from a client and servers, **respectively**.*

We can view 'perfect security' described in Goal 1 as security against leakages from *both* the client *and* the server(s), while 'strong security' described in Goal 2 as security against leakages from *either* the client *or* the server(s). We argue that their requirement is too strong, i.e., unnecessarily restrictive as Goal 2 is not the next best security in the absence of Goal 1. We can still have security against leakages from *both* the client *and* server(s) with some trade-off.

### Relation Between the LR-AKE Protocol and an $(n, n)$ Secret-Sharing Scheme

The reader might have observed that in the LR-AKE scheme, the $n$ shares of the secret password $pw$ are not separated uniformly among the $n - 1$ servers and the client. Therefore, leakage from a client should not be treated in the same way as leakage from a server – leakage of a stored secret from any server contains information about just one share whilst leakage from the client constitutes the entire stored secret, $h_i$. It should come as no surprise that the LR-AKE protocol will be insecure if there are leakages from the client (i.e., $n - 1$ shares are leaked) and one or more servers.

We can, however, relax this strong requirement to achieve perfect security to a certain extent. We termed this as *almost perfect security*, which can be formalized by splitting the Leak queries (as described in Section 3). By having a separate LeakC query for the client oracle and a separate LeakS query for the server oracle, we are able to formally state:

1. whether the leakage is from the client or the server, and
2. how many stored secrets are leaked.

Making the former explicit is useful because leakages from a server contain only information about a particular share, while leakage from a client contains information about $n - 1$ shares. Making the latter explicit is also useful because by knowing which client's stored secret has been compromised, we will know the corresponding compromise at the server(s). Consequently, this allows us to show that the original LR-AKE protocol proposed in [7] can achieve a stronger notion of leakage resilience (in the sense of 'almost perfect security' as described in Goal 3).

Goal 3. **Almost Perfect Security.** *Any AKE protocol with 'almost perfect security' remains secure even against leakages from **both** the client **and** up to $n-2$ servers, **simultaneously**.*

Since Goal 1 trivially implies Goal 3 and Goal 3 is a stronger notion than Goal 2, we now have the following result.

**Theorem 1.** The LR-AKE protocol achieves Goal 3 (almost perfect security) even when both the client and up to $n-2$ servers leak their corresponding stored secrets, as long as the leaked secret(s) $h_\iota$ of the client and leaked secret(s) of the server(s) $S_\jmath$ are such that $\jmath \neq \iota$.

*Proof Intuition.* Recall that:

- a LeakC$(\ell, \jmath)$ query allows the adversary $\mathcal{A}$ to learn $\ell$ $(1 \leq \ell \leq n-1)$ stored secrets $h_\iota$ of the Client, and the corresponding indices $\iota$ (for $\iota \in \{1, \ldots, n-1\}$) of these leaked secrets, thus as long as the LeakS queries are issued only to servers $S_\jmath$ for $\jmath \neq \iota$, there are insufficient shares (since number of leaked shares $< n$) to reveal the shared secret $pw$.
- a LeakS$(t, \iota)$ query allows the adversary $\mathcal{A}$ to learn $t$ $(1 \leq \jmath \leq n-1)$ stored secrets $h^{p(\jmath) \cdot \lambda_\jmath}$ of $t$ Servers $S_\jmath$, and the corresponding indices $\jmath$ (for $\jmath \in \{1, \ldots, n-1\}$) of these leaked servers, thus as long as the LeakC query returns only stored secrets $h_\iota$ of the client such that $\iota \neq \jmath$, there insufficient shares to reveal the shared secret $pw$. □

Although we cannot prove the protocol secure when leakages originate from both the client *and all* servers, we can prove that the protocol remains secure when the leakages originate from the client and up to $n-2$ servers, even in the case when the client leaks more than one (up to $n-2$) secret(s). The conditions necessary for achieving Goal 3 is that the total of the stored secrets leaked by the client and the servers cannot exceed $n-1$, and all their indices are different. Consequently, we can view Goal 3 as a special case of Goal 1 in the sense that we can still maintain security when we have leakages from both the client *and* the server(s) simultaneously.

**Traceability.** In our setting, the stored secrets can be leaked from either the client or server(s), or both. Although it is hard to prevent such leakages, the client would most likely to be interested to know which particular stored secret has been leaked. This is similar to the copyright violator identification and dispute resolution (arbitration) scenario (e.g., in buyer-seller protocols [6]). This allows us to handle cases where leakages are unavoidable, but future preventive measures can be taken by firstly identifying the compromised client or server devices.

In the context of the LR-AKE schemes, we should be able to determine the compromised site (i.e., which particular server) since every registered stored secret is unique. Consequently, we are able to demonstrate that the original LR-AKE scheme provides *traceability* (i.e., in the event of leakages that compromise the security of the password, it is possible to precisely pinpoint which server(s) leaked). For example, when a password has been compromised, we know that it is likely that the compromise is at the client site (except with negligible probability). We can, therefore, trace which particular server(s) had caused the leakage by simply checking which stored secret(s) of the client, $h_i$, is (are) leaked.

It appears that the original LR-AKE protocol [7] is the only scheme in their family that provides such a (traceability) feature as in the other variants (e.g., [8,9,10]), the Client stores only one secret instead of unique ones corresponding to each server in the case of [7].

## Acknowledgements

The first author thanks Kazukuni Kobara for clarifying issues related to the LR-AKE scheme and its notion of security. We also thank the anonymous referees for their feedback.

## References

1. Bellare, M., Pointcheval, D., Rogaway, P.: Authenticated Key Exchange Secure against Dictionary Attacks. In: Preneel, B. (ed.) EUROCRYPT 2000. LNCS, vol. 1807, pp. 139–155. Springer, Heidelberg (2000)
2. Canetti, R., Krawczyk, H.: Analysis of Key-Exchange Protocols and Their Use for Building Secure Channels. In: Pfitzmann, B. (ed.) EUROCRYPT 2001. LNCS, vol. 2045, pp. 453–474. Springer, Heidelberg (2001)
3. Choo, K.-K.R., Boyd, C., Hitchcock, Y.: Examining Indistinguishability-Based Proof Models for Key Establishment Protocols. In: Roy, B. (ed.) ASIACRYPT 2005. LNCS, vol. 3788, pp. 585–604. Springer, Heidelberg (2005)
4. Fathi, H., Shin, S.-H., Kobara, K., Chakraborty, S.S., Imai, H., Prasad, R.: Leakage-Resilient Security Architecture for Mobile IPv6 in Wireless Overlay Networks. IEEE Journal on Selected Areas in Communications 23(11), 2182–2193 (2005)
5. Itkis, G., Reyzin, L.: SiBIR: Signer-Base Intrusion-Resilient Signatures. In: Yung, M. (ed.) CRYPTO 2002. LNCS, vol. 2442, pp. 499–514. Springer, Heidelberg (2002)
6. Memon, N., Wong, P.W.: A Buyer-Seller Watermarking Protocol. IEEE Trans. on Image Processing 10(4) (2001)
7. Shin, S.-H., Kobara, K., Imai, H.: Leakage-Resilient Authenticated Key Establishment Protocols. In: Laih, C.-S. (ed.) ASIACRYPT 2003. LNCS, vol. 2894, pp. 155–172. Springer, Heidelberg (2003)
8. Shin, S.-H., Kobara, K., Imai, H.: A Simplified Leakage-Resilient Authenticated Key Establishment Protocol with Optimal Memory Size. In: Lorenz, P., Dini, P. (eds.) ICN 2005. LNCS, vol. 3421, Springer, Heidelberg (2005)
9. Shin, S.-H., Kobara, K., Imai, H.: A Simple Leakage-Resilient Authenticated Key Establishment Protocol, Its Extensions, and Applications. IEICE Transactions on Fundamentals of Electronics, Communications and Computer Sciences E88-A(3), 736–754 (2005)
10. Shin, S.-H., Kobara, K., Imai, H.: Efficient and Leakage-Resilient Authenticated Key Transport Protocol Based on RSA. In: Ioannidis, J., Keromytis, A.D., Yung, M. (eds.) ACNS 2005. LNCS, vol. 3531, pp. 269–284. Springer, Heidelberg (2005)

# A    Revised Security Proof

We now provide a sketch of the revised security proof demonstrating that the LR-AKE protocol provides both key establishment and mutual authentication.

**Theorem 2.** *The LR-AKE protocol is a secure mutual authentication and key establishment (MAKE) protocol if the underlying message authentication (MAC) scheme is secure in the sense of existential unforgeability under adaptive chosen message attack assuming the intractability of the DDH Problem.*

*Proof.* The proof for **key establishment** generally follows that of Shin *et al.* [9, Theorem 2]. We construct a forger $\mathcal{F}$ against the MAC, using an adversary $\mathcal{A}$ against the protocol. $\mathcal{F}$ now simulates the view of $\mathcal{A}$ in the game simulation. $\mathcal{F}$ answers all Send, Execute, Reveal, LeakC, LeakS, and Corrupt queries similar to the proof simulation of [9, Theorem 2]. At some stage of the game simulation, $\mathcal{A}$ decides to choose a session to be tested and asks the Test query, which is answered by $\mathcal{F}$ in almost the same fashion as the proof simulation presented in the proof for [9, Theorem 2]. Hence, whatever $\mathcal{F}$ can simulate in the proof for [9, Theorem 2], $\mathcal{F}$ can do the same here. After asking the Test query, $\mathcal{A}$ is allowed to further interact with the protocols by asking any Send, Execute, Reveal, LeakC, LeakS, and Corrupt queries of choice, with the exception that $\mathcal{A}$ is not allowed to trivially expose the Test session by asking any Reveal, LeakC, LeakS, or Corrupt queries to the partner or owner associated with the Test session. Eventually, $\mathcal{A}$ outputs the guess bit, $b'$.

It follows that whatever the MAC forger can simulate in the proof for [9, Theorem 2], our $\mathcal{F}$ can do the same although the converse is not true. Recall that the $SIDs$ of $A$ and $B$ for the protocol described in Fig. 1 are defined to be $y_1\|y_2\|v_1\|v_2$. Let Repeat be the event that a value of $SID$ repeats at some point during the game simulation. It is easy to see that the probability of Repeat happening occurs with probability upper bounded by $\frac{q_s^2}{2^k}$ (where $G$ and $q_s$ is the upper bound on the number of the sessions in the game simulation and $k$ is the security parameter) by a "birthday problem" calculation. Let the advantage of $\mathcal{A}$ in our game simulation be denoted by $\mathsf{Adv}^{\mathcal{A}}(k)$ and the advantage of $\mathcal{A}$ in the game simulation of [9, Theorem 2] be denoted by $\mathsf{Adv}^{\mathcal{A}}_{[9]}(k)$. It then follows easily that $\mathsf{Adv}^{\mathcal{A}}(k) \leq \mathsf{Adv}^{\mathcal{A}}_{[42]}(k) + \frac{q_s^2}{2^k}$. □

We now prove that the LR-AKE protocol achieves **mutual authentication**. We define as $\mathsf{Event}^{\mathsf{No-Matching}}$ the event that a fresh oracle, $\Pi_U^i$, who has been engaged in a conversation and has successfully finished the protocol with a session key output but without a partner oracle [1].

**Lemma 1.** *The LR-AKE protocol of Shin et al. [7] described in Fig. 1 achieves mutual authentication if $\Pr[\mathsf{Event}^{\mathsf{No-Matching}}]$ is negligible.*

*Proof.* Assume that an adversary can violate the mutual authentication with probability $\epsilon$ within a time bound $t$. Similar to our earlier proof, we construct a

MAC forger, $\mathcal{F}$, using such an adversary, $\mathcal{A}$. $\mathcal{F}$ now simulates the view of such an adversary, $\mathcal{A}$, in similar fashion as the earlier game simulation.

We consider the probability that $\mathcal{F}$ does not abort the simulation, which can happen under any of the scenarios: (1) abort when being asked some Reveal queries (2) abort when being asked some LeakC queries (3) abort when being asked some LeakS queries (4) abort when being asked some Corrupt queries. Let $q_N$ be the maximum number of sessions between any two parties in the protocol run and $q_P$ be the maximum number of players in the protocol run.

The probability that $\mathcal{F}$ does not abort for scenarios (1) to (3) are $(q_P^2 q_N - 2)/(q_P^2 q_N)$ respectively, and for (4) is $(q_P-2)/(q_P^2)$. One may further remark that the simulation is perfectly indistinguishable from a real game, except for a negligible probability. The probability for an oracle to have many partners is bounded by $q_P^2/q_N$. Therefore, if $\mathcal{F}$ is successful during the simulation (the probability is at least $\epsilon$), then there is a completed/accepted oracle $\Pi_U^i$ such that $\Pi_U^i$ has no matching oracle. Since there are at most $q_P^2 q_N$ oracles during the simulation, the probability for this oracle to be the oracle, $\Pi_{U_0}^i$, is $1/(q_P^2 q_N)$. Therefore, the advantage of $\mathcal{F}$ is at least $\epsilon(2^{2^k} - 1)(q_P - 2)((q_P^2 q_N - 2)/(q_P^2 q_N))^3(1/(q_P^7 q_N^3 2^{2^k}))$. However, we know that both $q_N$ and $q_P$ are polynomial in the security parameter $k$. Hence, the probability of $\Pr[\text{Event}^{\text{No-Matching}}]$ is negligible if the MAC is secure. □

# An Approach for Symmetric Encryption Against Side Channel Attacks in Provable Security

Wei Li and Dawu Gu

Department of Computer Science and Engineering,
Shanghai Jiao Tong University,
Shanghai 200240, China
{liwei2003,dwgu}@sjtu.edu.cn

**Abstract.** This paper defines perfect security against side channel attacks for a cryptosystem implementation, and discusses the implication of secure notions for a cryptosystem in provable security. Then we give some security notions for symmetric encryption against side channel attacks, UB-SCA (unbreakability in side channel attacks) and IND-CPA-SCA (indistinguishability of chosen plaintext attacks and side channel attacks). On the basis of these definitions, we propose and prove that IND-CPA + UB-SCA $\Rightarrow$ IND-CPA-SCA by reduction, and IND-CPA-SCA is stronger than IND-CPA or UB-SCA.

## 1 Introduction

During the last ten years a new class of attacks against cryptographic devices has become public [1,2]. These attacks exploit easily accessible information like power consumption[3], running time[4], and can be mounted by anyone using low–cost equipment. These *side–channel attacks* amplify and evaluate leaked information with the help of statistical methods, and are often much more powerful than traditional cryptanalysis. Examples show that a very small amount of side–channel information is enough to completely break a cryptosystem [5]. While many previously–known cryptanalytic attacks can be analyzed by studying algorithms, the vulnerabilities of side–channel attacks result from electrical behavior of transistors and circuits of an implementation. Therefore, it extends theoretically the current mathematical models of cryptography to the physical setting which takes into consideration side–channel attacks [6].

Indistinguishability of encryptions (IND), which captures a strong notion of privacy, formalizes that an adversary's inability to learn information about the plaintext given a challenge ciphertext in provable security[7]. Connecting an ability of an adversary with chosen-plaintext attack leads to security notions of symmetric encryption, eg. IND-CPA[8] etc. Likewise, the security of symmetric encryption against side channel attacks does not violate this definition as above[9–11]. However, it's difficult to limit the power of the adversary in implementation. As a result, the security goals and adversary models may be considered from other directions. The best we can hope to do is combining the security of designing with that of implementation.

W. Susilo, J.K. Liu, and Y. Mu. (Eds.): ProvSec 2007, LNCS 4784, pp. 178–187, 2007.

Therefore, in this paper we propose several notions of privacy for symmetric encryption: UB-SCA and IND-CPA-SCA. The former notion describes the security of a symmetric encryption against side channel attacks in implementation, while the latter notion gives us a notion for a secure symmetric encryption both in designing and implementation. We seek an approach that can put these attacks to a common foundation, since designing and implementation for a secure cryptosystem are not independent.

The rest of this paper is organized as follows. Section 2 and 3 focus on defining a cryptosystem implementation in perfect security against side channel attacks. Then we present security notions for a symmetric encryption based on IND-CPA in section 4, and further section 5 generalizes the relations by reductions. Finally we conclude some remarks about a secure cryptosystem.

# 2   Syntax of a Symmetric Encryption Scheme

Secure notions for symmetric encryption schemes against traditional attack are given in [12]. The definitions for the symmetric encryption include the syntax and formal security measures as follows. Let $\mathcal{SE}=(\mathcal{P}, \mathcal{C}, \mathcal{K}, \mathcal{E}, \mathcal{D})$ denote a symmetric encryption scheme. The key schedule $\mathcal{K}$ takes a security parameter $k \in N$ as its input and returns a key $K$, denoted as $K \leftarrow \mathcal{K}(k)$. The encryption algorithm $\mathcal{E}$ could be randomized or stateful. It takes the key $K$ and a plaintext $P$ as inputs to return a ciphertext $C$, denoted as $C \leftarrow \mathcal{E}_K(P)$. The decryption algorithm $\mathcal{D}$ is deterministic and stateless. It takes the key $K$ and a string $C$ as its input to return either the corresponding plaintext $P$ or the symbol $\perp$, denoted as $x \leftarrow \mathcal{D}_K(C)$ where $x \in \{0,1\}^* \bigcup \{\perp\}$. It requires $\mathcal{D}_K(\mathcal{E}_K(P)) = P$ for all $P \in \{0,1\}^*$.

# 3   Implementation of Security

## 3.1   Implementation of Perfect Security Against Side Channel Attacks

Side channel information is a kind of information leaked from the physical implementation of a cryptosystem.So an adversary concerns mostly how much side channel information contributes to the recovery of key. We present perfect security against side channel attacks for a cryptosystem implementation as follows.

**Definition 1.** *Let $(\mathcal{P}, \mathcal{C}, \mathcal{S}, \mathcal{K}, \mathcal{E}, \mathcal{D})$ be a cryptosystem implementation with side channel information $\mathcal{S}$. Let $H(\cdot)$ denote entropy of the information. If*

$$H(K|S) = H(K)$$

*where $K \in \mathcal{K}$ and $S \in \mathcal{S}$, then the cryptosystem implementation is perfect secure against side channel attacks.*                                                □

**Proposition 2.** *The following statement are equivalent:*

**(1)** $H(K|S) = H(K)$. *Given the side channel information, an adversary can not get any information of key.*

**(2)** $I(K;S) = 0$. *An adversary cannot get any mutual information between key and side channel information.*

**(3)** $H(S|K) = H(S)$. *Given a key, side channel information cannot be predicted.*

$\square$

### 3.2   Security Levels for a Symmetric Encryption

There are four security levers for a symmetric encryption as follows:

**(1)** Secure designing and secure implementation: it is the ultra aim that all cryptosystems pursue. Besides the designing principle, this kind of cryptosystem also considers implementation principle.

**(2)** Secure designing and insecure implementation: it is the region that most cryptosystems ignore now. In fact, implementation principle is as important as designing principle. It's high time that implementation principle should have its seat.

**(3)** Insecure designing and secure implementation: it is a dangerous region that a cryptosystem may exist some hidden trouble. A cryptosystem of insecure designing may suffer from one-off beaten once it is broken, and has no opportunity to be repaired and upgraded. So we had better not to use this cryptosystem.

**(4)** Insecure designing and insecure implementation: it is the best lesson for us to design and implement the new cryptosystem. It was maybe a milestone before, and yet now, it is behind the times on the development of theory and technology. So it provides a quick and good way to know the development of this field.

So the security levels remind us to pay more attention to countermeasure against threat from real world, and a secure cryptosystem in designing and implementation.

## 4   Secure Notions Against Side Channel Attacks

### 4.1   Privacy of a Symmetric Encryption Scheme

The privacy of a symmetric encryption scheme is measured by indistinguishability of the real-or-random model of [12]. It describes an adversary cannot distinguish a message from an equal-length random string in the encryption, which is called IND-CPA. Define the real-or-random encryption oracle $\mathcal{E}_K(RR(\cdot, b))$, where $b \in \{0, 1\}$, to take an input $x$ as follows:

If $b = 1$
    then it computes $C \leftarrow \mathcal{E}_K(\mathrm{x})$ and return $C$;
    else it computes $C \leftarrow \mathcal{E}_K(\mathrm{r})$ where $r \leftarrow \{0, 1\}^{|x|}$ and returns $C$.

The encryption scheme is good if no reasonable adversary can obtain significant advantage in distinguishing the cases $b = 0$ and $b = 1$ given access to the oracle.

**Definition 3 (IND–CPA).** *Let $\mathcal{SE}=(\mathcal{P}, \mathcal{C}, \mathcal{K}, \mathcal{E}, \mathcal{D})$ be a symmetric encryption scheme. Let $A$ be an adversary that has access to the oracles $\mathcal{E}_K(RR(\cdot,b))$, $b \in \{0,1\}$ and $k \in N$. Now, the following experiment is considered:*

$$\text{Experiment } \mathbf{Exp}_{\mathcal{SE},A_{cpa}}^{ind-cpa-b}(k)$$
$$K \leftarrow \mathcal{K}(k)$$
$$d \leftarrow A_{cpa}^{\mathcal{E}_K(RR(\cdot,b))}(k)$$
$$\mathbf{Return}\ d$$

The advantage of the adversaries is defined via

$$Adv_{\mathcal{SE},A_{cpa}}^{ind-cpa}(k) = \Pr[Exp_{\mathcal{SE},A_{cpa}}^{ind-cpa-1}(k) = 1] - \Pr[Exp_{\mathcal{SE},A_{cpa}}^{ind-cpa-0}(k) = 1].$$

The *advantage function* of the scheme is defined as follows. For any integers $t, q_e, u_e,$

$$Adv_{\mathcal{SE}}^{ind-cpa}(k, t, q_e, u_e) = \max_{A_{cpa}}\{Adv_{\mathcal{SE},A_{cpa}}^{ind-cpa}(k)\}.$$

Where the maximum is over $A_{cpa}$ with time complexity $t$, making at most $q_e$ queries to the $\mathcal{E}_K(RR(\cdot,b))$ oracle, totaling $u_e$ bits at most. The scheme is said to be IND-CPA secure if the function $Adv_{SE,A}^{ind-cpa}(\cdot)$ is negligible for any adversary $A_{cpa}$ whose time complexity is polynomial in $k$.  □

### 4.2  Implementation Privacy of a Symmetric Encryption Scheme

Now we specify security definitions for one implementation of a symmetric encryption scheme $\mathcal{SE}=(\mathcal{P}, \mathcal{C}, \mathcal{S}, \mathcal{K}, \mathcal{E}, \mathcal{D})$. It is convenient to define an algorithm $K' \leftarrow \mathcal{S}_K^*(\cdot)$, whose input is side channel information $S$ and output is key $K' \in \{0,1\}^* \bigcup\{\perp\}$.

The scheme is good in implementation if no reasonable adversary can obtain significant advantage to break the total key given access to the oracles. Here, $UB$ means unbreakability of the key.

**Definition 4 (UB-SCA).** *Let $\mathcal{SE}=(\mathcal{P}, \mathcal{C}, \mathcal{S}, \mathcal{K}, \mathcal{E}, \mathcal{D})$ be the implementation of symmetric encryption scheme with side channel information algorithm $\mathcal{S}$. Let $b \in \{0,1\}$ and $k \in N$. Let $A_{sca}$ to be an adversary that has access to the oracle $\mathcal{S}_K^*(\cdot)$. Now, the following experiment is considered:*

$$\text{Experiment } \mathbf{Exp}_{\mathcal{SE},A_{sca}}^{ub-sca}(k)$$
$$K \leftarrow \mathcal{K}(k)$$
$$K' \leftarrow A_{sca}^{\mathcal{E}_K(\cdot),\mathcal{S}_K^*(\cdot)}(k)$$
$$\text{If } K = K' \text{ then } return\ 1$$
$$\text{else } return\ 0$$

The advantage of the adversaries is defined via

$$Adv_{\mathcal{SE},A_{sca}}^{ind-sca}(k) = \Pr[Exp_{\mathcal{SE},A_{sca}}^{ind-sca}(k) = 1].$$

The advantage function of the scheme is defined as follows. For any integers $k, t, q_e, u_e, q_s, u_s$

$$Adv_{\mathcal{SE}}^{ind-sca}(k, t, q_s, u_s, q_s, u_s) = \max_{A_{sca}}\{Adv_{\mathcal{SE},A_{sca}}^{ind-sca}(k)\},$$

where the maximum is over all $A_{sca}$ with time complexity $t$. It makes at most $q_e$ encryption queries to the $\mathcal{E}_K(\cdot)$ oracle (totaling at most $u_e$ bits), and at most $q_s$ implementation queries to the $\mathcal{S}_K^*(\cdot)$ (totalling $u_s$ bits at most). The scheme is UB–SCA secure if the function $Adv_{\mathcal{SE},A}^{ind-sca}(\cdot)$ is negligible for any adversary $A_{sca}$ whose time complexity is polynomial in $k$.    □

### 4.3    Privacy of a Symmetric Encryption Scheme in Both Designing and Implementation

We specify IND–CPA–SCA that an adversary cannot distinguish a message from an equal–length string of garbage against side channel attacks in the implementation of encryption. Formally, we define an SCA oracle $S^*$ and a real-or-random oracle $\mathcal{E}_K(RR(\cdot,b))$, where $b \in \{0,1\}$, to take an input $x$ as follows:

If $b = 1$
    then it computes $C \leftarrow \mathcal{E}_{S^*(.)}(x)$ and return $C$;
    else it computes $C \leftarrow \mathcal{E}_{S^*(.)}(r)$ where $r \leftarrow \{0,1\}^{|x|}$ and returns $C$.

The scheme is "good" in designing and implementation if no "reasonable" adversary can obtain "significant" advantage in distinguishing the cases $b = 0$ and $b = 1$ given access to the oracles.

**Definition 5 (IND–CPA–SCA).** *Let $\mathcal{SE}=(\mathcal{P}, \mathcal{C}, \mathcal{S}, \mathcal{K}, \mathcal{E}, \mathcal{D})$ be a symmetric encryption scheme with side channel information. Let $b \in \{0,1\}$ and $k \in N$. Let $A_{cpa-sca}$ to be an adversary that has access to the oracles $\mathcal{E}_K(RR(\cdot,b))$ and $S_K^*(\cdot)$. Now, the following experiment is considered:*

$$\begin{aligned}
&\text{Experiment } \boldsymbol{Exp}_{\mathcal{SE},A_{cpa-sca}}^{ind-cpa-sca-b}(k)\\
&\quad K \leftarrow \mathcal{K}(k)\\
&\quad d \leftarrow A_{cpa-sca}^{\mathcal{E}_K(RR(\cdot,b)),S_K^*(\cdot)}(k)\\
&\quad \boldsymbol{Return}\ d
\end{aligned}$$

The advantage of the adversaries is defined via

$$Adv_{\mathcal{SE},A_{cpa-sca}}^{ind-cpa-sca}(k) = \Pr[Exp_{\mathcal{SE},A_{cpa-sca}}^{ind-cpa-sca-1}(k)=1] - \Pr[Exp_{\mathcal{SE},A_{cpa-sca}}^{ind-cpa-sca-0}(k)=1].$$

The advantage function of the scheme is defined as follows. For any integers $t, q_e, u_e, q_s, u_s,$

$$Adv_{\mathcal{SE}}^{ind-cpa-sca}(k, t, q_e, u_e, q_s, u_s) = \max_{A_{cpa-sca}}\{Adv_{\mathcal{SE},A_{cpa-sca}}^{ind-cpa-sca}(k)\}.$$

Where the maximum is over all $A_{cpa-sca}$ with time complexity $t$. It makes at most $q_e$ queries to the $\mathcal{E}_K(RR(\cdot, b))$ oracle (totaling at most $u_e$ bits), and at most $q_s$ queries to the $\mathcal{S}_K^*(\cdot)$ (totalling at most $u_s$). The scheme is said to be IND–CPA–SCA secure if the function $Adv_{SE,A}^{ind-sca}(\cdot)$ is negligible for any adversary $A_{cpa-sca}$ whose time complexity is polynomial in $k$.                     □

### 4.4   Notation for Adversary Execution

In reduction we often make an adversary $A'$ executing another adversary $A$. The adversary $A'$ maintains the execution state of $A$. Whenever $A$ makes an oracle query, $A'$ stops $A$, returns a reply to this oracle query, and then continues running $A$. We give some program for $A'$ as follows:

   For $i = 1, \ldots, q_e$ do
      When $A$ makes oracle query $x_i$
         [Some code computing a value $y_i$]
         $A \Leftarrow y_i$
      EndWhile
   $A \Rightarrow b$

The notation $A \Leftarrow y_i$ means that $A$ is designed a value $y_i$ in response to its oracle query $x_i$. It is assumed here that $A$ makes a total of $q_e$ queries. The notation $A \Rightarrow b$ means that $A$ is returning a value $b$.

## 5   Reduction Among the Notions

**Theorem 6 (UB–SCA $\wedge$ IND–CPA $\longrightarrow$ IND–CPA–SCA).** *For any scheme $SE=(\mathcal{P}, \mathcal{C}, \mathcal{S}, \mathcal{K}, \mathcal{E}, \mathcal{D})$, if $SE$ is IND–CPA secure and UB–SCA secure, then it is IND–CPA–SCA secure. Concretely,*

$$Adv_{SE}^{\text{ind-cpa-sca}}(k,t,q_e,u_e,q_s,u_s) \leq 2 \cdot Adv_{SE}^{\text{ub-sca}}(k,t,q_e,u_e,q_s,u_s)$$
$$+ Adv_{SE}^{\text{ind-cpa}}(k,t,q_e,u_e) \tag{1}$$

*Proof* Let $SE=(\mathcal{P}, \mathcal{C}, \mathcal{S}, \mathcal{K}, \mathcal{E}, \mathcal{D})$ be a symmetric encryption scheme implementation. To any adversary $A$ attacking the scheme in the *IND-CPA-SCA* notion, we associate two adversaries, $A_{sca}$ which attacks $SE$ in the *UB-SCA* sense, and $A_{cpa}$ which attacks $SE$ in the *IND-CPA* sense, so that inequation (1) is concluded. Furthermore, if $A$ runs in time $t$ using $q_e$ encryption and $q_s$ implementation queries (totalling $\mu_e, \mu_s$ bits respectively), then $A_{sca}$ runs in time $t$ using $q_e$ encryption and $q_s$ implementation queries (totalling $\mu_e$ and $\mu_s$ bits respectively), and $A_{cpa}$ runs in time $t$ using $q_e$ encryption queries (totalling $\mu_e$ bits).

   The two adversaries $A_{sca}$ and $A_{cpa}$ uses $A$ to achieve their goals. Specifically, $A_{sca}$, whose goal is to get a key from the oracle $\mathcal{S}_K^*(\cdot)$, will simply use $A$'s query to the oracle $\mathcal{S}_K^*(\cdot)$ as its own. Thus if $A$ gets a key, so does $A_{sca}$. Similarly,

$A_{cpa}$, whose goal is to figure out whether the encryption of the message or that of the random string of equal length, directly depends on $A$ to do so.

The constructions for $A_{cpa}$ and $A_{sca}$ are as follows.

> Adversary $A_{sca}^{\mathcal{E}_K(\cdot), \mathcal{S}_K^*(\cdot)}(k)$
>     $b' \leftarrow \{0, 1\}$
>     For $i = 1, \dots, q_e + q_s$ do
>         When $A$ makes a query $M_{i,0}, M_{i,1}$ to its
>         ind encryption oracle do
>             $A \Leftarrow \mathcal{E}_K(M_{i,b'})$
>         When $A$ makes a query $S_i$ to its
>         implementation oracle do
>             $K' \leftarrow \mathcal{S}_K^*(S_i)$
>             If $K! = K'$
>                 then $A \Leftarrow \perp$;
>                 else stop.
>
> Adversary $A_{cpa}^{\mathcal{E}_K(RR(\cdot,b))}(k)$
>     For $i = 1, \dots, q_e + q_s$ do
>         When $A$ makes a query $M_{i,0}, M_{i,1}$ to its
>         ind encryption oracle do
>             $A \Leftarrow \mathcal{E}_K(RR(M_{i,b}, b))$
>         When $A$ makes a query $S_i$ to its oracle do
>             $A \Leftarrow \perp$
>     $A \Rightarrow b'$
>     Return $b'$.

Now we prove inequation (1). Let $Pr[\cdot]$ denote the probability in $\mathbf{Exp}_{\mathcal{SE}, A_{cpa\text{-}sca}}^{ind\text{-}cpa\text{-}sca\text{-}b}(k)$ where $b \in \{0, 1\}$ and let $b'$ denote the bit output by $A$ in this experiment. Let $F$ denote the event that $A$ makes at least one query, i.e. a query $S$ such that $\mathcal{S}_K^*(S) = K$. Let $Pr_p[\cdot]$ denote the probability in $\mathbf{Exp}_{\mathcal{SE}, A_{cpa}}^{ind\text{-}cpa\text{-}b}(k)$ and let $Pr_s[\cdot]$ denote the probability in $\mathbf{Exp}_{\mathcal{SE}, A_{sca}}^{ub\text{-}sca}(k)$.

We claim

$$Pr[b' = b \wedge F] \le Pr[F]$$
$$= Pr_s[A_{sca}\, succeeds]$$
$$= Adv_{\mathcal{SE}, A_{sca}}^{ub-sca}(k) \qquad (2)$$

and

$$Pr[b' = b \wedge \neg F] \le Pr_p[b' = b]$$
$$= \frac{1}{2} Adv_{\mathcal{SE}, A_{cpa}}^{ind-cpa}(k) + \frac{1}{2}. \qquad (3)$$

We finish the proof given this and then return to the justification. That is,

$$\frac{1}{2} Adv_{SE}^{ind-cpa-sca}(k) + \frac{1}{2} = Pr[b' = b]$$
$$= Pr[b' = b \wedge F] + Pr[b' = b \wedge \neg F]$$
$$\leq Adv_{SE,A_{cpa}}^{ub-sca}(k) + \frac{1}{2} Adv_{SE}^{ind-cpa}(k) + \frac{1}{2}.$$

Some algebraic manipulation leads to inequation (1). We justify the claimed inequations (2) and (3) by analyzing each of them in turn.

To justify the inequations (2), we observe that $A_{sca}$ simulates $A$ in the exact same environment as that of the experiment $\mathbf{Exp}_{SE,A_{cpa-sca}}^{ind-cpa-sca-b}(k)$. Therefore, if $A$ submits a valid $S$ as a oracle query (i.e. the event $F$ occurs), $A_{sca}$ uses this $S$ as a query to its oracle, and so inequation (2) follows. (Once this output equals $K$, $A_{sca}$ stops and the simulation does not accurate more.) Similarly, for the inequation (3), when then event $F$ does not occur, $A_{cpa}$ simulates $A$ in the exact same environment as that of the experiment $\mathbf{Exp}_{SE,A_{cpa-sca}}^{ind-cpa-sca-b}(k)$. Therefore, if $A$ is able to guess the correct bit $b' = b$, so is $A_{cpa}$, and inequation (3) follows. This concludes the proof for inequation (1).

To justify the claimed resource complexities of $A_{sca}$ and $A_{cpa}$, each of $A_{sca}$ and $A_{cpa}$ uses the same number of queries as that of A. For time complexity, we measure the time for each entire experiment. There, inequation (1) leads to Theorem 6. □

**Theorem 7 (IND-CPA-SCA ⟶ IND-CPA).** *For any scheme* $SE=(P, C, S, K, E, D)$, *if* $SE$ *is* IND-CPA-SCA *secure, then it is* IND-CPA *secure. Concretely,*

$$Adv_{SE}^{\text{ind-cpa}}(k, t, q_e, u_e) \leq Adv_{SE}^{\text{ind-cpa-sca}}(k, t, q_e, u_e, q_s, u_s). \qquad (4)$$

*Proof* The adversary $A$ depends on $A_{cpa}$ to achieve its goal. Specifically, $A$'s goal is to figure out whether the message or the random string has been encrypted in an implementation.

The constructions for $A$ are as follows.

$$\text{Adversary } A^{\mathcal{E}_K(RR(\cdot,b)),S_K(\cdot)}(k)$$
$$\text{For } i = 1, \ldots, q_e \text{ do}$$
$$\text{When } A_{cpa} \text{ makes a query } M_{i,0}, M_{i,1} \text{ to its}$$
$$\text{ind encryption oracle do}$$
$$A_{cpa} \Leftarrow \mathcal{E}_K(RR(M_{i,b}, b))$$
$$A_{cpa} \Rightarrow b'$$
$$\text{Return } b'.$$

For $A_{cpa-sca}$'s advantage, we have

$$Adv_{SE,A_{cpa-sca}}^{ind-cpa-sca}(k) \geq Pr[Exp_{SE,A_{cpa}}^{ind-cpa-1}(k) = 1] - Pr[Exp_{SE,A_{cpa}}^{ind-cpa-0}(k) = 1]$$
$$= Adv_{SE,A_{cpa}}^{ind-cpa}(k).$$

Since $A_{cpa}$ is an arbitrary adversary, the claimed relation of the advantage follows.

□

**Theorem 8 (IND-CPA-SCA $\longrightarrow$ UB-SCA).** *For any scheme $\mathcal{SE}=(\mathcal{P}, \mathcal{C}, \mathcal{S},$ $\mathcal{K}, \mathcal{E}, \mathcal{D})$, if $\mathcal{SE}$ is* IND-CPA-SCA *secure, then it is* UB-SCA *secure. Concretely,*

$$Adv_{\mathcal{SE}}^{\text{ub-sca}}(k, t, q_e, u_e) \leq Adv_{\mathcal{SE}}^{\text{ind-cpa-sca}}(k, t, q_e, u_e, q_s, u_s) \tag{5}$$

*Proof* The adversary $A$ depends on $A_{sca}$ to achieve its goal. Specifically, $A$ whose goal is to figure out whether the message or the random string has been encrypted in an implantation.

The constructions for $A$ are as follows.

> Adversary $A^{\mathcal{E}_K(RR(\cdot,b)),\mathcal{S}_K(\cdot)}(k)$
> > For $i = 1, \ldots, q_e + q_s$ do
> > > When $A_{sca}$ makes a query $M_{i,0}, M_{i,1}$ to its
> > > ind encryption oracle do
> > > > $A \Leftarrow \mathcal{E}_K(RR(M_{i,b}, b)$
> > >
> > > When $A_{sca}$ makes a query $S_i$ to its
> > > implementation oracle do
> > > > $K' \leftarrow \mathcal{S}_K^*(S_i)$
> > > > If $K! = K'$
> > > > > then $A_{sca} \Leftarrow \perp$;
> > > > > else stop.
> > >
> > $A_{sca} \Rightarrow b'$
> > Return $b'$.

For $A_{cpa-sca}$'s advantage, we have

$$Adv_{\mathcal{SE}, A_{cpa-sca}}^{ind-cpa-sca}(k) \geq \Pr[Exp_{\mathcal{SE}, A_{sca}}^{ind-sca}(k) = 1] = Adv_{\mathcal{SE}, A_{sca}}^{ub-sca}(k).$$

Since $A_{sca}$ is an arbitrary adversary, the claimed relation of the advantage follows.

□

From the reduction as above, we conclude that "IND–CPA + UB–SCA $\Rightarrow$ IND–CPA–SCA", and IND–CPA–SCA notion is stronger than IND–CPA or UB–SCA. Our results has not only theoretical interest but also can be useful when one prove the IND–CPA–SCA securities of symmetric encryption scheme implementation.

## 6  Conclusion

This paper discusses the relationship of secure notions between traditional cryptanalysis and side channel attacks. Implementation of security for a symmetric encryption is introduced, including implementation of perfect security and security levels. Then we propose the security notions UB–SCA and IND–CPA–SCA for symmetric encryption based on IND–CPA, and further generalize the relations by reductions. These notions provide an approach for symmetric encryption against side channel attacks.

# Acknowledgement

This work is supported by the National Natural Science Foundation of China under Grant No.60573031 and New Century Excellent Talent Program of Education Ministry of China under Grant NCET–05–0398. The authors wish to acknowledge the anonymous referees for helpful suggestions.

# References

1. Hess, E., Janssen, N., Meyer, B., Schütze, T.: Information Leakage Attacks Against Smart Card Implementations of Cryptographic Algorithms and Countermeasures– A Survey. In: Proceedings of EUROSMART Security Conference (2000)
2. Kocher, P., Jaffe, J., Jun, B.: Differential power analysis. In: Wiener, M.J. (ed.) CRYPTO 1999. LNCS, vol. 1666, pp. 388–397. Springer, Heidelberg (1999)
3. Kocher, P.: Timing attacks on implementations of Diffie-Hellman, RSA, DSS, and other systems. In: Koblitz, N. (ed.) CRYPTO 1996. LNCS, vol. 1109, pp. 104–113. Springer, Heidelberg (1996)
4. Kelsey, J., Schneier, B., Wagner, D., Hall, C.: Side Channel Cryptanalysis of Product Ciphers. In: Quisquater, J.-J., Deswarte, Y., Meadows, C., Gollmann, D. (eds.) ESORICS 1998. LNCS, vol. 1485, pp. 97–110. Springer, Heidelberg (1998)
5. Micali, S., Reyzin, L.: Physically Observable Cryptography, Cryptology ePrint Archive of IACR, No. 120 (2003), available at http://eprint.iacr.org/2003/120
6. Goldwasser, S., Micali, S.: Probabilistic encryption. Journal of Computer and System Sciences 28(2), 270–299 (1984)
7. Bellare, M., Desai, A., Jokipii, E.: A concrete security treatment of symmetric encryption. In: FOCS 1997, pp. 394–405. IEEE Press, Los Alamitos (1997)
8. Clavier, C., Joye, M.: Universal Exponentiation Algorithm. In: Koç, Ç.K., Naccache, D., Paar, C. (eds.) CHES 2001. LNCS, vol. 2162, pp. 300–308. Springer, Heidelberg (2001)
9. Micali, S., Reyzin, L.: Phyiscal observable Cryptography. In: Naor, M. (ed.) TCC 2004. LNCS, vol. 2951, pp. 278–296. Springer, Heidelberg (2004)
10. Standaert, F.X., Peeters, E., Archambeau, C., et al.: Towards Security Limits in Side-Channel Attacks. In: Goubin, L., Matsui, M. (eds.) CHES 2006. LNCS, vol. 4249, pp. 30–45. Springer, Heidelberg (2006)
11. Standaert, F.X., Malkin, T.G., Yung, M.: A Formal Practice-Oriented Model for the Analysis of Side-Channel Attacks. Cryptology ePrint Archive, Report 2006/139 (2006)

# On the Notions of **PRP-RKA**, **KR** and **KR-RKA** for Block Ciphers

Ermaliza Razali[1], Raphael C.-W. Phan[2], and Marc Joye[3]

[1] Information Security Research (iSECURES) Lab
Swinburne University of Technology, Sarawak campus, Kuching, Malaysia
erazali@swinburne.edu.my
[2] Laboratoire de sécurité et de cryptographie, EPFL
Station 14 - Building INF, 1015 Lausanne, Switzerland
raphael.phan@epfl.ch
[3] Thomson R&D France
Technology Group, Corporate Research, Security Laboratory
1 avenue de Belle Fontaine, 35576 Cesson-Sévigné Cedex, France
marc.joye@thomson.net

**Abstract.** Security of commonly used block ciphers is typically measured in terms of their resistance to known attacks. While the provable security approach to block ciphers dates back to the first CRYPTO conference (1981), analysis of modern block cipher proposals basically do not benefit fully from this, except for a few cases. This paper considers the security of recently proposed PRP-RKA secure block ciphers and discusses how they relate to existing types of attacks on block ciphers.

**Keywords:** Provable security, pseudorandom permutation (PRP), key recovery (KR), block cipher, related key attacks (RKA).

## 1 Introduction

The right approach to analyzing the security of public-key encryption schemes and protocols is by reduction, in a given security model, to an underlying hard problem: the so-called the provable security approach. In the symmetric-key setting, while formal definitions of security do exist (e.g., Luby and Rackoff), security of a modern block cipher is often measured by its resistance to known attacks. Thus, from the perspective of the provable security community, the security of modern block ciphers may seem heuristic.

This paper considers the formal provable security approach to analyzing block ciphers. The advantage is clear. Security of a block cipher can be proved in a generic sense, by specifying bounds on the adversary's resources, without assuming the exact approach taken by the adversary. It encompasses all possible attacks mountable by the adversary given those resources. This compares favorably with the heuristic case where a primitive is designed to resist some list of attacks but may later fall to attacks not considered by the designer. Historically, building on work by Luby and Rackoff, the provable security of block ciphers

W. Susilo, J.K. Liu, and Y. Mu. (Eds.): ProvSec 2007, LNCS 4784, pp. 188–197, 2007.

have been analyzed with respect to the notion of pseudorandomness (PRP). This is advantageous since PRP implies security against key recovery (KR).

Except for a few cases (e.g., [8,1,11,12,9]), we are however not aware of any work that analyzes the security of modern block ciphers in the context of PRP. We also note that the assumption that the underlying block cipher is a PRP was used in the security analysis of CBC-MAC [2]. To the best of our knowledge, the earliest result on provable security analysis of block ciphers is by Hellman *et al.* [5]. In particular, the security was formalized in the ideal cipher model (a.k.a. Shannon model or black-box model) and in terms of an adversary winning a key-recovery game. The formalization of the security of block ciphers against related-key attacks in fact dates back to the work of Winternitz and Hellman [15], also considered in the context of a key-recovery game in the ideal cipher model, but here in the presence of related-key oracles. The first known block cipher with a provable security proof of pseudorandomness (PRP) is DESX [8].

Since the bulk of block cipher analysis is dedicated to key-recovery attacks, it is sensible to formally cast these PRP-RKA ciphers also in the context of resistance to key-recovery attacks either in the presence of related-key oracles (KR-RKA) or not (KR). Interestingly, doing so brings us back to where it started, since the first results [5,15] on provable security of block ciphers were in the context of KR and KR-RKA.

The rest of this paper is organized as follows. In the next section, we introduce some notation and review different security notions for block ciphers. Section 3 is the core of our paper. We describe several key recovery attacks on some PRP-RKA secure ciphers and relate the corresponding success probability with the security bound derived from a generic attacker. Finally, we conclude in Section 4.

## 2    Definitions

Consider a family of functions $F : \mathbb{K} \times \mathbb{D} \to \mathbb{R}$, where $\mathbb{K} = \{0,1\}^k$ is the set of keys of $F$, $\mathbb{D} = \{0,1\}^l$ is the domain of $F$ and $\mathbb{R} = \{0,1\}^L$ is the range of $F$, and where $k$, $l$ and $L$ are the key, input and output lengths in bits. We use $F_K(\mathbb{D})$ as a shorthand for $F(K, \mathbb{D})$. By $K \xleftarrow{\$} \mathbb{K}$, we denote the operation of selecting a string $K$ at random from $\mathbb{K}$. Similar notations apply for a family of permutations $E : \mathbb{K} \times \mathbb{D} \to \mathbb{D}$, where $\mathbb{K} = \{0,1\}^k$ is the set of keys of $E$ and $\mathbb{D} = \{0,1\}^l$ is the domain and range of $E$.

### 2.1    Related Keys

The *related-key-deriving* (RKD) function $\phi \in \Phi$ is a map $\phi : \mathbb{K} \to \mathbb{K}$, where $\Phi$ is a subset of functions mapping $\mathbb{K}$ to $\mathbb{K}$. Given $F$ and $K \in \mathbb{K}$, the *related-key oracle* $F_{\mathrm{RK}(K,\cdot)}(\cdot)$ takes two arguments: a function $\phi : \mathbb{K} \to \mathbb{K}$ and an element $P \in \mathbb{D}$, and returns $F_{\phi(K)}(P)$, where $\mathrm{RK}(K, \phi) = \phi(K)$. An attack exploiting access to the oracle $F_{\mathrm{RK}(K,\phi)}(\cdot)$ where $\phi \in \Phi$ is called a $\Phi$-restricted related-key attack (RKA). Similar definitions apply for $E$.

## 2.2   Security Notions

Suppose that $E : \mathbb{K} \times \mathbb{D} \to \mathbb{D}$ is a family of permutations on $\mathbb{D}$. A PRP adversary $\mathcal{A}$ gets access to an oracle, which, on input $P \in \mathbb{D}$, either returns $E_K(P)$ for a random key $K \in \mathbb{K}$ or returns $G(P)$ for a random permutation $G$ on $\mathbb{D}$. The goal of $\mathcal{A}$ is to guess the type of oracle it has — by convention, $\mathcal{A}$ returns 1 if it thinks that the oracle is computing $E_K(\cdot)$. The adversary's advantage is defined by:

$$\mathbf{Adv}_E^{\mathsf{PRP}}(\mathcal{A}) = \Pr\big[K \xleftarrow{\$} \mathbb{K} : \mathcal{A}^{E_K(\cdot)} = 1\big] - \Pr\big[G \xleftarrow{\$} \mathrm{Perm}(\mathbb{D}) : \mathcal{A}^{G(\cdot)} = 1\big] \ .$$

$E$ is said PRP-secure if $\mathbf{Adv}_E^{\mathsf{PRP}}(\mathcal{A})$ is sufficiently small.

Extension of this to include RKAs allows the PRP-RKA adversary $\mathcal{A}$ to make related-key oracle queries of the form $(\phi, P)$ for a related-key deriving function $\phi : \mathbb{K} \to \mathbb{K}$, $\phi \in \Phi$, and $P \in \mathbb{D}$. We so have:

$$\mathbf{Adv}_{\Phi,E}^{\mathsf{PRP-RKA}}(\mathcal{A}) = \Pr\big[K \xleftarrow{\$} \mathbb{K} : \mathcal{A}^{E_{\mathsf{RK}(\cdot,K)}(\cdot)} = 1\big]$$
$$- \Pr\big[K \xleftarrow{\$} \mathbb{K}; G \xleftarrow{\$} \mathrm{Perm}(\mathbb{K},\mathbb{D}) : \mathcal{A}^{G_{\mathsf{RK}(\cdot,K)}(\cdot)} = 1\big] \ .$$

When the inverse of $E$ is available, security under chosen-ciphertext (related-key) attacks (namely, PRP-CCA or PRP-CCRKA) can be similarly defined:

$$\mathbf{Adv}_E^{\mathsf{PRP-CCA}}(\mathcal{A}) = \Pr\big[K \xleftarrow{\$} \mathbb{K} : \mathcal{A}^{E_K(\cdot),E_K^{-1}(\cdot)} = 1\big]$$
$$- \Pr\big[G \xleftarrow{\$} \mathrm{Perm}(\mathbb{D}) : \mathcal{A}^{G(\cdot),G^{-1}(\cdot)} = 1\big]$$

and

$$\mathbf{Adv}_{\Phi,E}^{\mathsf{PRP-CCRKA}}(\mathcal{A}) = \Pr\big[K \xleftarrow{\$} \mathbb{K} : \mathcal{A}^{E_{\mathsf{RK}(\cdot,K)}(\cdot),E_{\mathsf{RK}(\cdot,K)}^{-1}(\cdot)} = 1\big]$$
$$- \Pr\big[K \xleftarrow{\$} \mathbb{K}; G \xleftarrow{\$} \mathrm{Perm}(\mathbb{K},\mathbb{D}) : \mathcal{A}^{G_{\mathsf{RK}(\cdot,K)}(\cdot),G_{\mathsf{RK}(\cdot,K)}^{-1}(\cdot)} = 1\big] \ .$$

For security against key recovery, a KR adversary $\mathcal{A}$ is given a list $\mathcal{L}$ of $p$ pairs of plaintext/ciphertext

$$\mathcal{L} = \big\{ \langle P_1, C_1 \rangle, \ldots, \langle P_p, C_p \rangle \big\}$$

where $C_i = E_K(P_i)$ for $1 \le i \le p$. The goal of $\mathcal{A}$ is to find a key $\hat{K}$ that is *consistent* with $\mathcal{L}$, that is, a key such that, for all $\langle P_i, C_i \rangle \in \mathcal{L}$, $E_{\hat{K}}(P_i) = C_i$. We let $\mathrm{Cons}_E(\mathcal{L})$ denote the set of all keys consistent with $\mathcal{L}$. The advantage of KR adversary $\mathcal{A}$ is then given by:

$$\mathbf{Adv}_E^{\mathsf{KR}}(\mathcal{A}) = \Pr\Big[K \xleftarrow{\$} \mathbb{K}; \mathcal{L} \leftarrow \big\{\langle P_i, E_K(P_i)\rangle\big\} : \mathcal{A}^{\mathcal{L}} = \hat{K} \in \mathrm{Cons}_E(\mathcal{L})\Big] \ .$$

$E$ is KR-secure if $\mathbf{Adv}_E^{\mathsf{KR}}(\mathcal{A})$ is sufficiently small. Again, this can be extended to include RKAs:

$$\mathbf{Adv}_{\Phi,E}^{\mathsf{KR-RKA}}(\mathcal{A}) = \Pr\Big[K \xleftarrow{\$} \mathbb{K}; \mathcal{L} \leftarrow \big\{\langle P_i, E_K(P_i)\rangle\big\} :$$
$$\mathcal{A}^{\mathcal{L},E_{\mathsf{RK}(\cdot,K)}(\cdot)} = \hat{K} \in \mathrm{Cons}_E(\mathcal{L})\Big] \ .$$

# 3    Security of Existing **PRP-RKA** Block Ciphers

In [5], it was shown that the advantage $\mathbf{Adv}_E^{\mathsf{KR}}(\mathcal{A})$ of any KR adversary $\mathcal{A}$ mounting a *generic* attack depends on the number $t$ of verifications made to the block cipher $E$ (i.e., evaluations of the form $E_{K_i}(P_i)$ for any text $P_i$ and any key $K_i$ of the adversary's choice), and on the key bit-length $k$. More specifically, it was shown that:

$$\mathbf{Adv}_E^{\mathsf{KR}}(\mathcal{A}) \leq \frac{t}{2^k} + \frac{1}{2^k - t} \; .$$

This bounds the advantage of a generic adversary. We see that both terms on the right side of the inequality remain small as long as $t \ll 2^k$. As $t$ relates to an exhaustive key search, this means that a generic adversary must exhaust a significant fraction of key candidates to have a reasonable chance to recover the actual key. This also means that having an advantage significantly better than by exhaustive search requires to exploit the specific structure of the block cipher under attack.

Similarly, in [15], it was shown that the advantage $\mathbf{Adv}_{\Phi,E}^{\mathsf{KR-RKA}}(\mathcal{A})$ of any KR-RKA adversary $\mathcal{A}$ mounting a generic related-key attack is bounded by:

$$\mathbf{Adv}_{\Phi,E}^{\mathsf{KR-RKA}}(\mathcal{A}) \leq \frac{mt}{2^k} + \frac{1}{2^k} \; ,$$

where $m$ is the number of related-key oracle queries to block cipher $E$. Analogously, we see that the advantage of a generic adversary remains small as long as $mt \ll 2^k$.

In the sequel, we analyze and discuss the security of the constructions depicted on Fig. 1.

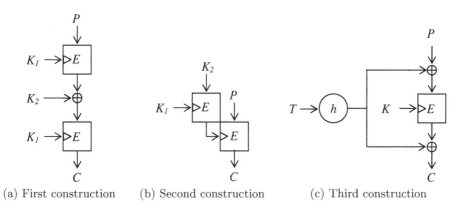

(a) First construction        (b) Second construction        (c) Third construction

**Fig. 1.** Block-cipher based constructs

## 3.1   First Construction

In [1], Bellare and Kohno analyzed a PRP-RKA secure block-cipher based construct that is essentially a generalization of the 2-key variant of DES-EXE [13] structure (see Fig. 1-a). In particular, they proved:

**Theorem 1 (Bellare-Kohno).** *Let $E : \{0,1\}^k \times \{0,1\}^l \rightarrow \{0,1\}^l$ be a block cipher. Let $E' : \{0,1\}^{k+l} \times \{0,1\}^l \rightarrow \{0,1\}^l$ be the block cipher defined as*

$$E'_{K_1 \| K_2}(P) = E_{K_1}\big(E_{K_1}(P) \oplus K_2\big)$$

*where $K_1$ is $k$ bits long and $K_2$ is $l$ bits long. Let $\Phi$ be any set of RKD functions over $\{0,1\}^{k+l}$ that modify only $K_2$ and that are independent of $K_1$. Then, for any adversary $\mathcal{A}$ against $E'$ that queries its related-key oracle with at most $r$ different RKD transformations and at most $q$ times per transformation, we can construct an adversary $\mathcal{B}_{\mathcal{A}}$ against $E$ such that*

$$\mathbf{Adv}^{\mathrm{PRP-RKA}}_{\Phi, E'}(\mathcal{A}) \leq \mathbf{Adv}^{\mathrm{PRP}}_E(\mathcal{B}_{\mathcal{A}}) + \frac{16r^2q^2 + rq'(q'-1)}{2^{l+1}}$$

*and $\mathcal{B}_{\mathcal{A}}$ makes $2rq$ oracle queries and runs in the same time as $\mathcal{A}$ and $q'$ is $q$ times the maximum over all $K, K' \in \{0,1\}^{k+l}$, of the number of $\phi \in \Phi$ mapping $K$ to $K'$.* □

The result above shows the existence of block ciphers secure against certain classes of $\Phi$-restricted related-key attacks. PRP-RKA security of the resulting cipher comes with a restriction that the set of RKD functions $\Phi$ defining an RKA adversary only modifies the second part of the key (i.e., $K_2$). This is a weaker notion of RKA security compared to previous works [6,7,14] where no such restriction is made.

With DES-EXE like structures, one may wonder if existing attacks [13,4] on DES-EXE apply to this variant. We answer this in the affirmative. First, we describe a meet-in-the-middle (MITM) attack that does not require related-key queries. Next, we present a differential RKA with similar effort.

MITM ATTACK.

1. Let $\langle P, C \rangle$ and $\langle P', C' \rangle$ be any two pairs of plaintext/ciphertext in $\mathcal{L}$ with $C = E'_{K_1 \| K_2}(P)$ and $C' = E'_{K_1 \| K_2}(P')$.
2. For each key guess, $\hat{K}_1 \in \{0,1\}^k$, do the following.
   (a) Evaluate

$$S_1 = E_{\hat{K}_1}(P) \oplus E_{\hat{K}_1}(P') \quad \text{and} \quad S_2 = E^{-1}_{\hat{K}_1}(C) \oplus E^{-1}_{\hat{K}_1}(C')$$

   and check whether $S_1 = S_2$.
   (b) If so, let $\hat{K}_2 = E^{-1}_{\hat{K}_1}(C) \oplus E_{\hat{K}_1}(P)$ and validate the guessed key $\hat{K}_1 \| \hat{K}_2$ on all pairs of $\mathcal{L}$.
3. If the guessed key is validated, return (the consistent key) $\hat{K}_1 \| \hat{K}_2$.

If the above MITM adversary tries all possible keys $\hat{K}_1 \in \{0,1\}^k$ at Step 2, it will win the key recovery game with probability 1. As a result, the success probability of this adversary is $\rho$, the proportion of guessed keys.

Recalling the results in [5], when considering a generic adversary, any block cipher $E'$ of key length $k + l$ bits is expected to provide the following security bound:

$$\mathbf{Adv}_{E'}^{\mathsf{KR}}(A) \leq \frac{t}{2^{k+l}} + \frac{1}{2^{k+l} - t},$$

where $t$ denotes the number of verifications. A closer look at the proof offered in [5] shows that if the generic adversary makes verifications with distinct key candidates then the bound can be sharpened as:

$$\mathbf{Adv}_{E'}^{\mathsf{KR}}(\mathcal{A}) \leq \frac{t}{2^{k+l}} + \frac{1 - \frac{t}{2^{k+l}}}{2^{k+l} - t} = \frac{t}{2^{k+l}} + \frac{1}{2^{k+l}}.$$

If we let $t$ denote the number of times Step 2 in the MITM attack is performed (i.e., the number of times distinct key candidates are being manipulated), then the success probability is given by:

$$\mathbf{Adv}_{E'}^{\mathsf{KR}}(\mathrm{MITM}) = \rho = \frac{t}{2^k}.$$

Interestingly, we observe that

$$\mathbf{Adv}_{E'}^{\mathsf{KR}}(\mathrm{MITM}) = \frac{t}{2^k} > \frac{t}{2^{k+l}} + \frac{1}{2^{k+l}},$$

and so the block-cipher based construct of Fig. 1-a does not give the best possible security against key recovery.

## DIFFERENTIAL RKA ATTACK (DRKA)

1. Let $\langle P, C \rangle$ be any pairs of plaintext/ciphertext in $\mathcal{L}$ with $C = E'_{K_1 \| K_2}(P)$.
2. Query the related-key oracle with $(P', \Delta)$ and obtain the pair $(P', C')$ with $C' = E'_{K_1 \| K_2 \oplus \Delta}(P)$.
3. For each key guess, $\hat{K}_1 \in \{0, 1\}^k$, do the following.
   (a) Check whether
   $$E_{\hat{K}_1}^{-1}(C) \oplus E_{\hat{K}_1}^{-1}(C') = \Delta.$$

   (b) If so, let $\hat{K}_2 = E_{\hat{K}_1}^{-1}(C) \oplus E_{\hat{K}_1}(P)$ and validate the guessed key $\hat{K}_1 \| \hat{K}_2$ on all pairs of $\mathcal{L}$.
4. If the guessed key is validated, return (the consistent key) $\hat{K}_1 \| \hat{K}_2$.

According to [15], we know that any block cipher $E'$ of key length $k + l$ bits is expected to provide the following security against generic related-key attacks:

$$\mathbf{Adv}_{\Phi, E'}^{\mathsf{KR-RKA}}(\mathcal{A}) \leq \frac{mt}{2^{k+l}} + \frac{1}{2^{k+l}},$$

where $m$ denotes the number of calls to the related-key oracle and $t$ the number of verifications. Interestingly, in a way similar to the analysis of the previous attack, we get that, for $m = 1$, the success probability of our differential related-key attack (DRKA) satisfies

$$\mathbf{Adv}_{E'}^{\mathsf{KR-RKA}}(\mathrm{DRKA}) = \frac{t}{2^k} > \frac{t}{2^{k+l}} + \frac{1}{2^{k+l}} \ .$$

Again, we conclude that the block-cipher based construct of Fig. 1-a does not offer the best possible security against key recovery, in this case, in the presence of related-key oracles.

### 3.2   Second Construction

Lucks [11] argued that Theorem 1 only applies for large $l$. For practical values of $l$, one may have that $\mathbf{Adv}_{\Phi,E'}^{\mathsf{PRP-RKA}}(\mathcal{A}) - \mathbf{Adv}_{E}^{\mathsf{PRP}}(\mathcal{B}_\mathcal{A})$ is not small. He therefore considered a construction that yields more meaningful security bound. See Fig. 1-b.

**Theorem 2 (Lucks).** *Let $E : \{0,1\}^l \times \{0,1\}^l \to \{0,1\}^l$ be a block cipher. Let $E' : \{0,1\}^{2l} \times \{0,1\}^l \to \{0,1\}^l$ be the block cipher defined as*

$$E''_{K_1 \| K_2}(P) = E_{E_{K_1}(K_2)}(P)$$

*where $K_1$ and $K_2$ are $l$ bits long. Let $\Phi$ be any set of RKD functions over $\{0,1\}^{k+l}$ that modify only $K_2$ and that are independent of $K_1$. Then, for any adversary $\mathcal{A}$ against $E'$ that queries its related-key oracle with at most $r$ different RKD transformations, we can construct an adversary $\mathcal{B}_\mathcal{A}$ against $E$ such that*

$$\frac{\mathbf{Adv}_{\Phi,E''}^{\mathsf{PRP-RKA}}(\mathcal{A})}{r+1} \leq \mathbf{Adv}_{E}^{\mathsf{PRP}}(\mathcal{B}_\mathcal{A}) \ .$$

*and $\mathcal{B}_\mathcal{A}$ makes no more oracle queries than $\mathcal{A}$ and runs in the same running time as $\mathcal{A}$.*                                                                                                        □

The encryption of key $K_2$ under key $K_1$ is used as the final secret key to encrypt the plaintext $P$, i.e., $C = E_{E_{K_1}(K_2)}(P)$. Further, note that although a $2l$-bit key $K_1 \| K_2$ is used, essentially the adversary just needs to recover the final $l$-bit secret key $\widetilde{K} := E_{K_1}(K_2)$ that is used to key the encryption of $P$, which leads to a total break. For an attacker performing an exhaustive search (XS) on $\widetilde{K}$, we have

$$\mathbf{Adv}_{E''}^{\mathsf{KR}}(\mathrm{XS}) = \frac{t}{2^l},$$

where $t$ denotes the number of guessed keys. This has to be compared with the security bound given by a generic KR adversary against a $2l$-bit key cipher $E''$:

$$\mathbf{Adv}_{E''}^{\mathsf{KR}}(\mathcal{A}) \leq \frac{t}{2^{2l}} + \frac{1}{2^{2l} - t} \ .$$

We see that the above XS attacker has a substantially larger success probability.

## 3.3    Third Construction

Kim *et al.* [9] analyzed another block-cipher based construct. See Fig. 1-c. It is more efficient than the two previous ones as it only requires a single call to the underlying $E$.

**Theorem 3 (Kim *et al.*).** *Let* $E : \{0,1\}^k \times \{0,1\}^l \to \{0,1\}^l$ *be a block cipher and let* $\mathcal{H} : \{0,1\}^t \to \{0,1\}^l$ *be an* $\epsilon$-*almost 2-xor universal* ($\epsilon$-$\mathrm{AXU}_2$) *family with* $\epsilon \geq \frac{1}{2^l}$. *Let* $E''' : \{0,1\}^{k+t} \times \mathcal{H} \times \{0,1\}^l \to \{0,1\}^l$ *be the block cipher defined as*

$$E'''_{K\|T,h}(P) = E_K(P \oplus h(T)) \oplus h(T)$$

*where* $K$ *is* $k$ *bits long and* $T$ *is* $t$ *bits long. Let* $\Phi$ *be any set of RKD functions over* $\{0,1\}^{k+t}$ *that modify only* $T$ *and that are independent of* $K$. *Then, for any adversary* $\mathcal{A}$ *against* $E'''$ *that queries its oracles with at most* $q$ *queries, we can construct a chosen-ciphertext adversary* $\mathcal{B}_\mathcal{A}$ *against* $E$ *such that*

$$\mathbf{Adv}^{\mathrm{PRP-CCRKA}}_{\Phi,E'''}(\mathcal{A}) \leq \mathbf{Adv}^{\mathrm{PRP-CCA}}_E(\mathcal{B}_\mathcal{A}) + 3\epsilon q^2$$

*and* $\mathcal{B}_\mathcal{A}$ *makes the same number of oracle queries and runs in the same running time as* $\mathcal{A}$. □

Recall that DESX [8] is defined as:

$$\mathrm{DESX}(P, K_1\|K\|K_2) = K_2 \oplus E_K(P \oplus K_1)$$

where $K_1$ and $K_2$ are the pre- and post-whitening keys, respectively, and $K$ is the key to the inner $E$ encapsulated by the two outer whitening (XOR) operations. The basic structure of the above construction is like DESX [8] except that the pre- and post-whitening keys equal each other and is the result of applying an $\epsilon$-$\mathrm{AXU}_2$ hash function $h$ to the input tweak $T$:

$$K_1 = K_2 = h(T) \ .$$

In other words, this construction can be viewed as 2-key DESX where the secret key is equivalently $K$ and $h(T)$, thus the total key length is $|K| + |h(T)|$.

There is a restriction attached to this construction as well. Namely, the key $K$ to $E_K(\cdot)$ cannot be varied by an RKA adversary; only $T$ is allowed to vary.

An advanced slide attack [3] was applied to DESX. It is basically a MITM attack. We show that a variant also applies here.

MITM ATTACK. We first make some observations. Consider a pair of plaintexts $P$ and $P'$ such that the corresponding ciphertexts, $C$ and $C'$, satisfying the relation $C \oplus C' = h(T)$. Such a pair is called a *slid pair*. For such a slid pair $\langle P, C \rangle$ and $\langle P', C' \rangle$, we have

$$C = C' \oplus h(T) = E_K\big(P' \oplus h(T)\big) \quad \text{and} \quad C' = C \oplus h(T) = E_K\big(P \oplus h(T)\big)$$

which yields

$$h(T) \oplus P \oplus P' = E_K^{-1}(C) \oplus P = E_K^{-1}(C') \oplus P' \ .$$

Based on this, we can mount the following attack.

1. Let $\mathcal{L} = \langle P_i, C_i \rangle_{1 \le i \le p}$ be a list of $p$ known pairs of plaintext/ciphertext with, $C_i = E'''_{K\|T,h}(P_i)$.
2. For each key guess, $\hat{K} \in \{0,1\}^k$, do the following.
   (a) For each $1 \le i \le p$, evaluate $E_{\hat{K}}^{-1}(C_i) \oplus P_i$ and insert

$$\langle E_{\hat{K}}^{-1}(C_i) \oplus P_i, i \rangle$$

   into a hash table keyed by the first component, and check whether there is a coincidence (collision) in the table.
   (b) If so, assuming that the collision occurs for indexes $i$ and $j$, namely, $E_{\hat{K}}^{-1}(C_i) \oplus P_i = E_{\hat{K}}^{-1}(C_j) \oplus P_j$, let $h(\hat{T}) = C_i \oplus C_j$ and validate the guessed key $\hat{K}\|\hat{T}$ on all pairs of $\mathcal{L}$.
3. If the guessed key is validated, return (the consistent key) $\hat{K}\|\hat{T}$.

The probability to have at least one coincidence (i.e., to find at least one slid pair $\langle P_i, C_i \rangle$ and $\langle P_j, C_j \rangle$ in $\mathcal{L}$) is about

$$1 - \exp(-p^2/2^{l+1}) \quad \text{with } p = |\mathcal{L}| \ .$$

As a result, if $t/2^k$ denotes the proportion of keys guessed at Step 2, the success probability of our MITM attacker is

$$\mathbf{Adv}^{\mathsf{KR}}_{E'''}(\mathrm{MITM}) \approx \frac{t}{2^k}\left(1 - \exp(-p^2/2^{l+1})\right) \ .$$

RESISTANCE AGAINST RKA. On the positive side, it appears that the construction of Fig. 1-c seems to resist differential RKAs since the key $K$ to the inner $E_K$ is not allowed to vary and although $T$ is allowed to vary, the actual key difference due to $h(T)$ cannot be predicted.

## 4   Concluding Remarks

We have discussed key recovery attacks on some recent proposals to construct a block cipher secure in the sense of PRP-RKA from a block cipher (not necessarily secure against related-key attacks). Our results emphasize that known constructions specifically designed for provable security against related-key attacks do not have optimal key-recovery resilience.

Furthermore, all PRP-RKA secure constructions proposed so far do not allow the key component of the underlying cipher $E$ to be varied. An open problem is to prove (or disprove) the existence of PRP-RKA secure constructions allowing this.

**Acknowledgments.** We would like to thank Jongsung Kim for sending a copy of [9]. We are also grateful to the anonymous referees for useful comments.

# References

1. Bellare, M., Kohno, T.A.: Theoretical treatment of related-key attacks: RKA-PRPs, RKA-PRFs, and applications. In: Biham, E. (ed.) EUROCRPYT 2003. LNCS, vol. 2656, pp. 491–506. Springer, Heidelberg (2003), available at http://www-cse.ucsd.edu/users/mihir/papers/rka.html
2. Bellare, M., Kilian, J., Rogaway, P.: The security of the cipher block chaining message authentication code. J. Comput. Syst. Sci. 61(3), 362–399 (2000)
3. Biryukov, A., Wagner, D.: Advanced slide attacks. In: Preneel, B. (ed.) EURO-CRYPT 2000. LNCS, vol. 1807, pp. 589–606. Springer, Heidelberg (2000)
4. Choi, J., Kim, J., Sung, J., Lee, S., Lim, J.: Related-key and meet-in-the-middle attacks on Triple-DES and DES-EXE. In: Gervasi, O., Gavrilova, M., Kumar, V., Laganà, A., Lee, H.P., Mun, Y., Taniar, D., Tan, C.J.K. (eds.) ICCSA 2005. LNCS, vol. 3481, pp. 567–576. Springer, Heidelberg (2005)
5. Hellman, M.E., Karnin, E.D., Reyneri, J.M.: On the necessity of exhaustive search for system-invariant cryptanalysis. In: Advances in Cryptology – A Report on CRYPTO 1981, U.C. Santa Barbara, Dept. of Elec. and Computer Eng., ECE Report No 82-04, pp. 2–6 (1982)
6. Kelsey, J., Schneier, B., Wagner, D.: Key-schedule cryptanalysis of IDEA, G-DES, GOST, SAFER, and Triple-DES. In: Koblitz, N. (ed.) CRYPTO 1996. LNCS, vol. 1109, pp. 237–251. Springer, Heidelberg (1996)
7. Kelsey, J., Schneier, B., Wagner, D.: Related-key cryptanalysis of 3-WAY, Biham-DES, CAST, DES-X, NewDES, RC2, and TEA. In: Han, Y., Quing, S. (eds.) ICICS 1997. LNCS, vol. 1334, pp. 233–246. Springer, Heidelberg (1997)
8. Kilian, J., Rogaway, P.: How to protect DES against exhaustive key search (an analysis of DESX). J. Cryptology 14(1), 17–35 (2001)
9. Kim, J., Sung, J., Lee, S., Preneel, B.: Pseudorandom permutation and function families secure against related-key attacks. Unpublished manuscript
10. Liskov, M., Rivest, R.L., Wagner, D.: Tweakable block ciphers. In: Yung, M. (ed.) CRYPTO 2002. LNCS, vol. 2442, pp. 31–46. Springer, Heidelberg (2002)
11. Lucks, S.: Ciphers secure against related-key attacks. In: Roy, B., Meier, W. (eds.) FSE 2004. LNCS, vol. 3017, pp. 359–370. Springer, Heidelberg (2004)
12. Phan, D.H., Pointcheval, D.: About the security of ciphers (semantic security and pseudo-random permutations). In: Handschuh, H., Hasan, M.A. (eds.) SAC 2004. LNCS, vol. 3357, pp. 182–197. Springer, Heidelberg (2004)
13. Phan, R.C.-W.: Related-key attacks on triple-DES and DESX variants. In: Okamoto, T. (ed.) CT-RSA 2004. LNCS, vol. 2964, pp. 15–24. Springer, Heidelberg (2004)
14. Razali, E., Phan, R.C.-W.: On the existence of related-key oracles in cryptosystems based on block ciphers. In: Meersman, R., Tari, Z., Herrero, P. (eds.) OTM 2006 Workshops. LNCS, vol. 4277, pp. 425–438. Springer, Heidelberg (2006)
15. Winternitz, R.S., Hellman, M.E.: Chosen-key attacks on a block cipher. Cryptologia 11(1), 16–20 (1987)

# Practical Threshold Signatures Without Random Oracles

Jin Li[1,*], Tsz Hon Yuen[2], and Kwangjo Kim[1]

[1] International Research center for Information Security (IRIS)
Information and Communications University(ICU)
103-6 Munji-Dong, Yuseong-Gu, Daejeon, 305-732, Korea
sysjinli@hotmail.com, kkj@icu.ac.kr
[2] School of Information Technology and Computer Science
University of Wollongong, NSW 2522 Australia

**Abstract.** We propose a secure threshold signature scheme without trusted dealer. Our construction is based on the recently proposed signature scheme of Waters in EUROCRYPT'05. The new threshold signature scheme is more efficient than the previous threshold signature schemes without random oracles. Meanwhile, the signature share generation and verification algorithms are non-interactive. Furthermore, it is the first threshold signature scheme based on the computational Diffie-Hellman (CDH) problem without random oracles.

**Keywords:** Threshold Signature, Bilinear groups, CDH problem.

## 1 Introduction

Digital signatures can be produced by a group of players rather then by one party by using a threshold signature scheme. In contrast to the regular signature schemes where the signer is a single entity which holds the secret key, in $(k, n)$-threshold signature schemes the secret key is shared by a group of $k$ players. In order to produce a valid signature on a given message $m$, individual players produce their partial signatures on that message, and then combine them into a full signature on $m$. A distributed signature scheme achieves threshold $k$, if no coalition of $k-1$ (or less) players can produce a new valid signature, even after the system has produced many signatures on different messages. A signature resulting from a threshold signature scheme is the same as if it was produced by a single signer possessing the full secret signature key. In particular, the validity of this signature can be verified by anyone who has the corresponding unique public verification key. In other words, the fact that the signature was produced in a distributed fashion is transparent to the recipient of the signature.

Threshold cryptography and secret sharing have been given considerable attention since they were proposed. The first threshold secret sharing schemes,

---

[*] This work was partially supported by the 2nd stage of Brain Korea 21 Project sponsored by the Ministry of Education and Human Resources Development, Korea.

W. Susilo, J.K. Liu, and Y. Mu. (Eds.): ProvSec 2007, LNCS 4784, pp. 198–207, 2007.

based on the Lagrange interpolating polynomial and linear project geometry, were proposed by Shamir [11]. Many efficient digital signature and threshold signature schemes are proved secure in the random oracle model. However, several papers proved that some popular cryptosystems previously proved secure in the random oracle are actually provably insecure when the random oracle is instantiated by any real-world hashing functions [2]. Therefore, provably secure threshold signature scheme in the standard model attracts a great interest.

**Related Work.** Recently, [13] gave the first threshold signature without random oracles. However, the threshold signature scheme requires that the users generate the signature interactively. Meanwhile, the correctness of these generated signature shares cannot be verified. Ideally, there is no other interaction in the threshold signature scheme, namely the players need not talk to each other during signing. Such threshold systems are called non-interactive. Often one requires that threshold signature be robust [8], namely if threshold signature fails, the combiner can identify the signing players that supplied invalid partial signatures. In [12], a practical threshold signature scheme based on RSA was proposed, which is non-interactive. However, it required a trusted dealer.

**Contributions.** In this paper, we propose a new practical threshold signature scheme without trusted dealer. The threshold signature has the following properties:

1. It is provably secure without relying on the random oracle model;
2. Signature share generation and verification are completely non-interactive;
3. The scheme is the first threshold signature scheme based on the CDH problem without random oracles;
4. Signature share generation and verification algorithms are very efficient.

## 2 Preliminaries

### 2.1 Security Definitions and Notions

We shows the definition as follows:

**Definition 1.** *A $(k, n)$-threshold signature scheme consists of algorithms (DKG, SS, SV, SC, Vrfy). These algorithms are specified as follows:*

1. *DKG is the distributed key generation algorithm. On input security parameter $1^\lambda$, $k, n$ it outputs public key pk and secret key sk. Meanwhile, it also outputs the private value $sk_i$ and verification key $vk_i$ of player $i$ such that the values $(sk_1, \cdots, sk_n)$ form a $(k, n)$-threshold secret sharing of sk. The public output of the protocol contains the public key pk and verification key $VK = (vk_1, \cdots, vk_n)$.*
2. *SS is the signature share generation algorithm run by player $i$, on input secret share $sk_i$, a message $m$, it returns $\sigma_i$ as the shared signature.*
3. *SV is the signature share verification, on input public key pk, verification key $vk_i$, a message $m$, $\sigma_i$, output 1 if it is valid. Otherwise, output 0.*

4. *SC is the signature share combining algorithm, on input $|\Phi|$ different shares $\{\sigma_i\}_{i \in \Phi}$, where $\Phi \subset \{1, 2, \cdots, n\}$ is a set and $|\Phi| \geq k$, a message $m$, it returns $\sigma$ as the signature.*
5. *Vrfy is the signature verification algorithm, on input $pk$, $m$, $\sigma$, returns 1 if it is valid, otherwise, returns 0.*

DKG makes use of an appropriate distributed secret-sharing technique to generate shares of the private key as well as verification keys that will be used for checking the validity of signature shares. The signing server then keeps their private key shares secret but publishes the verification keys. Given a message for signing, the signing servers then run the signature share generation algorithm SS taking the message as input and send the resulting signature shares to the combiner. Note that the validity of the shares can be checked by running the signature share verification algorithm SV. When the user collects valid signature shares from at least $k$ servers, the signature can be reconstructed by running the share combining algorithm SC. Notice that our model explicitly requires that the generation and verification of signature shares is completely non-interactive.

We work with a static corruption model: the adversary must choose which players to corrupt at the very beginning of the attack.

Unforgeability for $(k, n)$-threshold signature is defined as in the following game involving an adversary $\mathcal{A}$.

We have a set of $n$ players, indexed $1, \cdots, n$, a trusted dealer, and an adversary $\mathcal{A}$. There is also a share signing algorithm SS, a share verification algorithm SV, a share combining algorithm SC, and a signature verification algorithm Vrfy.

At the beginning of the game, the adversary selects a subset of $k - 1$ players to corrupt. In the dealing phase, the dealer generates a public key $pk$ along with secret key shares $sk_1, \cdots, sk_n$, and verification keys $\mathsf{VK} = \{vk_1, \cdots, vk_n\}$. The adversary obtains the secret key shares of the corrupted players, along with the public key and verification keys. After the dealing phase, the adversary submits signing requests to the uncorrupted players for messages of his choice. Upon such a request, a player outputs a signature share for the given message.

We say that the adversary forges a signature if at the end of the game he outputs a valid signature on a message that was not submitted as a signing request to the uncorrupted players. We say that the threshold signature scheme is unforgeable if it is computationally infeasible for the adversary to forge a signature.

## 2.2   Pairings and Problem

Let $G, G_T$ be cyclic groups of prime order $p$, writing the group action multiplicatively. Let $g$ be a generator of $G$. A bilinear map $\hat{e} : G \times G \to G_T$ is also defined.

**Definition 2.** *(Computational Diffie-Hellman **CDH** Assumption) The Computational Diffie-Hellman assumption is that, given $g, g^x, g^y \in (G)^3$ for unknown $x, y \in Z_p^*$, it is hard to compute $g^{xy}$.*

## 2.3   Brief Review of Waters Signature Scheme

In EUROCRYPT'05, Waters [14] proposed an identity based encryption scheme. From the private key extraction algorithm, a signature scheme without random oracles has been constructed [14].

1. **Gen.** Choose $\alpha \in Z_p$ and let $g_1 = g^\alpha$. Additionally, two random values $g_2, u' \in G$ and a random $n$-length vector $U = (u_i)$, whose elements are chosen at random from $G$. The public key is $pk = (g_1, g_2, u', U)$ and the secret key is $g_2^\alpha$.
2. **Sign.** To generate a signature on message $M = (\mu_1, \cdots, \mu_n) \in \{0,1\}^n$, pick $s \in_R Z_p^*$ and output the signature as $\sigma = (g_2^\alpha \cdot (u' \prod_{j=1}^n u_j^{\mu_j})^s, g^s)$ with his secret key $g_2^\alpha$.
3. **Verify.** Given a signature $\sigma$ on message $M = (\mu_1, \cdots, \mu_n) \in \{0,1\}^n$, it first parses $\sigma = (\sigma_1, \sigma_2)$. Then it checks if the following equation holds: $\hat{e}(\sigma_1, g) = \hat{e}(g_2, g_1) \cdot \hat{e}(u' \prod_{i=1}^n u_i^{\mu_i}, \sigma_2)$. Output 1 if it is valid. Otherwise, output 0.

## 2.4   Brief Review of GJKR's DKG

Before we give the description of GJKR's DKG, we review two fundamental secret sharing schemes:

A. **Shamir's Secret Sharing [11]:** Given a secret $\alpha$, choose at random a degree $k - 1$ polynomial function $f \in Z_p[X]$ such that $x = f(0)$. Give to player $P_i$ a share $x_i = f(i) \bmod p$, where $p$ is a prime. We will write $(x_1, \cdots, x_n) \leftrightarrow (x)$ to denote such a sharing.
B. **Feldman Verifiable Secret Sharing [6]:** Like Shamir's secret sharing scheme, it generates for each player $P_i$ a share $x_i = f(i) \bmod p$, such that $(x_1, \cdots, x_n) \leftrightarrow (x)$. If $f(x) = \sum_{i=0}^{k-1} a_i x^i$, then the dealer broadcasts the values $A_i = g^{a_i}$, where $g$ is subgroup generator. This will allow the players to check that the values $x_i$ really define a secret by checking that $g^{x_i} = \prod_{j=0}^{k-1} A_j^{i^j}$. It will also allow detection of incorrect shares at reconstruction time. In the following we will refer to this protocol by Feldman-VSS.

Pedersen proposed a DKG protocol in [9]. The basic idea in Pedersen's DKG protocol is to have $n$ parallel executions of Feldman-VSS protocol in which each player $P_i$ acts as a dealer of a random secret $z_i$ that he picks. The secret value $x$ is taken to be the sum of the properly shared $z_i's$. Since Feldman-VSS has the additional property of revealing $y_i = g^{z_i}$, the public value $y$ is the product of the $y_i$'s that correspond to those properly shared $z_i's$.

In spite of its use in many protocols, Pedersen's DKG [9] cannot guarantee the correctness of the output distribution in the presence of an adversary. Specifically, Gennaro et al. [7] showed a strategy for an adversary to manipulate the distribution of the resulting secret $x$ to something quite different from the uniform distribution. In contrast to the Pedersen's DKG, Gennaro et al. [7] presented the GJKR's DKG protocol that enjoys a full proof of security. It starts by running a commitment stage where each player $P_i$ commits to a $(k-1)$-degree polynomial $f_i(z)$ whose constant coefficient is the random value, $z_i$, contributed by $P_i$ to the jointly generated secret $\alpha$. To realize the above commitment stage it used the information-theoretic verifiable secret sharing protocol due to Pedersen's DKG. After the value $x$ is fixed the parties can efficiently and securely compute $y = g^x$. Most importantly, this guarantees that no bias in the output $x$ or $y$ of the protocol is possible, and it allows to present a full proof of security based on a careful simulation argument. Each honest party $P_j$ computes its share $x_j$ of $x$, and we have that for the set of shares $R$: $x = \sum_{j \in R} \lambda_j x_j$. Meanwhile, for each share $x_j$, the value $g^{x_j}$ can be computed from publicly available information broadcast.

We now describe in detail the secure distributed key generation [7](GJKR's DKG):

1. In order to generating a secret key $x$, each player $P_i$ performs interactively as follows:
   (a) $P_i$ chooses two random polynomials $f_i(z)$, $f_i'(z)$ over $Z_p$ of degree $k-1$:
   $f_i(z) = a_{i0} + a_{i1}z + \cdots + a_{i,k-1}z^{k-1}$, $f_i'(z) = b_{i0} + b_{i1}z + \cdots + b_{i,k-1}z^{k-1}$.
   Let $z_i = a_{i0} = f_i(0)$. $P_i$ broadcasts $C_{it} = g^{a_{it}}h^{b_{ik}} \bmod p$ for $t = 0, \cdots,$
   $k-1$. $P_i$ computes the shares $s_{ij} = f_i(j)$, $s_{ij}' = f_i'(j) \bmod p$ for $j = 1, \cdots, n$ and sends $s_{ij}, s_{ij}'$ to player $P_j$.
   (b) Each player $P_j$ verifies the shares he received from the other players. For each $i = 1, \cdots, n$, $P_j$ checks if $g^{s_{ij}}h^{s_{ij}'} = \prod_{t=0}^{k-1}(C_{it})^{j^t} \bmod p$. If the check fails for an index $i$, $P_j$ broadcasts a complaint against $P_i$.
   (c) Each player $P_i$ who, as a dealer, received a complaint from player $P_j$ broadcasts the values $s_{ij}, s_{ij}'$.
   (d) Each player marks as disqualified any player that either received more than $k-1$ complaints in Step 1b, or answered to a complaint in Step 1c with invalid values.
   (e) Each player $P_i$ then builds the same set of non-disqualified players $QUAL$ and sets his share of the secret as $x_i = \sum_{i \in QUAL} s_{ji} \bmod p$, and the value $x_i' = \sum_{i \in QUAL} s_{ji}' \bmod p$.
2. Finally, they extract $y = g^x \bmod p$ as follows:
   (a) Each player $i \in QUAL$ exposes $y_i = g^{z_i} \bmod p$ via Feldman VSS and broadcasts $A_{it} = g^{a_{it}} \bmod p$ for $t = 0, \cdots, k-1$. Then $P_j$ verifies the values broadcast by the other players in $QUAL$, namely, for each $i \in QUAL$, $P_j$ checks if $g^{s_{ij}} = \prod_{t=0}^{k-1}(A_{it})^{j^t} \bmod p$. If the check fails for an index $i$, $P_j$ complains against $P_i$ by broadcasting the values $s_{ij}, s_{ij}'$.
   (b) For players $P_i$ who receive at least one valid complaint, the other players run the reconstruction phase of Pedersen-VSS to compute $z_i, f_i(z), A_{it}$ for $t = 0, \cdots, k-1$ in the clear.
   (c) For all players in $QUAL$, set $y_i = A_{i0} = g^{z_i} \bmod p$. Compute $y = \prod_{i \in QUAL} y_i \bmod p$.

   The above argument shows that the secret $x$ can be efficiently reconstructed, via interpolation, out of any $k$ correct shares.

We need to show that we can tell apart correct shares from incorrect ones. For this we show that for each share $x_j$, the value $g^{x_j}$ can be computed from publicly available information broadcast in Step 2a: $g^{x_j} = g^{\sum_{i \in QUAL} s_{ij}} = \prod_{i \in QUAL} g^{s_{ij}}$ $= \prod_{i \in QUAL} \prod_{t=0}^{k-1} (A_{it})^{j^t} \mod p$. Thus the publicly available value $g^{x_j}$ makes it possible to verify the correctness of share $x_j$ at reconstruction time.

Meanwhile, for any set $R$ of $k$ correct shares, $z_i = \sum_{j \in R} \lambda_j \cdot s_{ij} \mod p$, where $\lambda_j$ are appropriate Lagrange interpolation coefficients for the set $R$. Since each honest party $P_j$ computes its share $x_j$ as $x_j = \sum_{i \in QUAL} s_{ij}$, then we have that for the set of shares $R$: $x = \sum_{i \in QUAL} z_i = \sum_{i \in QUAL} (\sum_{j \in R} \lambda_j \cdot s_{ij}) = \sum_{j \in R} \lambda_j \cdot (\sum_{i \in QUAL} s_{ij}) = \sum_{j \in R} \lambda_j x_j$.

## 3  The Threshold Signature Scheme with Trusted Dealer

Let $G$ be a bilinear group of prime order $p$. Given a pairing: $\hat{e} : G \times G \to G_T$. A random generator $g \in G$ is also selected.

1. **DKG.** To generate public key, the trusted dealer picks $\alpha \in Z_p$ and computes $g_1 = g^\alpha$. Additionally, two random values $g_2, u' \in G$ and a random $n$-length vector $\mathsf{U} = (u_i)$, whose elements are chosen at random from $G$, are also generated.

   a. It chooses a $k - 1$ degree function $f(x) \in Z_p(x)$ such that $\alpha = f(0)$ and computes $n$ secret key share $(i, sk_i)$ for $1 \le i \le n$ by using Shamir secret sharing scheme, which is defined as $sk_i = g_2^{f(i)}$.

   b. The public verification key $\mathsf{VK}$ consists of the $n$-tuple $(g^{f(1)}, \cdots, g^{f(n)})$. Then, it sends to player $P_i$ a share $g_2^{f(i)}$ for $1 \le i \le n$.

   c. The public key is $(g_1, g_2, u', \mathsf{U}, \mathsf{VK})$ and the secret key shares are $sk_i$ for $1 \le i \le n$.

2. **SS.** To generate a signature on message $M = (\mu_1, \cdots, \mu_n) \in \{0,1\}^n$, player $i$ picks $r_i \in_R Z_p^*$ and outputs the partial signature as $\sigma_i = (sk_i \cdot (u' \prod_{j=1}^{n} u_j^{\mu_j})^{r_i}, g^{r_i})$ with its secret key share $sk_i$.

3. **SV.** On input $\sigma_i = (\sigma_{i,1}, \sigma_{i,2})$, verification key $vk_i$, the verifier checks if the following equation holds: $\hat{e}(\sigma_{i,1}, g) = \hat{e}(g_2, vk_i) \cdot \hat{e}(u' \prod_{j=1}^{n} u_j^{\mu_j}, \sigma_{i,2})$. Output 1 if it is valid. Otherwise, output 0.

4. **SC.** Let $\lambda_1, \cdots, \lambda_k \in Z_p$ be the Lagrange coefficients so that $\alpha = f(0) = \sum_{i=1}^{k} \lambda_i f(i)$. Assume signature share combination algorithm has $|\Phi|$ valid signature shares $\sigma_i = (\sigma_{i,1}, \sigma_{i,2})$, where $|\Phi| \ge k$. Without loss of generality we assume that player $i = 1, \cdots, k$ were used to generate the shares. The signature combination algorithm computes the signature on message $M$ as $\sigma = (\prod_{i=1}^{k} (\sigma_{i,1})^{\lambda_i}, \prod_{i=1}^{k} (\sigma_{i,2})^{\lambda_i})$.

5. **Vrfy.** Given a signature $\sigma$ on message $M = (\mu_1, \cdots, \mu_n) \in \{0,1\}^n$, it first parses $\sigma = (\overline{\sigma}_1, \overline{\sigma}_2)$. Then it checks if the following equation holds: $\hat{e}(\overline{\sigma}_1, g) = \hat{e}(g_2, g_1) \cdot \hat{e}(u' \prod_{i=1}^{n} u_i^{\mu_i}, \overline{\sigma}_2)$. Output 1 if it is valid. Otherwise, output 0.

## 3.1  Efficiency Analysis

The new threshold signature scheme is non-interactive. Furthermore, signature share generation algorithm requires only two exponentiation computation for each player. Though [12] also gave a practical non-interactive threshold signature scheme with trusted dealer based on RSA problem, it required one exponentiation with zero-knowledge proof, which is actually not very efficient. Recently, a short threshold signature scheme [13] has been proposed, however, it is very inefficient for it requires the players generate signature shares interactively.

## 3.2  Security Result

**Theorem 1.** *Under the CDH assumption, the proposed practical threshold signature scheme is a secure (unforgeable and robust) threshold signature scheme resistant to $k - 1$ faults against a static malicious adversary, when the number of player is $n \geq 2k - 1$.*

*Proof.* Our algorithm $\mathcal{C}$ described below solves CDH problem for a randomly given instance $\{g, X = g^x, Y = g^y\}$ and asked to compute $g^{xy}$.

*Setup*: First, $\mathcal{C}$ defines $g_1 = X$ and sets an integer, $m = 4q_S$, chooses an integer, $k'$, uniformly at random between 0 and $n$. Choose a random $n$-length vector, $\overrightarrow{a} = (a_i)$, all are chosen uniformly at random between 0 and $m - 1$. Then, the simulator chooses a random $b' \in Z_p$ and an $n$-length vector, $\overrightarrow{b} = (b_i)$, where the elements of $\overrightarrow{b}$ are chosen at random in $Z_p$. It then assigns $u' = g_1^{p-km+a'} g^{b'}$ and the parameter $U$ as $u_i = g_1^{a_i} g^{b_i}$. The system parameters params$= (g, g_1, u', (u_i))$ are sent to $\mathcal{A}$. Two pairs of functions are defined for a message $M = \{\mu_1, \cdots, \mu_n\} \in \{0, 1\}^n$. We define $F(M) = (p - mk) + a' + \sum_{i=1}^{n} a_i^{\mu_i}$. Next, we define $J(M) = b' + \sum_{i=1}^{n} b_i^{\mu_i}$. Finally, define a binary function K(M) as $K(M) = \begin{cases} 0, & \text{if } a' + \sum_{i=1}^{n} a_i^{\mu_i} \equiv 0 \ (mod \ m); \\ 1, & \text{otherwise.} \end{cases}$

We assume w.l.o.g. that the adversary corrupted the first $k-1$ players $P_1, \cdots, P_{k-1}$. Then, C generates the secret key shares for the $k - 1$ corrupt players in S. To do so, C first picks $k - 1$ random integers $x_1, \cdots, x_{k-1} \in Z_p$. Let $f \in Z_p[X]$ be the degree $k - 1$ polynomial implicitly defined to satisfy $f(0) = x$ and $f(i) = x_i$ for $i = 1, \cdots, k - 1$. Algorithm C gives A the $k - 1$ secret key shares $sk_i = g_2^{x_i}$. These keys are consistent with this polynomial $f$ since $sk_i = g_2^{f(i)}$ for $i = 1, \cdots, k - 1$.

Finally, C constructs the verification key VK, which is a n-vector $(vk_1, \cdots, vk_n)$ such that $vk_i = g^{f(i)}$ for the polynomial $f$ defined above, as follows:

For $i \in S$, computing $vk_i$ is easy since $f(i)$ is equal to one of the $x_1, \cdots, x_{k-1}$, which are known to C. Thus, $vk_1, \cdots, vk_{k-1}$ are easy for C to compute.

For $i \notin S$, algorithm C needs to compute the Lagrange coefficients $\lambda_{0,i}, \lambda_{1,i}, \cdots, \lambda_{k-1,i} \in Z_p$ such that $f(i) = \lambda_{0,i} f(0) + \sum_{j=1}^{k-1} \lambda_{j,i} f(j)$; these Lagrange coefficients are easily calculated since they do not depend on $f$. Algorithm C then sets $vk_i = g_1^{\lambda_{0,i}} vk_1^{\lambda_{1,i}} \cdots vk_{k-1}^{\lambda_{k-1,i}}$, which entails that $vk_i = g^{f(i)}$ as required.

Once it has computed all the $vk_i$'s, C gives to A the verification key VK $=$ $(vk_1, \cdots, vk_n)$.

*Signature Share Query*: A issues up to $q_S$ signature share generation queries to the uncorrupt players. Consider a signature share generation query to player $i \notin S$. Let $M=(\mu_1, \cdots, \mu_n) \in \{0,1\}^n$ be the message for signature share query. If $K(M) = 0$, $\mathcal{C}$ will abort. Otherwise, $\mathcal{C}$ computes the simulated signature share for $M$ as follows: Algorithm B needs to return $(i, (\sigma_{i,0}, \sigma_{i,1}))$ where $\sigma_{i,0} = g_2^{x_i} \cdot (u' \prod_{j=1}^{n} u_j^{\mu_j})^{r_i}$, $\sigma_{i,1}=g^{r_i}$.

To do so, B first computes the Lagrange coefficients $\lambda_0, \lambda_1, \cdots, \lambda_{k-1} \in Z_p$ such that $f(i) = \lambda_{0,i} f(0) + \sum_{j=1}^{k-1} \lambda_{j,i} f(j)$. Pick $r_i' \in Z_p^*$ and output the simulated signature share as $\sigma_i = (g_2^{-\lambda_{0,i} \frac{J(M)}{F(M)}} (u' \prod_{i=1}^{n} u_i)^{r_i'} \cdot g_2^{\sum_{j=1}^{k-1} \lambda_{j,i} f(j)}, g_2^{\frac{-\lambda_{0,i}}{F(M)}} g^{r_i'})$. The correctness of the signature can be easily verified.

Finally, the adversary outputs a forged signature $(\sigma_1^*, \sigma_2^*)$ on message $M^* = (\mu_1^*, \cdots, \mu_n^*)$. If $a' + \sum_{i=1}^{n} a_i \mu_i^* \neq km$, the challenger will abort. Otherwise, $\mathcal{C}$ will compute $g^{xy} = \frac{\sigma_1^*}{(\sigma_2^*)^{J(M)}}$.

For the simulation to complete without aborting, we require that all signature queries on $M$ will have $K(M) \neq km$, that forgery signature on message $M^*$ has $K(M^*) = 0 \mod p$. In fact, the probability analysis is very similar to [23]. So, we can get the probability of solving computational CDH problem as $\epsilon' = \frac{\epsilon}{16(q_E+q_S)q_S(n+1)(m+1)}$ if the adversary success with probability $\epsilon$.

# 4   The Threshold Signature Scheme Without Trusted Dealer

We have construct a threshold signature scheme with trusted dealer in last section. However, in some situations, it does not have trusted dealer. So, in order to generate threshold signature, the players should generate the public key jointly. We assume that the involved n participants are connected by a broadcast channel. Furthermore, any one pair of the participants is connected by a private channel. We also assume that there is a universal clock such that each participant knows the absolute time, and the communication channel is (partially) synchronous by rounds.

It is also assumed that an adversary can corrupt up to $k-1$ of the $n$ players in the network, for any value of $k-1 < \frac{n}{2}$ (this is the best achievable threshold or resilience for solutions that provide both secrecy and robustness). We consider a malicious adversary that may cause corrupted players to divert from the specified protocol in any way. We assume that the computational power of the adversary is adequately modelled by a probabilistic polynomial time Turing machine. Furthermore, we consider a static adversary who chooses corrupted participants at the beginning of each time period. For the robustness, it means that the scheme can be successfully finished even if the adversary corrupts $k-1$ participants at most.

GJKR's DKG protocol of [7] is based on the ideas similar to the protocol of Pedersen [9], has comparable complexity, but provably fixes the weakness of the latter. So, we use the GJKR's DKG protocol in [7] to distributedly generate the shared secret keys and output public keys. The system parameters are the same with the scheme in section 3.

- **DKG.** To generate public key, $n$ servers jointly generate user public key $g_1 = g^\alpha$ by using GJKR's DKG. Meanwhile, Each player $P_i$ broadcasts $g^{f(i)}$ for a random jointly generated degree $k-1$ polynomial $f \in Z_p[X]$ such that $\alpha = f(0)$. Additionally, two values $g_2, u' \in G$ and a $n$-length vector $\mathsf{U} = (u_i)$, whose elements are from $G$, are also generated by using GJKR's DKG algorithm, respectively. Furthermore, player $P_i$ gets its secret share $sk_i = g_2^{f(i)}$ for $1 \le i \le n$. The public verification key VK=$(vk_1, \cdots, vk_n)$ consists of the $n$-tuple $(g^{f(1)}, \cdots, g^{f(n)})$. The public key is $(g_1, g_2, u', \mathsf{U}, \mathsf{VK})$ and the shared secret keys are $sk_i$ for $1 \le i \le n$.
- **SS, SV, SC, Vrfy** algorithms are the same with section 2.4.

Correctness is obvious. Next, we will prove its robustness and unforgeablity.

## 4.1    Security Result

We also prove the unforgeability by using the concept of simulatable adversary view [16] proposed by Gennaro et al.

**Theorem 2.** *Under the CDH assumption, the proposed practical threshold signature scheme is a secure (unforgeable and robust) threshold signature scheme resistant to $k-1$ faults against a static malicious adversary, when the number of player is $n \ge 2k-1$.*

*Proof.* The robustness is evident.
The construction of DKG is the same with [7], which has been proved to be simulatable. Next, we prove the protocol SS is simulatable:

Given public key $(g_1, g_2, u', \mathsf{U}, \mathsf{VK})$, message $m = (\mu_1, \cdots, \mu_n) \in \{0, 1\}^n$, signature $\sigma = (\overline{\sigma}_1, \overline{\sigma}_2)$, $k-1$ shares $(\alpha_1, \cdots, \alpha_{k-1})$ of the corrupted players, it picks random values $r_i \in Z_p$ and computes $\sigma_i = g_2^{\alpha_i} \cdot (u' \prod_{j=1}^n u_j^{\mu_j})^{r_i}, g^{r_i})$ for $i = 1, \cdots, k-1$. From the values $\sigma = (\overline{\sigma}_1, \overline{\sigma}_2)$, and $\sigma_i$ for $i = 1, \cdots, k-1$, simulator generates $\sigma_j = \frac{\sigma}{\sigma_i^{\lambda_{j,i}}}$, for $j = k, \cdots, n$, with known Lagrange interpolation coefficients $\lambda_{j,i}$.

## 5    Conclusion

A secure threshold signature scheme without trusted dealer is proposed in this paper. Our construction is based on the recently proposed signature scheme of Waters [14], combined with the new technique [3]. It is provably secure without relying on the random oracle model. Additionally, signature share generation and verification is completely non-interactive. The new threshold signature scheme is more efficient than the previous threshold signature schemes without random oracles. Furthermore, it is the first threshold signature scheme based on the CDH problem without relying on random oracles.

# References

1. Abe, M., Fehr, S.: Adaptively secure Feldman VSS and applications to universally-composable threshold cryptography. In: Franklin, M. (ed.) CRYPTO 2004. LNCS, vol. 3152, pp. 317–334. Springer, Heidelberg (2004)
2. Bellare, M., Boldyreva, A., Palacio, A.: An Uninstantiable Random-Oracle-Model Scheme for a Hybrid-Encryption Problem. In: Cachin, C., Camenisch, J.L. (eds.) EUROCRYPT 2004. LNCS, vol. 3027, pp. 171–188. Springer, Heidelberg (2004)
3. Boneh, D., Boyen, X., Halevi, S.: Chosen ciphertext secure public key threshold encryption without random oracles. In: Pointcheval, D. (ed.) CT-RSA 2006. LNCS, vol. 3860, pp. 226–243. Springer, Heidelberg (2006)
4. Canetti, R., Gennaro, R., Jarecki, S., Krawczyk, H., Rabin, T.: Adaptive security for threshold cryptosystems. In: Wiener, M.J. (ed.) CRYPTO 1999. LNCS, vol. 1666, pp. 98–115. Springer, Heidelberg (1999)
5. Desmedt, Y., Frankel, Y.: Threshold cryptosystems. In: Brassard, G. (ed.) CRYPTO 1989. LNCS, vol. 435, pp. 307–315. Springer, Heidelberg (1990)
6. Feldman, P.: A Practical Scheme for Non-Interactive Verifiable Secret Sharing. In: Proc. 28th FOCS, pp. 427–437.
7. Gennaro, R., Jarecki, S., Krawczyk, H., Rabin, T.: Secure Distributed Key Generation for Discrete-Log Based Cryptosystem, In: Stern, J. (ed.) EUROCRYPT 1999. LNCS, vol. 1592, pp. 295–310. Springer, Heidelberg (1999)
8. Gennaro, R., Jarecki, S., Krawczyk, H., Rabin, T.: Robust threshold DSS signatures. Information and Computation 164(1), 54–64 (1996)
9. Pedersen, T.: A threshold cryptosystem without a trusted party. In: Davies, D.W. (ed.) EUROCRYPT 1991. LNCS, vol. 547, pp. 522–536. Springer, Heidelberg (1991)
10. Pedersen, T.: Non-interactive and information-theoretic secure verifiable secret sharing. In: Feigenbaum, J. (ed.) CRYPTO 1991. LNCS, vol. 576, pp. 129–140. Springer, Heidelberg (1992)
11. Shamir, A.: How to Share a Secret. Communications of the ACM 22, 612–613 (1979)
12. Shoup, V., Gennaro, R.: Securing Threshold Cryptosystems against Chosen Ciphertext Attack. Journal of Cryptology 15, 75–96 (2002)
13. Wang, H., Zhang, Y., Feng, D.: Short Threshold Signature Schemes Without Random Oracles. In: Maitra, S., Madhavan, C.E.V., Venkatesan, R. (eds.) INDOCRYPT 2005. LNCS, vol. 3797, pp. 297–310. Springer, Heidelberg (2005)
14. Waters, B.: Efficient Identity based Encryption without random oracles. In: Cramer, R.J.F. (ed.) EUROCRYPT 2005. LNCS, vol. 3494, pp. 114–127. Springer, Heidelberg (2005)

# Aggregate Proxy Signature and Verifiably Encrypted Proxy Signature

Jin Li[1,*], Kwangjo Kim[1], Fangguo Zhang[2], and Xiaofeng Chen[3]

[1] International Research center for Information Security (IRIS)
Information and Communications University(ICU)
103-6 Munji-Dong, Yuseong-Gu, Daejeon, 305-732, Korea
sysjinli@hotmail.com, kkj@icu.ac.kr
[2] Department of Electronics and Communication Engineering
Sun Yat-Sen University, Guangzhou, 510275, P.R. China
[3] Department of Computer Science
Sun Yat-Sen University, Guangzhou, 510275, P.R. China

**Abstract.** An aggregate signature is a single short string that convinces any verifier that, for all $1 \le i \le n$, signer $i$ signed message $m_i$, where the $n$ signers and $n$ messages are distinct. The main motivation of aggregate signatures is compactness. In this paper, the concept of aggregate proxy signature (APS) is first proposed to compact the proxy signatures. Furthermore, a concrete APS scheme is constructed, which can be proved to be secure under the security model of APS. Additionally, as an application of APS, the concept of verifiably encrypted proxy signature (VEPS) is also first proposed in this paper, which can be used in contract signing. The VEPS allows the original signer to delegate another to sign the contract on its behalf. Finally, a VEPS construction is derived from the APS, which can be easily proved to be secure from the security of APS.

**Keywords:** Proxy signature, Aggregate signature, Random oracle, Bilinear pairings.

## 1 Introduction

A proxy signature protocol allows an original signer to delegate its signing power to another entity, called proxy signer, to sign messages on its behalf. The delegated proxy signer can compute a proxy signature that can be verified by anyone with access to the original signer's public key. Proxy signatures have many practical applications such as in distributed system etc. [10] and are one of important cryptographic protocols. The concept of proxy signature was first introduced by Mambo, Usuda, and Okamoto [8] in 1996. After Mambo et al.'s first scheme was published, many various types of proxy signature schemes have been proposed such as short proxy signature scheme [5,7], one-time proxy signatures [16]. Also, there are a lot of proxy signature schemes were found flaws such as [11].

---

* This work was partially supported by the 2nd stage of Brain Korea 21 Project sponsored by the Ministry of Education and Human Resources Development, Korea.

W. Susilo, J.K. Liu, and Y. Mu. (Eds.): ProvSec 2007, LNCS 4784, pp. 208–217, 2007.

The main reason is the lack of formal security model. Until 2003, the formal security model was proposed in [1]. In this security model, a public key infrastructure setting (PKI) is also assumed, where each entity holds a public and secret key pair.

The notion of aggregate signature schemes was introduced in 2003 by Boneh, Gentry, Lynn and Shacham [3]. Basically, aggregating signatures means compressing $n$ signatures on $n$ distinct messages from $n$ distinct users into a unique (shorter) signature. This is useful in many real-world applications. For example, certificate chains in a hierarchical PKI of depth $n$ consist of $n$ signatures by $n$ different CAs on $n$ different public keys. By using an aggregate signature scheme, this chain can be compressed down to a single aggregate certificate. After the concept of aggregate signatures was proposed, many types of aggregate signatures have been presented such as identity-based aggregate signatures [4], sequential aggregate signatures [13].

In this paper, the concept of aggregate proxy signature (APS) is first proposed. Consider the following situations: $n$ proxy signers have generated $n$ proxy signatures on $n$ different messages on behalf of the same original signer. To verify these proxy signatures, the ordinary method is to verify them one by one, which costs large storage and computation. Reducing the amount of memory required to store these proxy signatures and the computational time required to verify their validity is the motivation for the concept of APS. An APS is obtained from $n$ different initial proxy signatures, ideally in such a way that: (1) the length of the aggregate proxy signature is smaller than the sum of the length of the $n$ initial proxy signatures; (2) verifying the correctness of the aggregate proxy signature costs less than verifying the $n$ initial proxy signatures one by one. If an aggregate proxy signature is verified as valid, then the receiver is convinced that the $n$ initial signatures are valid. On the other hand, if the aggregate signature is invalid, the receiver is convinced that some initial proxy signature is not valid.

Next, we show an application of APS to verifiably encrypted proxy signature (VEPS). It is known that verifiably encrypted signatures can be used in applications such as online contract signing [8]. Suppose Alice wants to show Bob that she has signed a message, but does not want Bob to possess her signature of that message. Alice can achieve this by encrypting her signature using the public key of a trusted third party, and sending this to Bob along with a proof that she has given him a valid encryption of her signature. Bob can verify that Alice has signed the message, but cannot deduce any information from her signature. Later, in the protocol, if Alice is unwilling or unable to reveal her signature, Bob can ask the third party to reveal Alice's signature.

However, consider the following situation: If either Alice or Bob is busy, they can delegate their signing power to the other party, which is called as proxy signer, to sign the contract on behalf of him or her. So, the concept of VEPS is first presented in this paper to solve this problem. In this case, the proxy signer of Alice, for example, wants to show Bob that it has signed a message on behalf of Alice, but does not want Bob to possess its proxy signature on that message. The proxy signer can achieve this by encrypting its proxy signature using the public key of a trusted third party, and sending this to Bob along with a proof that it has given him a valid encryption of its proxy signature. Bob can verify that the proxy signer has signed the message on behalf of Alice, but cannot deduce any information from the encrypted signature. Later, in the protocol, if the proxy signer is unwilling or unable to reveal its signature, Bob can ask the third party to reveal its proxy signature.

**Contributions.** In this work we introduce the notion and security model of APS. Roughly speaking, the new concept allows to efficiently manage multiple proxy signatures addressed to a specific verifier. Furthermore, a concrete construction is presented, which can be proved to be secure in the security model. Additionally, the concept of VEPS is first proposed in this paper, which can be used in contract signing. It allows the original signer to delegate another to sign the contract on its behalf. A VEPS construction is also derived from the APS, which can be easily proved to be secure from the security of APS.

## 2   Preliminaries

### 2.1   Definition

**Definition 1 (APS).** *An APS scheme consists of 7 algorithms: (KeyGen, (D,P), PSign, PVerify, Aggregate, Verify). The algorithms are specified as follows:*

- *KenGen The key generation algorithm, on input security parameter $1^k$, outputs user's public key $pk$ and corresponding secret key $sk$.*
- *(D,P) is a pair of interactive algorithms forming the proxy-designation protocol. The input to each algorithm includes two public keys $pk_o, pk_i$. D also takes as input the secret key $sk_o$, and P also takes as input the secret key $sk_i$. As result of the interaction, the expected local output of P is $sk_p$, a proxy signing key that user $pk_i$ uses to produce proxy signatures on behalf of user $pk_o$.*
- *PSign The proxy signature generation algorithm, that takes as input a secret key $sk_p$, a message $m$, returns the signature $\sigma$.*
- *PVerify The proxy signature verification algorithm, that takes input public key $pk_o$, $pk_i$, a message $m$ and a proxy signature $\sigma$, outputs 1 if it is a valid proxy signature for $m$ relative to $pk$. Otherwise, output 0.*
- *Aggregate The aggregate algorithm, that takes as input $n$ different proxy signatures $\sigma_1, \cdots, \sigma_n$ of distinct messages $m_1, \cdots, m_n$ correctly signed by different users $pk_1, \cdots, pk_n$, outputs an aggregate proxy signature $\sigma$;*
- *Verify The aggregate proxy signature verification algorithm, that takes as input $pk_o$, $pk_1, \cdots, pk_n$, $n$ messages $m_1, \cdots, m_n$ and $\sigma$, returns 1 or 0 for accept or reject, respectively.*

### 2.2   Security Requirements

Adversary's attack capabilities are modelled by providing it access to certain oracles. We now introduce the oracles we will need and provide the adversary with different subsets of this set of oracles.

- $\mathcal{APS}$ Oracle: The aggregate proxy signing oracle, on input message $m_1$, $\cdots$, $m_n$, $pk_o$, $\mathcal{L} = \{y_1, \cdots, y_n\}$ for aggregate proxy signature, returns an aggregate proxy signature $\sigma$ such that $\mathsf{APV}(pk_o, \mathcal{L}, m_1, \cdots, m_n, \sigma) = 1$.
- $\mathcal{KR}$ Oracle: The key registration oracle, on input key pair $(pk, sk)$, first checks if $sk$ is indeed the secret key of $pk$. Then it stores $(pk, sk)$ as a valid registered key pair if it is. Otherwise, reject and output a special symbol $\perp$.
- $\mathcal{DE}$ Oracle: The delegation oracle, on input any registered public key $pk_i$, and original public key $pk_o$, its secret key $sk_o$, returns a delegation on the public key $pk_i$.
- $\mathcal{RA}$ Oracle: The random oracle, on input $m_i$, outputs a randomly value $r_i$ chosen in the domain of the hash function.

There are two types of unforgeability to consider in APS: *Delegation unforgeability* and *aggregate proxy signature unforgeability*. *Delegation unforgeability* means that even if the adversary asks for polynomial users' delegation, it is still hard to output a forgery delegation that the original signer has not delegated. *Aggregate proxy signature unforgeability* means that, except the proxy signers, anyone else (even if the origin signer) cannot generate valid aggregate proxy signature on behalf of these proxy signers.

### 2.2.1 Delegation Unforgeability

*Delegation unforgeability* for aggregate proxy signature is defined as in the following game involving an adversary $\mathcal{A}$.

1. Let $(pk_o, sk_o) \leftarrow \mathsf{KenGen}(1^k)$. $\mathcal{A}$ is given $pk_o$ and the public parameters.
2. $\mathcal{A}$ accesses to $\mathcal{RA}$ Oracle, $\mathcal{DE}$ Oracle, and $\mathcal{KR}$ Oracle.

The adversary $\mathcal{A}$ wins the game if he can output $m_1^*, \cdots, m_n^*$, $\mathcal{L} = (pk_1, \cdots, pk_n,)$, such that $\mathcal{L}$ includes a public key $pk_i$ that is not equal to any query of $\mathcal{DE}$ oracle and $\sigma^*$ is a valid aggregate proxy signature with respect to $pk_o$. The advantage of the adversary is the probability that he wins the game.

**Definition 2.** *(Delegation Unforgeability) An aggregate proxy signature scheme is delegation unforgeability secure if no probabilistic polynomial time (PPT) adversary has a non-negligible advantage in the above game.*

### 2.2.2 Aggregate Proxy Signature Unforgeability

We formalize this intuition as the aggregate chosen-key security model. In this model, the adversary $\mathcal{A}$ is given a single proxy signer's public key. His goal is the existential forgery of an aggregate proxy signature. We give the adversary power to choose all public keys except the challenge public key. The adversary is also given access to a proxy signing oracle on the challenge key. His advantage, $Adv^{AggSig}(A)$, is defined to be his probability of success in the following game.

- *Setup*: The aggregate forger $\mathcal{A}$ is provided with the challenge proxy signer's public key $pk_1$ and original signer's key pair $(sk_o, pk_o)$, generated at random.

- $\mathcal{A}$ requests proxy signatures with $pk_1$ on behalf of original signer $pk_o$, adaptively.
- $\mathcal{A}$ accesses to $\mathcal{RA}$ Oracle and $\mathcal{KR}$ Oracle.
- Finally, $\mathcal{A}$ outputs $n-1$ additional public keys $pk_2, \cdots, pk_n$, which have been queried to $\mathcal{KR}$ Oracle. Here $n$ is at most $N$, a game parameter. These keys, along with the initial key $pk_1$, will be included in $\mathcal{A}$'s forged aggregate. $\mathcal{A}$ also outputs messages $m_1^*, \cdots, m_n^*$, and, finally, an aggregate proxy signature $\sigma^*$ by the $n$ users on behalf of $pk_o$, each on his corresponding message. The forger wins if the aggregate signature $\sigma^*$ is a valid aggregate on messages $m_1^*, \cdots, m_n^*$ under public keys $pk_1, \cdots, pk_n$, and $\sigma^*$ is nontrivial, i.e., $\mathcal{A}$ did not request a proxy signature on $m_1^*$ under $pk_1$.

An aggregate forger $\mathcal{A}$ $(t, q_H, q_S, n, \epsilon)$-breaks an $n$-user APS scheme in the aggregate chosen-key model if: $\mathcal{A}$ runs in time at most $t$; $\mathcal{A}$ makes at most $q_H$ queries to the random oracle and at most $q_S$ queries to the $\mathcal{APS}$ oracle; $Adv^{AggSig}(A)$ is at least $\epsilon$; and the forged aggregate signature is by at most $N$ users. An aggregate signature scheme is $(t, q_H, q_S, n, \epsilon)$-secure against existential forgery in the aggregate chosen-key model if no forger $(t, q_H, q_S, n, \epsilon)$-breaks it.

**Definition 3.** *An APS is secure if $Adv^{AggSig}(A)$ is negligible for any PPT adversary $\mathcal{A}$.*

## 2.3   Preliminaries

Before present our results, we review the definitions of groups equipped with a bilinear pairings and a related assumption. Let $G$ be a (multiplicative) cyclic group of prime order $p$. Let $g$ be a generator of $G$. We also let $\hat{e}$ be a bilinear map such that $\hat{e} : G \times G \to G_1$ with the following properties:

1. *Bilinearity:* For all $u, v \in G$ and $a, b \in Z$, $\hat{e}(u^a, v^b) = \hat{e}(u, v)^{ab}$.
2. *Non-degeneracy:* $\hat{e}(g, g) \neq 1$.
3. *Computability:* There exists an efficient algorithm to compute $\hat{e}(u, v)$.

**Definition 4. Computational Diffie-Hellman Assumption:** *Given $g$, $g^x$, $g^y \in (G)^3$ for unknown $x, y \in_R Z_p^*$, it is hard to compute $g^{xy}$ for any PPT algorithm.*

## 3   An APS Scheme

Let $G$ be a bilinear group where $|G| = p$. Define a bilinear map $\hat{e} : G \times G \to G_1$. Meanwhile, define two collision-resistant hash functions $H_1 : G \to G$ and $H_2 : \{0,1\}^* \to G$. The construction of such hash function can be found in [2]. Then the system parameters are params=$(G, G_1, \hat{e}, g, H_1, H_2)$.

1. **KenGen.** For original signer, it picks $x_o \in Z_p$ and outputs $(x_o, y_o = g^{x_o})$ as its key pair. The original signer's secret key is $x_o$ and the public key is $y_o$. For user $i$, it chooses $x_i \in Z_p$ and outputs $(x_i, y_i = g^{x_i})$ as its key pair. The user $i's$ secret key is $x_i$ and the public key is $y_i$.

2. **D.** In order to delegate his signing capability to user $i$, the original signer $y_o$, on input $y_i$, computes $S_i = [H_1(y_i)]^{x_o}$ as the corresponding delegation.
3. **P.** Given $S_i$, the user $i$ computes its proxy signing key as $sk_i = (x_i, S_i)$.
4. **PSign.** Assuming the proxy signer $i$ with public key $y_i$ wants to generate signature on message $m$ on behalf of $y_o$, it computes $H_2(m)^{x_i}$ and outputs the proxy signature $\sigma = S_i \cdot H_2(m)^{x_i}$.
5. **PVerify.** On input the aggregate proxy signature $\sigma$, message $m$ and $y_o$, $y_i$, accept if $\hat{e}(\sigma, g) = \hat{e}(H_1(y_i), y_o)\, \hat{e}\, (H_2(m), y_i)$.
6. **Aggregate.** On input $n$ proxy signatures $\sigma_1, \cdots, \sigma_n$ on $n$ different messages $m_1, \cdots, m_n$ by $n$ distinct proxy signers $y_1, \cdots, y_n$, output $\sigma = \sigma_1 \cdots \sigma_n$ as the aggregate proxy signatures.
7. **Verify.** On input $\sigma$ on $n$ different messages $m_1, \cdots, m_n$ by $n$ distinct proxy signers $y_1, \cdots, y_n$, accept if $\hat{e}(\sigma, g) = \prod_{i=1}^{n}(\hat{e}(H_1(y_i), y_o)\, \hat{e}\, (H_2(m_i), y_i))$.

### 3.1   Security Results

**Theorem 1.** *In random oracle model, the APS scheme is delegation unforgeable if CDH assumption holds in bilinear groups.*

*Proof.* If there exists an adversary $\mathcal{A}$ breaks the scheme, then we show there exists an algorithm $\mathcal{C}$ that, by interacting with $\mathcal{A}$, solves the CDH problem. Our algorithm $\mathcal{C}$ described below solves CDH problem for a randomly given instance $\{g, g^x, g^y\}$ and asked to compute $g^{xy}$. The details are as follows.

$\mathcal{C}$ runs $\mathcal{A}$ on input $y_o = g^x$ as target user's public key, handling all of $\mathcal{A}$'s requests and answering all $\mathcal{A}$'s queries as follows:

– H-queries: Assume $\mathcal{A}$ makes at most $q_{H_1}$ times to $H_1$-oracle and $q_{H_2}$ times to $H_2$-oracle, respectively. When $\mathcal{A}$ queries $m_i$ to $H_2$-oracle, $\mathcal{C}$ answers $H_2(m_i) = g^{\hat{m}_i}$ for a random $\hat{m}_i \in Z_p$. Furthermore, $\mathcal{C}$ randomly chooses a $s \in [1, q_{H_1}]$ and prepares $t_i \in Z_p$ for $1 \le i \le q_{H_1}$. When $\mathcal{A}$ queries $y_i$ to $H_1$-oracle, $\mathcal{C}$ answers $H_1(y_i) = g^{t_i}$ if $i \ne s$. Otherwise, $H_1(y_s) = g^y$ if $i = s$.
– Key Registration Queries: If $\mathcal{A}$ requests to register a new user $i$ by outputting $(x_i, y_i)$, $\mathcal{C}$ stores these keys as valid registered key pair.
– Delegation Queries: If $\mathcal{A}$ requests to designates $i$ with registered public key $y_i$, it assumes $\mathcal{A}$ has requested $H_1$ query on $y_i$. If $i \ne s$, $\mathcal{C}$ knows the value $t_i$ such that $H_1(y_i) = g^{t_i}$. So cert is $y_o^{t_i}$. Otherwise, it aborts.

Finally, $\mathcal{A}$ outputs a forgery of aggregate proxy signature $(m_1^*, \cdots, m_n^*, \mathcal{L}, \sigma^*)$, such that $\mathcal{L}$ includes a public key $y^*$ that is not equal to any query of $\mathcal{DE}$ Oracle and $\sigma^*$ is a valid aggregate proxy signature with respect to $pk_o$ and $\mathcal{L}$ on message $m^*$. Assume $\mathcal{L} = \{y_1, \cdots, y_n\}$, such that $y_s = y^*$. It satisfies $\hat{e}(\sigma^*, g) = \prod_{i=1}^{n}(\hat{e}(H_1(y_i), y_o)\, \hat{e}\, (H_2(m_i^*), y_i))$, which implies $\sigma^* = \prod_{i=1}^{n} H_1(y_i)^x H_2(m_i^*)^{x_i}$. Because $H_2(m_i) = \hat{m}_i$, $H_1(y^*) = g^y$, and $H_1(y_i) = g^{t_i}$ for $y_i \ne y^*$, we can compute $g^{xy} = \sigma^* / \prod_{i=1}^{n} y_i^{\hat{m}_i^*} \prod_{i \in \{1, \cdots, n\} \backslash s} y_o^{t_i}$ and solve the CDH problem.

It is easy to see that if $\mathcal{A}$ outputs a forgery of aggregate proxy signature with probability $\epsilon$, then CDH problem can be solved with probability about $\frac{1}{q_{H_1}} \cdot \epsilon$. So, we can say that the APS scheme is delegation unforgeability secure in the random oracle if CDH assumption holds.

**Theorem 2.** *In random oracle model, the APS scheme is aggregate proxy signature unforgeable if CDH assumption holds in bilinear groups.*

*Proof.* We show there exists an algorithm $\mathcal{C}$ that, if there exists an adversary $\mathcal{A}$ breaks the scheme, by interacting with $\mathcal{A}$, solves the CDH problem. Our algorithm $\mathcal{C}$ described below solves CDH problem for a randomly given instance $\{g, g^x, g^y\}$ and asked to compute $g^{xy}$.

$\mathcal{C}$ chooses $x_o$ and computes $y_o = g^{x_o}$. Then it sends $(x_o, y_o)$ to the adversary. $\mathcal{C}$ runs $\mathcal{A}$ on input $y_1 = g^x$ as target proxy user's public key, handling all of $\mathcal{A}$'s requests and answering all $\mathcal{A}$'s queries as follows:

- H-queries: Assume $\mathcal{A}$ makes at most $q_{H_1}$ times to $H_1$-oracle and $q_{H_2}$ times to $H_2$-oracle, respectively. When $\mathcal{A}$ queries $y_i$ to $H_1$-oracle, $\mathcal{C}$ answers $H_1(y_i) = g^{r_i}$ for a random $r_i \in Z_p$. Furthermore, $\mathcal{C}$ randomly chooses a $s \in [1, q_{H_2}]$. When $\mathcal{A}$ queries $m_i$ to $H_2$-oracle, $\mathcal{C}$ answers $H_2(m_i) = g^{t_i}$ if $i \neq s$. Otherwise, $H_2(m_s) = g^y$ if $i = s$.
- Key Registration Queries: If $\mathcal{A}$ requests to register a new user by outputting $(x, y = g^x)$, $\mathcal{C}$ stores these keys as valid registered key pair.

Finally, $\mathcal{A}$ outputs a forgery of aggregate proxy signature $(m_1^*, \cdots, m_n^*, \mathcal{L} = \{y_1, \cdots, y_n\}, \sigma^*)$, such that $\sigma^*$ is a valid aggregate proxy signature with respect to $pk_o$ and $\mathcal{L}$ on message $m_1^*, \cdots, m_n^*$. It satisfies $\hat{e}(\sigma^*, g) = \prod_{i=1}^n (\hat{e}(H_1(y_i), y_o) \, \hat{e} \, (H_2(m_i^*), y_i))$. If $m_1^* = m_s$, we have $H_2(m_1^*) = g^y$ and $H_2(m_i^*) = g^{t_i}$ for $m_i \neq m_s$. Finally, $\mathcal{C}$ can compute $g^{xy} = \sigma/(\prod_{i \in \{1, \cdots, n\}} y_o^{r_i} \prod_{i \in \{1, \cdots, n\} \setminus s} y_i^{t_i})$. Otherwise, $\mathcal{C}$ aborts.

It is easy to see that if $\mathcal{A}$ outputs a forgery of APS with probability $\epsilon$, then CDH problem can be solved with probability about $\frac{1}{q_{H_2}} \cdot \epsilon$. So, we can say that the APS scheme is secure in the random oracle if CDH assumption holds.

In this paper, we only deal with the proxy signatures on behalf the same original signer. But, in many applications, the proxy signatures on behalf different signers are also practical. So, we think how to solve this question is also interesting, including its security model and scheme. We do not show details here for space.

## 4    Verifiably Encrypted Proxy Signature Scheme

Next, we show an application of APS to VEPS. Verifiably encrypted signatures (VES) are used in applications such as online contract signing [8]. However, if one of the two party is busy, they can delegate their signing power to the other party, which is called as proxy signer, to sign the contract on behalf of him or her. So, the concept of VEPS is first presented to solve this problem. From the APS, a VEPS can be easily constructed.

**Definition 5 (VEPS).** *A VEPS comprises nine algorithms: KeyGen, (D,P), PSign, PVerify, AdjKeyGen, VEPSigCreate, VEPSigVerify, and Adjudicate, provide the verifiably encrypted signature capability. The algorithms are described below. We also refer to the trusted third party as the adjudicator.*

- *KeyGen, (D,P), PSign, and PVerify are the same with their corresponding definitions in APS.*
- *AdjKeyGen. This algorithm generates key pair (ASK, APK) for the adjudicator.*
- *VEPSigCreate. Given a proxy signing key $sk_p$, message $m$, adjudicator's public key APK, it outputs the verifiably encrypted proxy signature $\sigma$.*
- *VEPSigVerify. Given original public key $pk_o$, proxy signer's public key $pk_i$, a message $m$, an adjudicator's public key APK, and a signature $\sigma$, verify if $\sigma$ is a valid verifiably encrypted proxy signature on $m$.*
- *Adjudicate. Given an adjudicator's secret key ASK, and a verifiably encrypted proxy signature $\sigma$ on some message $m$, extract and output $\sigma'$, an ordinary proxy signature on $m$ of proxy signer $pk_i$ on behalf of $pk_o$.*

We require three security properties of VEPS: validity, unforgeability, and opacity, which is similar to [3].

- Validity requires that ordinary proxy signature verify, verifiably encrypted proxy signatures verify, and that adjudicated verifiably encrypted signatures verify, i.e., that PVerify(m,PSign(m)), VESigVerify(m,VESigCreate(m)) and PVerify(m,Adjudicate(VESigCreate(m))) hold for all $m$.
- There are two types of unforgeability, including delegation unforgeability and verifiably encrypted proxy signature unforgeability. Delegation unforgeability requires that it be difficult to forge a valid verifiably encrypted proxy signature of an unauthorized user. Verifiably encrypted proxy signature unforgeability requires that it be difficult to output a verifiably encrypted proxy signature by anyone else, even the original user, except the right proxy signer.
- Opacity requires that it be difficult, given a VEPS, to extract an ordinary proxy signature on the same message, given access to a VEPS creation oracle and an adjudication oracle, maybe along with a hash (random) oracle. The opacity can easily be achieved in our construction based on the assumption that given an APS of $n$ signatures it is difficult to extract the individual proxy signatures.

Let $G$ be a bilinear group where $|G| = p$. Define a bilinear map $\hat{e} : G \times G \rightarrow G_1$. Meanwhile, define two collision-resistant hash functions $H_1 : \{0,1\}^* \rightarrow G$ and $H_2 : \{0,1\}^* \rightarrow G$. The system parameters are params=$(G, G_1, \hat{e}, g, H_1, H_2)$.

1. **KenGen.** For original signer, it picks $x_o \in Z_p$ and outputs $(x_o, y_o = g^{x_o})$ as its key pair. The original signer's secret key is $x_o$ and the public key is $y_o$.
2. **D.** In order to delegate his signing capability to user with registered public key pair $(x, y = g^x)$, then original signer, on input $y$, computes $S = [H_1(y)]^{x_o}$ as the corresponding delegation.
3. **P.** Given $S$, the user computes its proxy signing key as $sk_p = (x, S)$.
4. **PSign.** Assume the proxy signer wants to generate proxy signature on message $m$ on behalf of original signer with public key $y_o$. It computes the proxy signature $\sigma = S \cdot [H_2(m)]^x$.

5. **PVerify.** On input $\sigma$, a message $m$ and $y_o, y$, accept if $\hat{e}(\sigma, g) = \hat{e}(H_1(y), y_o)$ $\hat{e}$ $(H_2(m), y)$.
6. **AdjKeyGen.** For adjudicator, it picks $x_a \in Z_p$ and outputs $(x_a, y_a = g^{x_a})$ as its key pair. The adjudicator's secret key is $x_a$ and the public key is $y_a$.
7. **VEPSigCreate.** Given a proxy signing key $sk_p = (x, S)$, a message $m \in \{0,1\}^*$, and adjudicator's public key $y_a$, it signs as follows:

   a. Compute $h = H_2(m)$, where $h \in G$, and $\sigma = h^x \cdot S$.
   b. Select $r$ at random from $Z_p$, set $u = g^r$ and compute $\sigma' = (y_a)^r$.
   c. Aggregate $\sigma$ and $\sigma'$ as $\omega = \sigma\sigma'$.

   Finally, the verifiably encrypted proxy signature is the pair $(\omega, u)$. (This can also be viewed as ElGamal encryption of $\sigma$ under the adjudicator's key.)
8. **VEPSigVerify.** Given public keys $y_o, y$, a message $m$, adjudicator's public key $y_a$, and a verifiably encrypted proxy signature $(\omega, u)$, set $h = H_2(m)$; accept if $\hat{e}(\omega, g) = \hat{e}(y_o, H_1(y)) \cdot \hat{e}(y, h) \cdot \hat{e}(u, y_a)$ holds.
9. **Adjudicate.** Given adjudicator's private key $x_a$, and a verifiably encrypted proxy signature $(\omega, u)$ on some message $m$, ensure that the verifiably encrypted proxy signature is valid by running algorithm VEPSigVerify; then output the proxy signature $\sigma = \omega/u^{x_a}$.

### 4.1   Security Results

Our VEPS scheme depends on the assumption that given an aggregate signature of $k$ signatures it is difficult to extract the individual signatures. We posit that it is difficult to recover the individual signatures $\sigma_i$ given their aggregate $\sigma$, and the messages. In fact, for the VEPS is only constructed from an aggregate proxy signature of 2 proxy signatures, its security can be reduced to the following problem [3].

**Definition 6.** *Given $g^a, g^b, g^x, g^y$, and $g^{ax+by} \in G$, it is hard to output the value $g^{ax}$.*

In the bilinear aggregate proxy signature scheme, it is difficult to extract individual proxy signatures, under the aggregate extraction assumption [3]. For more details, the reader can be referred to [3]. We can get the following two security results easily from the security of APS with the above aggregate extraction problem [3]:

**Theorem 3.** *In random oracle model, the VEPS scheme is unforgeable (delegation unforgeable and verifiably encrypted proxy signature unforgeable) if CDH assumption holds in bilinear groups.*

**Theorem 4.** *In random oracle model, the VEPS scheme achieves opacity if CDH assumption holds in bilinear groups.*

# 5   Conclusion

In this paper we introduce the notion and security model of APS, which allows to compress the proxy signatures on different messages from different proxy signers into one. Meanwhile, a concrete APS scheme is presented, and it can be proved to be secure in the security model. Additionally, as an application of APS, the concept of verifiably encrypted proxy signature is also proposed in this paper, which can be used in contract signing. It allows the original signer to delegate another to signing the contract. A VEPS construction is also derived from the APS and can be easily proved to be secure from the properties of the corresponding APS.

# References

1. Boldyreva, A., Palacio, A., Warinschi, B.: Secure Proxy Signature Schemes for Delegation of Signing Rights. Cryptology ePrint Archive, Report 2003/096 (2003), available at http://eprint.iacr.org
2. Boneh, D., Lynn, B., Shacham, H.: Short Signatures from the Weil Pairing. In: Boyd, C. (ed.) ASIACRYPT 2001. LNCS, vol. 2248, pp. 514–532. Springer, Heidelberg (2001)
3. Boneh, D., Gentry, C., Shacham, H., Lynn, B.: Aggregate and verifiably encrypted signatures from bilinear maps. In: Biham, E. (ed.) EUROCRPYT 2003. LNCS, vol. 2656, pp. 416–432. Springer, Heidelberg (2003)
4. Gentry, C., Ramzan, Z.: Identity-Based Aggregate Signatures. In: Yung, M., Dodis, Y., Kiayias, A., Malkin, T.G. (eds.) PKC 2006. LNCS, vol. 3958, pp. 257–273. Springer, Heidelberg (2006)
5. Huang, X., Mu, Y., Susilo, W., Zhang, F., Chen, X.: A Short Proxy Signature Scheme: Efficient Authentication in the Ubiquitous World. In: EUC Workshops, pp. 480–489. Springer, Heidelberg (2005)
6. Kang, B.G., Park, J.H., Hahn, S.G.: A Certificate-Based Signature Scheme. In: Okamoto, T. (ed.) CT-RSA 2004. LNCS, vol. 2964, pp. 99–111. Springer, Heidelberg (2004)
7. Li, J., Wang, Y.: A short provably secure proxy signature scheme. Chinese Journal of Electronics 15(4), 721–724 (2006)
8. Mambo, M., Usuda, K., Okamoto, E.: Proxy signatures for delegating signing operation. In: Proceedings of the 3rd ACM Conference on Computer and Communications Security (CCS), pp. 48–57. ACM Press, New York (1996)
9. Malkin, S., Obana, S., Yung, M.: The hierarchy of key evolving signatures and a characterization of proxy signatures. In: Cachin, C., Camenisch, J.L. (eds.) EUROCRYPT 2004. LNCS, vol. 3027, pp. 306–322. Springer, Heidelberg (2004)
10. Neuman, B.C.: Proxy based authorization and accounting for distributed systems. In: Proceedings of the 13th International Conference on Distributed Computing Systems, pp. 283–291 (1993)
11. Wang, G., Bao, F., Zhou, J., Deng, R.H.: Security Analysis of Some Proxy Signatures. In: Lim, J.-I., Lee, D.-H. (eds.) ICISC 2003. LNCS, vol. 2971, pp. 305–319. Springer, Heidelberg (2004)
12. Wang, H.X., Pieprzyk, J.: Efficient One-time proxy signatures. In: Laih, C.-S. (ed.) ASIACRYPT 2003. LNCS, vol. 2894, pp. 507–522. Springer, Heidelberg (2003)
13. Zhu, H., Bao, F., Li, T., Wu, Y.: Sequential aggregate signatures for wireless routing protocols. In: IEEE WCNC 2005, pp. 2436–2439 (2005)

# Formal Security Treatments for Signatures from Identity-Based Encryption

Yang Cui[1], Eiichiro Fujisaki[2], Goichiro Hanaoka[1],
Hideki Imai[1], and Rui Zhang[1]

[1] Research Center for Information Security (RCIS),
National Institute of Advanced Industrial Science and Technology (AIST), Japan
{y-cui,hanaoka-goichiro,h-imai,r-zhang}@aist.go.jp
[2] NTT Information Sharing Platform Laboratories, NTT Corporation, Japan
fujisaki.eiichiro@lab.ntt.co.jp

**Abstract.** In a seminal paper of identity based encryption (IBE), Boneh and Franklin [4] mentioned an interesting transform from an IBE scheme to a signature scheme, which was observed by Naor. In this paper, we give formal security treatments for this transform and discover several implications and separations among security notions of IBE and transformed signature. For example, we show for such a successful transform, one-wayness of IBE is an essential condition. Additionally, we give a sufficient and necessary condition for converting a semantically secure IBE scheme into an existentially unforgeable signature scheme. Our results help establish strategies on design and automatic security proof of signature schemes from (possibly weak) IBE schemes. We also show some separation results which strongly support that one-wayness, rather than semantic security, of IBE captures an essential condition to achieve secure signature.

## 1 Introduction

*Identity-based encryption* (IBE) [17,4] is a public key encryption scheme where a user's public key can be any bit string, such as an email address. Although IBE was originally advocated to simplify public key certificate management, it has now been shown a powerful tool constructing various cryptographic applications: key-insulated encryption, forward secure encryption and public key encryption with keyword search , etc. In this paper, we investigate another application of IBE, whose observation was attributed to Naor, saying that *"an IBE scheme can immediately be converted into a public key signature scheme"* [4].

In IBE, a *private key generator* (PKG) uses his master key $msk$ to issue a decryption key $d$ which corresponds to an arbitrary bit string "ID". Here, $msk$ can also be seen as a signing key of the PKG, and by letting ID $= M$ ($M$ is a message), $d$ becomes the PKG's signature for $M$. The signature verification can be done by checking if $d$ functions properly as a correct decryption key for identity "$M$" by encrypting a random plaintext and checking if the ciphertext can be decrypted to the original plaintext. We hereafter call this transformation

W. Susilo, J.K. Liu, and Y. Mu. (Eds.): ProvSec 2007, LNCS 4784, pp. 218–227, 2007.

the *Naor Transform* (NT), and denote $NT(\Pi)$ as a signature scheme derived from an IBE scheme $\Pi$ via NT (A detailed description is give in Sec. 3).

## 1.1 IBE and Naor-Transformed Signatures

**IBE.** Boneh and Franklin [4] defined the security model and proposed the first full-fledged IBE, using bilinear maps and assuming random oracles. Independently, Cocks [9] also presented an IBE scheme based on the decisional quadratic residue assumption. Gentry and Silverberg [12] generalized the model of IBE with a hierarchical structure, and proposed hierarchical IBE (HIBE) schemes. Canetti, Halevi, and Katz [7] proposed an IBE whose security can be proven without random oracles but in a weaker security notion, called the selective-ID (sID) model [7]. Interestingly, sID IBE implies chosen ciphertext security (CCA) [15,16,8]. IBE The first fully secure (adaptively chosen ID secure) IBE system without random oracles was presented [3]. Waters [18] subsequently simplified the scheme from [3]. Recently, Gentry [11] presented a more efficient scheme with tight security reduction, relying on a stronger assumption.

**Naor-Transfromed Signatures.** Boneh, Lynn, and Shacham applied NT to the Boneh-Franklin IBE [4], and proposed the famous short signature [5]. Gentry and Silverberg proposed a hierarchical identity-based signature (HIBS) scheme from their HIBE scheme via NT [12]. Furthermore, Waters [18] presented the first (efficient) signature scheme whose security can be reduced to hardness of the computational Diffie-Hellman (CDH) problem. A subsequent paper [6] strengthened the Waters signature to have strong unforgeability.

Boneh and Franklin [4], and Waters [18] remarked (in an informal way) the security of Naor-transformed signatures: "*If IBE is semantically secure against adaptive chosen identity and adaptive chosen ciphertext attacks (*IND-ID-CCA*) [4], then the signature scheme is existentially unforgeable against adaptive chosen message attacks (*UF-CMA*) [14]*".

Posed a deeper consideration, the statement is *true*, yet with some subtle aspects that we later clarify. More importantly, since we are interested in "generic" applications of NT, we further wonder whether this statement admits of a broader interpretation. Namely, we would like to ask, for example, the following question: *What are sufficient and/or necessary conditions for underlying IBE to achieve* UF-CMA *signature?* Previous rich body of research on IBE seems not to have ready answers for such kind of "general questions". In particular, it should be noted that the security of signatures from [5,12,18,6] was analyzed individually and was very specific to their schemes.

## 1.2 Our Contributions

The main theoretical results are relations among security notions for IBE and signature, which are depicted in Figure 1. Our results help understand both primitive better, especially on the nature of a signature scheme with a randomized verification algorithm, which was rarely studied before. Throughout this paper,

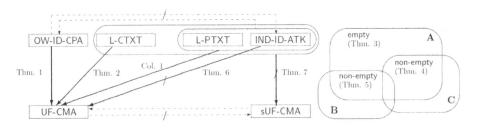

Solid arrows denote implication and separation with respect to the NT with a single varication, where the symbol "$_{NT}$" is omitted in the above figure for simplicity, and ATK $\in$ {CPA, CCA}. Dotted arrows denote trivial implications or separations. **A**, **B**, and **C** denote {$\Pi|\Pi$ is IND-ID-CPA $\wedge$ $NT(\Pi)$ is UF-CMA}, {$\Pi|\Pi$ is L-PTXT}, and {$\Pi|\Pi$ is L-CTXT}, respectively.

**Fig. 1.** Relations among Security notions for IBE and Signature

we limit our scope within only basic NT with a *single* encrypt-then-decrypt verification for some reasons (See Sec. 3). As an important remark, some of our separation results may not hold if one considers other verification procedures. Especially, IND-ID-CPA implies UF-CMA if iterative encrypt-then-decrypt verification is introduced.

Let "$X \rightarrow_{NT} Y$" denote "a signature scheme $NT(\Pi)$ always satisfies condition $Y$ if an IBE scheme $\Pi$ satisfies condition $X$", "$X \nrightarrow_{NT} Y$" denote "there exists $\Pi$ such that $NT(\Pi)$ may not satisfy $Y$ even if $\Pi$ satisfies $X$", and OW-ID-CPA (resp. IND-ID-CPA) [4] denotes one-wayness (resp. semantic security) against adaptive chosen identity and adaptive chosen plaintext attacks.

**Implications.** We show implications among notions for IBE and signature. We notice that most of the time, even very weak IBE implies strong digital signature. These supports the belief that IBE is a significantly stronger cryptographic primitive than signature.

1. OW-ID-CPA $\rightarrow_{NT}$ UF-CMA (Theorem 1). This is, strongly secure signatures can be derived from considerablyweak IBE schemes. An immediate corollary states that IND-ID-CPA $\wedge$ L-PTXT $\rightarrow_{NT}$ UF-CMA (Corollary 1), where we say $\Pi$ satisfies L-PTXT if $1/|\mathcal{M}|$ is negligible ($\mathcal{M}$ and $|\mathcal{M}|$ are the message space of $\Pi$ and the cardinality of $\mathcal{M}$, respectively).
2. L-CTXT $\rightarrow_{NT}$ UF-CMA (Theorem 2). Roughly speaking, $\Pi$ satisfies condition L-CTXT if it is even hard to generate a "fake key" (without using PKG's master key) which maps a randomly chosen valid ciphertext onto $\mathcal{M}$. See Def. 4 for details. It is not difficult to determine whether an IBE scheme satisfies L-CTXT or not.
3. If $\Pi$ is GOAL-ID-ATK and $NT(\Pi)$ is UF-CMA, then $\Pi$ satisfies L-PTXT $\vee$ L-CTXT (Theorem 3), where GOAL $\in$ {OW, IND} and ATK $\in$ {CPA, CCA}. This implies L-PTXT $\vee$ L-CTXT is necessary and sufficient condition to achieve UF-CMA from IND-ID-CPA. It should be also noted that $\Pi$ is not required to have a large message space if it satisfies L-CTXT.
4. There exists $\Pi$ such that $\Pi$ and $NT(\Pi)$ satisfy IND-ID-CPA $\wedge$ $\neg$L-PTXT and UF-CMA, respectively (Theorem 4). On the other hand, there exists

$\Pi$ such that $\Pi$ and $NT(\Pi)$ satisfy IND-ID-CPA $\wedge$ ¬L-CTXT and UF-CMA, respectively (Theorem 5).

**Separations.** We also show separations among security notions, which as usual, are demonstrated by counterexamples. However, these counterexamples are quite natural and non-trivial, which we believe form good guidance in building practical signature schemes from IBE.

5. IND-ID-CCA $\not\rightarrow_{NT}$ UF-CMA (Theorem 6). This implies that $NT(\Pi)$ is not always secure even if $\Pi$ satisfies the strongest security (i.e. IND-ID-CCA) for IBE. Actually, the separation is demonstrated by constructing various IND-ID-CCA secure IBE schemes that satisfy ¬L-PTXT $\wedge$ ¬L-CTXT. It should be noticed that it is easy to achieve L-PTXT from IND-ID-CCA IBE by a simple modification: just enlarge the input plaintext domain by encrypting in parallel. However, this modification is considered as a method to acquire one-wayness from semantic security, and this fact supports our first result "OW-ID-CPA $\rightarrow_{NT}$ UF-CMA", which establishes an essential relation between IBE and signatures.
6. IND-ID-CCA $\wedge$ L-PTXT $\wedge$ L-CTXT $\not\rightarrow_{NT}$ sUF-CMA (Theorem 7). Interestingly, this shows even the strongest IBE does not imply sUF-CMA secure Naor-transformed signature. This immediately implies that OW-ID-CPA$\not\rightarrow_{NT}$ sUF-CMA. Here, roughly speaking, sUF-CMA [1] means inability of adversaries to forge any signature even for any message signed before.

**Applications.** The first application is to provide automatic proof for signature schemes derived from IBE via NT. In the future, if a new IBE scheme is designed, a signature scheme corresponding to this IBE scheme will be constructed automatically with a proof. However, we note that our security proof may afford a price of a possibly stronger assumption. As another important application, one can relax requirements for a secure channel between a user and PKG. In an IBE system, each user's decryption key has to be securely transferred from PKG, therefore, a secure channel is needed. However, a user's decryption key can be also considered as PKG's signature based on NT, and consequently, only a channel with confidentiality is required for PKG.

## 2   Definitions

Define $x \xleftarrow{R} X$ as $x$ being generated randomly and uniformly from a finite set $X$. If $A$ is an algorithm, $x \leftarrow A$ means that the output of $A$ is $x$. When $y$ is not a finite set nor an algorithm, $x \leftarrow y$ is an assignment operation. $|\cdot|$ is defined as the bit length if "·" is an element of a finite set (respectively, the cardinality of the set if "·" is a finite set). Let "$||$" denote string concatenation. When we say that $\epsilon(k)$ is negligible, it means that for any constant $c$ there exists $k_0 \in \mathbb{N}$, such that $\epsilon < (1/k)^c$ for any $k > k_0$.

## 2.1   Identity-Based Encryption

An identity-based encryption (IBE) scheme $\Pi$ consists of four probabilistic poly-
nomial time (PPT) algorithms: $\Pi = (\mathsf{Setup}, \mathsf{Ext}, \mathsf{Enc}, \mathsf{Dec})$. The setup algorithm
$\mathsf{Setup}$ takes as input $1^k$, and generates public system parameter $\mathsf{PK}$ and master key $\mathsf{msk}$, where $k$ is a security parameter. The key extraction algorithm $\mathsf{Ext}$
takes as input $\mathsf{msk}$, $\mathsf{ID} \in \{0,1\}^*$ and $\mathsf{PK}$, and returns the corresponding decryption key $\mathsf{SK}_{\mathsf{ID}}$. The encryption algorithm $\mathsf{Enc}$ takes as input $\mathsf{ID}$, $M \in \mathcal{M}$, $\mathsf{PK}$,
and outputs ciphertext $C \in \mathcal{C}$, where $\mathcal{M}$ and $\mathcal{C}$ are the plaintext and cipher-
text spaces, respectively. The decryption algorithm $\mathsf{Dec}$ takes as input $\mathsf{SK}_{\mathsf{ID}}$, $C$
and $\mathsf{PK}$, and outputs $M$ or $\perp$, where $\perp$ is a special symbol. We require that
for all $(\mathsf{msk}, \mathsf{PK})(= \mathsf{Setup}(1^k))$, all $\mathsf{ID}$, all $\mathsf{SK}_{\mathsf{ID}}(= \mathsf{Ext}(\mathsf{msk}, \mathsf{ID}, \mathsf{PK}))$, all $M$, and
$C(= \mathsf{Enc}(\mathsf{ID}, M, \mathsf{PK}))$, $\mathsf{Dec}(\mathsf{SK}_{\mathsf{ID}}, C, \mathsf{PK}) = M$.

**One-wayness.** We define one-wayness for IBE, i.e., OW-ID-CPA [4]. Let $\mathcal{A} =$
$(\mathcal{A}_1, \mathcal{A}_2)$ and $k$ be an adversary and the security parameter, respectively. Now
consider the following experiment:

**Experiment** $\mathsf{Exp}_{\mathcal{A},\Pi}^{\mathsf{ow\text{-}id\text{-}cpa}}(k) : [(\mathsf{PK}, \mathsf{msk}) \leftarrow \mathsf{Setup}(1^k);$

$$(\mathsf{ID}^*, s) \leftarrow \mathcal{A}_1^{\mathcal{O}_e}(\mathsf{PK}); M \xleftarrow{R} \mathcal{M}; C^* \leftarrow \mathsf{Enc}(\mathsf{ID}^*, M, \mathsf{PK});$$

$$M' \leftarrow \mathcal{A}_2^{\mathcal{O}_e}(s, C^*); \text{return } 1 \text{ if } M' = M, \text{ or } 0 \text{ otherwise}],$$

where $\mathcal{O}_e$ is a key extraction oracle which for a given identity $\mathsf{ID}$, returns $\mathsf{SK}_{\mathsf{ID}}(=$
$\mathsf{Ext}(\mathsf{msk}, \mathsf{ID}, \mathsf{PK}))$. The only restriction is that $\mathsf{ID}^*$ is not allowed to submit to
$\mathcal{O}_e$. We define $\epsilon_{owe,\mathcal{A}} = \Pr[\mathsf{Exp}_{\mathcal{A},\Pi}^{\mathsf{ow\text{-}id\text{-}cpa}}(k) = 1]$.

**Definition 1 (OW-ID-CPA).** *We say $\Pi$ is $(t, q_e, \epsilon)$-OW-ID-CPA secure if for
any adversary $\mathcal{A}$ in time bound $t$ with at most $q_e$ queries to $\mathcal{O}_e$, $\epsilon_{owe,\mathcal{A}} \leq \epsilon$. As
shorthand, we say that $\Pi$ is OW-ID-CPA secure if $\epsilon$ is negligible.*

**Indistinguishability.** Semantic security [13] for IBE, i.e. IND-ID-ATK [4] where
$\mathsf{ATK} \in \{\mathsf{CPA}, \mathsf{CCA}\}$, is defined as follows. Let $\mathcal{A} = (\mathcal{A}_1, \mathcal{A}_2)$ and $k$ be an adversary and the security parameter, respectively. For $\mathsf{atk} \in \{\mathsf{cpa}, \mathsf{cca}\}$, consider the
following experiment:

**Experiment** $\mathsf{Exp}_{\mathcal{A},\Pi}^{\mathsf{ind\text{-}id\text{-}atk}}(k) : [(\mathsf{PK}, \mathsf{msk}) \leftarrow \mathsf{Setup}(1^k);$

$$(\mathsf{ID}^*, M_0, M_1, s) \leftarrow \mathcal{A}_1^{\mathcal{O}_e, \mathcal{O}_d}(\mathsf{PK}); b \xleftarrow{R} \{0,1\}; C^* \leftarrow \mathsf{Enc}(\mathsf{ID}^*, M_b, \mathsf{PK});$$

$$b' \leftarrow \mathcal{A}_2^{\mathcal{O}_e, \mathcal{O}_d}(s, C^*); \text{return } 1 \text{ if } b' = b, \text{ or } 0 \text{ otherwise}],$$

where $\mathcal{O}_e$ and its restriction are the same as the above, $\mathcal{O}_d$ is a decryption oracle
which for given $(\mathsf{ID}, C)$, returns $M(\text{or } \perp)(= \mathsf{Dec}(\mathsf{SK}_{\mathsf{ID}}, C, \mathsf{PK}))$ if $\mathsf{atk} = \mathsf{cca}$, or
a random bit string if $\mathsf{atk} = \mathsf{cpa}$. The only restriction is that $(\mathsf{ID}^*, C^*)$ is not
allowed to submit to $\mathcal{O}_d$. We define $\epsilon_{ind\text{-}atk,\mathcal{A}} = |\Pr[\mathsf{Exp}_{\mathcal{A},\Pi}^{\mathsf{ind\text{-}id\text{-}atk}}(k) = 1] - 1/2|$.

**Definition 2** (IND-ID-ATK). *We say $\Pi$ is $(t, q_e, q_d, \epsilon)$-IND-ID-CCA (resp. $(t, q_e, \epsilon)$-IND-ID-CPA) secure, if for any $\mathcal{A}$ in time bound $t$ with at most $q_e$ queries to $\mathcal{O}_e$ and $q_d$ queries to $\mathcal{O}_d$, $\epsilon_{ind\text{-}cca,\mathcal{A}} \leq \epsilon$ (resp. $\epsilon_{ind\text{-}cpa,\mathcal{A}} \leq \epsilon$). As shorthand, we say that $\Pi$ is IND-ID-CCA (resp. IND-ID-CPA) secure if $\epsilon$ is negligible.*

Above security definitions have mainly considered adaptive chosen ID (ID) attack, however one can easily adjust the definitions to selective ID (sID) attack [7]. The only difference between the two attack model is that for sID attack, the target identity $\mathsf{ID}^*$ must be selected by $\mathcal{A}$ before the key generation algorithm Setup is run.

**Largeness of Plaintext and Ciphertext Spaces.** Interestingly, security of Naor-transformed signatures is significantly influenced by sizes of the plaintext and the ciphertext spaces of the underlying IBE. In following experiments, let $\Pi = (\mathsf{Setup}, \mathsf{Ext}, \mathsf{Enc}, \mathsf{Dec})$ be an IBE scheme.

**Definition 3** (L-PTXT). *We say an IBE scheme $\Pi$ is $\gamma$-L-PTXT if $1/|\mathcal{M}| \leq \gamma$. As shorthand, we say that $\Pi$ is L-PTXT if $\gamma$ is negligible.*

Now consider the following experiment:

> **Experiment** $\mathsf{Exp}_{\mathcal{A},\Pi}^{\text{l-ctxt}}(k) : [(\mathsf{PK}, \mathsf{msk}) \leftarrow \mathsf{Setup}(1^k);$
>
> $(\mathsf{ID}^*, \mathsf{SK}'_{\mathsf{ID}^*}) \leftarrow \mathcal{A}^{\mathcal{O}_e}(\mathsf{PK}); M \xleftarrow{R} \mathcal{M}; C^* \leftarrow \mathsf{Enc}(\mathsf{ID}^*, M, \mathsf{PK});$
>
> $M' \leftarrow \mathsf{Dec}(\mathsf{SK}'_{\mathsf{ID}^*}, C^*, \mathsf{PK}); \text{return } 1 \text{ if } M' \in \mathcal{M}, \text{ or } 0 \text{ otherwise}],$

where $\mathcal{O}_e$ and its restriction are the same as the above. We define $\epsilon_{\ell\text{-}ctxt,\mathcal{A}} = \Pr[\mathsf{Exp}_{\mathcal{A},\Pi}^{\text{l-ctxt}}(k) = 1]$.

**Definition 4** (L-CTXT). *We say $\Pi$ is $(t, q_e, \epsilon)$-L-CTXT if for any $\mathcal{A}$ in time bound $t$ with at most $q_e$ queries to $\mathcal{O}_e$, $\epsilon_{\ell\text{-}ctxt,\mathcal{A}} \leq \epsilon$. As shorthand, we say that $\Pi$ is L-CTXT if $\epsilon$ is negligible.*

## 2.2 Digital Signature

**Signature.** A signature scheme $\Sigma$ consists of three PPT algorithms: $\Sigma = (\mathsf{Gen}, \mathsf{Sig}, \mathsf{Ver})$. The key generation algorithm $\mathsf{Gen}$ takes as inputs $1^k$, and generates signing key $\mathsf{SigK}$ and verification key $\mathsf{VK}$. The signing algorithm $\mathsf{Sig}$ takes as inputs $\mathsf{SigK}$, $m \in \{0,1\}^*$, and $\mathsf{VK}$, and outputs $(\sigma, m)$, where $m$ is a message to be signed. The verification algorithm $\mathsf{Ver}$ takes as inputs $\mathsf{VK}$, $\sigma'$, and $m'$, and outputs accept or reject. We require that for all $(\mathsf{SigK}, \mathsf{VK})(= \mathsf{Gen}(1^k))$, all $m$, all $(\sigma, m)(= \mathsf{Sig}(\mathsf{SigK}, m, \mathsf{VK}))$, we have $\mathsf{Ver}(\mathsf{VK}, \sigma, m) = \text{accept}$.

**Unforgeability.** Here, we define unforgeability for signature UF-CMA [14], and its stronger version, sUF-CMA [1]. Let $\Sigma = (\mathsf{Gen}, \mathsf{Sig}, \mathsf{Ver})$ be a signature scheme.

Let $\mathcal{A}$ and $k$ be an adversary and the security parameter, respectively. For goal $\in \{\mathsf{uf}, \mathsf{suf}\}$, consider the following experiment:

**Experiment** $\mathsf{Exp}_{\mathcal{A}, \Sigma}^{\mathsf{goal\text{-}cma}}(k) : [(\mathsf{SigK}, \mathsf{VK}) \leftarrow \mathsf{Gen}(1^k);$

$$(\sigma^*, m^*) \leftarrow \mathcal{A}^{\mathcal{O}_s}(\mathsf{PK}); \text{return } \mathsf{Ver}(\mathsf{VK}, \sigma^*, m^*)],$$

where $\mathcal{O}_s$ is a signing oracle which for a given message $m$, returns $(\sigma, m)$. The only restriction is that $m^*$ is not allowed to submit to $\mathcal{O}_s$ if goal $= \mathsf{uf}$, or that $(\sigma^*, m^*)$ is not allowed to be one of responses from $\mathcal{O}_s$ if goal $= \mathsf{suf}$. We define $\epsilon_{goal\text{-}cma, \mathcal{A}} = \Pr[\mathsf{Exp}_{\mathcal{A}, \Sigma}^{\mathsf{goal\text{-}cma}}(k) = \mathtt{accept}]$ for goal $\in \{\mathsf{uf}, \mathsf{suf}\}$.

**Definition 5 ((s)UF-CMA).** *We say $\Sigma$ is $(t, q_s, \epsilon)$-UF-CMA (resp. sUF-CMA) if for any $\mathcal{A}$ in time bound $t$ with at most $q_s$ queries to $\mathcal{O}_s$, $\epsilon_{uf\text{-}cma, \mathcal{A}} \leq \epsilon$ (resp. $\epsilon_{suf\text{-}cma, \mathcal{A}} \leq \epsilon$). As shorthand, we say that $\Sigma$ is UF-CMA (resp. sUF-CMA) secure if $\epsilon$ is negligible.*

## 3   A Generic Conversion from IBE to Signature

Let $\Pi = (\mathsf{Setup}, \mathsf{Ext}, \mathsf{Enc}, \mathsf{Dec})$ be an IBE scheme. Then, a Naor-transformed signature scheme $NT(\Pi) = (\mathsf{Gen}, \mathsf{Sig}, \mathsf{Ver})$ consists of three algorithms, which are depicted in Table 1.

**Table 1.** Algorithms of $NT(\Pi)$

| Algorithm $\mathsf{Gen}(1^k)$ | Algorithm $\mathsf{Sig}(\mathsf{SigK}, m, \mathsf{VK})$ | Algorithm $\mathsf{Ver}(\mathsf{VK}, \sigma, m)$ |
|---|---|---|
| $(\mathsf{PK}, \mathsf{msk}) \leftarrow \mathsf{Setup}(1^k);$ | $\mathsf{ID} \leftarrow m;$ | $\mathsf{ID} \leftarrow m; \mathsf{SK}'_{\mathsf{ID}} \leftarrow \sigma; M \xleftarrow{R} \mathcal{M};$ |
| $\mathsf{SigK} \leftarrow \mathsf{msk};$ | $\mathsf{SK}_{\mathsf{ID}} \leftarrow \mathsf{Ext}(\mathsf{SigK}, \mathsf{ID}, \mathsf{VK});$ | $C \leftarrow \mathsf{Enc}(\mathsf{ID}, M, \mathsf{VK});$ |
| $\mathsf{VK} \leftarrow \mathsf{PK};$ | $\sigma \leftarrow \mathsf{SK}_{\mathsf{ID}};$ | $M' \leftarrow \mathsf{Dec}(\mathsf{SK}'_{\mathsf{ID}}, C, \mathsf{VK});$ |
| return $(\mathsf{SigK}, \mathsf{VK})$ | return $(\sigma, m)$ | if $M' = M$, return $\mathtt{accept};$ |
| | | else      return $\mathtt{reject}$ |

NT can be also extended to other types of IBE schemes. For example, applying NT to an $(\ell+1)$-level HIBE scheme [12], one gains an $\ell$-level HIBS scheme. Applying NT to an sID secure IBE scheme [7,2], a signature scheme with "selective unforgeability" is then acquired. In this paper, we regard the above transformation as Naor Transform (NT), since it is the most natural and basic formalization of the intuitive explanation of [4] and [18]. We also discuss some variants of NT in the full paper [10].

## 4   Implication Results

Denote the IBE scheme $\Pi$ and a corresponding signature $NT(\Pi)$ as $\Pi = (\mathsf{Setup}, \mathsf{Ext}, \mathsf{Enc}, \mathsf{Dec})$ and $NT(\Pi) = (\mathsf{Gen}, \mathsf{Sig}, \mathsf{Ver})$. We present several theorems regarding implications among security definitions regarding $\Pi$ and $NT(\Pi)$. For the limitation of space, the proofs are given in the full paper [10].

**Theorem 1** (OW-ID-CPA $\rightarrow_{NT}$ UF-CMA). *If an IBE scheme $\Pi$ is $(t+O(\tau), q, \epsilon)$-OW-ID-CPA secure, $NT(\Pi)$ is $(t, q, \epsilon)$-UF-CMA secure. Here $\tau$ is the upper bound of time for one decryption operation.*

**Corollary 1** (IND-ID-CPA $\wedge$ L-PTXT $\rightarrow_{NT}$ UF-CMA ). *If an IBE scheme $\Pi$ is $(t+O(\tau), q, \frac{\epsilon-\gamma}{2-2\gamma})$-IND-ID-CPA secure and $\gamma$-L-PTXT, then $NT(\Pi)$ is $(t, q, \epsilon)$-UF-CMA secure. Here, $\tau$ is the upper bound of time for one decryption operation.*

One may wonder in order to build a secure signature $NT(\Pi)$ from semantically secure IBE $\Pi$ that is not L-PTXT, whether one has to first enlarge the plaintext space, e.g., by adopting interactive verifications. However, this is sometimes unnecessary. L-CTXT alone implies $NT(\Pi)$ is UF-CMA secure, namely,

**Theorem 2** (L-CTXT $\rightarrow_{NT}$ UF-CMA). *If IBE $\Pi$ is $(t, q, \epsilon)$-L-CTXT secure, then $NT(\Pi)$ is $(t, q, \epsilon)$-UF-CMA secure.*

The following theorem implies L-CTXT is a "properly correct" condition for IBE schemes to derive secure signatures. More precisely, L-CTXT $\vee$ L-PTXT is a necessary and sufficient condition for extracting UF-CMA secure signature from IND-ID-CPA secure IBE.

**Theorem 3.** *If IBE $\Pi$ is GOAL-ID-ATK secure (GOAL$\in\{$OW,IND$\}$, ATK$\in\{$CPA,CCA$\}$) and $NT(\Pi)$ is UF-CMA secure, then $\Pi$ always satisfies L-PTXT or L-CTXT.*

The following theorem shows L-CTXT is actually a natural and sufficiently weak notion. Many weak IBE schemes actually meet L-CTXT.

**Theorem 4.** *There exists an IBE scheme $\Pi$ such that $\Pi$ and $NT(\Pi)$ satisfy IND-ID-CPA $\wedge$ ¬L-PTXT and UF-CMA, respectively.*

**Theorem 5.** *There exists an IBE scheme $\Pi$ such that $\Pi$ and $NT(\Pi)$ satisfy IND-ID-CPA $\wedge$ ¬L-CTXT and UF-CMA, respectively.*

# 5   Separation Results

Here, we show impossibility of proving UF-CMA security of Naor-transformed signatures (with a single verification) solely based on indistinguishability of underlying IBE. This result supports that indistinguishability is not an essential requirement to provide secure Naor-transformed signatures but one-wayness is. For the limitation of space, the proofs are left to the full paper [10].

**Theorem 6** (IND-ID-CCA $\nrightarrow_{NT}$ UF-CMA). *There exists an IND-ID-CCA secure IBE scheme $\Pi$ such that $NT(\Pi)$ is not UF-CMA secure.*

In addition, we present separation results on the relation among security notions for IBE and sUF-CMA security of signature, even if this IBE meets both L-PTXT and L-CTXT.

**Theorem 7** (IND-ID-CCA $\wedge$ L-PTXT $\wedge$ L-CTXT $\nrightarrow_{NT}$ sUF-CMA). *There exists* IND-ID-CCA *secure IBE* $\Pi$, *such that* $\Pi$ *is both* L-PTXT *and* L-CTXT, *but* $NT(\Pi)$ *is not* sUF-CMA *secure.*

# References

1. An, J.H., Dodis, Y., Rabin, T.: On the Security of Joint Signature and Encryption. In: Knudsen, L.R. (ed.) EUROCRYPT 2002. LNCS, vol. 2332, pp. 83–107. Springer, Heidelberg (2002)
2. Boneh, D., Boyen, X.: Efficient Selective-ID Secure Identity-Based Encryption Without Random Oracles. In: Cachin, C., Camenisch, J.L. (eds.) EUROCRYPT 2004. LNCS, vol. 3027, pp. 223–238. Springer, Heidelberg (2004)
3. Boneh, D., Boyen, X.: Secure Identity Based Encryption Without Random Oracles. In: Franklin, M. (ed.) CRYPTO 2004. LNCS, vol. 3152, pp. 443–459. Springer, Heidelberg (2004)
4. Boneh, D., Franklin, M.: Identity-Based Encryption from the Weil Pairing. In: Kilian, J. (ed.) CRYPTO 2001. LNCS, vol. 2139, pp. 213–229. Springer, Heidelberg (2001)
5. Boneh, D., Lynn, B., Shacham, H.: Short Signatures from the Weil Pairing. In: Boyd, C. (ed.) ASIACRYPT 2001. LNCS, vol. 2248, pp. 514–532. Springer, Heidelberg (2001)
6. Boneh, D., Shen, E., Waters, B.: Strongly Unforgeable Signatures Based on Computational Diffie-Hellman. In: Yung, M., Dodis, Y., Kiayias, A., Malkin, T.G. (eds.) PKC 2006. LNCS, vol. 3958, pp. 229–240. Springer, Heidelberg (2006)
7. Canetti, R., Halevi, S., Katz, J.: A Forward Secure Public Key Encryption Scheme. In: Biham, E. (ed.) EUROCRPYT 2003. LNCS, vol. 2656, pp. 255–271. Springer, Heidelberg (2003)
8. Canetti, R., Halevi, S., Katz, J.: Chosen-Ciphertext Security from Identity-Based Encryption. In: Cachin, C., Camenisch, J.L. (eds.) EUROCRYPT 2004. LNCS, vol. 3027, pp. 207–222. Springer, Heidelberg (2004)
9. Cocks, C.: An Identity Based Encryption Scheme Based on Quadratic Residues. In: Honary, B. (ed.) IMA 2001. LNCS, vol. 2260, pp. 360–363. Springer, Heidelberg (2001)
10. Cui, Y., Fujisaki, E., Hanaoka, G., Imai, H., Zhang, R.: Formal Security Treatments for IBE-to-Signature Transformation: Relations among Security Notions. Full version of this paper, available as Eprint Report 2007/030.
11. Gentry, C.: Practical Identity-Based Encryption Without Random Oracles. In: Vaudenay, S. (ed.) EUROCRYPT 2006. LNCS, vol. 4004, pp. 445–464. Springer, Heidelberg (2006)
12. Gentry, C., Silverberg, A.: Hierarchical ID-Based Cryptography. In: Zheng, Y. (ed.) ASIACRYPT 2002. LNCS, vol. 2501, pp. 548–566. Springer, Heidelberg (2002)
13. Goldwasser, S., Micali, S.: Probabilistic encryption. Journal of Computer Security 28, 270–299 (1984)
14. Goldwasser, S., Micali, S., Rivest, R.: A Digital Signature Scheme Secure Against Adaptive Chosen-Message Attacks. SIAM Journal of Computing 17(2), 281–308 (1988)
15. Naor, M., Yung, M.: Public-Key Cryptosystems Provably-Secure against Chosen-Ciphertext Attacks. In: STOC 1990, pp. 427–437 (1990)

16. Rackoff, C., Simon, D.: Non-interactive Zero-knowledge Proof of Knowledge and Chosen Ciphertext Attack. In: Feigenbaum, J. (ed.) CRYPTO 1991. LNCS, vol. 576, pp. 433–444. Springer, Heidelberg (1992)
17. Shamir, A.: Identity-Based Cryptosystems and Signature Schemes. In: Blakely, G.R., Chaum, D. (eds.) CRYPTO 1984. LNCS, vol. 196, pp. 47–53. Springer, Heidelberg (1985)
18. Waters, B.: Efficient Identity-Based Encryption Without Random Oracles. In: Cramer, R.J.F. (ed.) EUROCRYPT 2005. LNCS, vol. 3494, pp. 114–127. Springer, Heidelberg (2005)

# Decryptable Searchable Encryption

Thomas Fuhr[1] and Pascal Paillier[2]

[1] Direction Centrale de la Sécurité des Systèmes d'Information
thomas.fuhr@sgdn.pm.gouv.fr
[2] Cryptography & Innovation, Gemalto Security Labs
pascal.paillier@gemalto.com

**Abstract.** As such, public-key encryption with keyword search (a.k.a
PEKS or searchable encryption) does not allow the recipient to decrypt
keywords *i.e.* encryption is not invertible. This paper introduces searchable encryption schemes which enable decryption. An additional feature
is that the decryption key and the trapdoor derivation key are *totally independent*, thereby complying with many contexts of application. We put
forward a seemingly optimal construction for decryptable searchable encryption which makes use of one KEM, one IDKEM and a couple of hash
functions. We define a proper security model for decryptable searchable
encryption and show that basic security requirements on the underlying
KEM and IDKEM are enough for our generic construction to be strongly
secure in the random oracle model.

## 1 Introduction

*Background.* Among the most recent developments of public-key cryptography,
the mechanisms for ID-based encryption [19,5,6,13,3] and public-key encryption
with keyword search (PEKS) have become increasingly attractive thanks to their
connections with many other (still unsolved) design issues. It seems that the
idea of encryption with keyword search, also known as *searchable encryption* [4],
appeared as a natural application of what one could achieve with bilinear maps,
which already provided the basis for ID-based encryption. A more recent work
[1] shows that these mechanisms are intimately related in the sense that they
are induced by a common primitive known as an anonymous IDKEM [8].

Informally, a searchable encryption $c$ of a keyword $w$ can only be tested by the
recipient who uses her private key to detect whether $c$ matches $w$ or not. This
ability is transferrable to anyone under the form of a keyword-specific trapdoor
$\mathsf{T}(w)$ which enables the search for encryptions of $w$. In a typical application of
searchable encryption, the entity holding $\mathsf{T}(w)$ receives lots of encrypted keywords and filters out encryptions of $w' \neq w$. Searchable encryption, as currently
achieved, does not require ciphertexts to be decryptable.

*Our Contributions.* This paper introduces searchable encryption schemes that
enable decryption. We mention that the decryption key and the trapdoor derivation key are independent of each other, thereby complying with various contexts

W. Susilo, J.K. Liu, and Y. Mu. (Eds.): ProvSec 2007, LNCS 4784, pp. 228–236, 2007.

of application. We put forward a generic construction for decryptable searchable encryption. To achieve our goal, we make use of generic cryptographic primitives such as key encapsulation mechanisms (a.k.a. KEMs) [10] and identity-based versions of KEMs (IDKEMs). Our construction also employs a couple of hash functions. We define a proper security model for decryptable searchable encryption and investigate under which security requirements on the underlying KEM and IDKEM blocks our construction yields a maximally secure scheme. All security proofs considered in this paper stand in the random oracle model.

*Applications of Our Work.* Decryptable searchable encryption (DSE for short) extends the notion of PEKS and may therefore be used in every single application of PEKS. We may also find applications in the management of encrypted databases. In particular, since the decryption key and the trapdoor derivation key are generated independently from one another, data can be decrypted by an entity and trapdoors be generated by some other party. An illustrative example of this feature is as follows. Assume Bob is a telephone operator, Alice a subscriber, Charlie a state agency and Daniel a police inspector whose role consists in identifying subscribers belonging to the Mafia. Assume that Bob stores Alice's telephone statement encrypted with DSE, and that the decryption key belongs to Alice and the trapdoor derivation key belongs to Charlie. Alice is the only person who can decrypt it, but Charlie can issue trapdoors for some phone numbers and give them to Daniel to help him find out whether Alice is connected to the Mafia, without learning anything about the other numbers Alice has called. The same scenario is applicable to the secure management of money transfers, wherein a maximal level of secrecy about account numbers involved in transactions is guaranteed, while leaving to a designated authority the ability to trace encrypted transactions made to or from well-identified bank accounts.

*Outline.* We start in Section 2 by a number of definitional facts about KEMs and IDKEMs. Section 3 describes our generic construction and provides a security analysis. Section 4 provides an example of instantiation based on ElGamal and BDOP [4]. Section 5 concludes on a number of questions left open by this work.

# 2 Preliminaries on Encapsulation Mechanisms

## 2.1 Key Encapsulation Mechanisms (KEMs)

*Definition.* A KEM is a basic cryptographic primitive by the means of which one can publicly and securely encapsulate a randomly generated session key. The owner of the private key (the decapsulation key) can later recover the session key given the encapsulation. KEMs make use of decapsulation keys, encapsulation keys, random numbers, ciphertexts and secret values (that may be symmetric keys). Here we will not describe their inner structure, but rather give a general description of the primitive. We identify a KEM to a tuple of probabilistic algorithms $\mathsf{KEM} = (\mathsf{KEM.Gen}, \mathsf{KEM.Encap}, \mathsf{KEM.Decap})$ defined as follows.

**Key generation.** $\mathsf{KEM.Gen}(1^k)$ takes a security parameter $k \in \mathbb{N}$ and outputs a public key $\mathsf{pk}_K \in \mathsf{KEM}.\mathcal{PK}$ and a decapsulation key $\mathsf{sk}_K \in \mathsf{KEM}.\mathcal{SK}$.

**Encapsulation.** $\mathsf{KEM.Encap}(\mathsf{pk}_K, r)$ takes as input a public key $\mathsf{pk}_K$ and a random $r \in \mathsf{KEM}.\mathcal{R}$ and returns an encapsulation $c \in \mathsf{KEM}.\mathcal{C}$ and the encapsulated value $s \in \mathsf{KEM}.\mathcal{S}$.

**Decapsulation.** $\mathsf{KEM.Decap}(\mathsf{sk}_K, c)$ takes as input a decapsulation key $\mathsf{sk}_K$ and an encapsulation $c$ and returns the matching decapsulated value $s \in \mathsf{KEM}.\mathcal{S}$.

It is well-known that the notion of KEM is equivalent to the one of public-key encryption. There has been a recent interest in lightening the relations between hybrid encryption and various forms of key encapsulations [2].

*Security Notions for KEMs.* As for other cryptographic primitives, one may define several security notions for KEMs. In particular, active attacks are defined similarly to chosen-ciphertext attacks against public-key encryption schemes. In this work, we mainly take interest in two security notions for KEMs which we describe under the form of games. The first security notion captures the property that the encapsulation function $\mathsf{KEM.Encap}$ cannot be inverted under an active attack:

**Game 1 (r-OW-CCA.KEM).** *A probabilistic algorithm $\mathcal{A}$ is given a random key pair $(\mathsf{pk}_K, \mathsf{sk}_K) \leftarrow \mathsf{KEM.Gen}(1^k)$ as well as random $(c^*, s^*)$ and attempts to recover $r^* \in \mathsf{KEM}.\mathcal{R}$ such that $\mathsf{KEM.Encap}(\mathsf{pk}_K, r^*) = (c^*, s^*)$.*

Unless otherwise stated, we denote by $\mathbf{Succ}(\mathcal{A}, k)$ the probability (taken over the random coins of $\mathcal{A}$ and its challenger) under which $\mathcal{A}$ wins a given security game. For any security notion SEC for any cryptographic primitive PRIM defined by such a game, we define $\mathbf{InSec}(\text{SEC.PRIM}, k) = \max_{\mathcal{A}} \mathbf{Succ}(\mathcal{A}, k)$ where the maximum is taken over all polynomial time adversaries $\mathcal{A}$ playing the above game. PRIM is said to be SEC-secure if $\mathbf{InSec}(\text{SEC.PRIM}, k)$ is a negligible function of $k$.

The second security notion also relates to active attacks. It is quite similar to plaintext-checking attacks against public-key cryptosystems. It states that the decapsulation procedure is hard to compute without the decapsulation key, even when one is given an oracle that tells when the wanted decapsulated value is found.

**Game 2 (s-OW-PCA.KEM).** *A probabilistic algorithm $\mathcal{A}$ is given $\mathsf{pk}_K$ where $(\mathsf{pk}_K, \mathsf{sk}_K) \leftarrow \mathsf{KEM.Gen}(1^k)$ as well as a random encapsulation $c^*$, and attempts to recover the decapsulated value $s^*$ matching $c^*$. During the game, the adversary $\mathcal{A}$ is given access to a distinguisher (or distinction oracle) which, given a pair $(c, s)$, tells whether $c$ encapsulates $s$. The oracle can be invoked without restrictions by $\mathcal{A}$.*

## 2.2 Identity-Based Key Encapsulation Mechanisms (IDKEM)

*Definition.* An IDKEM is an identity-based KEM. Definitionally, IDKEMs can be defined as *searchable* KEMs, a primitive providing the trapdoor mechanism underlying searchable encryption. Because this aspect of IDKEMs is important with regard to this work, we make use of the widest definition. An ID-KEM is identified to a tuple of probabilistic algorithms IDKEM = (IDKEM.Gen, IDKEM.Trap, IDKEM.Encap, IDKEM.Decap) defined as follows.

**Key generation.** IDKEM.Gen($1^k$) takes a security parameter $k$ and outputs a public key $\mathsf{pk_I} \in$ IDKEM.$\mathcal{PK}$ and a trapdoor derivation key $\mathsf{tk_I} \in$ IDKEM.$\mathcal{TK}$.

**Trapdoor derivation.** IDKEM.Trap($\mathsf{tk_I}, w$) makes use of the trapdoor derivation key to compute a decapsulation trapdoor $\mathsf{T}(w) \in$ IDKEM.$\mathcal{T}$ for the keyword $w \in \{0,1\}^w$. Trapdoor derivation may be probabilistic.

**Encapsulation.** IDKEM.Encap($\mathsf{pk_I}, w, r$) takes a public key, a keyword $w \in \{0,1\}^w$ and a random $r \in$ IDKEM.$\mathcal{R}$ and outputs an encapsulation $c \in$ IDKEM.$\mathcal{C}$ and the encapsulated value $u \in$ IDKEM.$\mathcal{U}$.

**Decapsulation.** IDKEM.Decap($\mathsf{T}(w), c$) takes an encapsulation $c$ and a decapsulation trapdoor $\mathsf{T}(w)$ and returns the decapsulated value $u$ matching $w$ and $c$.

*Security Notions.* As in the case of ID-based encryption schemes, security notions come in two different flavors for IDKEMs. A first family of adversarial goals captures different levels of privacy with respect to the decapsulated value (one-wayness, indistinguishability, etc.). The others are defined in a similar way but relate to the privacy of the keyword $w$ itself, and resistance to these goals is identified as a form of anonymity.

**Game 3 (s-OW-CCA.IDKEM).** *The adversary $\mathcal{A}$ is given a public key $\mathsf{pk_I}$ where $(\mathsf{pk_I}, \mathsf{tk_I}) \leftarrow$ IDKEM.Gen($1^k$) and later outputs a keyword $w^+ \in \{0,1\}^w$. The challenger randomly selects $r^+ \leftarrow$ IDKEM.$\mathcal{R}$ and computes $(c^+, u^+) =$ IDKEM.Encap $(\mathsf{pk_I}, w^+, r^+)$. The challenge $c^+$ is sent to $\mathcal{A}$ and $\mathcal{A}$ attempts to recover $u^+$. Throughout the game, the adversary is given access to two oracles; a distinction oracle which tells whether a tuple $(w, c, u)$ is consistent in the sense that $c$ encapsulates $u$ under keyword $w$; the adversary has also access to a trapdoor derivation oracle but is not allowed to request a trapdoor corresponding to $w^+$.*

**Game 4 (ANON-CCA.IDKEM).** *The adversary $\mathcal{A}$ is given a public key $\mathsf{pk_I}$ where $(\mathsf{pk_I}, \mathsf{tk_I}) \leftarrow$ IDKEM.Gen($1^k$) and later returns two different keywords $w_0, w_1 \in \{0,1\}^w$. The challenger picks a random bit $b$, randomly selects $r \leftarrow$ IDKEM.$\mathcal{R}$ and computes $(c_b, u_b) =$ IDKEM.Encap($\mathsf{pk_I}, w_b, r$). The encapsulation $c_b$ is sent to the adversary. The adversary later outputs a guess $\hat{b}$ and wins the game if $\hat{b} = b$. During the game, the adversary is allowed to query two oracles: a trapdoor derivation oracle for $w \neq w_0, w_1$ and a decapsulation oracle for $w \in \{w_0, w_1\}$ and $c \neq c_b$ which returns the decapsulation $u$ of $c$. Here $\mathbf{Succ}(\mathcal{A}, k)$ is defined as the difference between the probability that $\mathcal{A}$ wins the game and $1/2$, the probability for a random response to be true.*

## 3   Decryptable Searchable Encryption

### 3.1   Definition and Security Model

We identify a decryptable searchable encryption scheme DSE to a tuple of probabilistic algorithms

$$\mathsf{DSE} = (\mathsf{DSE.Gen}, \mathsf{DSE.Enc}, \mathsf{DSE.Dec}, \mathsf{DSE.Trap}, \mathsf{DSE.Test})$$

enjoying the following properties.

**Key generation.** $\mathsf{DSE.Gen}(1^k)$ takes a security parameter $k$ and outputs a public key pk, a decryption key dk and a trapdoor derivation key tk.

**Encryption.** $\mathsf{DSE.Enc}(\mathsf{pk}, w, r)$ takes as input a public key pk, a message $w \in \{0,1\}^w$ and $r \in \mathsf{DSE.R}$ and returns a ciphertext $c$.

**Decryption.** $\mathsf{DSE.Dec}(\mathsf{dk}, c)$ takes a decryption key dk and a ciphertext $c$ and returns the message $w \in \{0,1\}^w$ that $c$ encrypts or $\bot$ if $c$ is invalid.

**Trapdoor derivation.** $\mathsf{DSE.Trap}(\mathsf{tk}, w)$ requires a trapdoor derivation key tk and a message $w \in \{0,1\}^w$ to compute a search trapdoor $\mathsf{T}(w)$. The trapdoor $\mathsf{T}(w)$ may be probabilistic in which case $\mathsf{DSE.Trap}$ also requires randomness.

**Test.** $\mathsf{DSE.Test}(\mathsf{pk}, \mathsf{T}(w), c)$ takes as input a public key pk, a search trapdoor $\mathsf{T}(w)$ for $w$, a ciphertext $c$ and returns 1 if $c$ encrypts $w$. Otherwise 0 is returned.

We focus on the strongest possible notion of security for decryptable searchable encryption which we capture by the following game:

**Game 5** (IND-CCA.DSE). *A set of keys* $(\mathsf{pk}, \mathsf{dk}, \mathsf{tk}) \leftarrow \mathsf{DSE.Gen}(1^k)$ *is randomly selected and* $\mathcal{A}$ *is executed over* pk. $\mathcal{A}$ *outputs* $w_0, w_1 \in \{0,1\}^w$ *with* $w_0 \neq w_1$. *The challenger randomly picks* $b \in \{0,1\}$ *and outputs* $c_b$. $\mathcal{A}$ *then outputs its guess* $\hat{b} \in \{0,1\}$ *and wins if* $\hat{b} = b$. *Throughout the game,* $\mathcal{A}$ *may send queries* $w \notin \{w_0, w_1\}$ *to a trapdoor derivation oracle* $\mathsf{DSE.Trap}(\mathsf{tk}, \cdot)$ *and queries* $c \neq c_b$ *to a decryption oracle* $\mathsf{DSE.Dec}(\mathsf{dk}, \cdot)$.

### 3.2   A Generic Construction from KEMs and IDKEMs

We suggest a construction using one KEM, one IDKEM and a couple of hash functions $H_1, H_2$. These ingredients have to be *compatible* in the sense that $H_1$ must map elements of IDKEM.$\mathcal{U}$ to elements of KEM.$\mathcal{R}$, and elements of KEM.$\mathcal{S}$ to elements of $\{0,1\}^w \times$ IDKEM.$\mathcal{R}$. We also require an additional property for the IDKEM:

*Property 1.* Given $(w_0, w_1) \in \{0,1\}^w$ and $(c_0, c_1) \in$ IDKEM.$\mathcal{C}$, it is easy to check whether for some $s \in$ IDKEM.$\mathcal{S}$, the first component $c$ of

$$(c, u) = \mathsf{IDKEM.Encap}(\mathsf{pk_I}, w_i, s)$$

is equal to $c_i$ for $i = 0, 1$, this holding for any public key $\mathsf{pk_I}$.

This property is achieved for most existing IDKEMs. We denote by $\odot$ a revertible composition law over IDKEM.$\mathcal{R}$ such as a group law or $\oplus$. We define our construction DSE as follows.

**Key generation.** DSE.Gen$(1^k)$ runs KEM.Gen$(1^k)$ and IDKEM.Gen$(1^k)$ and sets pk $= (\mathsf{pk}_K, \mathsf{pk}_I)$, dk $= \mathsf{sk}_K$ and tk $= \mathsf{tk}_I$.

**Encryption.** DSE.Enc(pk, $w, r$) runs KEM.Encap($\mathsf{pk}_K, r$) resulting in an encapsulation $c_1$ and a decapsulated value $s$. One computes $(s_1, s_2) = H_1(s)$, $c_2 = s_1 \oplus w$, $(c_3, u) = $ IDKEM.Encap($\mathsf{pk}_I, w, s_2$) and $c_4 = r \odot H_2(u)$. The ciphertext is $(c_1, c_2, c_3, c_4)$.

**Decryption.** DSE.Dec(dk, $(c_1, c_2, c_3, c_4)$) first decapsulates $c_1$ by running KEM.Decap($\mathsf{sk}_K, c_1$) to recover $s$. One then computes $(s_1, s_2) = H_1(s)$, $w = s_1 \oplus c_2$, and $(c', u) = $ IDKEM.Encap($\mathsf{pk}_I, w, s_2$). The algorithm checks that $c' = c_3$, computes $r' = H_2(u)^{-1} \odot c_4$ and finally checks that KEM.Encap($\mathsf{pk}_K, r'$) $= (c_1, s)$ before returning $w$. In case one of these conditions is not fulfilled, $\perp$ is returned.

**Trapdoor derivation.** DSE.Trap(tk, $w$) returns IDKEM.Trap($\mathsf{tk}_I, w$).

**Test.** DSE.Test(pk, $\mathsf{T}(w), (c_1, c_2, c_3, c_4)$) computes

$$u' = \text{IDKEM.Decap}(\mathsf{T}(w), c_3) \,, \quad r' = c_4 \odot H(u')^{-1} \,,$$

$(c_1', s') = $ KEM.Encap($\mathsf{pk}_K, r'$) and $(s_1, s_2) = H_1(s')$. One then checks whether $c_1' = c_1$ and $(c_3, u) = $ IDKEM.Encap($\mathsf{pk}_I, c_2 \oplus s_1, s_2$). DSE.Test returns 1 if these conditions are fulfilled, 0 otherwise.

**Theorem 1.** *Assuming that* KEM *is* r-OW-CCA *and* s-OW-PCA-*secure and that* IDKEM *is* s-OW-CCA *and* ANON-CCA-*secure,* DSE *as per the above construction is* IND-CCA-*secure. More precisely,*

$$\mathbf{InSec}(\text{IND-CCA.DSE}, k) \leq 2 \cdot \mathbf{InSec}(\text{s-OW-PCA.KEM}, k)$$
$$+ 2 \cdot \mathbf{InSec}(\text{s-OW-CCA.IDKEM}, k) + \mathbf{InSec}(\text{r-OW-CCA.KEM}, k)$$
$$+ \mathbf{InSec}(\text{ANON-CCA.IDKEM}, k) + \mathsf{negl}(k) \,.$$

We give a full proof of Theorem 1 in the full version of this work [12].

# 4    An Efficient Instantiation of DSE Using Bilinear Maps

We now give a specific scheme using our general construction. To this end, we will use existing examples of KEMs and IDKEMs.

## 4.1    Description of Our Scheme

We now consider the decryptable searchable encryption scheme as per our construction of Section 3 using IDKEM $=$ BDOP [4] over a bilinear group system

$\mathcal{S} = (\mathbb{G}_1, g_1, \mathbb{G}_2, g_2, \mathbb{G}_t, e\,(\cdot, \cdot))$ and a KEM defined over $\mathbb{G}_1$ and relying on El-Gamal encryption [11]. It is easily seen that BDOP satisfies Property 1. The revertible operator $\odot$ is taken as addition modulo $q = |\mathbb{G}_1| = |\mathbb{G}_2| = |\mathbb{G}_t|$. The security parameter $k$ is set to $\log q$. We also employ three hash functions $F, G, H$ viewed as random oracles which domain and range are implicitly defined by the following description.

**Key generation.** DSE.Gen randomly selects $x \leftarrow \mathbb{Z}_q$ and $x' \leftarrow \mathbb{Z}_q$ and sets the decryption key to $\mathsf{dk} = x$ and the trapdoor derivation key to $\mathsf{tk} = x'$. Noting $y = g_1^x$, $y' = g_1^{x'}$, the public key is $\mathsf{pk} = (y, y')$.

**Encryption.** For $w \in \{0, 1\}^{\mathsf{w}}$ and $r \in \mathbb{Z}_q$, DSE.Enc($\mathsf{pk}, w, r$) computes $c_1 = g_1^r$, $(s_1, s_2) = G(y^r)$, $c_2 = s_1 \oplus w$, $c_3 = g_1^{s_2}$, $u = e\,(y'^{s_2}, F(w))$ and $c_4 = H(u) + r \bmod q$. The encryption is $c = (c_1, c_2, c_3, c_4)$.

**Decryption.** Given $c = (c_1, c_2, c_3, c_4)$, DSE.Dec($x, c$) computes $s = c_1^x$, $(s_1, s_2) = G(s)$ and $w = c_2 \oplus s_1$. If $c_3 \neq g_1^{s_2}$, DSE.Dec($x, c$) returns $\perp$. Otherwise, one computes $u = e\,(y'^{s_2}, F(w))$, $r = c_4 - H(u) \bmod q$ and checks whether $c_1 = g_1^r$. If this condition is satisfied, DSE.Dec($x, c$) returns $w$. Otherwise $\perp$ is returned.

**Trapdoor derivation.** Given $w \in \{0, 1\}^{\mathsf{w}}$ and $x'$, DSE.Trap($x', w$) returns $\mathsf{T}(w) = F(w)^{x'} \in \mathbb{G}_2$.

**Test.** Given $c = (c_1, c_2, c_3, c_4)$ and $\mathsf{T}(w) \in \mathbb{G}_2$, DSE.Test($\mathsf{pk}, \mathsf{T}(w), c$) computes $u = e\,(c_3, \mathsf{T}(w))$ and $r = c_4 - H(u) \bmod q$. If $c_1 \neq g_1^r$, 0 is returned. Otherwise one computes $s = y^r$, $(s_1, s_2) = G(s)$ and $w = c_2 \oplus s_1$. If $c_3 \neq g_1^{s_2}$, 0 is returned. Otherwise 1 is returned.

### 4.2  Security Analysis

*The Gap-Diffie-Hellman Problem* GDH. Let $\mathbb{G}$ be a group of prime order $q$ and let $g$ be a generator of $\mathbb{G}$. The computational problem CDH is defined as the problem of computing $g^{ab}$ given $(g^a, g^b) \in \mathbb{G}$. DDH consists in distinguishing the two distributions $D = (g^a, g^b, g^{ab})$ and $R = (g^a, g^b, g^t)$ for randomly selected $a, b, t \leftarrow \mathbb{Z}_q$. The gap problem GDH is defined as the problem of solving CDH given an oracle that solves DDH. These problems are classical in cryptography and we refer the reader to an extensive literature [9,18,14,7] for applications of GDH to public-key design. We finally note that GDH $\equiv$ CDH over bilinear map groups.

*The Gap-Bilinear-Diffie-Hellman Problem* GBDH. Let $\mathcal{S}$ be a bilinear group system as above. The computational problem CBDH is defined as the problem of computing $e\,(g_1, g_2)^{abc}$ given $g_1^a, g_1^b \in \mathbb{G}_1$ and $g_2^c \in \mathbb{G}_2$. CBDH admits a decisional version DBDH which consists in distinguishing the two distributions $D = (g_1^a, g_1^b, g_2^c, e\,(g_1, g_2)^{abc})$ and $R = (g_1^a, g_1^b, g_2^c, e\,(g_1, g_2)^t)$ for randomly selected $a, b, c, t \leftarrow \mathbb{Z}_q$. It is easily shown that DBDH $\Leftarrow$ CBDH, which allows one to define the gap problem GBDH as the problem of solving CBDH given an oracle that solves DBDH.

We now claim the following facts: *a)* ElGamal (defined over the group $\mathbb{G}_1$) is s-OW-PCA-secure under the assumption that GDH is intractable over $\mathbb{G}_1$; *b)* it is also r-OW-CCA-secure under the discrete log assumption over $\mathbb{G}_1$; *c)* one has $\mathbf{InSec}(\text{ANON-CCA.BDOP}, k) = 0$ for any $k \in \mathbb{N}$; *d)* BDOP is s-OW-CCA-secure under the assumption that GBDH is intractable over $\mathcal{S}$ in the random oracle model; *e)* the GBDH problem over $\mathcal{S}$ is reducible to the GDH problem over $\mathbb{G}_1$; *f)* DSE[ElGamal, BDOP] is IND-CCA-secure under the GBDH assumption over $\mathcal{S}$ and the GDH assumption over $\mathbb{G}_1$ in the random oracle model.

As a direct application of the above, we state:

**Theorem 2.** DSE[ElGamal, BDOP] *is* IND-CCA-*secure under the* GDH *assumption over* $\mathbb{G}_1$ *in the random oracle model.*

We refer to the full version of this work [12] for more details and proper proofs of these statements.

# 5    Conclusion and Open Issues

We introduced the concept of decryptable searchable encryption and showed how to generically implement this new primitive using one KEM, one IDKEM and hash functions. We provided a precise security proof in which we relate IND-CCA-security to the security properties of the inner primitives. Decryptable searchable encryption finds applications in the secure management of encrypted databases, among others. We mention that ID-based decryptable searchable encryption is obtained as a side effect of our generic construct. This is done by replacing the underlying KEM by a second IDKEM which keyword input is fed with ID strings. The trapdoor derivation key of this IDKEM is then the master secret key of the whole ID-based encryption scheme.

We see several open research topics associated to our work. First, one may ask whether more efficient constructions exist that achieve general-purpose DSE. Optimizing the ciphertext size is a pending issue in this respect. Second, we would consider as a major breakthrough to come up with a DSE which security does not rely on random oracles. Although seemingly hard to find, such a scheme would benefit from a security standing in the standard model and would consequently avoid the threat of recent separation results [15,16,17].

# References

1. Abdalla, M., Bellare, M., Catalano, D., Kiltz, E., Kohno, T., Lange, T., Malone-Lee, J., Neven, G., Paillier, P., Shi, H.: Searchable encryption revisited: Consistency properties, relation to anonymous ibe, and extensions. In: Shoup, V. (ed.) CRYPTO 2005. LNCS, vol. 3621, pp. 205–222. Springer, Heidelberg (2005)
2. Abe, M., Gennaro, R., Kurosawa, K., Shoup, V.: Tag-kem/dem: A new framework for hybrid encryption and a new analysis of the kurosawa-desmedt kem. In: Cramer, R.J.F. (ed.) EUROCRYPT 2005. LNCS, vol. 3494, pp. 426–442. Springer, Heidelberg (2005)

3. Boneh, D., Boyen, X., Goh, E.-J.: Hierarchical identity based encryption with constant size ciphertext. In: Cramer, R.J.F. (ed.) EUROCRYPT 2005. LNCS, vol. 3494, pp. 440–456. Springer, Heidelberg (2005)
4. Boneh, D., Di Crescenzo, G., Ostrovsky, R., Persiano, G.: Public key encryption with keyword search. In: Cachin, C., Camenisch, J.L. (eds.) EUROCRYPT 2004. LNCS, vol. 3027, pp. 506–522. Springer, Heidelberg (2004)
5. Boneh, D., Franklin, M.: Identity-based encryption from the Weil pairing. In: Kilian, J. (ed.) CRYPTO 2001. LNCS, vol. 2139, pp. 213–229. Springer, Heidelberg (2001)
6. Boyen, X.: Multipurpose identity-based signcryption (a swiss army knife for identity-based cryptography). In: Boneh, D. (ed.) CRYPTO 2003. LNCS, vol. 2729, pp. 383–399. Springer, Heidelberg (2003)
7. Cha, J.C., Cheon, J.H.: An identity-based signature from gap diffie-hellman groups. In: Desmedt, Y.G. (ed.) PKC 2003. LNCS, vol. 2567, pp. 18–30. Springer, Heidelberg (2002)
8. Chen, L., Cheng, Z., Malone-Lee, J., Smart, N.P.: An efficient ID-KEM based on the sakai-kasahara key construction. In: Cryptology ePrint Archive, Report 2005/224 (2005), http://eprint.iacr.org/
9. Coron, J.-S., Handschuh, H., Joye, M., Paillier, P., Pointcheval, D., Tymen, C.: Optimal chosen-ciphertext secure encryption of arbitrary-length messages. In: Naccache, D., Paillier, P. (eds.) PKC 2002. LNCS, vol. 2274, pp. 17–33. Springer, Heidelberg (2002)
10. Cramer, R., Shoup, V.: Design and analysis of practical public-key encryption schemes secure against adaptive chosen-ciphertext attacks. SIAM Journal on Computing 33(1), 167–226 (2003)
11. ElGamal, T.: A public key cryptosystem and signature scheme based on discrete logarithms. IEEE Transactions on Information Theory 31, 469–472 (1985)
12. Fuhr, T., Paillier, P.: Decryptable searchable encryption. Cryptology ePrint Archive (2007), http://eprint.iacr.org/
13. Gentry, C., Silverberg, A.: Hierarchical ID-based cryptography. In: Zheng, Y. (ed.) ASIACRYPT 2002. LNCS, vol. 2501, pp. 548–566. Springer, Heidelberg (2002)
14. Okamoto, T., Pointcheval, D.: The gap-problems: A new class of problems for the security of cryptographic schemes. In: Kim, K.-c. (ed.) PKC 2001. LNCS, vol. 1992, pp. 104–118. Springer, Heidelberg (2001)
15. Paillier, P., Vergnaud, D.: Discrete-log-based signatures may not be equivalent to discrete log. In: Roy, B. (ed.) ASIACRYPT 2005. LNCS, vol. 3788, pp. 1–20. Springer, Heidelberg (2005)
16. Paillier, P., Villar, J.: Trading one-wayness against chosen-ciphertext security in factoring-based encryption. In: Lai, X., Chen, K. (eds.) ASIACRYPT 2006. LNCS, vol. 4284, pp. 252–266. Springer, Heidelberg (2006)
17. Paillier, P.: Impossibility proofs for RSA signatures in the standard model. In: Abe, M. (ed.) CT-RSA 2007. LNCS, vol. 4377, pp. 31–48. Springer, Heidelberg (2006)
18. Pointcheval, D.: Chosen-ciphertext security for any one-way cryptosystem. In: Imai, H., Zheng, Y. (eds.) PKC 2000. LNCS, vol. 1751, pp. 129–146. Springer, Heidelberg (2000)
19. Shamir, A.: Identity-based cryptosystems and signature schemes. In: Blakely, G.R., Chaum, D. (eds.) CRYPTO 1984. LNCS, vol. 196, pp. 47–53. Springer, Heidelberg (1985)

# Author Index

# Lecture Notes in Computer Science

Sublibrary 4: Security and Cryptology

Vol. 4219: D. Zamboni, C. Krügel (Eds.), Recent Advances in Intrusion Detection. XII, 331 pages. 2006.

Vol. 4189: D. Gollmann, J. Meier, A. Sabelfeld (Eds.), Computer Security – ESORICS 2006. XI, 548 pages. 2006.

Vol. 4176: S.K. Katsikas, J. López, M. Backes, S. Gritzalis, B. Preneel (Eds.), Information Security. XIV, 548 pages. 2006.

Vol. 4117: C. Dwork (Ed.), Advances in Cryptology - CRYPTO 2006. XIII, 621 pages. 2006.

Vol. 4116: R. De Prisco, M. Yung (Eds.), Security and Cryptography for Networks. XI, 366 pages. 2006.

Vol. 4107: G. Di Crescenzo, A. Rubin (Eds.), Financial Cryptography and Data Security. XI, 327 pages. 2006.

Vol. 4083: S. Fischer-Hübner, S. Furnell, C. Lambrinoudakis (Eds.), Trust and Privacy in Digital Business. XIII, 243 pages. 2006.

Vol. 4064: R. Büschkes, P. Laskov (Eds.), Detection of Intrusions and Malware & Vulnerability Assessment. X, 195 pages. 2006.

Vol. 4058: L.M. Batten, R. Safavi-Naini (Eds.), Information Security and Privacy. XII, 446 pages. 2006.

Vol. 4047: M.J.B. Robshaw (Ed.), Fast Software Encryption. XI, 434 pages. 2006.

Vol. 4043: A.S. Atzeni, A. Lioy (Eds.), Public Key Infrastructure. XI, 261 pages. 2006.

Vol. 4004: S. Vaudenay (Ed.), Advances in Cryptology - EUROCRYPT 2006. XIV, 613 pages. 2006.

Vol. 3995: G. Müller (Ed.), Emerging Trends in Information and Communication Security. XX, 524 pages. 2006.

Vol. 3989: J. Zhou, M. Yung, F. Bao (Eds.), Applied Cryptography and Network Security. XIV, 488 pages. 2006.

Vol. 3969: Ø. Ytrehus (Ed.), Coding and Cryptography. XI, 443 pages. 2006.

Vol. 3958: M. Yung, Y. Dodis, A. Kiayias, T.G. Malkin (Eds.), Public Key Cryptography - PKC 2006. XIV, 543 pages. 2006.

Vol. 3957: B. Christianson, B. Crispo, J.A. Malcolm, M. Roe (Eds.), Security Protocols. IX, 325 pages. 2006.

Vol. 3956: G. Barthe, B. Grégoire, M. Huisman, J.-L. Lanet (Eds.), Construction and Analysis of Safe, Secure, and Interoperable Smart Devices. IX, 175 pages. 2006.

Vol. 3935: D.H. Won, S. Kim (Eds.), Information Security and Cryptology - ICISC 2005. XIV, 458 pages. 2006.

Vol. 3934: J.A. Clark, R.F. Paige, F.A.C. Polack, P.J. Brooke (Eds.), Security in Pervasive Computing. X, 243 pages. 2006.

Vol. 3928: J. Domingo-Ferrer, J. Posegga, D. Schreckling (Eds.), Smart Card Research and Advanced Applications. XI, 359 pages. 2006.

Vol. 3919: R. Safavi-Naini, M. Yung (Eds.), Digital Rights Management. XI, 357 pages. 2006.

Vol. 3903: K. Chen, R. Deng, X. Lai, J. Zhou (Eds.), Information Security Practice and Experience. XIV, 392 pages. 2006.

Vol. 3897: B. Preneel, S. Tavares (Eds.), Selected Areas in Cryptography. XI, 371 pages. 2006.

Vol. 3876: S. Halevi, T. Rabin (Eds.), Theory of Cryptography. XI, 617 pages. 2006.

Vol. 3866: T. Dimitrakos, F. Martinelli, P.Y.A. Ryan, S. Schneider (Eds.), Formal Aspects in Security and Trust. X, 259 pages. 2006.

Vol. 3860: D. Pointcheval (Ed.), Topics in Cryptology – CT-RSA 2006. XI, 365 pages. 2006.

Vol. 3858: A. Valdes, D. Zamboni (Eds.), Recent Advances in Intrusion Detection. X, 351 pages. 2006.

Vol. 3856: G. Danezis, D. Martin (Eds.), Privacy Enhancing Technologies. VIII, 273 pages. 2006.

Vol. 3786: J.-S. Song, T. Kwon, M. Yung (Eds.), Information Security Applications. XI, 378 pages. 2006.

Vol. 3108: H. Wang, J. Pieprzyk, V. Varadharajan (Eds.), Information Security and Privacy. XII, 494 pages. 2004.

Vol. 2951: M. Naor (Ed.), Theory of Cryptography. XI, 523 pages. 2004.

Vol. 2742: R.N. Wright (Ed.), Financial Cryptography. VIII, 321 pages. 2003.